CW00621634

AFRICA IN THE N.

About this series

The books in this series are an initiative by CODESRIA, the Council for the Development of Social Science Research in Africa, to encourage African scholarship relevant to the multiple intellectual, policy and practical problems and opportunities confronting the African continent in the twenty-first century.

Publishers: CODESRIA in association with Zed Books

Titles in the series

African Intellectuals: Rethinking Politics, Language, Gender and Development *edited by Thandika Mkandawire* (2005)

Urban Africa: Changing Contours of Survival in the City *edited by A.M. Simone and A. Abouhani* (2005)

Liberal Democracy and Its Critics in Africa: Political Dysfunction and the Struggle for Social Progress *edited by Tukumbi Lumumba-Kasongo* (2005)

Negotiating Modernity: Africa's Ambivalent Experience *edited by Elísio Salvado Macamo* (2005)

Insiders and Outsiders: Citizenship and Xenophobia in Contemporary Southern Africa *Francis B. Nyamnjoh* (2006)

African Anthropologies: History, Critique and Practice *edited by Mwenda Ntarangwi, David Mills and Mustafa Babiker* (2006)

Intellectuals and African Development: Pretension and Resistance in African Politics *edited by Björn Beckman and Gbemisola Adeoti* (2006)

Africa and Development Challenges in the New Millenium: The NEPAD Debate *edited by J.O. Adésínà, A. Olukoshi and Yao Graham* (2006)

Kenya: The Struggle for Democracy *edited by Godwin R. Murunga and Shadrack W. Nasong'o* (2007)

Ghana: One Decade of the Liberal State *edited by Kwame Boafo-Arthur*

About CODESRIA

The Council for the Development of Social Science Research in Africa (CODESRIA) is an independent organisation whose principal objectives are facilitating research, promoting research-based publishing and creating multiple forums geared towards the exchange of views and information among African researchers. It challenges the fragmentation of research through the creation of thematic research networks that cut across linguistic and regional boundaries.

CODESRIA publishes a quarterly journal, *Africa Development*, the longest standing Africa-based social science journal; *Afrika Zamani*, a journal of history; the *African Sociological Review*; *African Journal of International Affairs* (AJIA); *Africa Review of Books*; and the *Journal of Higher Education in Africa*. It co-publishes the *Africa Media Review* and *Identity, Culture and Politics: An Afro-Asian Dialogue*. Research results and other activities of the institution are disseminated through 'Working Papers', 'Monograph Series', 'CODESRIA Book Series', and the *CODESRIA Bulletin*.

About this book

The path towards democracy in Kenya has been long and often tortuous. Though it has been trumpeted as a goal for decades, democratic government has never been fully realised, largely as a result of the authoritarian excesses of the Kenyatta, Moi and Kibaki regimes.

This uniquely comprehensive study of Kenya's political trajectory shows how the struggle for democracy has been waged in civil society, through opposition parties, and amongst traditionally marginalised groups like women and the young. It also considers the remaining impediments to democratisation, in the form of a powerful police force and damaging structural adjustment policies. Thus, the authors argue, democratisation in Kenya is a laborious and non-linear process.

Kenyans' recent electoral successes, the book concludes, have empowered them and reinvigorated the prospects for democracy, heralding a more autonomous and peaceful twenty-first century.

Kenya

The Struggle for Democracy

edited by Godwin R. Murunga and Shadrack Wanjala Nasong'o

CODESRIA BOOKS
Dakar

in association with

ZED BOOKS
London & New York

Kenya: The Struggle for Democracy was first published in 2007
by Zed Books Ltd, 7 Cynthia Street, London N1 9JF, UK and
Room 400, 175 Fifth Avenue, New York, NY 10010, USA.
www.zedbooks.co.uk

in association with

CODESRIA, Avenue Cheikh Anta Diop, X Canal IV,
BP3304, Dakar, 18524 Senegal

www.codesria.org

Editorial copyright © CODESRIA, 2007
Individual chapters © individual contributors, 2007

The rights of the contributors to be identified as the authors
of this work have been asserted by them in accordance with the
Copyright, Designs and Patents Act, 1988

CODESRIA would like to express its gratitude to the Swedish
International Development Co-operation Agency (SIDA/SAREC), the
International Development Research Centre (IDRC), the Ford Foundation,
the MacArthur Foundation, the Carnegie Corporation, the Norwegian
Ministry of Foreign Affairs, the Danish Agency for International Development
(SANISA), the French Ministry of Cooperation, the United Nations
Development Programme (UNDP), the Netherlands Ministry of Foreign
Affairs, the Rockefeller Foundation, FINIDA, NORAD, CIDA, IIEP/ADEA,
OECD, IFS, OXFAM America, UN/UNICEF and the Government of
Senegal for supporting its research, training and publication programmes.

Cover designed by Andrew Corbett
Typeset by Exeter Premedia Services Private Ltd., Chennai, India
Printed and bound in Malta by Gutenberg Press Ltd

Distributed in the USA exclusively by Palgrave Macmillan, a division of
St. Martin's Press, LLC, 175 Fifth Avenue, New York 10010

All rights reserved

No part of this publication may be reproduced, stored in a retrieval
system or transmitted, in any form or by any means, electronic or otherwise,
without the prior permission of the publisher.

A catalogue record for this book is available from the British Library
US CIP data is available from the Library of Congress

ISBN-13: 978-1-84277-832-6 Hb Zed Books
ISBN-13: 978-1-84277-857-9 Pb Zed Books
ISBN-13: 978-2-86978-203-7 Pb CODESRIA

Contents

List of Tables and Figures   ix

Acknowledgements   x

List of Abbreviations   xii

Preface   xvi

PART I   Introduction

1   Prospects for Democracy in Kenya
   **Shadrack Wanjala Nasong'o and
   Godwin R. Murunga**   3

PART II   Civil Society and the Politics of Opposition

2   Negotiating New Rules of the Game: Social Movements,
   Civil Society and the Kenyan Transition
   Shadrack Wanjala Nasong'o   19

3   Religious Movements and Democratisation in Kenya:
   Between the Sacred and the Profane
   Margaret Gathoni Gecaga   58

4   The Contemporary Opposition in Kenya:
   Between Internal Traits and State Manipulation
   Adams G.R. Oloo   90

**PART III   Major Constituencies in the
Democratisation Process**

5   Leaders of Tomorrow? The Youth and Democratisation
   in Kenya
   Mshaï S. Mwangola   129

6   Women in Kenya's Politics of Transition
   and Democratisation
   **Shadrack Wanjala Nasong'o and
   Theodora O. Ayot**   164

7   Intellectuals and the Democratisation Process in Kenya
    Maurice N. Amutabi   197

8   The Role of the Police in Kenya's Democratisation
    Process
    Edwin A. Gimode   227

                    PART IV   **Donors and the Politics of**
                              Structural Adjustment

9   Governance and the Politics of Structural Adjustment
    in Kenya
    Godwin R. Murunga   263

10 From Demiurge to Midwife: Changing Donor Roles
    in Kenya's Democratisation Process
    Stephen Brown   301

    About the Contributors   331

    Index   333

Tables and Figures

Table 2.1   Democracy and governance civil organisations
             formed in Kenya in the 1990s   35
Table 2.2   Presidential vote distribution in Kenya's 1992
             elections   39
Table 2.3   Presidential election results in Kenya's 2002
             elections   47
Table 3.1   Typical Mungiki prayer   72
Table 6.1   Women in Kenya's ninth parliament, 2002–07   187

Figure 10.1 Official development assistance to Kenya
             (all donors, 1978–90)   305
Figure 10.2 Official development assistance to Kenya
             (all donors, 1990–2002)   312

Acknowledgements

This book grew from a CODESRIA National Working Group (NWG), the first ever successful NWG on Kenya. As co-ordinators of the NWG, we are enormously grateful to CODESRIA for the confidence it showed in our ability to co-ordinate the NWG and edit the manuscript. We live in an academic environment where few institutions have any faith in first timers. This being our very first time editing a book, we understand the risk CODESRIA took in commissioning and funding this project and are very grateful to the institution. In particular, we wish to thank Adebayo Olukoshi, Ebrima Sall, Sheila Bunwaree and Francis Nyamnjoh for supporting the project. We also wish to extend our gratitude to the staff at CODESRIA in Dakar who assisted us in realising our objective and to the editorial group at Zed Books in London for the excellent work in converting the manuscript into this book.

In the course of research, writing and editing, the contributors to this study were assisted by many people in providing data, and in reading and commenting on the drafts. Many of these people must, for lack of space, remain nameless, but their contribution to the successful completion of this work is reflected in the product and we sincerely thank them. The editors wish to thank the contributors for their dedicated research and timely submission of chapters. Thanks also to Lisa Asili Aubrey for editorial assistance and to our families for withstanding the necessary withdrawal from normal family life to concentrate on finishing this project.

Finally, this book is as much about heroes and sheroes of the struggle for democracy in Kenya as it is about the villains. Our aim has been to interrogate and celebrate the knowledge that democratisation in Kenya, as in Africa at large, has been a process fraught with trials, travails and tribulations as well as expectations and achievements. None of the Kenyan political actors embody this struggle and process better than Ms Philomena Chelagat Mutai and Mr Martin Shikuku, two s/heroes of the democratisation struggle who have not yet been given due intellectual recognition. These two politicians distinguished themselves in the days of state authoritarianism as unrelenting spokespersons of the masses. Long before civil society became a buzzword for all kinds of groups and people and mobilisation for gender equity became a rallying point for women's emancipation, Ms Mutai was a leading activist, journalist and legislator in a predominantly male arena who challenged the repressive state when most male politicians were silent accomplices. Ms Mutai also suffered detention on trumped-up charges. On the other hand, Martin Shikuku's political career, in which he is popularly recognised as the people's watchman, spans the colonial and post-colonial times. Throughout, he has remained steadfast in fighting political corruption and demanding a new constitutional dispensation in Kenya. It is only fitting that we dedicate this book to Mutai's and Shikuku's vision, strength and commitment to the cause of liberty in Kenya.

Godwin R. Murunga
Shadrack W. Nasong'o
2006

Abbreviations

ADEC	Agency for Development Education and Communication
AG	Attorney-General
BWI	Bretton Woods Institution(s)
CCCC	Citizens Coalition for Constitutional Change
CCGD	Collaborative Centre for Gender and Development
CID	Criminal Investigations Department
CKRC	Constitution of Kenya Review Commission
CLARION	Centre for Legal Aid and Research International
CLEAN	Centre for Legal Education and Aid Networks
CODESRIA	Council for Development of Social Science Research in Africa
COTU	Central Organisation of Trade Unions
CRIC	Civic Resources and Information Centre
CSO	civil society organisation(s)
DEMO	Democratic Movement
DG	democracy and governance
DP	Democratic Party
DSI	Directorate of Security Intelligence
DTM	December Twelve Movement
DYM	Dini ya Msambwa
EAA	East African Association
ECK	Electoral Commission of Kenya
ECWD	Education Centre for Women in Democracy
EFK	Evangelical Fellowship of Kenya
FIDA-K	International Federation of Women Lawyers-Kenya
FORD	Forum for Restoration of Democracy
FORD-A	Forum for Restoration of Democracy Asili
FORD-K	Forum for Restoration of Democracy in Kenya
FORD-P	Forum for Restoration of Democracy for the People
GBM	Green Belt Movement
GDP	gross domestic product

GEMA	Gikuyu, Embu and Meru Association
GNP	gross national product
GSU	General Service Unit
IBEACO	Imperial British East African Company
ICEDA	Institute for Civic Education in Africa
IED	Institute for Education in Democracy
IFI	International Financial Institution(s)
IGAD	Intergovernmental Authority on Development
IMF	International Monetary Fund
IPPG	Inter-Parties Parliamentary Group
IPU	Inter-Parliamentary Union
KACA	Kenya Anti-Corruption Authority
KADU	Kenya African Democratic Union
KANU	Kenya African National Union
KAR	Kenya African Rifles
KASU	Kenya African Study Union
KAU	Kenya African Union
KBC	Kenya Broadcasting Corporation
KDC	KANU Disciplinary Committee
KEC	Kenya Episcopal Conference
KENDA	Kenya National Democratic Alliance
KFA	Kenya Farmers Association
KGGCU	Kenya Grain Growers Cooperative Union
KHRC	Kenya Human Rights Commission
KISA	Kikuyu Independent School Association
KLWV	Kenya League of Woman Voters
KKEA	Kikuyu Karing'a Education Association
KNC	Kenya National Congress
KNSCDF	Kenya National Schools and Colleges Drama Festival
KPTC	Kenya Post and Telecommunication Corporation
KPU	Kenya People's Union
KSC	Kenya Social Congress
KTG	Kamirithu Theatre Group
KTPWA	Kavirondo Tax Payers Welfare Association
KYFM	Kenya Youth Foundation Movement
LDP	Liberal Democratic Party
LG	Lost Generation
LHG	Lancaster House Generation
LKWV	League of Kenya Women Voters

LPK   Labour Party of Kenya
LRF   Legal Resources Foundation
LSA   Literature Students Association
LSK   Law Society of Kenya
MMD   Movement for Multiparty Democracy
MODAN   Movement for Dialogue and Non-violence
MoU   Memorandum of Understanding
MP   member(s) of parliament
MVOA   *Matatu* Vehicle Owners Association
MYWO   Maendeleo ya Wanawake Organisation
NAK   National Alliance (Party) of Kenya
NARC   National Alliance Rainbow Coalition
NCCK   National Council of the Churches of Kenya
NCEC   National Convention Executive Council
NCPB   National Cereals and Produce Board
NCPC   National Convention Preparatory Committee
NCSW   National Commission on the Status of Women
NCWK   National Council of the Women of Kenya
NDP   National Development Party
NEMU   National Election Monitoring Unit
NGO   non-governmental organisation(s)
NIC   newly industrialising countries
NPK   National Party of Kenya
NRM   new religions movement(s)
NSIS   National Security Intelligence Services
NUKS   National Union of Kenya Students
NYM   National Youth Movement
NYPSC   National Youth Policy Steering Committee
ODA   official development assistance
OECD   Organisation for Economic Cooperation and
           Development
OP   Office of the President
PAC   Public Accounts Committee
PAF   Policy Advisory Foundation
PCK   People's Commission of Kenya
PIC   Public Investments Committee
PICK   Party of Independent Candidates of Kenya
PS   Permanent Secretary
RPP   Release Political Prisoners
SDP   Social Democratic Party

SAP	structural adjustment programme(s)
SAL	structural adjustment lending
SAREAT	Series on Alternative Research in East Africa Trust
SODNET	Social Development Network
SONU	Student Organization of Nairobi University
SUPKEM	Supreme Council of Kenyan Muslims
UASU	Universities Academic Staff Union
UG	Uhuru Generation
UNDP	United Nations Development Programme
UNESCO	United Nations Educational, Scientific and Cultural Organisation
UoN	University of Nairobi
WB	World Bank
YA	Youth Agenda
YK '92	Youth for KANU '92
YKA-a	Young Kavirondo Association
YKA-b	Young Kikuyu Association
YWCA	Young Women's Christian Association

Preface

The ideas contained in this volume are penned by authors who identify with a newer generation of Kenyan scholarship. The chapters are shaped by the experiences of the individual authors. By experiences, we refer to the contexts of their training within institutions of higher learning in and out of Kenya and the ways these contexts have shaped or been shaped by the wider political environment within which higher education institutions operate. Except for two colleagues, one a senior Kenyan scholar and the other a Canadian Africanist, the chapters in this volume are authored by a 'younger' generation of Kenyan scholars. Most of them recently received their doctoral degrees or are just about to receive them. Indeed, in constituting the CODESRIA National Working Group on Kenya under whose umbrella this volume was researched and written, we aimed to tap into the energy and bring forth the perspectives of this generation of scholars.

Most of the time, this generation is dismissed as young and inexperienced, in complete disregard of the contexts of its training. Many of these researchers attended initial university education in Kenya at a time when higher education was in deep crisis. Thus, most of us were in fact trained under extremely harsh conditions characterised by decreased public expenditure on higher education and limited access to faculty, libraries and other basic learning facilities. This hostile situation has been linked to mismanagement of national economies that was accompanied by increasing state authoritarianism, a situation that also spawned internal authoritarianism and mismanagement within universities – crowded lecture rooms, decaying physical infrastructure, regular student riots punctuated by university closures and, most importantly, high rates of brain drain that denied students the opportunity to be tutored by the very best that Kenya could produce. The products that we are and the ideas we pen in this volume are, by and large, the work of a generation of Kenyan scholarship that was orphaned at a critical stage of their development.

We begin this preface with a declaration of our identity not to excuse cavalier work but to locate our intentions in the words of the great African revolutionary, Frantz Fanon, who famously stated that 'each generation must out of relative obscurity discover its mission, fulfil it or betray it'. Fanon's words ring true of what Kenyan scholarship urgently needs to do. It needs to facilitate the emergence of a new generation of thinkers and dreamers dedicated to realising their mission. For a long time, and with very few notable exceptions, a gerontocratic grip has stalled the emergence of this generation both in politics and in scholarship. This grip is evident in most humanities and social science disciplines in which senior scholars have not lived up to the expectation of nurturing and mentoring younger scholars. First, due to the harsh and authoritarian rule, some leading scholars were forced to flee into exile, others were hounded out of the university system, while still others left on account of demoralisation by the increasingly intolerant political environment. Second, other scholars simply opted to seek greener pastures provided by international agencies, research organisations, non-governmental organisations or private tertiary colleges in the face of increased work demands and low remuneration at the public universities. Third, scholars who suffered detention but survived it and rejoined the academy, but whose detention experience impacted negatively on them, transforming them from vibrant and engaging scholars into cynics with an overly pessimistic worldview. That there were good reasons for some scholars to leave the university is not in doubt. What we need to discuss are the consequences such actions had on the nurturing of a new generation of scholars, because understanding the reasons for this abandonment has not shielded us from its consequences.

The significance of mentoring a new generation of Kenyan scholars cannot be overemphasised. It is notable that within the local public universities in Kenya, many senior scholars are preoccupied by hierarchies of seniority and distinguish themselves by their superciliousness. Socialised in a culture where hierarchy takes precedence over a collegial attitude, some of these scholars prefer to emphasise their seniority. As a consequence, some have limited the possibilities of mentoring through close teacher–student interaction and the potential to bring forth a new well-trained and well-equipped generation to advance knowledge and take over the endeavours already initiated. Teacher–student interaction, especially at the postgraduate level, has been limited by the general crisis situation affecting many Kenyan universities and by a section of the professoriate that has been complicit in the dictatorial tendencies exhibited by successive university administrations. Thus, a significant portion of the blame also rests on senior faculty who have not sufficiently played their role in teaching students the basic skills in critical reading, thinking and writing, and introducing them to the art of writing grant proposals, articles and book manuscripts. Some senior scholars have not successfully supervised a single postgraduate student in their long careers or are simply incapable of doing so. There is also the well-known endemic one-book-in-career or no-book-at-all syndrome among senior scholars.

Such shortfalls among senior faculty have in turn been reflected among students. For instance, in its inaugural competition for the award of a prize for the best doctoral dissertation written on the continent, a CODESRIA panel of eminent scholars decided that none of the dissertations submitted qualified for the 2003 award. In other cases, major funding organisations like Rockefeller and SIDA-SAREC have observed that proposals submitted to some of the programmes they sponsor have poor theoretical and methodological orientation. A Rockefeller report went further to call for 'the creation of intergenerational learning and research communities around thematic concerns'. CODESRIA, which sources most of its constituents from African universities (and Kenya supplies a sizeable cohort), has praised proposals for their thematic richness but observed that this richness 'is in a total mismatch with the theoretical, methodological, and bibliographical poverty'. While many of these complaints are attributable to poor infrastructure within higher education in Africa, admirable results from some sites of higher learning in Africa suggest that there is more to this problem than infrastructure.

The choice of themes for this text was influenced by a consideration of the conditions, highlighted above, under which our generation was trained. This experience has a lot to do with the state–university relations and the role of actors within the state, universities and society in general in shaping political trends. There is no doubt that the experience of many students at any given university is directly influenced by its relationships with the state and the society. After all, this has been a repressive state whose relations with the wider society are defined by an arrogant misuse of political power. Scholars have not sufficiently analysed the sense of loss and confusion for scholarship generated by the developmental losses of the so-called lost decade. Kenya is perhaps the only African country with a considerably well-developed

epistemic community that is often ignored as Western scholars conduct major debates of immense national importance. This study implicitly
addresses some of the questions arising from the indelible impressions
and sense of loss associated with this decade especially as they relate to
the conduct of politics and the production of knowledge. We see this
as an important part of the process of celebrating the achievements and
also addressing the shortfalls of the previous generations of scholars.

There were two other considerations in choosing to study the
prospects of democratisation in Kenya. First, with researchers of limited direct experience in politics, it was judged that their assessment of
politics and democratisation processes might be detached and dispassionate and therefore different from extant literature. Of the previous
generations we write about above, many went to school with occu-
piers of state power. Some of their contemporaries, using their first
timer connections, have taken up key political appointments in
government and positions within the civil society from where they
launched their 'struggle' against the incumbent KANU regime. But is
this not simply an intra-class struggle that focuses on seizure of state
power rather than a radical change in the mode of politics? This situation leaves wide open the crucial question of what the alternative
agenda for power takeover really is for the intellectuals who use their
privileged position, either in the university or through civil society, to
assume the reins of power.

Closely related to the first explanation above is a second motivation
for this study. It concerns historiography as it relates to praxis. Upon
review of the literature on democratisation in Kenya, a certain flaw in
terms of the consistency of the writers' ideas with their actions in politics was detected. In the initial stages of this project, it was difficult to
assess this issue of consistency of ideas and actions and to connect it to
the need for dispassionate and detached research. After all, the intellectual climate at the time was one in which critical thinking about opposition politics played into the hands of a dictatorial KANU regime on
the one hand and risked being branded by opposition-aligned intellectuals as pro-KANU thinking on the other hand. But as Kenya went
into the 2002 general elections and the Moi regime was swept out of
power, subsequent political developments in the country have consistently confirmed the hunch that the Kenyan transition is beset by a
politics of selective blame that has, in turn, limited the emancipative
capacity of the new leadership. The transition has laid bare the disconnection between the ideas of opposition-aligned politicians, activists

and intellectuals with respect to democratisation and their actual practices and actions once in power. Our concern and contribution in this
text is that knowledge about democratisation must not just be comprehensive; it must also be consistent with the actions and practices of
those who articulate it. This consistency is seriously lacking among
many intellectuals and politicians.

A final area of concern is the connection of local knowledge to
wider continental debates on knowledge production and democratisation. The literature on the state, democratisation and economic
reform in Kenya suffers from too much exposure to intellectual fads
from the North and very little connection to research trends from
within Africa. This is especially true with respect to studies conducted
within the framework of CODESRIA programmes. Except for a few
articles, very few Kenyan scholars have been actively involved in the
numerous CODESRIA networks. It was only in the mid-1990s that a
new wave of young Kenyan scholars and students, mostly based at
Kenyatta University, began actively to take advantage of the amicable
and collegial scholarly environment provided by CODESRIA to
make their contributions. But among the path-breaking CODESRIA
publications on social movements, democratisation, economic reform,
labour, the military and agriculture, there is a notable absence of Kenyan
involvement and contribution. Yet CODESRIA is an acclaimed pre-
mier social science institution in Africa whose role in shaping scholarship on the continent, challenging Northern dominance in the study
of Africa, shifting theoretical and policy positions and also in engendering social sciences is, by now, widely acknowledged and respected.
Indeed, the nature of knowledge on democratisation and development as they relate to governance has been transformed under the
auspices of CODESRIA in association with similarly oriented institutions in Africa, Asia and Europe.

In looking to the North for intellectual inspiration, Kenyan scholarship on the state, democratisation and economic reform has largely
missed an inspiring critique of how Africanists 'manufacture African
studies and crises'. A section of the local Kenyan scholarship has most
of the time uncritically reproduced fads from the North. There are
studies that laud liberal democracy and uncritically embrace Western
discourses on human rights, women's rights and gender relations.
Indeed, not very many Kenyan scholars have been critical of the disastrous Western discourses on economic reform. Thus, in more ways
than one, the World Bank discourse on rolling back the state has found

an almost passive audience among sections of Kenyan politicians, intellectuals and civil society activists. While some local intellectuals, activists and politicians simply lacked the critical sensitivity to engage this donor discourse without relenting on the noble goal of fighting internal mismanagement, corruption and authoritarianism, others hoped to use the donor demands as leverage to fight the Moi/KANU regime. But they failed to offer credible alternatives to the donor-driven agenda whose aims are not consonant with local interests and needs and cannot therefore be beneficial to local communities. The result has been that non-Kenyan scholars, most of them schooled in Northern theories and methodologies that are not sensitive to local nuances, carry out most of the major studies on reform and structural adjustment in Kenya.

In order to provide analysis that respects the nuances of the local situation but remains critical of Northern fabrications and incantations of African crises, this study relied heavily on perspectives of African scholars working on the various themes examined herein. These thematic areas were decided on in the context of prevailing trends in Kenya's democratic transition. At the time, in mid-2001, a mixed air of expectation and resignation hung on the minds of most Kenyans about the prospects for real democratic transition. No one knew whether Moi would relinquish power under any amount of pressure. Also, very few people would have predicted that a formidable and united opposition would coalesce to prevent Moi from holding on to power by sponsoring a preferred successor. So much has changed since then. The pre-election pessimism was temporarily replaced by excessive optimism immediately before and after the 2002 elections. Thus, from the very start, we were aware of the limitations and prospects of the democratisation process in Kenya. As in the rest of Africa, it had notable gains as well as inherent limitations that needed to be identified, discussed and understood with a view to putting the future prospects in perspective. The interface between the pessimistic picture and the optimistic vision has therefore been critical to this study.

Godwin R. Murunga
Shadrack W. Nasong'o

PART I

Introduction

I

Prospects for Democracy in Kenya

Shadrack Wanjala Nasong'o and Godwin R. Murunga

Then, we knew we had a dictator as president and found ways to survive in a hostile, autocratic environment; today, our so-called liberators have proved to be no better than wolves in sheep's clothing. Our sense of betrayal today is far greater than it was even three years ago, because everyone we thought was on our side was actually only looking out for himself and herself. (Warah 2004: 14)

Introduction

The purpose of this chapter is twofold. First, it problematises two key concepts, democracy and democratic transition, that are extensively used in this study with a view to delineating their conceptual and practical applications. Second, it explores the general outlines of the transition from the Moi regime to the Kibaki regime and highlights the dilemmas and democratic prospects this transition has presented. We conclude that the prospects for democracy in Kenya are contingent, to a large extent, upon restructuring the institutions of governance and concomitantly devolving power from the presidency, a process that all governments in Kenya, including the Kibaki one, have been reluctant to shepherd. As the transition from Moi to Kibaki amply illustrates, a mere change of guard is not, in and of itself, a basis for a new mode of politics, notwithstanding the claims and promises of the new ruling elite to the contrary.

Theoretical and Conceptual Considerations

The quest for democratic governance is an almost universal pheno-menon. The ubiquitous nature of the wave of democratisation across the world at the end of the twentieth century and the concomitant burgeoning literature on transition politics illustrate this with clarity. Indeed, the honorific nature of the concept of democracy is such that all manner of political systems claim to be democracies. Even countries that have never held an election in decades, such as the former Zaire, are conveniently baptised 'democratic republics'. Others without a competitive party system, such as Uganda (1986–2006), call themselves 'non-party democracies'. Yet to others, the only genuine brand of democracy is the liberal variety with its emphasis on individual freedom and civil liberties. In fact, according to Francis Fukuyama (1989), until recently, liberal democracy is the highest form of human government that cannot be improved upon! Given the competing views of democracy including 'democracy with adjectives', 'liberal democracy', 'social democracy' 'progressive democracy' (Collier and Levitsky 1997), 'guided democracy' and 'non-party democracy', some scholars argue that we are living in an age of democratic confusion. Democracy, they assert, is a high-flown concept for something that does not exist in concrete reality (see Sartori 1987) or, at best, exists in the form of 'choiceless democracy' where economic realities negate the possibilities for political choice (Ake 1996a; Mkandawire 1999). What, then, is 'democracy' and what constitutes 'democratic transition'?

Conceptualising democracy

According to the liberal conceptualisation, the prerequisite for the concrete realisation of democracy lies in a number of institutional guarantees. These guarantees include (1) freedom to form and join organisations, be they political parties, social movements, or civic, professional and welfare associations; (2) freedom of expression and movement; (3) universal adult suffrage; (4) eligibility, in principle, of any citizen to seek public office; (5) right of political leaders to compete freely for support and votes; (6) existence of alternative sources of information; (7) free, fair and competitive elections; (8) accountable governmental decision-making institutions; (9) freedom of elected officials from overriding opposition from unelected officials (Dahl 1982; Harbeson 1999: 40). The more a country approximates these institutional guarantees, the more democratic it is. This form of liberal democracy, according to Ake (2000), is markedly different from genuine democracy even though it has significant affinities. The affinities include the notion of government by the consent of the governed, formal political equality, inalienable human rights including the right to political participation, accountability of power to the governed and the rule of law. 'None-theless, the differences are highly significant. Instead of the collectivity, liberal democracy focuses on the individual whose claims are ultimately placed above those of the group. It replaces government by the people with government based on the consent of the people. Instead of the sovereignty of the people it offers the sovereignty of "law" and operates by repudiating the very idea of popular power' (Ake 2000: 10; 1996b).

Claude Ake (1996a: 130) argues that even at its best, liberal democracy is inimical to people having effective decision-making power. The essence of liberal democracy is precisely the abolition of popular power and the replacement of popular sovereignty with the rule of law. As it evolved, liberal democracy became less democratic because its funda-mental elements, such as consent of the governed, accountability of power to the governed and popular participation, came under pressure from political elites all over the world as well as from mainstream social science which seemed more suspicious of democracy than political elites. On the pretext of clarifying the meaning of democracy, Western social science has constantly redefined it to the detriment of its democratic val-ues. For instance, the group theory of democracy evades the meaning of democracy and pushes the notion that the essence of democracy is the dynamics of group competition, which prevents the monopolisation of power and allows the accommodation of the broad concerns of many groups. According to the interest group theory of democracy, the citizen is no longer a real or potential lawmaker or a participant in sovereignty, but only a supplicant for favourable policy results in accordance with articulated interests. For the protective theory of democracy, the demo-cratic polity is one in which the citizen is protected against the state, espe-cially by virtue of a vibrant civil society. Popular sovereignty disappears, as does participation, as people settle for protection. It is this approach, Ake affirms, that celebrates apathy as being conducive to political stabil-ity or for being a mark of citizen satisfaction with rulers.

For Afrifa Gitonga (1987), democracy exists at three levels: abstract, practical and concrete levels. At the abstract level, democracy is an intellectual visualisation of a model of the possible and desirable in matters of governance. At the practical level, it consists of the ways and means of translating the democratic ideal into reality. And finally, at the concrete level, democracy comprises the balance sheet of past and present experiments of humanity to install a democratic order. In this regard, Ake's (1996a) conceptualisation of the kind of democracy suitable for Africa is most illuminating. Such democracy entails four key characteristics. First, it has to be a democracy in which people have some real decision-making power over and above the formal consent of electoral choice. This entails, among other things, a powerful legislature, decentralisation of power to local democratic formations, and considerable emphasis on the development of institutions for the aggregation and articulation of interests. Second, it has to be a social democracy that places emphasis on concrete political, social and economic rights, as opposed to a liberal democracy that emphasises abstract political rights (see Mafeje 1995). It has to be a social democracy that invests heavily in the improvement of people's health, education and capacity so that they can participate effectively. Third, it has to be a democracy that puts as much emphasis on collective rights as it does on individual rights. It has to recognise nationalities, subnationalities, ethnic groups and communities as social formations that express freedom and self-realisation, and thus grants them rights to cultural expression and political and economic participation. Fourth and finally, it has to be a democracy of incorporation – an inclusive politics that engenders inclusive participation and equitable access to state resources and ensures special representation in legislatures of mass organisations, especially the youth, the labour movement and women's groups, which are usually marginalised but without whose active participation there is unlikely to be democracy or development (Ake 1996a: 132).

The basic assumption is that the objective of the political transition phenomenon in Africa has been, or should be, geared towards maximising the actualisation of the kind of democracy as conceptualised by Ake. It was the expectation of a shift to this mode of politics in Kenya that informed the enthusiastic euphoria that accompanied the transition from the Moi regime to the Kibaki regime in December 2002. Nevertheless, as Ake posits, the attainment of this concrete form of democracy is a function, for the most part, of the extent to which Africans themselves, especially the non-elite, drive the process.

The transition paradigm

Carothers (2002) attributes the notion of democratic transition as an analytic model to the seminal work of O'Donnell and Schmitter (1986) which, in his view, marked the beginning of the emergent academic field of 'transitology'. The concept was derived from a general interpretation, on the part of scholars, policy makers and democracy advocates, of the patterns of democratic change that were taking place in Africa, Asia, Eastern Europe and Latin America. This change entailed shifting away from military dictatorship, statist developmentalism, single-party authoritarianism and communist totalitarianism to more open systems of governance. As a paradigmatic perspective, 'democratic transition' became a way of talking about, thinking about and designing interventions in processes of political change around the world (Carothers 2002: 6). Carothers notes that several assumptions mark the transition paradigm. First is the assumption that any country moving *away* from dictatorial rule can be considered a country in transition *towards* democracy. Second is the assumption that democratisation occurs in sequential stages. It begins with political *opening*, a period of democratic ferment and political liberalisation in which cracks appear in the ruling dictatorial regime, with the main fault line lying between the hardliners and softliners. This is followed by the *breakthrough* – the collapse of the regime and the emergence of a new democratic system, with the assumption of power by a new government through national elections and the establishment of a new democratic institutional structure, via the promulgation of a new constitution. This transition is then followed by *consolidation*, constitutive of a slow but purposeful process in which democratic forms are transformed into democratic substance. This is done by the reform of state institutions, regularisation of elections, strengthening of civil society and overall habituation of society to the new democratic rules of political engagement.

The third core assumption of the transition paradigm, as Carothers notes, is the belief in the determinative importance of elections. Harbeson (1999) elaborates this assumption more clearly than Carothers. According to Harbeson, the push for democratisation in the early 1990s suffered from a disproportionate emphasis on the conduct of initial, national-level multiparty elections. This temporally constrained, election-centric conception of the transition phase, according to Harbeson (1999: 42–3), lies in the implicit excessive expectations of this period. The expectations included the presumptions that, first, democratic transition would necessarily produce a regime change from an incumbent authoritarian regime to a new democratically inclined one. Second, that initial multiparty elections and/or regime change would generate the momentum necessary to produce subsequent, broader patterns of democratisation. Third, that this momentum would be sufficient to generate the means for the fulfilment of the broader array of democratisation tasks in the consolidation phase. Fourth, that the initial multiparty elections taking place at the national level would lead to democratisation at the sub-national levels. Fifth and finally, that the polity itself would remain sufficiently stable to sustain the transition and the subsequent consolidation phases of democratisation. Hence the euphoria that attended the onset of transition politics which was assumed to mark democratic resurgence in hitherto undemocratic regimes.

The assumption that any country moving *away* from authoritarianism is, ipso facto, undergoing transition *towards* democracy may, however, be mistaken. According to Colomer (2000), multiparty elections held in democratising countries within a context of non-democratic rules of the game constitute what he calls 'strategic transitions'. Colomer contends that in the quest for democratic transition, authoritarian incumbents and their democratic oppositions always arrive at an intermediate formula between dictatorship and democracy:

> In order to be agreeable, a provisional compromise must include the calling of a multiparty election not securing an absolute winner. On the one hand, the rulers can rely upon their advantage as incumbents to turn the compromise into a lasting 'semi-democratic' regime, which would allow them not to be expelled from power or even to recover some of their previously challenged positions. On the other side, the democratic opposition can envisage the agreement as a mere transitory stage, giving it some chance of gaining power and introducing further reforms, which can lead to the eventual establishment of a democratic regime. (Colomer 2000: 1–2)

It is in this sense that Ake (1996a) observes that in the hurry to globalise democracy following the end of the cold war, democracy has been reduced to the crude simplicity of multiparty elections to the benefit of some of the world's most notorious autocrats. In Africa, elections have produced democratic dictators (Ihonvbere 1996). These include Daniel arap Moi of Kenya and Paul Biya of Cameroon, both able to parade democratic credentials without reforming their repressive regimes. On the flip side, Colomer makes the assumption that opponents of authoritarian incumbents are committed democrats. This is not always the case. Given the exclusivist nature of African politics, the democratisation phenomenon may simply constitute an opening wedge for excluded politicians to successfully stage re-entry into power and perpetuate the same exclusivist politics. The expectation that they will introduce reforms towards the establishment of emancipatory politics is not guaranteed (Wamba-dia-Wamba 1992). Democratic transition is thus bound to be messy, fitful and frustrating, with many advances and setbacks along the way.

Prospects for Democracy in Kenya

The struggles for democracy in Kenya have been long and persistent. The results of the December 2002 elections in the country were a landmark in this struggle as they heralded expectations that a new political era of democracy had dawned in Kenya. For the first time, the incumbent Kenya African National Union (KANU) was defeated after four decades in power. Second, again for the first time in the country's history, a president retired from office. Third, the electoral defeat of KANU occurred against the backdrop of a united opposition under the aegis of the National Alliance Rainbow Coalition (NARC), a reality that promised to usher in a new political era of dialogue, consensus and power sharing. This new dispensation was encapsulated in the NARC Summit – the coalition's eight-member chief decision-making organ – and the memorandum of understanding (MoU) that committed the coalition partners to conclude the constitutional review process within 100 days of their assumption of power, create new institutions of governance, strengthen existing ones and devolve some of the overwhelming powers of the presidency (see Murunga and Nasong'o 2006 for details). It is this commitment to reduce the powers of the president through a new power-sharing arrangement that the MoU anticipated. As Ndegwa argues, 'had the constitutional-reform process not been going on at the time of the campaign, it is virtually inconceivable that any opposition leader would have agreed to give up his or her slim chance at the imperial presidency and settle for the certainty of exclusion in its shadow' (Ndegwa 2003: 154).

How has Kibaki performed since taking over power in January 2003? With respect to the task of transforming the state, Ndegwa (2003: 156) predicted that 'after the first series of major correctives, attempts to redesign the state will stall. Efforts to correct the institutionalised propensity for overcentralisation will be abandoned'. Less than two years after being elected, Kibaki abandoned the MoU and, with it, the power-sharing arrangement it promised. He also marginalised the Liberal Democratic Party allies of the coalition and invited die-hard Kanuists like Simeon Nyachae, Kipkalia Kones, William Ole Ntimama and John Koech into his government. They joined a cabal of largely Mount Kenya region politicians, popularly referred to as the 'Mount Kenya Mafia', to defeat the popular optimism that saw Kenya through the elections. Consequently, Kibaki's administration quickly acquired an ethno-regional bias, not different from Moi's and Kenyatta's before him. Far from fighting corruption, the vice became even more endemic under the Kibaki regime with revelations of a series of scandals perpetrated by President Kibaki's close associates using a shadowy company called Anglo Leasing and Finance. With respect to the constitution review process, infighting within the coalition stalled the process, which was eventually hijacked by the National Alliance (Party) of Kenya (NAK) wing of NARC that proceeded to amend the people-driven Bomas draft of the constitution with an eye to maintaining the institutional status quo especially with regard to presidential powers. This effort backfired when the revised draft was overwhelmingly rejected by citizens in a referendum in November 2005.

On account of the above political developments in Kenya following the transition from Moi to Kibaki, most Kenyans are overly disappointed with the Kibaki regime to the point of disillusionment. Nevertheless, despite some major limitations in the struggles for democracy in Kenya, there are a number of fundamental gains and the prospects for democracy are bright given the empowering experience for Kenyans of voting an incumbent party out of power in 2002 and handing the Kibaki regime defeat in the 2005 referendum on a new constitution. To analyse the gains, limitations and prospects of the struggles for democracy in Kenya, this book focuses on the intersecting dynamics between local and foreign initiatives geared towards checking the excesses of the Kenyatta, Moi and Kibaki regimes. It demonstrates that the democratisation process in Kenya has been waged in numerous sites, civil society being one but not always a consistently pro-democracy site. The chapters in this book are designed to address the trials, travails and tribulations attending the process, highlighting the twists and turns, the forward rushes, and the instant reversals that have characterised the process of democratisation in Kenya. In so doing, the chapters show that democratic transition is a laborious process that does not follow any linear path. Rather, we argue that anti-democratic forces emanating from within and also external forces, especially the multilateral and bilateral lenders have, while supporting democracy, also worked to bolster authoritarian tendencies, thereby pushing social movements in Kenya to adjust not just to internal impediments to democracy but also to external ones. The result has been a rich political experience, one that cannot be reduced to the Afro-pessimist labelling common in much of the Western Africanist literature.

This book is divided into four parts. The first part comprises the introduction to the book. Part II deals with the theme of civil society and the politics of opposition, and comprises Chapters 2–4. Chapters 5–8

constitute Part III of the book, which deals with the key constituencies in the democratisation process. Part IV comprises Chapters 9 and
10, and deals with the theme of donors and the politics of structural
adjustment.

Part II: Civil society and the politics of opposition

Part II begins with Shadrack Nasong'o's chapter on the role of civil
society in the democratisation process in Kenya. Nasong'o argues that the
prospects for democratic transition are inextricably linked to the negotiation of new rules of the political game. The realisation of concrete forms
of democracy is contingent upon the rules of the game that provide for
alternative political parties competing against one another for the chance
to govern within institutional structures that guarantee fair competition
and a genuine opportunity for alternation of power between parties.
Arguing that this is where civil society organisations (CSOs) have the
potential to make their most profound impact, Nasong'o delineates the
historical specificity of CSOs in Kenya and evaluates their role in negotiating new rules of politics in the Kenyan transition. He observes that
CSOs and the pro-democracy movement in Kenya generally have contributed modestly to opening up the political space within the context of
democratisation. This was largely a function of the window of political
opportunity afforded by the general movement for good governance.
Whereas the CSOs in Kenya had great potential to impact politics,
Nasong'o argues that they faced a number of constraints. These constraints
circumscribed the ability of the pro-democracy movement in Kenya
to effect fundamental changes to the strategic environment of political
engagement by way of constitutional engineering via mass action.

In Chapter 3, Margaret Gecaga grapples with the role of religious
movements in the process of democratisation with particular reference
to the Mungiki movement. She outlines the cultural and religious
beliefs and practices that informed the development of Mungiki and
analyses its sensibilities in the politics of transition in Kenya. Gecaga
notes that Mungiki attempted to resacralise the Agikuyu society
through redefining the sacred in the secular domain by using religion
to legitimise political ideals. She concludes, however, that the movement's violent nature and the propensity of its leaders to convert to
other mainstream religions like Christianity and Islam paint it as a
group constituted for instrumentalist and profane purposes. It is, in
essence, a highly eclectic and amorphous group mobilised by politicians to execute their own narrowly conceived political schemes.

Adams Oloo, in Chapter 4, focuses on opposition political parties in Kenya with particular emphasis on their internal traits and efforts by incumbent regimes to manipulate them. He proceeds from the conceptual premise that there cannot be democracy in a single-party state since, in such a system, elections amount simply to contests between personalities and are thus devoid of meaning with regard to democratic choice. It was this conviction that informed the push for the legalisation of opposition political parties in Kenya. Accordingly, Oloo analyses the country's experience with multiparty politics and the impact of multipartyism on the broad goal of enhancing democracy. He argues that opposition parties in Kenya have generally had an uninspiring experience characterised by elitism, factionalism, ethnocentrism and systematic manipulation by incumbents. He also notes that the first-past-the-post winner-takes-all electoral system used in Kenya works against opposition parties.

Part III: Major constituencies in the democratisation process

In Chapter 5, Mshaï Mwangola examines the role of the youth in enabling democracy in Kenya. Proceeding from her categorisation of actors on the Kenyan political scene into three generations – the Lancaster House Generation (LHG), the Lost Generation and the Uhuru Generation – she notes that within the context of the gerontocratic nature of Kenya's political leadership dominated by the LHG leaders, the political space for the participation of youth has remained overly circumscribed. The situation is compounded by religious and associated belief systems that emphasise traditional allegiance to male elders to further constrict the space available for youth representation in positions of leadership. The gerontocratic political elite are simply content with assuring the youth that they are the 'leaders of tomorrow'. Unfortunately for many youth, the future has come and gone with no signs of the old elite relinquishing positions of political leadership to them. Contending that the decade of the 1990s brought to the fore an aggressive youth discourse that has rejected prevailing perceptions of youth and demanded a reconfiguring of the social roles and responsibilities of this category, Mwangola identifies the spaces available for youth political action and delineates the dimensions of such youth action and their implications for Kenya's transition politics.

Chapter 6 focuses on women in Kenya's politics of transition and democratisation. Shadrack Nasong'o and Theodora Ayot note that women played a critical role in the politics of decolonisation, yet after independence the establishment of patrimonial authoritarianism engendered male dominance of all aspects of Kenyan society and denied women a chance to develop strategic initiatives and gain an audible political voice. The authors contend that the active participation of women in the democratisation process in Kenya is critical to ensuring substantial influence on the direction of national politics. The major constraints to this eventuality, in their estimation, include the social construction of politics as a man's game, complete with an ingrained culture of violence, differential levels of literacy and poverty, patriarchal ideologies of the postcolonial state, as well as lack of unity in the gender movement with regard to ethnicity, class, organisational capabilities, clearly stated unity of purpose and vision for the future.

In Chapter 7, Maurice Amutabi emphasises that intellectuals are affected by and interested in the political processes that attend the course of society's social development. Academicians have been on both sides of the political divide; some supporting the status quo while others remain at the forefront of agitation for political change. Some others simply engage in praising the dictatorial regimes through sophisticated intellectual propaganda or fashioning support systems for student and mass struggles. Proceeding from a taxonomic categorisation of intellectuals into organic/activist, bourgeois/authoritarian, academic/philosophical and generic/general, Amutabi locates Kenyan intellectuals in the country's political process and examines their role and impact in the democratisation process. In addition, he explores the social struggles that universities wage through student activism and their contribution to bridging the gap between the elite and the masses. Such activities have implications for the role of universities in general and intellectuals in particular, who manifest dual orientations of either fervently supporting the status quo or seeking to challenge it through ardent political activism.

The role of law enforcement agencies in the struggles for democracy in Kenya is an understudied theme. Edwin Gimode, in Chapter 8, reaches back to colonial times to understand the role of Kenya police in supporting the ideology of order, underpinning the colonial and postcolonial states. Law enforcement agencies were created to enforce colonial rule over the natives and this role was inherited and perfected by the postcolonial state in fighting political opposition. For Gimode, democratisation started with resistance to the colonial political forces, and the fight for *uhuru* (freedom) mirrored a fight for the democratic ideal of self-government. Concomitantly, the origins of oppressive practices by the police are traceable to these early decades. Gimode's main thesis is that law enforcement agencies have been used over time to impede the progress of democratic forces while simultaneously promoting dictatorship over Kenyans. He optimistically concludes that the defeat of Moi in 2002 has ushered in a new era of democracy in which the new regime has made efforts to reform the police force to serve the public better.

Part IV: Donors and the politics of structural adjustment

This part begins with Chapter 9. Godwin Murunga focuses on governance and the politics of structural adjustment. The movement for good governance and sustainable economic development in Africa emerged out of concern for the worsening economic situation in the continent. This was motivated by the economic stagnation beginning in the late 1970s and the decline at the turn of the decade in the 1980s. This problem was variously attributed to the crisis of governance in Africa, to lack of a development ethic, and to African culture generally. It was against this background that the World Bank and the International Monetary Fund launched several initiatives including structural adjustment programmes (SAPs) as a panacea for sub-Saharan Africa's economic problems. Murunga shows that the idea of governance was merely an afterthought addition to the economistic dictates of donor neo-liberalism. He examines the history and impact of SAPs on social movements, political choices and popular power in Kenya by contextualising the politics of structural adjustment within the broader framework of the agenda for political reform, and by evaluating the implications of structural adjustment for political transition and good governance in Kenya. In so doing, he unmasks the hypocrisy of adjustment prescriptors who have historically been part and parcel of the Kenyan (indeed African) problem.

In Chapter 10, Stephen Brown analyses the role played by Kenya's bilateral and multilateral lenders and donors in the country's democratisation process. Brown's main thesis is that the form and intensity of donor intervention in Kenya's democratisation process shifted several times between 1989 and 2002, resulting in contradictory effects. While at times donors helped bring about rapid political change, they simultaneously sought to shape the outcome of the democratisation process, sometimes holding back aid to prevent the process from taking a form of which they disapproved. Given this conjuncture, Brown aptly describes donors as having had one foot on the accelerator and the other on the brakes, and concludes that donors should neither expect Kenyan actors blindly to follow their preferred strategies, nor should Kenyan actors expect donors blindly to support their pro-democracy initiatives. While cognisant of the complexity and difficulty of finding common ground between external and local actors in the democratisation process, Brown rightly observes that greater attention to domestic priorities and strategies on the part of external actors is more likely to produce an effective road map to sustainable democracy in Kenya.

In the final analysis, the future of democratisation in Kenya resides in a power-sharing arrangement that brings together a popular decision-making unit akin to the NARC Summit; in devolving power, both political and economic, horizontally from the presidency to parliament, the bureaucracy and judiciary, and vertically to refashioned local government units; as well as in gradually including a new generation of leadership whose vision goes beyond the next general election to the next generation. This eventuality is contingent upon exertion of sustained public pressure on the political class, both in government and in the opposition, to put in place a vision for Kenya's transformation and a calculated understanding and strategic mobilising against entrenched external forces whose role in constricting the democratic space is too well known to require recapitulation. Towards this end, one very positive development in Kenya that can be described as ushering in a new dawn is the high level of consciousness and awareness among ordinary people about their role in Kenyan politics. The trap the NARC government drove itself into in the pre-election period in 2002 enhances this awareness. Upon assuming power, NARC had no option but to liberalise the airwaves and allow for greater freedom of speech and assembly. Furthermore, the very acts of successfully voting out Moi and KANU, and of defeating a government-sponsored but watered down draft constitution, has inspired a new sense of confidence in ordinary people to make a difference. This is important to sustain the initiative to transform the state, and it is herein that the prospects for democracy in Kenya lie.

References

Ake, C. (1996a) *Democracy and Development in Africa*, Washington, DC: The Brookings Institution.

———— (1996b) 'Rethinking African Democracy', in L. Diamond, and M.F. Plattner (eds), *The Global Resurgence of Democracy*, Baltimore, MD: The Johns Hopkins University Press.

Ake, C. (2000) *The Feasibility of Democracy in Africa*, Dakar: CODESRIA.

Carothers, T. (2002) 'The End of the Transition Paradigm', *Journal of Democracy*, vol. 13, no. 1.

Collier, D., and S. Levitsky (1997) 'Democracy with Adjectives: Conceptual Innovation in Comparative Research', *World Politics*, vol. 49.

Colomer, J.M. (2000) *Strategic Transitions: Game Theory and Democratization*, Baltimore, MD: The Johns Hopkins University Press.

Dahl, R. (1982) *Dilemmas of Pluralist Democracy*, New Haven, CT: Yale University Press.

Fukuyama, F. (1989) 'The End of History?', *The National Interest*, vol. 16.

Gitonga A. (1987) 'The Meaning and Foundations of Democracy', in W.O. Oyugi et al. (eds), *Democratic Theory and Practice in Africa*, London: Heinemann.

Harbeson, J.W. (1999) 'Rethinking Democratic Transitions: Lessons from Eastern and Southern Africa', in R. Joseph (ed.), *State, Conflict, and Democracy in Africa*, Boulder, CO: Lynne Rienner.

Ihonvbere, J.O. (1996) 'Where is the Third Wave? A Critical Evaluation of Africa's Non-transition to Democracy', *Africa Today*, vol. 43, no. 4.

Mafeje, A. (1995) 'Theory of Democracy and the African Discourse: Breaking Bread with My Fellow-Travellers', in E. Chole and J. Ibrahim (eds), *Democratisation Processes in Africa: Problems and Prospects*, Dakar: CODESRIA.

Mkandawire, T. (1999) 'Crisis Management and the Making of "Choiceless Democracies",' in R. Joseph (ed.), *State, Conflict, and Democracy in Africa*, Boulder, CO: Lynne Rienner.

Murunga, G.R., and S.W. Nasong'o (2006) 'Bent on Self-Destruction: The Kibaki Regime in Kenya', *Journal of Contemporary African Studies*, vol. 24, no. 1.

Ndegwa, S.N. (2003) 'Kenya: Third Time Lucky?', *Journal of Democracy*, vol. 14, no. 3.

O'Donnell, G., and P.C. Schmitter (1986) *Transitions from Authoritarian Rule: Tentative Conclusions about Uncertain Democracies*, Baltimore, MD: The Johns Hopkins University Press.

Sartori, G. (1987) *The Theory of Democracy Revisited*, Chatham, NJ: Chatham House Publishers.

Wamba-dia-Wamba, E. (1992) 'Beyond Elite Politics of Democracy in Africa', *Quest*, vol. 4, no. 1.

Warah, R. (2004). 'Ngugi in Exile: Home is Where the Art is', *The East African*, 30 August–5 September.

PART II

Civil Society and the Politics of Opposition

Negotiating New Rules of the Game: Social Movements, Civil Society and the Kenyan Transition

Shadrack Wanjala Nasong'o

Introduction

The literature on transition politics across the democratising world accords civil society pride of place in the process of democratisation. The extant literature on Africa posits that civil society is the missing key to sustained political reform, legitimate states, improved governance, viable state–society and state–economy relationships, and insurance of political renewal. Scholars taking this view hold that structural adjustment programmes (SAPs) initiated in Africa proved a fiasco largely because they failed to emphasise the political role of civil society. Instead, they consigned civil society to the realm of market economics and private enterprise. The propulsion of civil society to the centre stage of activism for political reform is thus informed by the belief that the political role of civil society is indispensable to effecting the transition from authoritarianism to democracy. The purpose of this chapter is to theorise and analyse the role of civil society in the Kenyan transition.

The chapter historically locates civil society as represented by non-governmental organisations (NGOs) and social movements in Kenya, and examines their role in the country's politics. The chapter attempts an exposition of the historical specificity and behavioural dynamics of civil society organisations (CSOs). It aims to provide insights into the nature of the linkages between the state and civil society, and between civil society and political economy. This background is a prerequisite to evaluating the significance of civil society to transition politics, and to demonstrating how the Kenyan masses have responded to the politics generated by the mediation born of CSO activities vis-à-vis the state. The main thesis is that the prospects for democratic transition are inextricably linked to the negotiation of new rules of the political game. In other words, the realisation of democracy is contingent upon rules of the game that provide for alternative political parties competing against one another for the chance to govern within institutional systems that serve the interests of the masses, ensure their effective participation in the political process, and guarantee fair competition and a genuine opportunity for alternation of power between parties. This is where CSOs have the potential to make their most profound impact.

Sketching the Conceptual Cornerstones

The conceptual meanings of 'democracy' and 'transition' have been mapped out in the introductory chapter and need not be repeated here. Nevertheless, two key terms employed in this chapter require elaboration: 'social movements' and 'civil society'.

The idea of social movements

A social movement is defined as '… a collective attempt to further a common interest or secure a common goal, through collective action outside the sphere of established institutions' (Giddens 1997: 511). However, whereas some social movements operate as illegal groups, most social movements operate within the rubric of existing legal parameters, resorting to extra-legal mechanisms only when they face intransigence from the established order. According to Mamdani (1995a: 7), a social movement entails '… the crystallisation of group activity autonomous of the state'. This view is most apt since it is inclusive and encompasses the distinctions not only between community and class or popular and elite movements but also between organised and unorganised, spontaneous or anomic movements, and, as such, it is rooted in concrete African social processes. Social movements often oppose formal, bureaucratic organisations with a view to having certain social institutions and processes changed either for the benefit of members of the social movement or for the general betterment of society. Some social movements seek to control the state or seek effective citizenship therein; others seek to defend and maintain their autonomy and rights against domination and violation (Amadiume 1995: 35; Olukoshi 1995). It is in this sense that some scholars view social movements as '… normatively oriented interactions between adversaries with conflicting interpretations and opposite societal models of a shared cultural field' (Touraine 1981: 31–2; Cohen and Arato 1992: 510). For our purposes, the constellation of all social forces fighting for democracy in Kenya constitutes the pro-democracy movement in the country.

Social movements evolve and develop through three key stages. First is the incubation period, which is usually led by 'men and women of words'. These are the intelligentsia and the ideologues who utilise their gift of the gab and the power of the written word to publicise existing social dysfunctions and to philosophise about how the dysfunctions can be fixed. According to Hoffer (1958), the 'men and women of words' seek to undermine the existing belief systems and institutional arrangement while simultaneously promoting 'hunger for faith' among masses. The key role played by these individuals is the provision of a body of organising principles and slogans around which people are organised for action. They play the crucial role of laying the groundwork for the emergence of a social movement by problematising social dysfunction and hypothesising remedial measures while at the same time inspiring those affected to take action in this regard. The second stage is the action phase. This stage is led by 'fanatics' whose skills and temperament are imperative for hatching and animating the actual movement. The fanatics take the ideology and words of the ideologues and translate them into comprehensible terms for the masses under stress. Katumanga (2000: 6) equates the 'fanatics' to what resistance movements in Africa call 'cadres', and argues that '[t]he salience of cadres lies in the fact that they can easily reach the society through their ability to use and talk the language of the people'. He contends that the ability of a movement to train a cadreship and pass on its objectives, and to convince and motivate them, can determine the movement's ability to survive and achieve its goals. The third stage is the institutionalisation phase. This is the phase in which the social movement becomes bureaucratised on account of its growth in age and size, as it attracts different elements in society. The increasingly routinised nature of the movement's activities in this stage calls for administrative and organisational skills on the part of the leadership. Consequently, this phase requires the leadership of 'practical men and women of action'. Without such leadership, a movement may lose its drive, become tame, experience paralysis and may ultimately atrophy.

There are three types of social movements. The first type is composed of transformative movements, which aim at far-reaching cataclysmic changes in social order. Their purpose is to turn the status quo upside down. They tend to employ violent means to bring about the desired change. Examples of such movements include revolutionary movements, radical religious movements such as *Dini ya Msambwa*[1] in Western Kenya and millenarian movements such as the Davidian sect of Waco, Texas. The second type is composed of redemptive movements, which seek to rescue people from ways of life seen as corrupting, debasing and against the will of God. Such movements target people's belief systems and appeal to their conscience, sense of morality and transcendentalism, with faith as their driving force. Examples of redemptive movements include religious movements such as the Pentecostal revivalist sects, which believe that the spiritual development of individuals is the true indication of their essential worth as human beings. The third type is composed of reformative movements, which aspire to alter only some aspects of the existing social order. The main preoccupation of reformative movements is specific kinds of socio-political inequality and injustice, which they seek to redress. Examples of reformative movements are many, including women's empowerment movements, development and human rights advocacy NGOs, and pro-democracy movements. All these seek to reform, in a particular way, intra-societal relations and/or state–society relations for the general good.

Overall, the success of social movements is a function of four key variables. The first is the nature of the objectives a movement seeks to achieve and the strategies designed to achieve them. The more clearly and realistically the objectives are defined, the greater the chances for crafting effective strategies for their realisation and hence the more likely the movement is to succeed. The second variable is the quality of leadership, which needs to be inspirational, with a capacity for strategic thinking and planning. The third variable is the movement's ideology or organising principles, which serve as the mobilising force. To succeed, the movement's ideology must be understood by the people, appropriated, internalised and deployed against the status quo forces. The fourth and final variable is the quality of a movement's followers, who may be classified into three groups: the ideologues, the militant followers and the passive sympathisers. Ideologues inspire and found social movements, while militant followers are those who act in the name of the movement. Success in this regard calls for the constant renewal, replenishment and widening of the base of militant followers by way of conversion of passive sympathisers. A social movement that fails to do so risks having little, if any, impact on the social order that it seeks to reform or transform.

Conceptualising civil society

The concept of civil society and the idea of empowerment have emerged as significant aspects of democratisation in Africa. Nonetheless, there is contestation over the definition of the concept of civil society. Some scholars celebrate what they posit as the actual and potential capacity of civil society to transform African politics towards greater democracy. They elevate the phenomenon of civil society to the position of a providential spirit dispatched to redeem a political world gone awry (see Callaghy 1994; Harbeson 1994; Diamond 1999; Nyang'oro 2000). Other scholars view the notion of civil society as a mere metaphor masquerading as a political player. They deny the concept concrete reality and contend that it is essentially a child of the anthropomorphic fertility of the social scientific mind. In this view, civil society is a theoretical construct lacking empirical locus, whose contemporary currency is only an intellectual fad that is inherently limited in heuristic value (see Bratton 1994a; Young 1994, 1999; Chabal and Daloz 1999; Nasong'o 2005). Yet, to other scholars, the current emphasis on the state–civil society dichotomy is an ideological strategy of the current neoliberal offensive. For instance, Beckman (1998: 46) argues:

> In an effort to delegitimise the principal ideological rival – economic nationalism – neoliberals seek to delegitimise the state, the main locus of nationalist aspirations and resistance to the neoliberal project. In order to undercut the claims by the state to represent the nation, its alien nature is emphasised. Its retrogressiveness is explained in terms of its separation from civil society … [its] rent-seeking, patrimonialism and … autonomy.

In the same vein, Mamdani (1995b) contends that the state–civil society perspective was not originally formulated to compare the West and the rest, yet it has been treated in Africanist scholarship as a turnkey project instead of being modified as an appropriate technology. Used as a turnkey project, it is guilty of the double manoeuvre of mythology and caricature. Given its unilinear evolutionist orientation that equates the rise of civil society with that of democracy and eschews struggles that inform the historical development of African societies, the state–civil society perspective mythologises European experience and caricatures African experience, in the process mutilating both (Mamdani 1995b: 609).

Whatever one's perspective, the contemporary currency of the concept of civil society in the discourse on democratisation is a political reality. Some scholars take a benign view of civil society and posit it as a bastion of liberty against the state as institutionalised authoritarianism. They see civil society as recruiting and training new leaders, as an agent of political change, and as a midwife of regime transformation (Harbeson 1994; Young 1994; Diamond 1999). For the purposes of this chapter, civil society entails organised social life that is voluntary, self-perpetuating and, though bound by a legal order, is beyond state control (see Diamond 1999: 239–50; Nasong'o 2005: 65–9). It is a realm of contradictory possibilities, replete with conflict between ethnicities, classes and other interests. The implication of this conceptualisation, according to Mamdani (1995b: 604), is clear: 'neither civil society nor movements that arise from it can be idealised. In contrast, movements within civil society demand concrete analysis to be understood, for they harbour contradictory possibilities'. The advantage of this view, as Chazan (1994) observes, is that it takes into account the interpenetrations between civil and political societies, the straddling of one over the other and vice versa. Accordingly, Mamdani (1995b: 604) contends, an analysis anchored in the view of civil society as a realm of contradictory possibilities is not content with highlighting demands of social movements, like those for democracy and human rights, as the general demands of civil society against the state. It calls for reaching beyond every general formulation to fathom and clarify the concrete meaning of a general demand like that of democracy from different viewpoints. It demands raising fundamental questions: what, for instance, is the meaning of democracy from the point of view of different classes and groups? What specific interests are organising behind the general demand for democracy?

Overall, in the grand scheme of Africa's democratisation, civil society is assigned the role of Lenin's strong vanguard Communist Party – that of political mobilisation and education (indoctrination in the case of Lenin's party) of the masses (see Wanyande 2002). As Nyang'oro (2000: 98) contends, the more the members of society organise themselves into groups to advance their particular interests, the less likely the state can function in an autonomous and unaccountable manner. The proliferation of organised interests, in his view, is a bulwark against unbridled state power. Nyang'oro holds that this autonomy may be one of the key principles in the building of democracy. The idea of civil society is thus an overarching concept that subsumes within it a variety of social formations including social movements, NGOs, trade unions, professional associations, student organisations and other civic organisations. All these social formations are collectively referred to in this chapter as CSOs. As Chandhoke (1998: 29) observes, if the literature on social movements describes a phenomenon of popular struggles, civil society provides the conceptual apparatus to comprehend the implications of these struggles on state–society relations.

Kenyan Civil Society: Historical Overview

Kenya's associational arena is a very vibrant one, with thousands of CSOs. The country's receptivity to contemporary CSOs is a function of its long history of organised voluntary activity. Pre-colonial politics in Kenya revolved around ascriptive and functional groups that varied widely in scope and organisational complexity. In traditional Kenyan societies, arrangements for the regulation of public affairs depended on horizontal social networks of kinship rights and obligations generated by the structure of the extended family. Within this social context, people were guaranteed access to the means of production. As Mamdani and Wamba-dia-Wamba (1995) and Chazan et al. (1988) demonstrate, people joined associations not only because they were born into them but also in order to promote their own interests, to enhance their own standing in the community, and to cope with new and unfamiliar environments. Deliberately constructed social institutions, especially the extended family system, kinship ties, the clan structure and the age-set system, provided social security and facilitated the diffusion of power and the inviolability of this egalitarian social order. This egalitarian structure promoted social democracy and thus did not create conditions under which social class exclusivism and state dictatorship could emerge. '… the social antagonisms that made the emergence of civil society in the form that it did, inevitable in Europe were nearly absent in pre-colonial Kenya like in much of Africa' (Owiti 2000: 8). However, colonialism, based as it was on a subjugative mission and a ruthless exploitative logic, altered this social order dramatically.

Emergence of dual societies

The imposition of colonialism on Kenya nurtured the emergence of dual societies. On the one hand was the capitalist economy dominated by the colonialists and on the other stood the pre-capitalist African society. Although there were realms of interpenetration as the former depended on the latter for labour, which was forcefully extracted, the colonial economy systematically worked against national institutional integration and thus engendered a conjuncture of exclusivist politics. This was buttressed by ethnic paddocking to constrain interethnic interaction and circumscribe cross-national political organisation. As Bratton (1994b) rightly observes, state agencies established by the British in Kenya and elsewhere in Anglophone colonial Africa enjoyed a great deal of autonomy. In most situations, the colonial government bypassed civil associations, establishing control directly over stringently demarcated local communities through the sophisticated employment of local collaborators. They adopted a top-down, central–local pattern of extraction and distribution that limited the flow of entitlements between the distinct and purportedly mutually exclusive local collectivities (Berman 1990). The frustration emanating from this colonial politics of exclusion accounted for the emergence of pioneer social movements in colonial Kenya between the 1920s and 1940s. Examples of these include the Young Kavirondo Association (later Kavirondo Taxpayers' Welfare Association), Young Kikuyu Association, Kikuyu Central Association, Ukambani Members Association and Taita Hills Association (Rosberg and Nottingham 1966). These pioneer movements were reformative in orientation. They sought inclusion in the socio-political dispensation of the moment and the amelioration of the depredations of the punitive colonial taxation and forced labour systems. In spite of the genuine and well-meaning nature of the leadership of these emergent social movements, they failed to squeeze any concessions from the colonial state. The new organisations were soon co-opted into a scheme of collaboration with the colonial regime and were thus compromised as vehicles for addressing African grievances (Muigai 1995: 165).

Consequently, more militant organisations emerged that were transformative in nature. Prime examples of these were *Dini ya Msambwa* (DYM) in Western Kenya and *Kikuyu Karing'a* (Orthodox Kikuyu) in Central Kenya (see Chapter 3 by Gecaga in this volume; Anderson 2005). These movements constructed a counterideology to colonial hegemony. They bastardised Christianity and recreated the Old Testament theology, which they infused with African myths of creation and religious ethos. They did this because of Christianity's foreign origin and its interference with the cultural practices and religious beliefs of the Africans as well as the alliance of the missionaries with colonial administrators. They pointed to the colonial robbery of their God-given land and the construction of an exclusive socio-economic system to legitimise all struggles that sought to overturn this scheme of things. Founded on and inspired by a deep-seated sense of injustice, the ideology of these movements found resonance among their followers. It was on account of this that DYM was able to attract cross-ethnic followers, not only among the Bukusu, the Kabras and the Tachoni sub-groups of the larger Luhyia ethnic group but also among the Sabaot, the Pokot and some communities of Eastern Uganda (see Were 1971; Wipper 1977). The colonial state responded to these developments by legislating tighter controls on registration of social organisations. Given the shrinking associational space, social organisations began to organise more discreetly, leading to the establishment of informal social groups like *Rika Ria Forty*,[2] which provided the organisational basis for the emergence of the more militant Mau Mau.

In the meantime, the colonial administration relied on the development of patronage systems based on elaborate hierarchies of personal power while simultaneously enabling the gradual emergence of a new, albeit contained, civil society around the colonial governmental edifice. At the same time, the colonial state stood aloof from rural development, focusing instead on the regulatory functions of maintaining law and order. Consequently, CSOs in the form of churches and missionary societies were the principal providers of health and education services, particularly in the rural areas. The colonial government's attitude towards these social formations ranged from laissez-faire to attempts to sever the links between the Church mission system and the nationalist movements (see Chazan et al. 1988; Bratton 1994b; Chazan 1994). These attempts were facilitated by the fact that though the Church was emerging as a legitimate voice in the politics of the moment, given the constrained ability of other social formations, it was not homogeneous. The Church was polarised between the Anglicans and the Catholics. This division was accentuated by the differentiated predominance of different denominations in certain regions of the country. 'Henceforth, the Church was forced to reflect the ethnic tendencies predominant in their areas of residence' (Katumanga 2000: 10). It was within this context that Kenya's first modern NGOs, as elements of organised civil society, sprang up to articulate the social demands of newly urbanised Africans (see Hodgin 1967; Lloyd 1969; Allen and Williams 1982).

These NGOs formed the building blocks of nationalist political parties and played an explicitly political role in contesting the authority of the colonial government. Indeed, political formations such as Abaluhyia Political Union, Maasai United Front, Kalenjin Political Alliance and Coast People's Party among others were a direct outgrowth of these ethnic welfare associations. In many respects, they constituted the harbingers of a new civil society that emerged in the post-colony.

The nature of the new social groups' transactions depended on the extent of group resources and the skills and goods held by other social forces or by the colonial state (see Rosberg and Nottingham 1966; Spencer 1985). Patterns of investing surplus generated by productive activities furnished an important indicator of the directions and substance of transactions at this juncture. According to Bratton (1994b), the transactions took place primarily along a vertical axis ranging from the local level to the colonial state. The religious and ethnic organisations established strong links with local constituencies while vying with each other and with other types of groups for access to avenues of communication with colonial authorities. While the forms of exchange were inherently unequal, these civil organisations occupied a clearly defined, albeit quite minuscule, middle space in social exchanges. The methods of exchange involved a degree of subordination and incorporation. This, Ekeh (1975) argues, intensified the disarticulation between the patronage-propelled colonial administration and the elementary civil society that was crystallising. According to Hodder-Williams (1984), the paradoxes inherent in the structure of these colonial exchanges generated a growing conflict between the middle-level social groups that made up civil society and the externally controlled administrative apparatus. Consequently, associational life flourished by arrangement, toleration, exclusion, evasion and default or muted resistance. The sphere of civil society was hence both discrete and contained. The small scale and limited cohesion of civil society at this time helped shape the image of the colonial state, which was in itself both precarious and aloof.

Overall, the process of emergence of a modern civil society in Kenya coincided with the creation of an array of social organisations, especially ethnic welfare and cultural associations, clustered around new urban areas. Whereas these were moderate in their orientation and sought to ameliorate the externalities of colonialism and inclusion in the socio-economic dispensation of the moment, those that emerged in the rural areas, such as DYM and Kikuyu Karing'a, were more radical and rejected out of hand colonial hegemony. They instead sought to reconstruct alternative institutions or a return to African traditionalism. Because of the exclusivist nature of the colonial state and its failure to respond to local demands for political inclusion, emergent social formations increasingly became radicalised as they amalgamated into a vibrant nationalist movement. Due to political factors and dynamics, both internal and external to Kenya, the nationalist movement accumulated sufficient political resources and the requisite momentum to effect the granting of political independence in 1963. The nationalist movement eventually coalesced into two major political parties on the eve of independence – Kenya African Democratic Union (KADU) and Kenya African National Union (KANU). This transformation of social formations into political organisations, Chazan (1994: 263) notes, left a partial vacuum at the intermediate societal level on the eve of independence, presaging a period of uncertainty and fluctuation in state–society transactions.

Shrinking associational space

The immediate post-colonial period in Kenya was characterised by efforts geared towards consolidation of political power on the part of the new ruling elite in a process that nurtured the emergence of an authoritarian regime. The Kenyatta regime failed to deconstruct the colonial state. Instead, it dismantled the *Majimbo* (regionalist) system of government that was agreed upon in the run-up to independence. The new regime adopted the colonial administrative apparatus, complete with its legal and statutory instruments and prerogatives. These legal instruments, together with the provincial administration, which remained under the direct control of the president, facilitated the regime's firm control over associational space. The failure to deconstruct the colonial state and reconstruct one consistent with the aspirations of the majority of Kenyans amounted to a betrayal of the nationalist movement (Nasong'o 2002). Power consolidation was buttressed by a series of constitutional amendments that culminated in the Constitutional Amendment Act No. 16 of 1969, which empowered President Kenyatta to control the civil service. The amendment made the civil service and local governments directly accountable to the president. Functions of local governments were transferred to the central government. The new independent regime, like its colonial predecessor, was thus able to establish effective control over the regions and closely monitored and controlled the registration and activities of associational organisations through the Societies Act (Ochieng 1995; Makinda 1996; Republic of Kenya 1998).

During the immediate post-independence era, middle-level social organisations continued to be based in the major cities. Their expansion and growth depended on their ability to recruit newcomers and branch out into smaller urban areas. However, given the authoritarian reality, although civil associations grew in number and variety at this juncture, they did not necessarily expand in size or increase in relative importance. Although the associational terrain became more heterogeneous during the Kenyatta era, independent social organisations were enveloped and their range of manoeuvrability severely constrained. Instead of enhancing the capacity of civil society to impact state performance, the opposite was the case. Against this background, civil organisations in Kenya employed two strategies in their relations with state agencies. The first strategy was retrenchment, with some civil organisations closing themselves off to unnecessary influences from above and nurturing their own dynamic arrangements backed by specific group values. The picture of NGO–state relations that emerged in the Kenyatta period was that of diverse and unequal social organisations that, in different circumstances, preyed on the state, dissociated themselves from its agents or, alternatively, succumbed to its dictates. The second strategy was patron–client ties. The disruption of competitive party politics in the immediate years following independence (see Chapter 4 by Oloo in this volume) and the restrictions placed on intermediate social groups meant that few institutional mechanisms were available for mediating between local communities and state organisations. Personalistic networks came to fill this void. It was within this context that Kenyan politics became highly ethnicised, with ethnic boss-men serving as links between their communities and the state and as conduits for the extraction of resources from the centre to the locality (see Nyangira 1987; Ochieng 1995; Adar 1998; Oyugi 1998).

Under the ethnic accumulation logic that the Kenyatta regime fostered, social movements were pulverised and political institutions perverted to serve the self-aggrandising interests of an ethnically based political elite (see Katumanga 2000; Nasong'o 2001; Murunga 2002). First, the trade union movement was muzzled through the Trade Union Disputes Act, which illegalised industrial action, and via the unification of trade unions under the umbrella of the Central Organisation of Trade Unions (COTU), whose leadership the regime had to approve. The opposition KADU was forced to dissolve itself in 1964 while the progressives among the political elite led by Oginga Odinga and Bildad Kaggia, who rooted for the restructuring of the colonial state, the economy and fundamental agrarian reform, were marginalised from power. When they reconstituted themselves into an opposition party – the Kenya People's Union (KPU) – it was banned in 1969 (Mueller 1984). Where threats to the Kenyatta regime and its dominant elite were manifested through individuals, they were assassinated or detained. Notable among the assassinated individuals were Pio Gama Pinto in 1965, Argwings Kodhek in 1966, Tom Mboya in 1969 and Josiah Mwangi Kariuki in 1975. Those detained by Kenyatta included Martin Shikuku, Jean Marie Seroney, Ngugi wa Thiong'o and George Anyona. The emergent political context was one that seriously curtailed the possibilities of organising social movements. Accordingly, radical social movements that survived after being banned were the now millenarian-oriented movements like DYM, which no longer posed a threat to the regime. This reality, coupled with the highly ethnicised nature of the Church, meant that the only credible opposition to the Kenyatta state within the ranks of civil society came from the Universities Academic Staff Union (UASU) and the Kamirithu Theatre Group (KTG). Whereas UASU opposed the regime's economic policy and uncritical pro-West foreign policy, KTG, organised by Ngugi wa Thiong'o, critiqued the same by satire and caricature through drama (see Chapter 7 by Amutabi in this volume).

This political eventuality in which the state came to reign supreme, with little if any challenge from civil society, was a function of three notions of development that informed political practice in post-colonial Africa. First, it was held that development was the principal national task of the time and politics was subsidiary to the development imperative. Hence in Kenya, *maendeleo na ujenzi wa taifa* (development and nation building) became the post-colonial ideology to which *siasa* (politics) was predicated. Second, development was considered a value-free social process and a desirable end. The fact that it could unleash its own patterns of social oppression was neither recognised nor appreciated. Third, the idea of development, as enunciated by the political elite, was premised on a pervasive belief that society needed to be guided towards desirable social goals because it was unable to either regulate itself or identify those goals. That society could be navigated in directions considered desirable by the elite was hardly questioned (see Chandhoke 1998). It was within this context that statism came to dominate the political realm. In view of this, and despite Barkan's (1992) attempt to put a positive spin on it, the Kenyatta state remained a contested space much like the colonial one it had replaced. It was a state in which the Gikuyu, Embu and Meru Association (GEMA) elite predominated (see Muigai 1995).

From imperial presidency to a personal state

On assumption of power, Moi sought to consolidate his regime by marginalising those who had campaigned to stop him from succeeding Kenyatta. He proceeded by reversing the gains this political elite had made under the former regime. Lacking a capital base of his own upon which he could build and maintain a patron–client network, and faced with shrinking economic opportunities, Moi resorted, according to Nyong'o, to 'robbing Kamau to pay Patel' (cited in Katumanga 2000) or, in Ajulu's (2000) words, 'looting from the original [Kikuyu] looters'. In so doing, Moi perpetuated the politics of exclusion and thereby created a basis for opposition to his regime from the very beginning. To hedge himself against opposition, he reconfigured the financial, legal, political and administrative institutions. For instance, the Constitutional Amendment Act No. 7 of 1982 made Kenya a one-party state by law, while the Constitutional Amendment Act No. 14 of 1986 removed the security of tenure for the Attorney-General, comptroller and auditor general, and High Court judges, making the holders of these offices personally beholden to the president. These developments had the effect of transforming the Kenyan state from an 'imperial presidency' under Kenyatta to a 'personal state' under Moi (see Chepkwony 1987; Anyang Nyong'o 1989).

Credible opposition to the Moi regime emanated from the radical wing of university lecturers under the aegis of UASU, sections of the Church fraternity, and the Law Society of Kenya (LSK) (see Sabar 2002; Amutabi 2004). In particular, UASU went out of its way to organise other workers and university students in its articulation of the interests of university staff and students, and opposition to foreign military bases on Kenyan soil. Because of its radical agenda, Moi banned UASU in 1982 as well as other social organisations defined as ethnic organisations including GEMA, Abaluhyia Football Club, Gor Mahia and Luo Union.[3] Following the 1982 attempted coup, the Moi regime launched a spirited attempt to control social forces such as trade unions, student associations and women's groups, which were seen as potential sources of political unrest. Henceforth, political loyalty became the litmus test for assuming and maintaining positions of leadership. Moi went further and transformed the Kenya Farmers Association (KFA) into the Kenya Grain Growers Cooperative Union (KGGCU). The logic of these actions was to impose a symbiotic relationship between the leaders of social organisations and the state for purposes of facilitating state control over CSOs (Widner 1992, 1994).

Nevertheless, the position of the state itself remained tenuous, confirming the close connection between weak and fragmented civil societies and ineffective states.[4] The fragility and precariousness of the state was manifested particularly in its efforts to dilute CSOs and render their capacity to impact the state ineffective. For instance, the Nyayo Bus Service Corporation was established in 1988 to compete with the partly British-owned Kenya Bus Service and the privately run *Matatu* (commuter taxi) industry. In the same vein, the *Matatu* Vehicle Owners Association (MVOA) was banned in 1991, making it difficult for the sector to organise. Growers of export crops were organised and had considerable bargaining power because of the government's heavy dependence on the revenues generated by these crops. These growers were potential advocates for political pluralism, because of the deterioration of the quality of agricultural services including fairness in pricing procedures, all of which were state controlled. The Moi regime defused the threat by banning or reorganising farmers' unions. Nyayo Tea Zones Development Corporation, for instance, was set up, limiting the bargaining power of the Central Province tea farmers by flooding tea factories with cheap leaves from government-controlled land. Similarly, KANU absorbed the Maendeleo ya Wanawake Organisation (MYWO), co-opted the COTU and interfered with the elections of the LSK to ensure election of pro-establishment individuals to head the Society (Aubrey 1997). Hence the degree to which opposition groups could draw upon the bargaining power of dissatisfied groups, including mobilisation against policies or against incumbent politicians, was effectively circumscribed (Widner 1994; Oanda 1999).

The above developments, coupled with the intensive crackdown on left-wing intellectuals and other radical elements following the abortive 1982 coup, forced social movements underground. The movements also shifted their reformative objectives to a transformative revolutionary agenda. They now sought to topple the incumbent regime by violent means. The first revolutionary movement to emerge was

Mwakenya, whose existence became public knowledge in 1985. The movement established a newsletter, *Mpatanishi* (Reconciliator), to promote its revolutionary agenda. The second movement was the December Twelve Movement (DTM), which also set up its mouthpiece *Pambana* (Struggle) (see Maren 1987). The key limitation on the part of these movements, however, is that they failed to train political and military cadres, with their leadership marooned in Europe and therefore disconnected from the social realities in Kenya. This limitation was compounded by the movements' failure or inability to set up effective organisational structures through which to mobilise the masses in pursuit of their stated objectives (see Ajulu 1992 for a critique of Mwakenya). 'It is indeed partly due to this immaturity that most of their activists were rounded up, tortured and jailed between 1986 and 1987' (Katumanga 2000: 17). Within the context of the crackdown on Mwakenya and other underground movements, Kenya was transformed into a police state. It was the high noon of authoritarianism in the country. In this event, only sections of the Church and elements within the LSK remained to articulate an alternative view against bad governance, corruption and human rights abuse.

The mid-1980s not only witnessed heightened political repression in Kenya but it was also a period that laid bare the fact that statist developmentalism had proved a fiasco. The country's dire economic conditions made both CSOs and the state experience what Chazan (1994: 263) describes as a process of implosion in which the scale of activities contracted, the range of contacts diminished and the linkage arrangements were undermined. This crisis opened up new political and economic spaces, which allowed for the emergence and strengthening of viable CSOs, especially at the communal level. Thus the period of SAPs (see Chapter 9 by Murunga in this volume) set the stage for the further expansion of CSOs, permitting the re-emergence of the outlines of these organisations in forms parallel to those that prevailed in Africa on the eve of independence. The growth of these social organisations was given great impetus by a new policy agenda on the part of foreign aid donors beginning in the decade of the 1990s. Arguing that state-led developmentalism had dismally failed, donors increasingly redirected the flow of their development resources to CSOs, which, it was reckoned, were cost effective because they were less bureaucratised than the state. Supporting CSOs, it was envisaged, would not only engender economic development but would also serve the complex task of promoting political change and social justice.

This policy shift on the part of donors witnessed a mushrooming of CSOs in the democracy and governance (DG) realm. Some of the DG organisations that emerged in the 1990s in Kenya in response to the emergent political aid industry are listed in Table 2.1.

With this new policy agenda, CSOs were thrust into the centre of the political economy of development in Africa with a specific agenda to mediate state–society relations and empower people, socially, economically and politically vis-à-vis the state. This new conjuncture led to the emergence of a vibrant DG sector of CSOs in Kenya that thrived on political aid. External donors, including bilaterals, multilaterals, private foundations and international NGOs, channelled resources to the Kenyan DG sector expressly to fund their political agenda. The agenda included advocacy for democracy and good governance, promotion of human rights, civic awareness, research, policy analysis, and publication.

Table 2.1 Democracy and governance civil organisations formed in the 1990s

Organisation	Date of formation	Nature of work
Release Political Prisoners (RPP)	1991	Rights and welfare of political prisoners
ABANTU	1991	Promotion of women in decision making and development policy issues, and strengthening women's NGOs through research, training and advice
Institute for Civic Education in Africa (ICEDA)	1992	Civic education, and advocacy for political rights, good governance and political pluralism
Kenya League of Women Voters (KLWV)	1992	Women's civil and political rights through sensitisation and civic education
Kenya Human Rights Commission (KHRC)	1992	Civil and political rights through sensitisation and civic education

Continued

Table 2.1 *Continued*

Organisation	Date of formation	Nature of work
National Commission on the Status of Women (NCSW)	1992	Gender sensitisation through publications, media and other civic education
Collaborative Centre for Gender and Development (CCGD)	1992	Women's political and economic advancement through training in gender planning, programming and capacity building
Centre for Legal Aid and Research International (CLARION)	1993	Constitutional reform through research, publication and civic education
Civic Resources and Information Centre (CRIC)	1994	Promotion of democratic change, and civic education through research, publication and documentation
Agency for Development Education and Communication (ADEC)	1994	Education for good governance and poverty elimination
Legal Resources Foundation (LRF)	1994	Human rights issues through education and advocacy
Centre for Legal Education and Aid Networks (CLEAN)	1995	Paralegal training, legal rights awareness and legal assistance
Youth Agenda (YA)	1996	Socio-economic and political rights of the youth
Social Development Network (SODNET)	1996	Policy analysis and dialogue in areas of poverty alleviation, and watchdog on government commitment to various international conventions
DARAJA	1996	Civic education

Table 2.1 *Continued*

Organisation	Date of formation	Nature of work
National Convention Executive Council (NCEC)	1997	Constitutional reform
Media Institute	1997	Media issues, advocacy on freedom of expression and training for journalists
National Youth Movement (NYM)	1997	Highlighting youth issues through advocacy
L'Étoile International	1998	Law and policy for contemporary problems at national, regional and global levels

Source: Compiled from Ngunyi and Nyaga 1998; Owiti 2000.

Civil Society and the Kenyan Transition

The elevation of civil society in the politics of transition in Kenya was, in a way, a turning of the tables. As a post-colony, Kenya is historically located in a dual and contradictory legacy. The first legacy is encapsulated in the ideology of statism. This is hinged on an elaborate system of control developed and perfected by the colonial state. The second legacy is embodied by the freedom movement, which challenged the authoritative conceptions of the political set forth by colonialism. As Chandhoke (1998) shows, if the first legacy bequeathed the post-colonial elite a model of statism and the notion of the centrality of the state, the second legacy gave to civil society the idea that states could be challenged successfully almost to the point of being rendered irrelevant. The tension between these two legacies constituted the substance of post-colonial politics in Kenya. Yet, in the working out of this tension, it is, quite paradoxically, the statist legacy that emerged victorious. However, in the context of transition politics, civil society was reinvented, 'empowered' and charged with the onus of 'deconstructing' the authoritarian state.

State deconstruction within the rubric of transition politics was aimed at realising a democratic political dispensation that guarantees people concrete political, social and economic rights. Such a democratic system of governance is contingent upon the rules of the game that provide for alternative political parties competing against one another for the chance to govern within institutional systems which guarantee fairness and a genuine opportunity for alternation of power between parties. The significance of such institutional design is borne out by the cases of Benin in 1991, Mali in 1992 and Madagascar in 1993 as well as Malawi, Mozambique and South Africa, all in 1994, where incumbent authoritarian regimes were defeated when social struggles for democracy successfully pushed the case for redesigning the rules of political engagement to make political competition fairer (see Nasong'o 2005: 120–5). Overall, CSOs in Kenya employed both conventional and unconventional modes of political activism. The first involved working within established legal parameters to champion the cause of democracy while the latter involved violence, mass protest, riots and demonstrations.[5]

The push for new rules of the game

Two forms of the movement for political change in Kenya in the 1990s can be discerned. The first was composed of reformist politicians who had been excluded from the political dispensation of the moment. This group agitated for the opening up of the political space to allow for their own inclusion or for purposes of replacing the incumbent elite. The main source of grievance for these politicians was the widely rigged 1988 elections, and their source of inspiration was the new international political context following the end of the cold war – the disintegration of the Soviet Union. It was within this context that Charles Rubia teamed up with Kenneth Matiba in 1990 to call for the freedom to form alternative political parties and stated their plan to hold a political rally in Nairobi on 7 July without a licence. Though the duo were detained prior to their intended meeting, people turned up for the meeting, which degenerated into skirmishes with the police, hence the making of the *Saba Saba* (July 7) riots.

The original Forum for Restoration of Democracy (FORD), led by Oginga Odinga, Masinde Muliro and Martin Shikuku among others, was emblematic of the reformist movement. FORD's activism led to the repeal of Section 2(A) of the constitution via the Constitutional Amendment Act No. 12 of 1991. However, though the FORD model managed to trump state obscurantism, it failed to evolve an organising ideology to inform its agenda. The movement sought to counter the state's ethnicised politics by ethnic coalition making; unwittingly, however, this strategy raised ethnic fears because of its vertical organisation and FORD's general failure to develop a horizontal unifying dynamic. Essentially, though FORD was a potent political force, it failed to develop an all-inclusive national political agenda. Once the constitution was amended to allow the existence of opposition political parties, the movement transformed itself into a political party. Jostling for positions within FORD led to its disintegration and the rush to register political parties that reflected politicians' ethnic bases (see Chapter 4 by Oloo in this volume). It was this fragmentation that led to incumbent victory in the 1992 presidential elections with only 36.9 per cent of the votes cast against a combined opposition of 63.1 per cent as shown in Table 2.2.

The second form of the movement for political change was composed of political activists, especially within civil society, who campaigned for far-reaching political change, bordering on the transformative. Political activism in this regard was geared towards restructuring the state and rewriting the constitution to reflect the changing political reality in Kenya. This push for new rules of the political game was spearheaded by the National Council of the Churches of Kenya (NCCK), which held two symposia in the run-up to the 1992 elections attended by a host of CSOs. Whereas the main objective of the NCCK, especially in regard to the first symposium, was to mobilise for opposition unity in the run-up to the 1992 elections, the CSOs that attended were more concerned with the release of political prisoners and the holding of a national convention to debate a new constitution. The Coalition for a National Convention emerged out of the two NCCK symposia to mobilise for a national convention. The coalition was led by

Table 2.2   Presidential vote distribution in Kenya's 1992 elections

Name/party	1992	% of total vote
Moi/KANU	1,927,640	36.91
Matiba/FORD-A	1,354,856	25.95
Kibaki/DP	1,035,507	19.83
Odinga/FORD-K	903,886	17.31
Total	5,221,889	100

Source: Compiled from Electoral Commission of Kenya figures (excludes figures for fringe presidential candidates whose votes were negligible).

the KHRC and the RPP group, with the support of the Kenya Youth Foundation Movement (KYFM), the Student Organisation of Nairobi University (SONU), the Policy Advisory Foundation (PAF) and the National Union of Kenya Students (NUKS) among others.

After the 1992 elections, 15 CSOs coalesced around KHRC to push for a new constitution. This group was energised by calls for a new constitution by the Catholic Church and the Church of the Province of Kenya. KHRC commissioned a constitutional lawyer to draft a model constitution as a basis for mobilisation. Consultations over the model constitution led to the establishment of the Citizens Coalition for Constitutional Change (4Cs), whose first meeting on 31 May 1996 transformed itself into the National Convention Preparatory Committee (NCPC) charged with engendering an all-inclusive constitutional review process. The management and control of the convention was delegated to individuals believed to have credible integrity to ensure neutrality, confidence and acceptability by all stakeholders. A panel of five convenors and a secretariat were established. The NCPC's tasks entailed: (1) drawing up minimum constitutional, legal and administrative reforms that were to constitute the framework around which reform agitation would be built prior to the general election of 1997; (2) proposing the means and strategies for attaining this minimum agenda; (3) suggesting the methodology for holding the convention to deliberate on comprehensive reforms; (4) proposing the modalities for participation in the review process; (5) drafting a programme for the convention and drawing up the timeframe for holding the same. In the initial stages, NCPC received support from all political formations, with the Safina party providing financial support to the secretariat.

The NCPC held the first 'National Convention Assembly' in Limuru on 15 November 1996 where a 'minimum constitutional reform agenda' was adopted to be implemented prior to the 1997 elections. The agenda included the reform of the Electoral Commission of Kenya (ECK), especially Sections 41 and 42(A) of the constitution to allow vetting of the nominations of members of the ECK; amendment of Sections 15, 16 and 19 of the constitution to allow for the formation of a coalition government; repeal of the Public Order Act (Cap 56), the Chief's Authority Act (Cap 128), the NGO Coordination Act (Cap 19 of 1990), the Societies Act (Cap 108), the Penal Code (Cap 63) and the Preservation of Public Security Act (Cap 57), and amendment of the National Assembly and Presidential Election Act

(Cap 107) among others. This agenda constituted the basis of discussion at the second NCPC National Convention in April 1997. The second convention, however, expanded the agenda to include the Films and Stage Act, the Plays Act, the Public Collections Act, the Election Code, resettlement of ethnic clashes victims, prohibition of illegal presidential decrees on elections, prevention of the provincial administration from interfering with the electoral process, release of all political prisoners, registration of unregistered parties and replacement of the 25 per cent rule with the 50 per cent rule.[6] Whereas the election-driven minimum reform agenda seemed to excite political parties, it did not attract much support from most CSOs, especially the youth movement, which argued the case for adopting resolutions calling for maximum reforms. These demands were rejected out of hand, particularly by the politicos in the pro-democracy movement, on account of 'lack of time' in the run-up to the 1997 elections.

The National Convention Assembly transformed the NCPC into the NCEC, which mobilised demonstrations and civil disobedience under the banner 'No Reforms No Elections' to put pressure on the KANU regime to effect the necessary constitutional reforms. Underlying the push for a defiant opposition against the regime was a section of the NCEC which had gone through the 4Cs' sessions on the 'zero option'.[7] The thrust of the 'zero option' model was that constitutional reform is the consequence of a crisis. However, granted that there was no crisis in the Kenyan context, the regime did not perceive the process of constitution making as a rational and necessary enterprise. Accordingly, the reform movement needed to engender a crisis, the magnitude of whose proportions would serve to circumscribe the regime's capacity for strategic manoeuvre and thus force it into constitutional review at zero option. The logic of this scheme was the reasoning that in the absence of a fundamental political and widespread crisis, the regime appeared legitimate in the public realm. It had thus to be confronted head-on to not only demystify it but also delegitimise it through its likely violent reaction to civil defiance (see Mutunga 1999; Murunga 2000). Accordingly, the NCEC called a meeting at Kamukunji Grounds, Nairobi on 3 May 1997. Predictably, the regime's response was violent. It unleashed paramilitary forces on citizens who defiantly turned out for the meeting despite the fact that the government had declared the meeting illegal. In the end, the NCEC demystified the notion held by some ethnic-minded politicians that they owned ethnic crowds and thus believed that their word would be enough to stop their co-ethnics from turning up for the meeting. Second, the NCEC disproved some religious leaders who held the view that their moral authority would not only dissuade the public from turning up for the rally but would also propel them to the centre stage of the reform process. Third, by defying the regime, the NCEC ipso facto delegitimised the regime in the court of public opinion. Furthermore, it forced the elite factions, both within and outside government, to seriously rethink their position on constitutional reform. Henceforth, constitutional reform became an agenda every opposition politician sought to identify with (see Katumanga 2000).

Bolstered by the gains of the first meeting, the NCEC called a second mass action rally on 31 May 1997 following the state's refusal to enter into dialogue on constitutional reform. In the resultant rally, two people were shot dead by the paramilitary General Service Unit (GSU). In protest at this violence, the NCEC called for the disruption of the national budget reading ceremony. It called on Kenyans to turn up on budget day, 19 June 1997, to disrupt and prevent budget reading. The NCEC contended that the reading of the budget was illegal to the extent that the state had over the years continued to read budgets without tabling its expenditure statements. Having refused to institute constitutional reforms, the NCEC argued, the regime thereby lost the legitimate right to table budget estimates. By taking its debate into the August House, the pro-reform movement had several objectives in mind. First, it sought to put the debate not only before the Kenyan public and to the president himself but also to the entire world, as represented by ambassadors accredited to Kenya. Second, it aimed at demonstrating to the nation at large, and to the diplomats assembled in particular, that the president was not in charge of the political process as he pretended to be. In a bid to respond to the threats of disruption by the NCEC, the state garrisoned parliament, and hired private thugs to prevent pro-reform crowds from assembling at the sealed-off parliamentary precincts. For the first time, a private vigilante group known as *Jeshi la Mzee* (Elder's Army) was unleashed on the public at the parliamentary precincts. But while the state thought that it had managed to contain the NCEC by unleashing the *Jeshi la Mzee*, it was surprised to find itself faced by demonstrators within the House itself, led by opposition members who demanded to listen to the heckling of demonstrators outside parliament. For the first time in the history of Kenya, the budget speech (which is always televised live) was switched off from the national airwaves.

The procrastination of the KANU regime in instituting reforms was followed by a fresh rally called by the NCEC on 7 July 1997. In the ensuing demonstrations, more than 14 Kenyans lost their lives. The disorder itself was an embarrassment to the head of state given that the Intergovernmental Authority on Development (IGAD) conference was taking place in Nairobi. The July 7 mass action had the net impact of achieving what the NCEC had sought from the onset: to legitimise the reform process while conversely de-legitimising the state as a result of its anti-reform activities, especially state violence against civilians. While these mass protests succeeded in tarnishing the regime's image, they did not succeed in forcing the hardliners in the regime to commit themselves to constitutional reform. The regime merely changed strategy. Instead of remaining obstinately against the constitutional reform issue, it agreed to reforms in principle and convened the ruling party's National Executive Council meeting to deliberate on the same. Consequently, KANU published a list of reforms it intended to pass to the government for implementation. These included the repeal of the Public Order Act, the Chief's Authority Act and the Presidential Elections Act. In addition, President Moi announced that he had lifted requirements for permits for public rallies. He also called upon religious leaders to take up a facilitative role to initiate dialogue between him and pro-reform movements. The president then requested the religious sector to urge the NCEC to call off a national strike scheduled for 8 August 1997.

The Attorney-General published a new bill seeking to establish a commission to review the constitution. Under this bill, the commission was to collect and collate views from Kenyans on the constitution and subsequently make recommendations to the national assembly. It was to be appointed by the president in consultation with other interested institutions and to complete its work within 24 months. With the benefit of hindsight, it is apparent that these measures on the part of the incumbent regime amounted to a public relations exercise. They were meant to placate donor pressure and public opinion at one level, while simultaneously driving a wedge between the CSO forces of change and moderate parliamentarians. Unfortunately, the NCEC did not have a clear strategy on how to deal with any change of strategy by the regime. Similarly, the religious and diplomatic sectors saw the reforms proposed by the KANU regime as an indication that the regime had finally accepted that it must embrace constitutional reform. Thus the two began exerting pressure on the NCEC leadership and moderate members of parliament to call off the strike that had been scheduled for 8 August 1997 and instead give dialogue by the bishops a chance. Nevertheless, the strike went ahead with the support of Raila Odinga, Mwai Kibaki, James Orengo and 30 other parliamentarians who appended their signatures to the strike call (see *East African Standard*, 8 August 1997). In the ensuing rally at Nairobi's Central Park, a policeman was killed and violent demonstrations were held in Nairobi, Kiambu, Nakuru and Kisumu. At this point, the government's attempt to paint the NCEC as a violent organisation spawning violence succeeded. It was within this context that a counter-movement to the NCEC was hatched, the Movement for Dialogue and Non-violence (MODAN) led by the KANU sympathiser lawyer P.L.O. Lumumba and KANU parliamentarian Joseph Misoi. It was supported and funded by foreign embassies in Nairobi, especially the Swedish embassy.

The IPPG and the NCEC paralysis

In the final analysis, President Moi was forced to capitulate and initiate some token changes under the aegis of the Inter-Parties Parliamentary Group (IPPG). Under IPPG, members of parliament resolved to repeal and/or revise some of the draconian colonial laws such as the Chief's Authority Act and the requirement for licences to hold political rallies. The IPPG package also provided, for the first time in Kenya's history, that political parties were to jointly nominate members of the Electoral Commission.[8] The issues covered by the IPPG were the same ones that constituted the minimum reform agenda on the part of CSOs at their first convention in Limuru in November 1996. The IPPG package had a number of effects. First, it enabled President Moi to pull the constitutional reform initiative away from the NCEC and the 4Cs. Second, it laid the foundation for further disagreements within opposition ranks. Some of the opposition leaders rightly argued that the IPPG package did not go far enough in overhauling the constitution. Third, the advocates of constitutional change, particularly the 4Cs, viewed the IPPG package as an appeasement of Moi and as such rejected its spirit on the grounds that it did not deal with the central contentious issues related to the constitution. Fourth, donors came out in support of the IPPG initiative calling it 'a step in the right direction' and in the process supported Moi and inadvertently helped him maintain himself in power (see Brown 2001). Once again

Moi solidified his grip on the direction of constitutional change, which meant operating under rules that greatly constrained the opposition (see Adar 1998). Against these developments, the NCEC now faced a crisis of paralysis.

The KANU government continued to play the game of musical chairs with the much-needed constitutional reform necessary for advancing democracy. Also working against fair political competition in Kenya were politically motivated ethnic clashes, threats by Moi against opposition zones on withholding national development resources, harassment of private print media and arrest of its publishers and editors, the skewed nature of opposition constituency representation, and lack of independence of the judiciary and the electoral commission from KANU. Against this reality, and given the first-past-the-post Kenyan electoral system, the incumbent President Moi secured victory with 37 per cent of the votes cast in the 1992 general elections compared to a combined opposition tally of 63 per cent. KANU won 100 of the parliamentary seats to the combined opposition's 88 seats. The same results were replicated in the 1997 general elections when President Moi once again secured victory with 40 per cent of the votes cast against 60 per cent for the combined opposition. Had electoral rules been changed to require an absolute majority to win the presidency, it is arguable that a run-off between Moi and his closest rival in 1992 could have produced an upset for the incumbent (see Table 2.3, p. 47).

One year after the 1997 elections, the parliament passed the Constitution of Kenya Review Act, which sought to create the Constitution of Kenya Review Commission (CKRC) to review the constitution. The problem, however, was that the process was to remain under parliamentary control. Given this, the NCEC and other CSOs contested both the procedural and constitutive provisions of the Constitutional Review Act, demanding an all-inclusive process that would culminate in a national conference. Contestations between the two sides over these issues culminated in a series of consultative meetings, including Bomas I and II and Safari Park I–IV. To placate those who stood for an all-inclusive process, and a National Constitutional Conference, the government agreed to establish District Consultative Forums composed of councillors and parliamentarians, and a National Consultative Forum comprising the Speaker of the National Assembly, the Attorney-General, parliamentarians and two representatives from each district. Nonetheless, CSOs were wary of the government's motivations and had no confidence in its commitment to reforms. Consequently, on 15 December 1999, 400 people representing CSOs and some opposition political parties convened at Ufungamano House, Nairobi, under Catholic, Hindu, Muslim and Protestant leaders and initiated a parallel reform process under the aegis of the 'People's Commission of Kenya' (PCK). This was subsequently dubbed the 'Ufungamano Initiative'. The PCK undertook to use mosques, temples and churches as forums for collecting and collating views from citizens for the constitutional review process (*Daily Nation*, 16 December 1999).

Fortunately, once Professor Yash Pal Ghai was appointed to chair the CKRC, he successfully brokered a merger between the Ufungamano Initiative and the CKRC, paving the way for the review to commence in 2000. However, as if to underscore the KANU regime's ambivalence towards the review process, the 2002 elections were called while the review process was in progress. In essence, the review process was thrown into a limbo as its time frame was coming to an end and required an Act of Parliament to extend, yet parliament now stood dissolved. In the same vein, whatever document was to emerge out of the process would need to be adopted by parliament for it to come into effect. Accordingly, as Harbeson (1999: 51) posits, Kenya '... provides one of the clearest examples in Africa of the precariousness of undertaking multiparty elections as the first step toward democracy before inter-party agreement has been forged and the fundamental rules of the game reformed. Lacking such an agreement, opposition parties and civil society have remained futilely dependent upon a manifestly unsympathetic government to initiate further democratisation'. He concludes that donor pressure upon the Kenyan government to permit multiparty elections should, in retrospect, have extended to fashioning broader multiparty agreement on reforming the rules of the game, and perhaps to electing a constituent assembly to draft a new constitution. The significance of redesigning the rules of the game is accentuated by the electoral outcome in the 2002 elections. Having been beaten twice in 1992 and 1997 even as they cumulatively got more votes, the opposition united into the National Alliance Rainbow Coalition (NARC) and rallied behind one presidential candidate resulting in a major victory over the incumbent party as illustrated in Table 2.3.

The slow march to regime change in Kenya is a function of the single-minded preoccupation with the replacement of incumbent leaders in

Table 2.3   Presidential election results in Kenya's 2002
elections

Name/party	Votes	% of total
Kibaki/NARC	3,647,658	62.21
Kenyatta/KANU	1,836,055	31.31
Nyachae/FORD-P	345,161	5.89
Orengo/SDP	24,568	0.42
Ng'ethe/CCU	10,030	0.17
Total	5,863,472	100

Source: Nasong'o, 2005: 139.

the democratisation wave in Africa, in which the focus on individuals
rather than institutions has been a disservice to the possibilities of
attaining true democracy. Once multiparty politics was legalised, most
opposition political formations broke ranks with CSOs to contest for
political power against incumbent regimes under rules of political
engagement that greatly circumscribed the possibilities for competitive
politics. Even after the opposition electoral victory in Kenya in 2002
under the NARC, the prospects for institutionalisation of democracy
in the country remain dim even on the most optimistic assumptions.
Indeed, one of the NARC's key campaign planks was a new constitutional dispensation for the country within the first one hundred days
of its presidency (given that the constitutional review process was
already at the advanced drafting stage). On assumption of power in
January 2003, however, the NARC regime reneged on this promise
and resorted to stonewalling the review process (see Nasong'o 2005:
165). At the end of the day, the NARC government heavily edited
the CKRC draft constitution before subjecting it to a referendum on
21 November 2005. The draft constitution was resoundingly rejected
by Kenyans.

Arguably therefore, countries that commence their multiparty politics with a fundamental restructuring of the rules of the game through
pacts that are broadly constructed in terms of scope and duration, as
happened in Benin, Mali, Malawi and Mozambique (see Nasong'o
2005), engender the best prospects for progress towards democratic
consolidation. The role of CSOs is crucial in this process of negotiating for new rules of the political game. Without such negotiation, '...
democratisation is bound to be gradual, messy, fitful, and slow, with
many imperfections along the way' (Young 1996: 60). The constitution

review debacle in Kenya, under both KANU and NARC, is ample testimony to this tragic reality. The task of deconstructing the authoritarian state on the part of civil society remains gigantic. For, though CSOs have successfully pushed Kenya through the political opening stage, the country is stuck at the threshold of the breakthrough stage on the transition spectrum, which requires the promulgation of a new constitutional dispensation. Until this is done, the consolidation phase remains only a political vision, a dream for the politically optimistic.

Limitations of the Civil Society Promise

Overall, CSOs have made a modest contribution to democratisation in Africa. Nevertheless, five key constraints exhibited by the pro-democracy movements circumscribe their capacity to effectively contribute to democratisation. The CSOs' limitations are closely tied to the factors that determine the success of social movements elaborated at the beginning of this chapter. The first factor comprises the objectives a movement seeks to attain and the strategies devised to attain them. The clearer and more realistic the objectives, the greater the chances of crafting effective strategies for their realisation. The Kenyan movement for democratisation, however, lacked a clear-cut definition of the objectives; hence there was no agreement on the strategies to be employed in pursuit of the objectives. More perceptive elements within CSO ranks correctly identified the key objective as deconstructing the authoritarian state through constitutional engineering. For opposition politicians, on the other hand, the key task at hand was the removal of Moi from power and the legalisation of multiparty politics. They had personal grievances against Moi for having marginalised them from power and were impatient with prescriptions for engaging in a more fundamental struggle for constitutional change.

Consequently, the democratisation effort in Kenya, as elsewhere in Africa, suffered from overpersonalisation of the crisis of governance and the contradictions inherent in African politics. In Kenya, the embodiment of the political crisis was seen as Moi, hence the slogan 'Moi Must Go!' In Ghana, it was Jerry Rawlings. In Nigeria, it was Ibrahim Babangida, then Sani Abacha. In Zaire, it was Mobutu; and in Zambia, it was Kaunda, hence the chants of 'Kaunda *walala*'.[9] To be sure, Ihonvbere (1997) argues, these leaders were noted for their corruption, repression, mismanagement and the suffocation of the popular will. However, as the Movement for Multiparty Democracy (MMD) found out after coming to power in Zambia, Kaunda simply represented a class, a political tradition and mode of politics. His removal did not stop or eliminate inefficiency and corruption, conflicts and contradictions between and within ethnic and other interests. After the fall of Kaunda, Chiluba was forced to sack 19 ministers and his government was plagued by allegations of drug trafficking, corruption and land grabbing. Similarly, in Kenya, the change from Moi to Kibaki did not meaningfully alter the mode of politics. Although a show was made of combating corruption, corruption was reinvented and became as endemic as it had been under the previous regime. Like Chiluba in Zambia, President Kibaki in Kenya had, by February 2006, been forced to sack four cabinet ministers linked to corruption (see Murunga and Nasong'o 2006).

The second limitation was the crisis of leadership within the pro-democracy movement in Kenya. As noted earlier, for a social movement to succeed in achieving its objectives, it requires quality leadership capable of strategic thinking and planning, effective mobilisation and inspiration. The pro-democracy movement in Kenya lacked such leadership to guide it towards its goals. Instead, the leadership was bifurcated between civil society personalities such as Kivutha Kibwana, Willy Mutunga and Wangari Maathai on the one hand, and politicians marginalised from politics such as Oginga Odinga, Masinde Muliro and George Nthenge among others, on the other hand. As a social movement for democracy, the original FORD in Kenya was a most potent force. The problem, however, was that it was dominated by politicians whose main interest was merely a quest for an opportunity to get a stab at power. Their immediate concern was not in favour of a profound agenda for democratisation of the Kenyan state. Once multipartyism was legalised, they transformed the social movement into a political party and each of the key figures in the new party sought to contest the presidency, leading to FORD's irredeemable disintegration and the dislocation of the transition momentum.

Third, a social movement's capacity for success is also a function of the movement's ideology or organising principles, which serve as the mobilising force. Such an ideology needs to be understood and internalised by followers, then deployed against the status quo. The Kenyan pro-democracy movement failed to articulate an ideology to unify its varied elements and catalyse the commitment of its followers to action for social change. In addition, most of the pro-democracy social groups lacked self-articulated political alternatives to the incumbent political agenda. Lacking such alternative conceptions, as Ihonvbere (1997) notes, CSOs simply capitalised on the unequal distribution of the externalities of SAPs and general socio-economic and political dislocation. The new movements did not come up with credible alternatives to existing policies. 'At best, like the Movement for Multiparty Democracy in Zambia before and since the 1991 elections, they adopt uncritically the monetarist prescriptions of the International Monetary Fund and the World Bank' (Ihonvbere 1997: 129). In Kenya, civil society actors tended to identify with any source of pressure directed at the incumbent KANU regime, including the aid crunch on the country and the shock therapy prescriptions of IMF/World Bank. This provided President Moi with effective ammunition to mock these actors as allies of external forces whose sole intention was to make life difficult for the ordinary citizen.

The fourth limitation of the pro-democracy movement in Kenya lay in the quality of the movement's followers. A movement's followers are grouped into ideologues, fanatics and passive sympathisers. The Kenyan pro-democracy movement did not lack ideologues. These are the men and women of letters who use their gift of the gab and intellectual abilities to problematise social dysfunction and inspire people to take remedial action. Perhaps the problem is that there were so many of these that none emerged as the foremost ideologue and clear leader of the movement, hence the movement remained in disarray. Whereas ideologues found movements and inspire hunger for change among individuals, fanatics constitute the engine that drives movements towards achieving their goals. They are the militants who are called to action in the name of the movement. The major constraint was that the pool of fanatics was narrow and limited to the unemployed and underemployed urban youth, largely in Nairobi, Kisumu, Kiambu and Nakuru, and was closely associated with specific politicians – Kenneth Matiba and Raila Odinga – a clear illustration of the bifurcated nature of the movement. Most Kenyans remained passive sympathisers of the pro-democracy movement. For a movement to succeed, it must constantly renew and replenish the pool of fanatical followers. This is where the Kenyan movement for democratisation failed. There was no deliberate strategy for converting passive sympathisers into active followers of the movement. Even the fanatics who existed were not mobilised and organised into cadres for dispersal into the population to mobilise the passives. This would have greatly boosted the successful implementation of the 'zero option' strategy for constitutional reform. The failure of the pro-democracy movement to force constitutional change through mass action was, to a large extent, a function of this limitation.

The fifth and final constraint was the external linkage of the pro-democracy movement. The reliance of CSOs on external sources of financial support forces them to strive to win the approval of Western donors, lenders, nations and international monitors, rather than the loyalty and support of domestic constituencies, turning them into programmatic appendages of international funding agencies. Given this reality, most of these organisations are unable to effectively counter accusations that they are in the service of foreign rather than local interests. The organisations' external linkages directly impinge upon their agendas and performance. It is noteworthy that it was the policy shift on the part of international development financiers in the late 1980s from channelling development resources via state apparatuses to channelling the same through civil organisations that thrust these social formations into the political arena as political norm setters and agents of political change. This policy shift on the part of donors was a function of the perception of the African state as too corrupt, opaque and overly bureaucratic. For their part, CSOs were envisioned as bastions of liberty, transparency and accountability, and thus regarded as the natural allies of the poor. Yet most of these organisations, just like the single-party state institutional legacy they seek to deconstruct, operate under highly personalised leaderships, which, though largely benevolent, are nevertheless unaccountable (see Ndegwa 1996; Nasong'o 2005). Under such circumstances, their contribution to democratic transition remains only incidental rather than fundamental.

Indeed, some CSOs share the alignment and project of the state-based elite in the form of self-advancement and personal accumulation. The emergence of what have come to be termed 'MONGOs' (my own NGO) that are run as personal or family outfits points to this. Accordingly, it is the chief executives of the NGOs who, in the process, get 'empowered' partly vis-à-vis the state but mainly vis-à-vis rank and file members of the civil society. The speed with which some NGO executives have transformed themselves from modest living standards to bourgeois lifestyles complete with state-of-the-art limousines and palace-like residences is a glaring pointer to the fact that some of these outfits are largely avenues for accumulation within civil society, much as the state has remained an arena for self-aggrandisement with regard to the political class. For example, in 2001, the executive director and trustees of SAREAT (Series on Alternative Research in East Africa Trust – an NGO committed to promoting good governance through research and publication) were taken to court by the Ford

Foundation for misappropriating millions of dollars in grants to the NGO. The NGO has since closed down.

There are other examples: NGO's receiving the bulk of their funding from the United States Agency for International Development and the Swedish International Development Agency, the two leading providers of political aid to Kenyan CSOs, shut up shop when financial and programmatic audits could no longer justify their continued existence and funds could not be accounted for.

Conclusion

Given the personalised nature of the democratic transition in Kenya, the prospects for democratic institutionalisation, defined in terms of establishment of the constitutional, legal and bureaucratic political order required for a fundamental shift of the governance paradigm, remain bleak. The democratisation process has so far failed to facilitate such a change because it has overly focused on multiparty elections and not on restructuring the strategic environment of political engagement. As Mbaku (1997) posits, to make certain that the present transitions in Africa lead to the establishment of viable political and economic systems, African countries must begin with proper constitution making. This process must include provision of appropriate facilities for all relevant population groups to effectively participate in constitutional discourse. 'Unless effective and self-enforcing social contracts which must flow from the political cultures of these polities are produced, the continent is unlikely to see any significant improvement in human development' (Mbaku 1997: 49).

Quite paradoxically, the opportunity for such constitutional engineering existed in Kenya but was squandered by opposition politicians who were more interested in merely replacing the incumbents. This moment of political opportunity obtained when the original FORD managed to push for the return to multiparty politics. At this juncture, the incumbent KANU regime was overly vulnerable and would easily have been pushed into acquiescing in rewriting the constitution before the first multiparty elections. The opposition failed to secure this window of opportunity, however, as they jostled amongst themselves to replace the incumbents. It is noteworthy that effective political institutions with well-defined powers and functions enshrined in a constitution are key to the emergence and sustenance of concrete forms of democratic governance as elaborated in Chapter 1. Such institutions provide a framework that shapes and stabilises people's expectations by providing a sense of continuity, reciprocity, equity and fairness in the distribution of societal values. They check and counterbalance one another and provide mechanisms for objective resolution of conflicts. Without routinising and institutionalising politics by way of devolving power to effective institutions, both vertical and horizontal, most African countries will remain marooned between what Ake (1996) calls a discredited authoritarian past and a democratic future that refuses to arrive.

Notes

1. *Dini ya Msambwa*, literally 'religion of ancestral spirits', is a religious movement that was founded by Elijah Masinde in the 1940s. Its ideology was crafted from the traditional Luhyia religious and social ethos and revolved around the rejection of Christianity, colonialism and what it stood for, and demanded the ejection of colonialists from Kenya.

2. *Rika Ria Forty* was the age group that was circumcised/initiated in the 1940s among the Kikuyu of Central Kenya. It was composed mainly of former war veterans like Bildad Kaggia and Fred Kubai among others, who were staunch trade unionists and great supporters of the Kikuyu Central Association and the Karing'a movement.

3. Abaluhyia Football Club and Gor Mahia were sports clubs associated with the Luhyia and Luo ethnic groups, respectively. Following their banning, the former re-registered as AFC (All-stars Football Club) Leopards and the latter as Golden Olympic Rangers (Gor) Football Club, while Luo Union became Reunion.

4. This reality contradicts Joel Migdal's (1988) 'weak states-strong societies' thesis.

5. Personal interview with David Makali, Director, Media Institute, Nairobi, 23 July 2003, revealing the intricate planning of strategies used in this mode of political activism.

6. The 25 per cent rule was introduced in April 1992 requiring a presidential winner to, in addition to garnering a simple majority of the votes cast, win at least 25 per cent of the votes cast in at least five of the country's eight administrative provinces. It is this rule that the CSOs wanted replaced by one simply requiring an overall majority (50% + 1) of the votes cast to win the presidency.

7. The idea of zero option was developed by researchers linked to the Institute for Policy Analysis and Research, Nairobi, who were consulted by the 4Cs on the constitutional reform project.

8. In this event, the number of ECK commissioners was increased from 5 to 21, with the additional commissioners nominated by political parties on the basis of their parliamentary strength, which meant that KANU still dominated the ECK.

9. Bemba for 'Kaunda no more'.

References

Adar, K.G. (1998) 'Ethnicity and Ethnic Kings: The Enduring Dual Constraint in Kenya's Multiethnic Democratic Electoral Experiment', *The Journal of Third World Spectrum*, vol. 5, no. 2.

Ajulu, R. (1992) 'The Left and the Question of Democratic Transition in Kenya: A Reply to Mwakenya', *Review of African Political Economy*, vol. 22, no. 64.

_____ (2000) 'Thinking Through the Crisis of Democratisation in Kenya: A Response to Adar and Murunga', *African Sociological Review*, vol. 4, no. 2.

Ake, C. (1996) 'Rethinking African Democracy', in L. Diamond and M.F. Plattner (eds), *The Global Resurgence of Democracy*, Baltimore, MD: The Johns Hopkins University Press.

Allen, C., and G. Williams (eds) (1982) *Sociology of Developing Countries: Sub-Saharan Africa*, New York, NY: Monthly Review Press.

Amadiume, I. (1995) 'Gender, Political Systems and Social Movements: A West African Experience', in M. Mamdani and E. Wamba-dia-Wamba (eds), *African Studies in Social Movements and Democracy*, Dakar: CODESRIA.

Amutabi, M.N. (2004) 'Crisis and Student Protest in Universities in Kenya: Examining the Role of Students in National Leadership and the Democratisation process', *African Studies Review*, vol. 45, no. 2.

Anderson, D. (2005) *Histories of the Hanged: The Dirty War in Kenya and the End of Empire*, New York, NY: W.W. Norton.

Anyang' Nyong'o, P. (1989) 'State and Society in Kenya: The Disintegration of the Nationalist Coalition and the Rise of Presidential Authoritarianism, 1963–78', *African Affairs*, vol. 88, no. 351.

Aubrey, L. (1997) *The Politics of Development Cooperation: NGOs, Gender and Partnership in Kenya*, London: Routledge.

Barkan, D. (1992) 'The Rise and Fall of a Governance Realm in Kenya', in G. Hyden and M. Bratton (eds), *Governance and Politics in Africa*, Boulder, Co: Lynne Rienner.

Beckman, B. (1998) 'The Liberation of Civil Society: Neo-Liberal Ideology and Political Theory in an African Context', in M. Mohanty et al. (eds), *People's Rights: Social Movements and the State in the Third World*, London: Sage.

Berman, B. (1990) *Control and Crisis in Colonial Kenya: The Dialectic of Domination*, London: James Currey.

Bratton, M. (1994a) 'Civil Society and Political Transitions in Africa', in J.W. Harbeson et al. (eds), *Civil Society and the State in Africa*, Boulder, CO: Lynne Rienner.

_____ (1994b) 'Peasant-State Relations in Post-Colonial Africa: Patterns of Engagement and Disengagement', in J.S. Migdal et al. (eds), *State Power and Social Forces: Domination and Transformation in the Third World*, Cambridge, UK: Cambridge University Press.

Brown, S. (2001) 'Authoritarian Leaders and Multiparty Elections in Africa: How Foreign Donors Help to Keep Kenya's Daniel arap Moi in power', *Third World Quarterly*, vol. 22, no. 5.

Callaghy, T.M. (1994) 'Civil Society, Democracy, and Economic Change in Africa: A Dissenting Opinion about Resurgent Societies', in J.W. Harbeson et al. (eds), *Civil Society and the State in Africa*, Boulder, CO: Lynne Rienner.

Chabal, P., and J.P. Daloz (1999) *Africa Works: Disorder as Political Instrument*, Oxford: James Currey.

Chandhoke, N. (1998) 'The Assertion of Civil Society Against the State: The Case of the Post-Colonial World', in M. Mohanty et al. (eds), *People's Rights: Social Movements and the State in the Third World*, London: Sage.

Chazan, N. (1994) 'Engaging the State: Associational Space in Sub-Saharan Africa', in J.S. Migdal et al. (eds), *State Power and Social Forces: Domination and Transformation in the Third World*, Cambridge, UK: Cambridge University Press.

Chazan, N., et al. (1988) *Politics and Society in Contemporary Africa*, Boulder, CO: Lynne Rienner.

Chepkwony, A. (1987) *The Role of NGOs in Development: A Study of the NCCK, 1963–78*, Uppsala: Scandinavian Institute of African Studies.

Cohen, J.L., and A. Arato (1992) *Civil Society and Political Theory*, Cambridge, MA: MIT Press.

Diamond, L. (1999) *Developing Democracy toward Consolidation*, Baltimore, MD: The Johns Hopkins University Press.

Ekeh, P. (1975) 'Colonialism and the Two Publics in Africa: A Theoretical Statement',*Comparative Studies in Society and History*, vol. 17, no. 1.

Giddens, A. (1997) *Sociology*, Cambridge, UK: Polity Press.

Harbeson, J.W. (1994) 'Civil Society and Political Renaissance in Africa', in J.W. Harbeson et al. (eds), *Civil Society and the State in Africa*, Boulder, CO: Lynne Rienner.

———— (1999) 'Rethinking Democratic Transitions: Lessons from Eastern and Southern Africa', in R. Joseph (ed.), *State, Conflict, and Democracy in Africa*, Boulder, CO: Lynne Rienner.

Hodder-Williams, R. (1984) *An Introduction to the Politics of Tropical Africa*, London: Allen & Unwin.

Hodgin, T. (1967) *Nationalism in Colonial Africa*, New York, NY: New York University Press.

Hoffer, E. (1958) *The True Believer*, New York, NY: Mentor Books.

Ihonvbere, J.O. (1997) 'On the Threshold of Another False Start? A Critical Evaluation of Pro-democracy Movements in Africa', in E.I. Udogu (ed.), *Democracy and Democratisation in Africa*, Leiden: Brill.

Katumanga, M. (2000) 'Civil Society and the Politics of Constitutional Reforms in Kenya: A Case Study of the National Convention Executive Council (NCEC)', Research Report, Institute of Development Studies, UK.

Lloyd, P.C. (1969) *Africa in Social Change*, Harmondsworth: Penguin.

Makinda, S.M. (1996) 'Democracy and Multiparty Politics in Africa', *Journal of Modern African Studies*, vol. 34, no. 4.

Mamdani, M. (1995a) 'Introduction', in M. Mamdani and E. Wamba-dia-Wamba (eds), *African Studies in Social Movements and Democracy*, Dakar: CODESRIA.

_____ (1995b) 'A Critique of the State and Civil Society Paradigm in Africanist Studies', in M. Mamdani and E. Wamba-dia-Wamba (eds), *African Studies in Social Movements and Democracy*, Dakar: CODESRIA.

_____ and E. Wamba-dia-Wamba (eds) (1995) *African Studies in Social Movements and Democracy*, Dakar: CODESRIA.

Maren, M.P. (1987) 'Kenya: The Dissolution of Democracy', *Current History*, May.

Mbaku, J.M. (1997) 'Effective Constitutional Discourse as an Important First Step to Democratisation in Africa', in E.I. Udogu (ed.), *Democracy and Democratisation in Africa*, Leiden: Brill.

Migdal, J.S. (1988) *Strong Societies and Weak States: State-Society Relations and State Capacity in the Third World*, Princeton, NJ: Princeton University Press.

Mueller, S.D. (1984) 'Government and Opposition in Kenya, 1966-9', *Journal of Modern African Studies*, vol. 22, no. 3.

Muigai, G. (1995) 'Ethnicity and the Renewal of Competitive Politics in Kenya', in H. Glickman (ed.), *Ethnic Conflict and Democratisation in Africa*, Atlanta, GA: The Africa Association Studies Press.

Murunga, G.R. (2000) 'Civil Society and the Democratic Experience in Kenya: Review Essay', *African Sociological Review*, vol. 4, no. 1.

_____ (2002) 'A Critical Look at Kenya's Non-transition to Democracy', *Journal of Third World Studies*, vol. XIX, no. 2.

_____ and S.W. Nasong'o (2006) 'Bent on Self-Destruction: The Kibaki Regime in Kenya', *Journal of Contemporary African Studies*, vol. 24, no. 1.

Mutunga, W. (1999) *Constitution Making from the Middle: Civil Society and Transition Politics in Kenya*, Nairobi and Harare: SAREAT/MWENGO.

Nasong'o, S.W. (2001) 'The Illusion of Democratic Governance in Kenya', in R. Dibie (ed.), *The Politics and Policies of Sub-Saharan Africa*, Lanham, MD: University Press of America.

_____ (2002) 'Political Consolidation and the Betrayal of Nationalism in Kenya: The Dynamics of External Linkages', in SORAC Conference on 'Internalist vs. Externalist Interpretations of African History and Culture', Montclair State University, Upper Montclair, NJ, September.

_____ (2005) *Contending Political Paradigms in Africa: Rationality and the Politics of Democratization in Kenya and Zambia*, New York and London: Routledge.

Ndegwa, S.N. (1996) *The Two Faces of Civil Society: NGOs and Politics in Africa*, West Hartford, CT Kumarian.

Ngunyi, M., and G. Nyaga (1998) *Democratic Audit Report*, Nairobi: SAREAT.

Nyangira, N. (1987) 'Ethnicity, Class, and Politics in Kenya', in M.G. Shatzberg (ed.), *The Political Economy of Kenya*, New York, NY: Praeger.

Nyang'oro, J.E. (2000) 'Civil Society, Structural Adjustment, and Democratisation in Kenya', in R.B. Kleinberg and J.A. Clark (eds),

Economic Liberalisation and Civil Society in the Developing World, New York, NY: St. Martin's Press.

Oanda, O. (1999) 'Economic Reform, Political Liberalisation and Economic Ethnic Conflict in Kenya', *Africa Development*, vol. XXIV, nos 1–2.

Ochieng, W.R. (1995) 'Structural and Political Changes', in B.A. Ogot and W.R. Ochieng (eds), *Decolonisation and Independence in Kenya, 1940–93*, London: James Currey.

Olukoshi, A. (1995) 'Bourgeois Social Movements and the Struggle for Democracy in Nigeria: An Inquiry into the Kaduna Mafia', in M. Mamdani and E. Wamba-dia-Wamba (eds), *African Studies in Social Movements and Democracy*, Dakar: CODESRIA.

Owiti, J. (2000) 'Political Aid and the Making and Re-making of Civil Society', Research Report, Institute of Development Studies, UK.

Oyugi, W.O. (1998) 'Ethnic Politics in Kenya', in Okwudiba Nnoli (ed.), *Ethnic Conflicts in Africa*, Dakar: CODESRIA.

Republic of Kenya (1998) *Constitution of Kenya*, Nairobi: Government Printer.

Rosberg Jr., C.G., and J. Nottingham (1966) *The Myth of 'Mau Mau'; Nationalism in Kenya*, New York, NY: Praeger.

Sabar, G. (2002) *Church, State, and Society in Kenya: From Mediation to Opposition, 1963–1993*, London: Frank Cass.

Spencer, J. (1985) *The Kenya African Union*, London: KPI.

Touraine, A. (1981) *The Voice and the Eye*, Cambridge: Cambridge University Press.

Wanyande, P. (2002) 'The Power of Knowledge: Voter Education and Electoral Behaviour in a Kenyan Constituency', in Ludeki Chweya (ed.), *Electoral Politics in Kenya*, Nairobi: Claripress.

Were, G.S. (1971) 'Politics, Religion and Nationalism in Western Kenya, 1942–1962', in Historical Association of Kenya Annual Conference.

Widner, J.A. (1992) *The Rise of a Party-State in Kenya: From 'Harambee!' to 'Nyayo!'* Berkeley, CA: University of California Press.

_____ (1994) 'Political Reform in Anglophone and Francophone African Countries', in J.A. Widner (ed.), *Economic Change and Political Liberalisation in Sub-Saharan Africa*, Baltimore, MD: The Johns Hopkins University Press.

Wipper, A. (1977) *Rural Rebels: A Study of Two Protest Movements in Kenya*, Nairobi: Oxford University Press.

Young, C. (1994) 'Democratisation in Africa: The Contradictions of a Political Imperative', in J.A. Widner (ed.), *Economic Change and Political Liberalisation in Sub-Saharan Africa*, Baltimore, MD: The Johns Hopkins University Press.

_____ (1996) 'Africa: An Interim Balance Sheet', *Journal of Democracy*, vol. 7, no. 3.

_____ (1999) 'The Third Wave of Democratisation in Africa: Ambiguities and Contradictions', in R. Joseph (ed.), *State, Conflict, and Democracy in Africa*, Boulder, CO: Lynne Rienner.

3

Religious Movements and Democratisation in Kenya: Between the Sacred and the Profane

Margaret Gathoni Gecaga

Introduction

The imposition of colonial domination had important effects on indigenous African political systems. In most African traditional societies, the ethnic group, its rulers and institutions were set within a sacred cosmic order. The patterns and sanctions for political organisations were often derived from a religious cosmology and the mythology that expressed and supported it. In addition, in some societies, the political leader was the channel through which ultimate forces operated for the welfare of society. The disruption of traditional integrationist systems produced by the intrusion of Western ideas and power had the effect of separating the religious and political components. This was the beginning of a complex process of secularisation whereby religion began to lose its hold at both levels of social institutions and human consciousness. Subsequently, religion was seen as a mere dimension of the social order. One of the consequences of this change was a shift from religious to military power as a basis for political authority. For instance, under Western rule colonies were held together by vastly superior military, technological, economic and administrative power. However, with the demise of colonialism, post-colonial states were faced with the crisis of legitimacy. To counteract this, secular ideologies were introduced to assume the legitimising functions of religion. Theories of social contract, representative government or other variations on the idea of democracy were most prominent, but there were also secular theories of authoritarianism. In this situation, religion shifted from the centre and thus became available to inspire social movements.

Studies of the early colonial period demonstrate the active role of religious-based ideologies and organisations in mobilising people to rebel against foreign rule. For example, *Kimbanguism* in Zaire (now Democratic Republic of Congo) was a religious quest for transcendental justice and order. In colonial Kenya, the cult of *Mumbo*, *Dini ya Msambwa* and the *Karing'a* movements led in the fight against colonial rule. These movements emerged in the context of political transition from a colonial to an independent government. They played a major role of mobilising citizens to win political power from the colonial administration. To the extent that such transfer relocated power into the hands of the citizenry, decolonisation was an important process in democratisation. However, subsequent events in the post-independence period shifted power from the citizenry to the ruling party and the presidency with unrestricted powers leading to authoritarianism (Anyang' Nyong'o 1989).

In the post-independence period, movements that claim to be 'religious' have emerged in the public realm of many African countries with important political implications. These movements include the Holy Spirit Mobile Forces of Alice Lakwena and the Lord's Resistance Army of John Kony, both in Uganda, the *Budu Dia Kongo* Movement in Zaire, the *Naprama* Movement in Mozambique and more recently the *Mungiki* in Kenya. These movements emerged at a time begging state reform due to multiple crises. These crises emanated from the political decay of single parties, and from the crumbling economies with their resultant prescriptive reform policies under the structural adjustment programmes (SAPs) (see Chapter 9 by Murunga in this volume), and massive corruption. Subsequently, beginning in the late 1990s, there was increased pressure on African countries to adopt democratic governance with conditionalities from many Western countries. This pressure led to an increase in social movements that called for greater democratisation of society, greater accountability in the management of national affairs and an end to corruption. Others protested against the effects of SAPs (Beckman 1991; Mkandawire 1992: 4).

This chapter evaluates the role of religious movements in the political process of democratisation, focusing particularly on the intersections between Christian religious groupings and the *Mungiki* movement. The chapter outlines the cultural and religious beliefs and practices that informed the development of *Mungiki* and analyses the movement's sensibilities in the politics of transition in Kenya. It situates the discussion of *Mungiki* in the broader context of transitional politics, which saw a shift in the perception of religion as simply a compartment of the social order. It argues that at different political transition periods in Kenya, religio-political groups have emerged to play positive or negative roles in democratisation.

Conceptualising Key Terms

In this chapter, I use the notion of democracy to refer to governance by the will of the people, observed through a representative system of government achieved through competitive politics, independent media, rule of law, liberty of the individual and a vibrant civil society. In theory, it is held that democratic leaders are trustees of the people and exercise power on their behalf. From this understanding, democratisation is a process by which a great majority of the citizens are empowered to participate substantively in social, economic and political issues and decision making (see Chapter 1 in this volume; De Gruchy 1995; Mande 1999; Akivaga 2002). Four other key concepts require explication: 'sacred' and 'profane', the idea of 'religio-political movements' and 'social mobilisation'.

Sacred and profane

The term 'sacred' has been used from a wide variety of perspectives and given varying descriptive and evaluative connotations by scholars. Durkheim (1915) identifies the sacred as the creation of society. Objects or people become sacred when human beings 'remove' or see them apart from ordinary use. Otto (1923) terms the sacred as the 'Holy' or the 'wholly other', and Eliade (1957) refers to the sacred space as qualitatively different from all other homogeneous spaces in which regular everyday occurrences and activities take place.

Phenomenologists of religion such as Otto (1923), Eliade (1957) and Wach (1944) hold sacrality to be the hallmark of religion and also its very essence. According to these theorists, cultural belief systems and traditional practices cannot be given the title religion if there is nothing that is deemed sacred by their adherents. For the phenomenological school, the sacred is comprehended as a dynamic force that manifests itself in feelings of religious awe, inexplicable sentiments of horror or dread on the one hand and of overwhelming ecstasy and fascination on the other (Anttonen 2000). This implies that for many religious systems the sacred involves the supernatural, a power that is beyond the laws of the observable universe. In this connection, 'profane' implies that which is not concerned with religion or religious matters. It is that which is secular and sometimes shows contempt for sacred things. In the latter sense, profane has a negative connotation. Anthropologists Steiner (1956) and Douglas (1966) argue how profane implies 'unclean', disorder and incoherence. However, for the purpose of this chapter, profane will refer to secular or worldly, non-sacred things.

It is important to note that the relationship between the sacred and the profane can be understood either abstractly as a mutual exclusion of spheres of reality or cognitively as a way of distinguishing between two aspects of that reality. In this case, the sacred and the profane are two levels, which are not inherently in competition or conflict. At the sacred level, reality is experienced as being under the governance of God. In this reality, God is intimately present as the object of religious faith and is experienced by the believer who enters into living communion with the Deity. The profane, on the other hand, is the same reality construed as being accessible to humanity (Shorter and Onyancha 1997). In this regard, the sacred and the profane are not intrinsically opposed. This theoretical assertion, however, is undermined by historical practice, especially the secularisation process that led to structural differentiation of social institutions including the economy, the polity, morality, justice, education, recreation, health maintenance and familial organisation (see Shiner 1966; Jules-Rosette 1991). Each of these operates with considerable autonomy as conceptions of the supernatural lose their sovereignty over human affairs.

Religio-political movements

According to Wipper (1977: 3), a religious movement exemplifies collective mobilisation with the objective of redefining humanity's relationships to questions of ultimate concern, the purpose of life, death, and people's relations to the cosmos and to each other. A political movement in turn exemplifies collective mobilisation with the objective of maintaining, restoring, modifying or changing the institutional structure of power in society.

A 'religio-political movement' contains both religious and political components. It has widespread grassroots adherence to religious ideas, symbols and rituals. These are inextricably linked to people's political beliefs. Examples of religio-political movements include *Dini ya Msambwa* of the Babukusu of Western Kenya and the *Karing'a* (Orthodox Kikuyu) movement among the Agikuyu (that led to the establishment of a nationalist movement – the Mau Mau in the 1950s). A more recent religio-political movement is the Holy Spirit Movement of Alice Lakwena in Northern Uganda.

Religion and social mobilisation

Emile Durkheim (1915) first propounded the functionalist theory of religion with respect to the Aborigines of Australia. Durkheim maintained that religious activity allowed the Aborigines to take cognisance of themselves as collectives. One of the functions of religion for such a people was that their myths and rituals permitted them to entertain collective sentiments and express a sense of unity. Religion then functioned to maintain social cohesion. It also prescribed moral norms, which were enjoined on the people as requirements of a higher supernatural order. In this sense, religion functions to legitimise the purpose and procedures of society (Cunningham et al. 1991).

Whereas Wilson (1982: 32) observes that religion has latent functions that arise unseen or unintended by people in their practice of religion, Smith (1971: 4) argues that individual religious leaders and clerical groups utilise sacred symbols to mobilise the masses for nationalist struggles, internal revolts and election campaigns. This is possible because religion is the centre of the order of symbols, values and beliefs which govern society. Reicher and Hopkins' (2001: 23) conception of a symbolic reserve is of relevance here. They suggest that just as nations have gold reserves to guarantee the value of their economic currencies, nations similarly use their symbolic reserves to give sense to situations, to legitimise their actions and to design their futures. This 'sense-making' process is facilitated by the existence of symbolic resources, and the creation of new meaning is affected by nations' relations to the old meanings. Thus, leaders find in religion a gateway to manipulate these symbolic reserves.

Religion provides powerful emotional symbols of group identity which bind people together even in the midst of great opposition. In historical circumstances, while awareness of oppression runs deep, reaction may appear erratic, diffuse and difficult to characterise. It is here that we must look beyond the conventionally explicit domains of 'political action' and consciousness. When expressions of dissent are prevented from attaining the level of open discourse, a subtle but systematic breach of authoritative cultural codes might make a statement of protest. In such contexts, ritual provides an appropriate medium through which the values and structures of a contradictory world may be manipulated. For example, all over Africa, political elites make use of religious communities for purposes of mobilising voters, creating clients or organising constituencies. In Senegal, the influence wielded by Marabouts or Islamic holy men belonging to the main Sufi brotherhoods has been recognised as a source of political influence for decades (O'Brien 1975). Similarly, during the liberation war in Zimbabwe, the advice of mediums said to be possessed by the spirits of ancestors played a vital role in securing the support of the population. In these two cases, religion served as a vehicle of political mobilisation through the enormous power of its symbols.

It is worth pointing out that just as religion has a potent force of mobilising people and sustaining their unity against any form of oppression, it can also cause conflict. Religion can create and enhance stress (Johnstone 1997). Religions have an essentially 'fissiparous quality'. In this view, religious beliefs create boundaries between people, not only when distorted or misused but also by their very nature; for religion binds persons together into 'partial wholes' of communities of those who believe in Jesus, Allah or Krishna. Religious communities with clearly drawn boundaries respond to this unease by providing clear answers to the questions 'Who am I?', 'Where do I belong?'. Their answers inevitably spill into other realms of life, including politics.

Emergence of Religious Movements in Kenya

New religious movements (NRMs) have emerged in the last one hundred years triggered by a variety of factors, chief among them being political and economic pressures afflicting society at specific points. The numbers of these movements grew at such times of stress, underpinned by sociological, political, economic, anthropological, religious and theoretical factors. Highlighted are causative factors such as psychological stress and conflicts felt by individuals in unfamiliar or rapidly changing situations, which make them confused, powerless and frustrated. Welbourn and Ogot (1966) provide ample evidence of the mediating role of movements under conditions of rapid, uneven transformation, as they act as buffers in the wake of social dislocation. In addition, Cunningham et al. (1991) have observed that religious groups can provide refuge from the pressures and fears, real and imagined, of social change.

In Kenya, two factors seem to loom large as causative factors in the rise of NRMs. They are also at the centre of three of the most pronounced of such movements in colonial Kenya: the *Mumbo* cult, *Dini ya Msambwa* (DYM) and the *Karing'a* movements. The factors are: (1) the need to resist cultural forms of neo-colonialism by rallying followers' traditional values to challenge the orthodoxy behind the mainstream churches as well as the injustices of the state; and (2) economic deprivation or exploitation, most importantly, the loss of land. The cult of Mumboism, for instance, was the first challenge to colonial authority in South Nyanza. Although it originated among the Luo, it got its direction among the Abagusii, specifically within the Bogonko clan. This was the largest and wealthiest clan of the Kitutu sub-tribe whose position and influence had suffered under colonialism (Wipper 1977: 58). Subsequently, members of the Bogonko clan became leaders of protests against the colonial regime.[1] Mumboism also attracted young men and women whose leadership roles were not recognized in the traditional set-up. The cult established other criteria for leadership through the status reversal theme.[2] In this case, young men and women lacking power and prestige saw in Mumbo an opportunity to acquire more satisfying roles. Mumboism also venerated Abagusii warriors and prophets who became its symbols of courage, strength and unity among the different groups for purposes of forming a formidable force against the British. However, in spite of Mumboism's blatant rejection of Christianity and the Europeans, it derived the millennial concept from Christian eschatology. This millennial ideology did not aim at changing the present order but abolishing it and ushering in a new social order, a kingdom of Mumboites (Wipper 1977: 83). Though it died out because of severe state repression, it represented the beginnings of political protest among the Abagusii, the articulation of social and economic injustices, and the building of embryonic movements towards democracy.

Dini ya Msambwa or 'the religion of ancestral spirits' emerged among the Babukusu (see Makila 1987) during the colonial period. Founded by Elijah Masinde, who was regarded as the people's protector and liberator from the injustices of the colonial order, the movement had support from many ethnic groups in Western Kenya including the Abaluhyia, the Suk, the Turkana, the Samburu, the Teso, the Abagusii and a number of communities in Eastern Uganda. DYM emerged out of the socio-economic and political injustices experienced by the people of Western Kenya including the loss of power and status, denigration of African religion and culture, absence of legitimate means to channel grievances, land alienation, and punitive agricultural reforms. DYM and the Bukusu Union protested many of the same grievances though their tactics were different. It is important to note that DYM's connection with the Bukusu Union and other organisations protesting similar issues lends weight to the contention that its (DYM) goals in colonial Kenya were mainly political.

DYM's beliefs were an eclectic combination of Western and indigenous political and religious ideas. DYM members refused to co-operate with the colonial government's policies whether it was in agriculture or in recruitment for World War II. They harassed settler farmers with strikes for better pay and working conditions. Through the late 1940s and 1950s, members of the movement were associated with anti-government activities leading to violent clashes. In 1948, DYM was proscribed after the Malakisi riots in which 11 followers were killed by the police. Subsequently, Masinde was detained for 13 years. In spite of the ban, a wave of arson in 1949 was attributed to DYM members. In the Trans Nzoia District, 16 cases were recorded involving the burning of stock, sheds, police huts, churches and schools. In 1950, a severe battle took place at Kolloa in Baringo District in which 29 Suk and 4 policemen were killed. Underground meetings and activities of the movement continued throughout the period of the State of Emergency. Masinde was released in 1961 and immediately took on the British government demanding compensation for wrongful incarceration and declared his intentions to reactivate DYM. In 1962, Masinde addressed a political meeting in Kitale following which he was arrested the same year together with a few of his followers. After independence in 1963, the ban on DYM was revoked. However, in 1972 the Kenyatta government enforced the ban again and Masinde was imprisoned. Masinde was disillusioned with the new government because the Babukusu did not get back their land in the Rift Valley, the Europeans did not leave Kenya and the same foreign (European) ideology continued in schools (Shimanyula 1978; Buijtenhuijs 1983).

Another movement, the Karing'a religio-political movement, also emerged out of the political, educational and cultural struggles of the 1920s and 1930s (see Rosberg and Nottingham 1966; Muga 1975; Tignor 1976; Kangethe 1981). The Agikuyu reacted to an oppressive situation that the colonial government and the missionaries had created. The Agikuyu, like other Africans, experienced problems of land alienation, forced labour, squatter and taxation system, unemployment, and gross violation of human rights (see Kanogo 1987; Anderson 2005). The missionaries condemned the Agikuyu religion and culture. By 1925, the Agikuyu political system and its administrative units were virtually disintegrated by the colonial political system, which set in motion a disorganisation of the Agikuyu social structure. In addition, substantial amounts of land had already been confiscated by the colonialists thus dislocating the Agikuyu kinship system.[3] The final blow came with the ultimate condemnation by the missionaries of a central rite in the Kikuyu community, namely, female circumcision, which was the central feature of the Agikuyu identity (see Kenyatta 1938; Kanogo 2005). Hence, the Karing'a movement was against white domination and demanded total socio-cultural independence from the Europeans.

The Agikuyu religion and culture played the primary role in the development of the Karing'a movement. Nine Agikuyu cultural and religious practices were utilised in the development of the movement including the Agikuyu concept of 'democracy' (refer to Chapter 5 by Mwangola in this volume), the sacredness of land, the social spirit of co-operation and communalism, songs, the Agikuyu concept of God, oathing, initiation rites, folk tales, and the prophetic tradition inherent in the Agikuyu society (Kangethe 1981: 467). The oaths and the traditions were of special significance (Maloba 1993). The administration of oaths was both a religious and a political act. The effectiveness of the oaths lay in their traditional and symbolic force. They were for the purpose of creating social and moral solidarity. Oathing involved personal loyalty to the resistance movement backed by powerful mystical sanctions. The Mau Mau used these mystically sanctioned oaths to enforce strict adherence to the movement. Renouncement of Christianity also contributed to the development of the Karing'a movement. To be baptised in the movement meant that one had made a decision to dissociate oneself from the missionaries and the abolitionists. As a result of the wide protest among the Agikuyu, the missionaries excommunicated members of the Karing'a movement from the churches and the children of members of the movement were sent away from schools. Two organisations emerged to meet the education crisis: the Kikuyu Karing'a Education Association (KKEA) and the Kikuyu Independent Schools Association (KISA) (see Anderson 1970). In these new schools, students were taught cultural and political education. The Kenya Teachers College in Githunguri, Kiambu District, was an emblem of the triumph of the Karing'a Movement (Kangethe 1981).

Origin and Growth of Mungiki

At the attainment of independence, many African political elites opted for the one-party system with the hope that this would guarantee national unity. This was done either through the acts of parliament or through what was viewed as the people's wish, whereby small parties such as the Kenya African Democratic Union (KADU) were absorbed by the ruling party (see Chapter 4 by Oloo, in this volume). Most post-independence African leaders, for the most part, did not seek to restructure the colonial state. Instead, they perpetuated the models of the former colonial governments which were characterized by misuse of power and oppression of the ruled. The one-party state served this purpose very well.

The constitutional amendments in the first few years of independence in Kenya gave the late President Kenyatta so much power that he became a monarch (see Wanjala 2002). As Nasong'o (see Chapter 2 in this volume) and Oloo (see Chapter 4 in this volume) discuss in detail, Kenyatta used his monolithic power to destroy or push into oblivion all pro-democracy and people-centred movements that had been involved in the struggle for independence and land rights, thereby emasculating institutions meant to provide checks and balances on the executive. When Daniel arap Moi took over power in 1978, Kenya was essentially a politically corrupt society in which most of the institutions and notions of democratic governance had been subverted by personal rule (Kibwana et al. 1996: 127). President Moi consolidated his powers and made the infamous 1982 constitutional amendment that made Kenya a de jure one-party state. As Gimode and Murunga show in this volume, there was total mismanagement of the economy and breakdown in the provision of essential services such as education, health and transportation, and Moi governed through violence, harassment, intimidation and increased use of state security organs for self-preservation. The violence culminated in the infamous 1992 politically instigated ethnic clashes. Faced with this repression, the pro-democracy movement flourished. The religious sector became the first to lay its criticism.

From the 1980s, the religious sector had been at the forefront of the pro-democracy forces that were challenging the autocratic Moi regime. The National Council of the Churches of Kenya (NCCK) and the Roman Catholic Church through the Kenya Episcopal Conference (KEC) co-operated in defending citizens and denouncing the government that had failed to defend them (Githiga 2002). They called for multipartyism as an attempt to help the country enter into a new era where the rights of citizens regardless of ethnic origin would be protected and where there would be an end to the ethnocentric system of government. In their offensive against state authoritarianism, the religious organisations questioned the dichotomy between politics and religion, showing that power does not rest in politics alone but also in religion. The NCCK and the KEC came up with literature that was soon circulated throughout the country in the form of posters, pamphlets and booklets (Githiga 2002: 110). These themes covered an in-depth discussion of civic education to create some awareness among a wide audience of Kenyans of the political rights they had lost. There were some religious organisations, however, such as the Evangelical Fellowship of Kenya (EFK) that sought to preserve the dichotomy between religion and politics (Ngunyi 1995). Their silence in many ways may be interpreted as support of the government as demonstrated by their antagonistic attitude towards the NCCK.

As several chapters in this volume show, even with the return to multiparty politics in 1992, authoritarianism persisted along with the entrenched socio-economic deprivation of the majority of Kenyans. Accordingly, it is within this context of poor economic performance, ineffectual provision of basic services, the collapse of social infrastructure, unbridled accumulation of power by the political elite and ethnic violence that the Mungiki emerged (see Kagwanja 1997). According to Wamue (2001: 254), Mungiki is a Gikuyu word that has its etymological root in the word *muingi*, meaning masses of people. 'Mungiki denotes a mass movement.' However, the fact that a majority of its followers are from the Gikuyu community negates this notion. Mungiki is not proto-nationalistic, it does not transcend the limitation of language and ethnicity as did DYM in Western Kenya. Thus, to a great extent, Mungiki is exclusivist in nature.

The making of Mungiki

The fact that Mungiki has attracted a high proportion of Kikuyu displaced by the 1992 and 1997 ethnic clashes is instructive. During the colonial period, the Agikuyu, like other ethnic groups in Kenya, experienced land alienation. This was concentrated in the central highlands and the fertile highlands of the Rift Valley. The net effect of land expropriation in these two regions was the creation of two agricultural corridors, which later developed incongruent forms of ethno-regional nationalism (Ngunyi 1996). When the colonial period drew to a close, the issue of independent distribution of land came to dominate Kenyan politics. Ethnic political leaderships allied with each other on the basis of their location, size and wealth. For instance, the Kikuyu political leaders in the Kenya African National Union (KANU) allied with the Luo leaders and sought to expand into Kalenjin areas. The Kalenjin allied with the Luhyia and formed the KADU and both had claims conflicting with those of the Kikuyu and the Luo (Gibbon 1995: 15). Although KADU was eventually absorbed into KANU, uneven rates of development continued to provoke ethnic hatred. President Kenyatta aggravated the regional inequalities through consolidating the Gikuyu, Embu and Meru domination of the country's economy, a process that further ethnicised political relations between the Kikuyu and other ethnic groups. When Moi eventually ascended to power in 1978, he held the GEMA people responsible for his exclusion from political prominence despite having been vice-president.[4] Hence he took the first opportunity to form his inner core of aides and supporters in order to contain the GEMA factionalists while establishing his own hegemony.

Ethnic welfare associations such as GEMA, Luo and Abaluhyia Unions were banned. Moi argued that 'tribal' associations disrupted national unity. Through disbanding GEMA and the promotion of non-Kikuyu in the military and civil service, the president alienated many people within the Kikuyu elite thereby constituting these as the basis of opposition to his rule. Other organisations with a large Kikuyu membership, such as the *Matatu* Vehicle Owners Association (MVOA), were de-registered while still others were either co-opted into state institutions or dissolved. Various punitive measures were put in place between 1979 and 1988 to effectively marginalise the Kikuyu. These included ethnically based quota systems of resource apportionment, and collapse of the agricultural sector through non-payment of farmers for milk, tea and coffee. Thus Moi used his state power to consolidate his presidency and to destroy the Kikuyu economic base. This was aimed at ensuring that the Kikuyu did not use their economic might to rebel or organise against his supremacy. The Kikuyu had to be made dependent on the *Nyayo* system of patronage of reward and punishment in order to be controlled (Kanyinga 1995).

The situation began to change in 1989 when pro-democracy forces began to agitate for multipartyism. In response, the government sponsored the infamous 1992–93 and 1997–98 ethnic clashes in the Rift Valley, Western Province and parts of the Coast Province to deal with communities not deemed as supporting the government. Moi had predicted in advance that multiparty politics would breed interethnic violence. These ethnic clashes confirmed Moi's prediction. Although they had many objectives, the clashes aimed to secure KANU domination of the whole of the Rift Valley. Their occurrence also coincided with the call for Majimboism, which intensified ethnic rivalries (see Ngunyi 1996). Kalenjin politicians warned that if multiparty democracy was established, non-natives (non-Kalenjins) would be driven out of the Rift Valley. Consequently, the already tenuous relations between ethnic groups deteriorated rapidly. Kikuyu, Luhyia and Luo communities bordering the Rift Valley became targets of Kalenjin and Maasai warriors' violence. The main point of harassment of opposition communities was to ensure that no opposition candidate would receive 25 per cent of the presidential vote in these provinces. For example, in Nakuru and Laikipia Districts where the Kikuyu formed a majority of the target population, it was imperative to minimise their vote in order to ensure that neither Mwai Kibaki nor Kenneth Matiba would secure 25 per cent of the vote in the Rift Valley (Throup and Hornsby 1998). The atrocities meted out against the Kikuyu, the Luo, the Luhyia and many other non-Kalenjin communities failed to escalate as planned because of the unexpected massive retaliation by the Kikuyu in defence of their land and property. Pushed to the wall, the displaced Kikuyu in Laikipia and Nakuru became easy targets for political mobilisation.

Mungiki arose out of the economic hardships and exclusion generated by the ethnic clashes. Mobilised on the basis of cultural heritage, Mungiki was founded in 1995 by Maina Njenga who claimed to have had a vision in which *Ngai* (God) commanded him to liberate his people from all forms of oppression. His claims to possessing special powers and a mandate from God are consistent with those of ritual specialists and prophets such as Elijah Masinde. Njenga's main message to his followers was that they had been elected by God to bring about social and political liberation to the people of Kenya and to Africans in general.

Some view Mungiki as a splinter group of the Tent of the Living God (Hema ya Ngai we Mwoyo), a Gikuyu religious group, led by Ngonya wa Gakonya, that later turned political.[5] It is argued that the main reason why some members of the Tent left to form Mungiki was the inability of wa Gakonya's group to respond to the political situation. Many members felt that the Tent was too conservative at a time when Kenya was at a political crossroads. Although Ngonya wa Gakonya later joined politics in 1992 and even formed the Democratic Movement

(DEMO), which was denied registration by the state, most members of the group wanted the movement to remain apolitical, insisting that there was a serious and urgent need to sensitise people, especially the youth, on Kikuyu cultural beliefs as a way of self-actualisation. By the mid-1990s at the height of political clashes in the Rift Valley, however, some members left the Tent to form Mungiki.

Initially, Mungiki sought the renaissance of the Gikuyu culture as a first step towards the liberation of the people. The movement is nativistic and rejects Western customs. It advocates the return to traditional beliefs and practices. It has thus been radical and virulent in condemning Christianity and its teachings. Like the Karing'a religio-political movement of the 1930s, Mungiki also turned to the past for inspiration and attempted some syncretism in its approach. It stresses the lost glory and dignity of the Agikuyu, which it seeks to re-establish in the 'Kirinyaga Kingdom'. To this extent, the Mungiki movement is millenarian in nature. At the same time, it can be viewed as 'revolutionary' and 'utopian' in rejecting the neo-colonial regime and in seeking to introduce new values and forms of leadership.

The fundamental principles of Mungiki are cultural self-determination, self-pride and self-reliance. Mungiki has utilized traditional methods such as prayers, songs, prophetic utterances, and oathing and initiation rites to censor the forces of neo-colonialism. These have been used to protect and uphold such basic values as belief in God (*Ngai*), reverence of ancestors, belief in the sacredness of land and respect for moral values. According to Mungiki tenets, the cultural re-engineering of the Agikuyu should apply to the whole country irrespective of differences in culture. The intermeshing of political and religious themes is evident in Mungiki hymns and prayers. Mount Kenya (Kirinyaga) is believed to be the holy dwelling place of *Ngai*. Members seek supernatural signs and potency as they face the mountain in prayers and hymns. They end their prayers with the traditional chant *Thaai, thai thaya Ngai thaai* (we beseech thee oh God [*Ngai*]; Table 3.1).

The songs have a religio-political overtone. They bear a strong religious consciousness expressing the omnipresence and omnipotence of *Ngai* in their struggle against neo-colonialism. They also use the songs to dramatise their cause of cultural renaissance. One such song is:

Our people let us return to
Our shrines let us remember
What Ngai the creator of Gikuyu
and Mumbi did for our heroes

as they fought for uhuru. Ngai will not
abandon us as long as
we return to our customs[6]

According to Anderson (2002) and Kagwanja (2003) Mungiki followers reflect a strong consciousness of the prophetic message of Mugo wa
Kabiru, the Gikuyu diviner and seer, who prophesied the coming of the
Europeans. He promised the destruction of the colonial order, the fall of
the Europeans and the establishment of a Kikuyu Kingdom. Mugo urged
the Agikuyu to treat the Europeans with courtesy spiced with suspicion
(Kenyatta 1938: 73). Kagwanja (2003) notes that the glorification of
the Gikuyu culture in the writings and activities of Gikuyu intellectuals,
particularly Jomo Kenyatta and Ngugi wa Thiong'o, has conferred
on Mungiki an ethnically exclusive cultural radicalism. Especially
important are Thiong'o's literary works *The River Between* and *Weep
Not Child*. Anderson (2002) specifically isolates the portrayal of the
prophecy of Mugo wa Kabiru as the ideological drive that makes
Mungiki ethnocentric. Consequently, Mungiki has advocated for the
restoration of Gikuyu indigenous practices as an indigenous refuge in
the face of colonial mental slavery of mainstream churches. Essentially,
Mugo's prophecy has become a beacon for Mungiki. The prophecies
infused the living with the courage and strength of past heroes. It has
also aroused a sense of unity and commitment among the Agikuyu and
helped in the development of Mungiki's personality, which was
initially uncompromising and unbending (until part of its rank and
file began to convert to Islam and more recently to Christianity).

To bring their millenarian dream to fruition, the Mungiki have
relied on rituals such as oaths. Oathing binds the members to culturally
important vows of secrecy and allegiance for which they are promised

Table 3.1   Typical Mungiki prayer

Prayer	Translation
Mwene nyaga twa kuhoya	Ngai we pray thee
Utuhe wendani – thaai	Give us love – we beseech thee
Utuhe irio – thaai	Give us food – we beseech thee
Utuhe mugunda – thaai	Give us land – we beseech thee
Thaai thaai Thaaai thaiya Ngai Thaai	We beseech thee oh God

Source: Personal interview with Mohamed Muroki, 15 November 2003.

supernatural protection. Oaths also help to sustain moral solidarity among the group members under the most adverse conditions. They also provide the occasion for teaching the members about the goals of the movement. Oaths are also used as a recruiting technique. It is reported that Mungiki conducted blood oaths at the height of land clashes in the Rift Valley. This was the traditionally dreaded oath *Kaurugo* (Kenyatta 1938: 21; see also Maloba 1993). To be 'baptised' into Mungiki means to believe in the socio-political, cultural and religious principles of the movement. This rite involves baptism in the river by ritual 'elders' and passing of the neophytes over fire.[7] Prominence is given to moral reform in the face of the breakdown of traditional codes and sanctions. Therefore Mungiki calls for the teaching of *Kirira*, which involves learning the consequences of abandoning African culture and religion. *Kirira*, according to Wamue (2001), leads to socio-religious cleansing rituals known as *guthera* (being clean). As a result, cleansing rituals are a common phenomenon among Mungiki followers. A goat or lamb is slaughtered and the blood is offered as libation to the ancestors. The meat is shared by all the members who have undergone the cleansing ceremony. The purpose of this ritual is to induct new members into the movement and invoke divine intervention in their mission. It is also meant to help retain cosmic harmony. The belief in this case is that these members were ritually unclean and they needed to be purified from the foreign cultural hegemony which was evil (*thahu*). Such cleansing rituals were not uncommon among the Agikuyu (see Kenyatta 1938). Through this kind of rituals the Mungiki not only claim to break with the influence of Western culture but also attempt to resacralise much of common life. It is an attempt to create cohesive forms of community in which religious values are more coherent and exercise a larger direct influence on social life. However, this has not succeeded. Many people loathe Mungiki because of its atavistic nature. Moreover, its association with violence in the recent past has left many Kenyans convinced that it is a terror gang. As a result, it has been labelled parochial and tribalist.

Mungiki: a contextual analysis

Mungiki's focus on cultural renaissance is not unique. *Bundu Dia Kongo* (a Congolese fundamentalist movement) sought to regenerate Kongo culture in a situation politically dominated and invaded by Lingala culture (see Wamba-dia-Wamba 1999). The question at this juncture is why the emphasis on ritual in religion. Religion is the core of the culture of a people. It must be consistent with and rooted in the culture and history of a people. A foreign religion (in this case Christianity) that is inconsistent with a people's history, their ancestors, messengers and teachings represents spiritual enslavement of the people. African people under the influence of 'colonial religion' are thus an enslaved people. Being so enslaved, their spiritual liberation can only be achieved by returning to their own. For instance, members of Mungiki profess that the spirit of the movement started with Waiyaki wa Hinga, the Kikuyu leader who first protested the encroachment on Kikuyuland by British settlers early in the twentieth century. The climax was the Mau Mau rebellion. Mungiki members refer to themselves as *thuna Cia Mau Mau* (Mau Mau offshoot), or *Atiriri Baruri* (the protectors of the nation), *njama* or *ngerewani* (young warriors), who are out to fight *ukombo wa meciria* (mental slavery). In this connection, the movement has attracted young men disillusioned with the current socio-economic and political situation. The prominence of the young generation in Mungiki is underscored by Mugo wa Kabiru's prophecy that a new generation of younger people with great wisdom would come into being. Consequently, the youth have challenged the leaders of the older generation who have governed Kenya for the past four decades. The young people have found in Mungiki an opportunity to acquire leadership roles that they were denied by the Kenyatta and Moi regimes.

The movement must therefore be seen as the effect of a much deeper structural malady in society. Looking at religious factors alone as the cause for the emergence of the movement narrows the parameters of the struggle by its ideological exclusivity. Moreover, religious conflicts are simply epiphenomena of a much deeper conflict (Sebidi 1986). In this case, economic dependency, economic exploitation and exclusion from politics should be points of concern in the study of the Mungiki movement. To some extent, material conditions of life are the root cause of the conflict between Mungiki and the public, and specifically the ruling class. The adherents of the movement consider themselves as the underprivileged and the disinherited of the earth. However, the class analysis approach errs not by acknowledging the determinative role of material conditions but by downplaying the determinative role of belief systems. A genuine synthesis of the interplay between ideology and economy is crucial. It is their concrete interrelationships, their dialectical relationships, that we should focus on.

Mungiki began as a quasi-religious organisation that was responding to a socio-economic and political structure that had debased members' humanity. The general objective of Mungiki, as already indicated, is to restore dignity to black people. Some of the beliefs, especially on the dignity of black people, are not dissimilar to the teachings of negritude and the Black Renaissance before it. The Mungiki have chosen the Agikuyu cultural tradition as the principal axis of African Renaissance. Wamue (2001) has observed that the educated Mungiki consult books on Agikuyu history as well as other writings by heroes such as Marcus Garvey and Martin Luther King. In this regard, she implicitly suggests that Mungiki has been influenced by the pan-Africanist ideas founded through the inspiration of Marcus Garvey. Garvey was instrumental in the development of the black political consciousness movement that emerged in the first quarter of the twentieth century and with subsequent movements such as Jamaica Rastafarianism. The *Rastafari* movement has become an important sub-culture both in Jamaica and in parts of Africa. Ras Tafari (Prince Tafari, later Emperor Haile Selassie) was the very symbol of liberation in the movement (Oosthuizen 1990). Apparently many Mungiki followers have been Rastafarians. Some brief remarks on the link between the two are given below.

The Mungiki movement first attracted Rastafarians in the major towns of Kenya because the objective(s) of Mungiki and Rastafarians are similar. Both movements aim to liberate blacks from mental slavery. Moreover, like Rastafarians, Mungiki emphasises sisterhood and brotherhood, a lifestyle based on black values, and self-evaluation and gravitation from institutions associated with colonialism and neo-colonialism. It has drawn membership from the Rastafarians in slums, many of whom are disadvantaged and seize opportunities to express their dissatisfaction and opposition to bourgeois liberal secularism. To some extent Rastafarian ideology has fuelled Mungiki's militancy. Nevertheless, Mungiki ideology has, in the long run, proved to be insufficient, as leading Mungiki members converted to Islam and Christianity.

The Role of Mungiki in Transition Politics

Scholars have studied the Mungiki movement from different perspectives. In her sociological study of the Mungiki movement, Wamue (2001) discusses its beliefs and practices as they relate to traditional religion and cultural practices of the Gikuyu people. She argues that

Mungiki is a fundamentalist movement with a religious, political and cultural agenda. Nevertheless, in the last few years Mungiki has not only become politicised but also entangled with urban vigilantism as the movement has fought with gangs for control of the city's *Matatu* (taxi-bus) routes. For their part, Turner and Brownhill (2001) view Mungiki as a representation of the downtrodden, poor, dispossessed and landless, and as a movement from 'below' that utilises its traditional resources to bring about change. They seem to glorify Mungiki as a rebirth of the Mau Mau spirit of resistance. However, many people have been suspicious of Mungiki due to its ethnocentrism and violence. Many Kenyans view the movement as retrogressive and subversive.

Anderson (2002) views Mungiki as one of the dreaded vigilante groups in Nairobi. He sketches its descent to political tribalism (Gikuyu interests) and how its activities have accentuated insecurity, violated human rights and disrupted public order. Anderson is, however, aware of its expression in the towns as a product of the decay so rampant in urban Kenya. Kagwanja (2003) moves a step beyond, tracing the movement's religious and ideological roots. He shows that the use of sectarian violence for political ends transformed the Mungiki's noble moral ethnicity into political tribalism. Kagwanja argues that the state under KANU leadership co-opted the movement and redirected its noble goals into political misuse. Kagwanja's argument is, however, an over-romanticisation of the Mungiki objectives. His idea of the state's hijack of Mungiki assumes that Mungiki actors have no agency in seeking political patronage, especially given the socio-economic circumstances that informed the rise of the movement. The transformation of Mungiki into a vigilante group serving political interests must be understood against the backdrop of state reform and its inability to provide basic security needs.

Mungiki partly reflects the kind of violent confrontations that accompanied the agitation for political pluralism. As the agitation for political reforms intensified in June 1990 culminating in the *Saba Saba* rally at the Kamukunji grounds on 7 July, so did the state's use of harassment, detention and violence increase. Meanwhile, the idle and unemployed youth saw violence as an opportunity for looting and engaging in other forms of criminal activities during the reform protests. Much of the violence was state sponsored or sanctioned or simply took advantage of the failure of the state to oversee public order. President Moi's response to calls to open up public space first consisted of increasing coercion and excessive use of the state apparatus to intimidate the citizenry. The police were called upon to break up democracy rallies, and on many occasions the police provoked riots and violence by their mishandling of peaceful pro-democracy demonstrators (see Chapter 8 by Gimode in this volume). The situation was worsened by the gradual development of ethnic tensions in the Rift Valley, Western Province and parts of the Nyanza Province. In early 1992 and until elections in December that year, armed ethnic gangs remained active in these parts of the country resulting in the ethnic clashes that led to death, displacement and terror among ethnic groups that were perceived to support the opposition.

The bloody clashes in the Rift Valley and parts of the Western and Nyanza Provinces in 1992 caused bitter political problems between the KANU government and the non-Kalenjin ethnic groups living in these regions. Over 1,500 people were killed and thousands were injured. There was large-scale displacement of the Kikuyu from Molo, Burnt Forest and other parts of Nakuru District and in the Enosoopukia area of Narok District. It is these internally displaced persons affected by the clashes in Njoro, Elburgon, Rongai, Eldoret and Narok in the period 1991–93 and in Njoro and Laikipia in 1998 who formed the core of Mungiki (Wamue 2001; Kagwanja 2003). In other words, the economic malaise affecting Kenya, by itself, does not explain the growth of Mungiki; the effects of ethnic clashes aggravated the situation in the areas named above and powered Mungiki.

If the ethnic clashes provide the context within which Mungiki grew, they also constitute the rationale for its transformation into a vigilante group. In response to government-initiated ethnic clashes, Mungiki began to mobilize its members against government violence. Like Mau Mau in the 1950s, Mungiki reportedly began administering oaths as a way of uniting members politically for the purpose of repulsing ethnic attacks. The oathing ceremonies forced the government to crack down on Mungiki followers. The Kikuyu procured weapons and organised small armed groups to protect themselves in anticipation of renewed violence in 1998. When violence broke out in the Rift Valley's Laikipia District in early 1997 for the second time, the then opposition politicians reportedly proclaimed that they were willing to contribute funds necessary to purchase weapons (*East African Standard*, 24 January 2000). In this regard, Mungiki organized themselves into a militia ostensibly to be able to defend their community against attack. Apparently because of Mungiki's activities in repulsing attacks, the 1998 ethnic clashes in Laikipia and Njoro were abated.

In the process, Mungiki members were arrested and denied bail on charges of taking illegal oaths (Amnesty International Kenya 1998).

In the urban areas, the vigilante identity of Mungiki grew because the state had abdicated from its role as a guarantor of security in Nairobi and its environs.[8] Mungiki took a tactical posture to occupy both rural and urban positions. But in urban areas, the movement appeared less as a protector against land clashes victims and more as an urban militia. The movement also shed its identity as a religious movement. Thus, in Nairobi as in many other towns, the movement did not just abandon its original objectives, it also became amenable to intrigue and manipulation both by its leaders seeking political favour and office and by politicians eager to constitute private armies for clandestine political activities. If politicians were eager for Mungiki's services, Mungiki was eager to reap benefits, especially financial ones, that accrued from this arrangement. In this way, and contrary to Kagwanja's argument, the transformation of Mungiki was akin to a transaction between a willing buyer and a willing seller.

Mungiki transformed in an environment that was proliferating with private armies and vigilante groups. The urban environment from the mid-1980s was characterised by criminal violence in the form of brutal attacks, armed bank robberies, carjacking, street muggings and housebreakings. This criminal violence reported in the daily mass media symbolised the problems and tensions of changes in the social, political and economic life of Kenya. Poverty-induced frustration, unemployment and increased school dropouts led many young people to engage in criminal activities (Nairobi Central Business Association 2001). The crisis of criminal violence and insecurity was also a crisis of governance. The result of this insecurity, as Gimode (2001: 298) observes, was an air of resignation on the part of citizens, given the apparent impotence of law enforcement authorities in the face of rising criminality. The role of the Kenyan police force in combating crime and fostering security was minimal (see Chapter 9 by Gimode in this volume) as some of the criminals were in league with renegade police officers who lent them uniforms and guns (*East African Standard*, 29 June 1991). Most Kenyans concluded that the government was unable to guarantee their security. Consequently, they instituted private initiatives to guarantee themselves a measure of security from criminals. This led to the proliferation of vigilante/urban militia groups.

Mungiki was one of the vigilante groups that re-emerged in Nairobi. Its activities encompassed crimes like robbery. In October 2002,

26 members of Mungiki were jailed for three months each for criminal activities in Nairobi city (*Daily Nation*, 5 October 2000). In another incident, eight members of Mungiki were arrested in Nairobi after an hour-long battle with the police on suspicion of violently robbing members of the public.[9] As Mungiki members unleashed violence on the public they did not spare the law enforcers. An estimated 700 members of Mungiki snatched a G3 rifle from the police in Kianja Village, Mathioya Division.[10] Mungiki involvement in criminal activities drew the wrath of the public. Consequently, Kenyans began to call upon the state to deal ruthlessly with the group. In October 2000, the then police commissioner, Philemon Abong'o outlawed Mungiki meetings. Police were directed to arrest and charge Mungiki members holding unlicensed meetings. In addition, the then minister of state in the Office of the President, Shariff Nassir, emphasised that the government's crackdown on the Mungiki followers would be intensified. This followed an incident in Kayole Estate, Nairobi, where Mungiki followers attacked and stripped naked six women wearing trousers.

One cannot overlook the broader political and economic context of Mungiki's transformation and politicisation. On the political front, the group transformed from one with peripheral interest in politics into a highly politically charged movement. This was not unique given the proliferation of similar vigilante groups that served politicians, especially in urban places. One indication of Mungiki's ideological shift from being apolitical to political was the involvement of politicians in the affairs of the group. For instance, the Akiwumi Commission linked Kihika Kimani, a former legislator from Molo, with organising Kikuyu youth in January 1998 to counter planned raids by Kalenjin warriors. Similarly, Embakasi legislator David Mwenje was charged along with 25 Mungiki followers with disrupting court proceedings in Machakos. Earlier on, Mwenje had been accused of inciting Nairobi City Council workers against the then minister for local government, Joseph Kamotho. When Mwenje was arraigned in court, his supporters whom the police claimed were Mungiki followers accompanied him. But he denied that his supporters were Mungiki members (*Daily Nation*, 5 October 2000).

Mungiki's political activities were facilitated by the insecure conditions in Nairobi and the general tendency of politicians recruiting ad hoc private armies of jobless youths as personal bodyguards. In the run-up to the 1992, 1997 and 2002 general elections, candidates used these groups to harass and rough up their opponents at political rallies. Such groups included the *Taliban*, the *Jeshi la Mzee* (Elder's Army), the *Baghdad Boys* and the *Kosovo Boys*. But the largest known vigilante group was Mungiki. As the group grew, it also diversified its realms of operation. From the year 2000, it took control of *Matatu* routes in Nairobi. To legitimise their actions, the Mungiki leadership argued that their aim was to restore order in this lucrative business. But in October 2000, Mungiki's attempt to take over the Dandora route in Nairobi's Eastlands provoked bloody clashes between its members and other interested groups such as *Kamjeshi*. Henceforth, Mungiki fought with other groups for the control of *Matatu* routes and continued to collect illegal levy from *Matatu* owners (see *Daily Nation*, 17 October 2001).

The existence of these tribal militias and vigilante groups tells a lot about the Kenyan state, politicians and governance. But equally interesting is the eclectic and shifting nature of Mungiki's ideological basis as its leadership toys with Islam and Christianity. On 2 September 2000, 13 of its leaders, among them Ndura Waruinge (renamed Ibrahim), converted to Islam. In the next few months many Mungiki followers converted to Islam. They argued that there were common grounds between them and their beliefs and Islamic tenets that made their conversion easy. The other reason for their conversion was to gain inclusion in a more universalised, non-communitarian faith and to shed off the 'tribal' stigma that the state was using to rationalise its harassment of Mungiki followers (Kagwanja 2003). Mungiki's followers admitted that they converted to Islam to avoid persecution by the state machinery.[11] However, the conversion of Mungiki followers to Islam was not without controversy. There was strong resistance from moderate Muslims as well as supporters of the ruling elite in KANU from the Coast, who accused the movement of using Islam as a 'hideout' (*Daily Nation*, 21 December 2000). Upon ascending to power, the Kibaki administration launched a half-hearted crackdown on Mungiki. On 12 January 2003, the *Sunday Nation* reported that the outlawed Mungiki movement had declared war on the Kibaki regime. Mungiki threatened to call a *Jihad* (Islamic Holy War) unless there was a let-up on the crackdown against their members. The threat was however denied by the chairman of the Supreme Council of Kenya Muslims (SUPKEM), Professor Abdulghfur el-Basaidy. He maintained that there was no collaboration between Mungiki and Muslims.

Mungiki's relationship with Christian institutions is hostile. It has maintained a strong anti-Christian stance arguing that Christianity has engendered mental slavery of Africans. Moreover, it encourages the traditional Kikuyu way of worship, facing Mount Kenya, oathing and female circumcision among other practices that are in deep contrast to the Christian faith. Mungiki have in the past even been accused of attacking Christians. In January 2000, its members attacked Christians attending an inter-denominational prayer meeting at Uhuru Park (*Daily Nation*, 24 April 2000). The criminal activities of Mungiki thus caused great concern among the mainstream churches. This was more so because the members of the movement were subscribing to Islamic laws and recruiting members from the established churches. As a result, the NCCK set up a committee to investigate Mungiki's activities. The NCCK leaders observed that Mungiki posed a great security threat both to the government and to Kenyans in general. The public outcry over the activities of Mungiki was followed by a government crackdown and the subsequent imprisonment of Mungiki leaders and some members. On 27 November 2001, Mungiki co-ordinator, Ndura Waruinge, was charged in a Machakos law court for promoting war-like activities (*East African Standard*, 27 November 2001). In January 2003, police raided the rural home of Waruinge, in Molo, and arrested his younger brother and four other members. Molo regional co-ordinator, Simon Karanja Wanyoike, was also arrested (*Daily Nation*, 17 January 2003). In the same month, 68 suspected Mungiki members were charged with offences linked to the outlawed organisation in various parts of the country (*Daily Nation*, 27 January 2003).

After many such incidents, Ndura Waruinge converted to Christianity towards the end of 2003. This was yet another of the many contradictions of Mungiki. Waruinge converted to Christianity by joining the Neno (word/gospel) Church under the leadership of James Maina Ng'ang'a in a well-televised ceremony. This was in spite of the fact that the Church had been at the forefront in calling upon the state to proscribe Mungiki. In addition, Mungiki was founded in rebellion against Christianity, which had undermined the African culture (*East African Standard*, 29 November 2003). From the brief history of Waruinge, it is difficult to gauge with certainty how long he will remain in the 'new faith'. It is argued that Waruinge is a besieged man who has sought temporary refuge in the Church after committing atrocities against innocent Kenyans. Overall, it is difficult to state what Mungiki represents, for it is not now grounded in African religion, Islam or Christianity. Could this be a temporary truce meant to hoodwink Kenyans as Mungiki prepares to change its tactics?

Mungiki's engagement with the Moi regime

From early 2000, Mungiki organisers and political leaders insinuated that government security services were infiltrating the sect and setting up pseudo-Mungikis to monitor its activities. The *East African* weekly newsmagazine reported incidents where Mungiki had attempted to hold prayer meetings and the police moved in almost before they had begun. This suggests that Mungiki had been infiltrated by security services (*The East African*, 15 November 2000). Waruinge alleged that some members of the armed forces from the regular police, Criminal Investigation Department and General Service Unit had joined Mungiki (*Daily Nation*, 25 August 2002).

Despite the alleged infiltration, in the run-up to the 2002 general elections, violent incidents involving Mungiki increased. On 3 March 2002, about 300 youths wielding machetes, axes and other crude weapons killed 23 people and injured 31 others. The majority of the dead and injured were from the Luo community. It was reported that Mungiki was avenging two of their members who had been killed by a largely Luo militia known as *Taliban* based in Kariobangi Estate.[12] As a result of this incident, ethnic tensions intensified and the government came under sharp criticism from the opposition parties for lax security in Nairobi. The police in Nairobi seemed to know the perpetrators and the sponsors of such political violence but they were reluctant to arrest them either because of bribery and inadequate evidence to link them to the offence or because of their connections with people in high places (Mwagiru et al. 2002). After the Kariobangi incident, the government banned Mungiki along with a number of other vigilante groups including the *Jeshi la Mzee*, the *Jeshi la Embakasi*, the *Baghdad Boys*, the *Sungu Sungu* and the *Kosovo Boys*. President Moi ordered the police to crack down on illegal organisations. He blamed the police and the provincial administration for failing to stop the killings at Kariobangi. Moi also blamed the Democratic Party (whose councillors were the majority in the Nairobi City Council) for failing to manage the affairs of the city.

However, a relationship that was emerging between KANU and Mungiki soon became public. Galaviri, in the *Daily Nation* of 7 March 2002, noted that vigilante groups had political masters who both appointed senior police officers and deployed the gangs for political ends. He accused the government of complicity in the Kariobangi massacre. Subsequently, Kenyans pointed out that Mungiki was being used to implement a political agenda quite inimical to the national interest. After the Kariobangi incident, Mungiki played a significant role in the politics of the city. In spite of being banned, it continued to be active and vocal.[13] As KANU intensified the struggle to secure power in Nairobi's constituencies where opposition was strong, further violence erupted. In this connection, Anderson (2002) observes that the KANU government did not need to manufacture an army to attack its opponents in Nairobi. Mungiki was already undermining the opposition very effectively by exposing the latter's inability to control the politics of the city or bring security to the lives of its population.

When KANU and the National Development Party (NDP) merged on 18 March 2002 and President Moi later decided on Uhuru Kenyatta as KANU's presidential candidate, the relationship between Mungiki and the ruling elite warmed up with Mungiki rallying its support around Uhuru. Indeed, some Kikuyu politicians like Stephen Ndichu of Juja and Kihika Kimani vowed to protect Uhuru, promising to use members of the outlawed Mungiki to take up arms and attack those opposed to Moi's choice of Uhuru. This prompted the *Daily Nation* to accuse the two legislators of war-mongering and criticised the government for applying double standards to the outlawed Mungiki.[14] In August 2002, several thousand Mungiki members, some armed with machetes and clubs, staged a demonstration in Nairobi in support of Uhuru's candidacy in the presence of the police. This was a violation of the Public Order Act which the police often enthusiastically cited to ban opposition rallies. There was a public outcry and Uhuru had to disassociate himself from Mungiki. Some alleged that the Mungiki demonstration had been sponsored by some opposition members to discredit Uhuru.[15]

In November 2002, Uhuru denied any relationship with Mungiki. He reminded Kenyans of the incident in August 2000 when Mungiki had burnt his effigy outside his father's mausoleum along Parliament Road in Nairobi (*East African Standard*, 11 November 2002). The burning of the effigy was one way by which Mungiki followers expressed their anger with Mzee Jomo Kenyatta's betrayal of Mau Mau leaders. This notwithstanding, Mungiki's national chairman Maina Njenga and its co-ordinator Ndura Waruinge unsuccessfully contested the Laikipia West and Molo parliamentary seats, respectively, on KANU tickets. It appeared as though the KANU government was using Mungiki leaders to mobilise members for its own political ends. Although Anderson (2002) argues that Mungiki's activities in Nairobi had a materialist, ethnic and political dimension, it is quite evident that the KANU government had allowed Mungiki to wreak havoc in Nairobi to drive home the point that the opposition had failed in governing the city.

The fortunes for Mungiki changed dramatically with the changes on the political scene after the 27 December 2002 elections. The new Kibaki regime declared a crackdown on Mungiki leaders (*Daily Nation*, 8 January 2003). On 13 January 2003 the *East African* weekly newsmagazine reported an incident where Mungiki followers were reported to have killed 23 people in Nakuru. Former Nakuru town legislator David Manyara was arrested in connection with this incident. Subukia legislator Koigi wa Wamwere described the group as a 'slave force out to make money for its leaders'. He alleged that Mungiki was an armed wing of KANU (*The East African*, 13–19 January 2003). At the height of the internal struggle between the National Alliance Party of Kenya (NAK) and the Liberal Democratic Party (LDP), Koigi wa Wamwere and his Tigania counterpart Peter Munya (Safina) and former Limuru legislator George Nyanja came under heavy criticism for holding a rally in Kiambu District in which Mungiki members participated. This event was interpreted as meant to cause fear and anxiety among the LDP leadership who were mounting a rebellion from within the ruling National Alliance Rainbow Coalition (NARC) over the failure of NAK to honour the MoU that required power sharing as agreed upon prior to the 2002 general election. Clearly, then, political elites in KANU and NARC have used Mungiki either to settle scores or consolidate their power base.

Conclusion

Mungiki emerged in the early 1990s as a religious movement at a moment of transition from a single-party state to a multiparty state. It had the Agikuyu traditional religion and culture as its basis. It advocated a politics of cultural emancipation and clearly showed that spiritual liberation requires political liberation. In this connection, it was attempting to resacralise the Agikuyu society by redefining the sacred in the secular domain by way of using religion to legitimise political ideals. Accordingly, Mungiki activities can be understood within the context of transitional politics in Kenya just as earlier movements have adopted similar strategies in previous transition times. For instance, the transition from colonialism to independence was characterised by political violence occasioned by the growth of anti-colonial revolts. Leading in the fight against white rule were the cult of Mumbo, Dini ya Msambwa and the Karing'a religio-political movement. Mungiki's philosophy has been traced to these movements. The common aspect among all these movements is that they have mobilised followers behind African traditional values to challenge the churches as well as the injustices of both colonial and post-colonial states. Mau Mau, the militant wing of the Karing'a movement, drew its core support from the squatters oppressed by the colonial agrarian system. Similarly, Mungiki draws its support from thousands of people displaced by the infamous ethnic clashes in the Rift Valley.

But somewhere along the line, Mungiki shed its initial objective of resacralising Agikuyu society and became an urban vigilante group. In its new form, Mungiki has been engaged in acts of violence, crime and political opportunism, showing a willingness to sell its services to the highest bidder. Mungiki began to engage in acts of lawlessness, especially in its endeavour to control *Matatu* routes in the country. Rivalry with other groups like Kamjeshi also eventually led to fierce battles in Eastlands causing deaths and looting of property (*Daily Nation*, 20 November 2002). In all of this, an element of government complicity is detected, as the state used the movement to hold public meetings in Thika and Nairobi. Thus, Mungiki has transformed drastically into a politically inclined militia group, constantly engaged in violent activities, with its leaders exhibiting malleability as seen in their ideological shifts to Islam and Christianity without denouncing their earlier beliefs. This makes it quite difficult to identify the ideological basis of Mungiki. It can only be described as a highly eclectic and amorphous group that is easily mobilised by politicians to execute their missions. Consequently, in the politics of transition, Mungiki under the control of the ruling elite has been responsible for human rights violations and widespread insecurity in Nairobi and Central Kenya.

Notes

1. On the various Gusii clans and their relationship to British rule, see W.R. Ochieng, *A Precolonial History of the Gusii of Western Kenya C.A.D. 1500–1914*, Nairobi: East African Literature Bureau, 1974.
2. For details on status reversal, see Wipper (1977: 66–78).
3. The Agikuyu kinship system was based on three units – the nuclear family, the lineage and the clan.
4. For details on the activities and power of GEMA politicians and Vice-President Moi, see Karimi and Ochieng (1980).
5. It is worth pointing out that the 'Tent of the Living God' is a misnomer. According to its members 'tent' here is a creation of the Kenyan media who literally translated *He na ma* (there is truth) directly into English. In spoken Kikuyu, these three syllables are pronounced 'heema' which is easily confused with 'hema' which means tent. Hence, 'Tent of the Living God'.
6. Personal interview with Ibrahim Wanyoike, 16 November 2003.
7. Personal interview with Kamanda Muriuki, 20 November 2003.
8. For details on crime in Nairobi, see Nairobi Central Business Association (2001); Gimode (2001).
9. Pan African News Agency, 'Kenya's Outlawed Sect Jailed after Battling Police', 13 November 2000.
10. M. Wachira and M. Mwati, 'Mungiki Attack Officer Dies', *Daily Nation*, 26 September 2000.
11. Personal interview with Ibrahim Kagwa, 22 November 2003.
12. Reuters, 6 March 2002, 'Kenya Police Arrest Sect Leader after Killings'.
13. UN Integrated Regional Information Network, 'Outrage over Mungiki Threats', 21 August 2002.
14. David Mageria, 'Kenyan Sect Banned by State but Still Defiant', Reuters, 19 April 2002.
15. Personal interview with Ndirangu Kamoche, 17 November 2003.

References

Akivaga, S.K. (2002) 'Towards a National Movement for Democratic Change', in Kioko Wanza et al. (eds), *Building an Open Society: The Politics of Transition in Kenya*, Nairobi: Claripress.

Amnesty International Kenya (1998), *Amnesty International Report 1998: Kenya*, Nairobi: Amnesty International.

Anderson, J. (1970) *The Struggle for the School: The Interaction of Missionary Colonial Government and Nationalist Enterprise in the Development of Formal Education in Kenya*, Nairobi: Longman.

Anderson, D. (2002) 'Vigilantes, Violence and Politics of Public Order in Kenya', *African Affairs*, vol. 101, no. 405.

———— (2005) *Histories of the Hanged: The Dirty War in Kenya and the End of Empire*, New York, NY: W.W. Norton.

Anttonen, V. (2000) 'Sacred', in W. Braun and T.R. McCutcheon (eds), *Guide to the Study of Religion*, New York, NY: Cassell Wellington House.

Anyang' Nyong'o, P. (1989) 'State and Society in Kenya: The Disintegration of the Nationalist Coalitions and the Rise of Presidential Authoritarianism 1963–78', *African Affairs*, vol. 88, no. 351.

Beckman, B. (1991) 'Empowerment or Repression?: The World Bank and the Politics of Adjustment', in *Africa Development*, vol. XVI, no. 1.

Buijtenhuijs, R. (1983) 'Dini ya Msambwa: Rural Rebellion or Counter Society?', *Canadian Journal African Affairs*, vol. 17, no. 2.

Cunningham, L.S., et al. (1991) *The Sacred Quest: An Invitation to the Study of Religion*, New York, NY: Macmillan Publishing Company.

De Gruchy, J.W. (1995) *Christianity and Democracy*, Cambridge, UK: Cambridge University Press.

Douglas, M. (1966) *Purity and Danger: An Analysis of Concepts of Pollution and Taboo*, London: Routledge and Kegan Paul.

Durkheim, E. (1915) *The Elementary Forms of Religious Life*, Translated by J.W. Swain, Glencoe, IL: The Free Press.

Eliade, M. (1957) *The Sacred and the Profane: The Nature of Religion*, Translated by Willard R. Trask New York, NY: World Inc.

Gibbon, P. (ed.) (1995) *Markets, Civil Society and Democracy in Kenya*, Uppsala: Nordiska Afrikainstitutet.

Gimode, E. (2001) 'Anatomy of Violent Crime and Insecurity in Kenya: The case study of Nairobi, 1985–1999', *Africa Development* vol. XXVI, nos. 1–2.

Githiga, G. (2002) *The Church as the Bulwark against Authoritarianism: Development of Church-State Relations in Kenya, with Particular Reference to the Years after Political Independence 1963–1992*, Oxford: Regnum Books.

Johnstone, R.L. (1997) *Religion in Society: A Sociology of Religion*, London: Prentice Hall Inc.

Jules-Rosette, B. (1991) 'Tradition and Continuity in African religions: The Case Study of New Religious Movements', in J.K. Olupona (ed.), *African Traditional Religions in Contemporary Society*, New York, NY: Paragon House.

Kagwanja, P. (1997) 'Politics of Marionettes: Extra-Legal Violence and the 1997 Elections in Kenya', in M. Ruttem et al. (eds), *Out for the Count: The 1997 General Elections and Prospects for Democracy in Kenya*, Kampala: Fountain Publishers.

———— (2003) 'Facing Mt. Kenya or Facing Mecca? The Mungiki Ethnic Violence and Politics of Moi Succession 1987–2002', *African Affairs*, vol. 102, no. 406.

Kangethe, K.wa. (1981) 'The Role of the Agikuyu Religion and Culture in the Development of the Karing'a Religio-political Movement, 1900–1950 with Particular Reference to the Agikuyu Concept of God and the Rite of Initiation', Unpublished PhD Thesis, Kenyatta University.

Kanogo, T. (1987) *Squatters and the Roots of Mau Mau*, Nairobi: Heinemann.

——— (2005) *African Womanhood in Colonial Kenya, 1900–50*, Oxford: James Currey.

Kanyinga, K. (1995) 'The Changing Development Space in Kenya: Socio-Political Change and Voluntary Development Activities', in P. Gibbon (ed.), *Markets, Civil Society and Democracy in Kenya*, Uppsala: Nordiska Afrikainstitute.

Karimi, J., and P. Ochieng (1980) *The Kenyatta Succession*, Nairobi: Trans Africa Publishers.

Kenyatta, J. (1938) *Facing Mt. Kenya: The Traditional Life of the Gikuyu*, London: Martin Secker and Warburg Ltd.

Kibwana, K., et al. (eds) (1996) *The Anatomy of Corruption in Kenya*, Nairobi: Claripress.

Makila, F.E. (1987) *An Outline History of the Babukusu of Western Kenya*, Nairobi: Kenya Literature Bureau.

Maloba, W.O. (1993) *Mau Mau and Kenya: An Analysis of a Peasant Revolt*, Bloomington, IN: Indiana University Press.

Mande, W.M. (1999) 'The Church and Democratic Liberties in Uganda', in L. Magesa and Z. Nthamburi (eds), *Democracy and Reconciliation: A Challenge for African Christianity*, Nairobi: Acton Publishers.

Mkandawire, T. (1992) 'Democratisation Process in Africa: Prospects and Problems', Paper presented at the Seventh General Assembly of CODESRIA on Democratisation Process in Africa: Problems and Perspectives, Dakar, 10–14 February.

Muga, E. (1975) *African Response to Western Christian Religion: A Socio-logical Analysis of African Separatist Religious and Political Movements in East Africa*, Nairobi: East African Literature Bureau.

Mwagiru, M., et al. (2002) *Facts About Majeshi ya Wazee*, Nairobi: Friedrich Ebert Stiftung (FES).

Nairobi Central Business Association (2001) 'Crime Survey Report', June.

Ngunyi, M. (1995) 'Religious Institutions and Political Liberalisation in Kenya', in P. Gibbon (ed.), *Markets, Civil Society and Democracy in Kenya*, Uppsala: Nordiska Afrikainstitute.

——— (1996) 'Resuscitating the Majimbo Debate: The Politics of Deconstructing the Unitary State of Kenya', in A.O. Olukoshi and L. Laakso (eds), *Challenges to the Nation-State in Africa*, Uppsala: Nordiska Afrikainstitute.

O'Brien, D.B. (1975) *Saints and Politicians: Essays in the Organization of a Senegalese Peasant Society*, Cambridge, UK: Cambridge University Press.

Oosthuizen, G. (1990) *Rastafarian*, Zululand: University of Zululand.

Otto, R. (1923) *The Idea of the Holy: An Inquiry into the Non-rational Factor in the Idea of the Divine and its Relation to the Rational*, Translated by John W. Harvey, London: Oxford University Press.

Reicher, S., and N. Hopkins (2001) *Self and Nation Categorization, Contestation, and Mobilization*, London: Sage Publications.

Rosberg, C., and R. Nottingham (1966) *The Myth of Mau Mau Nationalism in Kenya*, Nairobi: East African Publishing House.

Sebidi, L. (1986) 'The Dynamics of the Black Struggle and its Implications for Black Theology', in I. Mosala and B. Tihagale (eds), *Black Theology from South Africa*, New York, NY: Orbis Books.

Shimanyula, J.B. (1978) *Elijah Masinde and the Dini ya Msambwa*, Nairobi: Trans Africa.

Shiner, L. (1966) 'The Concept of Secularization in Empirical Research', *Journal for Scientific Study of Religion*, vol. 6: 207–20.

Shorter, A., and E. Onyancha (1997) *Secularism in Africa. A Case Study: Nairobi City*, Nairobi: Pauline Publications.

Smith, D.E. (1971) *Religion, Politics and Social Change in the Third World: A Source Book*, London: Macmillan Publishers.

Steiner, F. (1956) *Taboo*, London: Cohen and West.

Tignor, R.L. (1976) *The Colonial Transformation of Kenya*, Princeton, NJ: Princeton University Press.

Throup, D., and C. Hornsby (1998) *Multiparty Politics in Kenya*, Nairobi: East African Educational Publishers.

Turner, T.E., and L.S. Brownhill (2001) 'African Jubilee: Mau Mau Resurgence and the Fight for Fertility in Kenya, 1986–2002', *Canadian Journal of Development Studies*, vol. 22 (Special issue).

Wach J. (1944) *Sociology of Religion*, Chicago, IL: University of Chicago Press.

Wamba-dia-Wamba, E. (1999) 'Bundi Dia Kongo: A Kongolese Fundamentalist Religious Movement', in T. Spear and I. Kimambo (eds), *East African Expressions of Christianity*, Nairobi: East African Educational Publishers.

Wamue, G. (2001) 'Revisiting our Indigenous Shrines Through Mungiki', *African Affairs* vol. 100, no. 400.

Wanjala, S. (2002) 'Elections and the Political Transition in Kenya', in Kioko Wanza et al. (eds), *Building on Open Society: The Politics of Transition in Kenya*, Nairobi: Claripress.

Wellbourn, F.B. and B. Ogot (1966) *A Place to Feel at Home: A Study of Two Independent Churches in Western Kenya*, Nairobi: Oxford University Press.

Wilson, B. (1982) *Religion in Sociological Perspective*, London: Oxford University Press.

——— (1992) 'Cults of Violence and Counter Violence in Mozambique', *Journal of South African Studies*, vol. 18, no. 3.

Wipper, A. (1977) *Rural Rebels: A Study of Two Protest Movements in Kenya*, Nairobi: Oxford University Press.

4

The Contemporary Opposition in Kenya:
Between Internal Traits and State Manipulation

Adams G.R. Oloo

Introduction

Since the early 1990s, a worldwide process of transformation and change in political systems has been visible. The collapse of the socialist regimes not only brought about fundamental and sweeping changes in the affected countries of central, east and southeast Europe but also affected Latin American and African countries. Likewise, it also brought existing international power hierarchies to an end. These dramatic developments signified the end of the cold war and undermined a crucial basis on which many regimes in Africa rested, namely almost unconditional propping up of unrepresentative and unaccountable African governments by cold war protagonists as part of their strategy for maximising global advantages.

The 1990s witnessed a series of developments in Africa that culminated in the return to liberalised forms of politics. Many developments largely centred on dismantling constitutional or de facto one-party regimes, terminating a number of military-led or military-dominated governments and embracing a multiparty framework. The associated end of the cold war and subsequent spread of multiparty politics created an international climate that was far more conducive to and tolerant of internal political reforms in Africa than the previous cold war period. When domestic pressures for change began to build up in various African countries, pressures that took the form of massive and sustained public protests, the latter dovetailed with an emerging post-cold war mood that accommodated internal political dissent and change. The collapse of socialist regimes led to victory in the ideological rivalry between state capitalism as represented by the former socialist countries on the one hand, and market capitalism as represented by Western liberal democracies on the other hand. To this end, it is the ideas, structures, concepts and instruments of liberal democracy and market economics that triumphed as championed by the US. Thus we can argue that liberal democracy as a form of government was given a boost after 1989.

Structurally and institutionally, political parties are the basis of political democracy. Indeed, in a liberal democracy, the existence of political parties is indispensable. This is premised on the fact that the election of representatives of the people is best facilitated by the existence of political parties, which makes elections meaningful to the electorate as they offer two or more alternative programmes from which to choose. Hence, the post-1989 period received a boost with the reintroduction of multiparty politics and opening up of political space that came with the triumph of liberal democracy. This chapter broadly assesses Kenya's experience with multiparty politics and opposition political dynamics in particular. It seeks to examine the extent to which the restoration of multipartyism in Kenya has enhanced the democratisation process. The opposition has generally had an uninspiring experience that has been characterised by elitism, factionalism, ethnocentrism and systemic manipulation by incumbents. The focus of this chapter is on the experience of opposition politics in Kenya from 1992 to 2004. Consequently, it analyses the internal dynamics of opposition parties in Kenya and the subsequent impacts on their broad goal of enhancing democracy.

Political Parties: A Conceptual Framework

The principle of representation in a democracy hinges on the existence of parties. The representation of the people, who are the source of power, can only be effected by the election of representatives. For this, political parties are inescapably necessary. The term 'political party' can be used to describe organisations whose aim is to exert a permanent influence on the formation of public opinion and hence require permanent organisational structures and programmes. The main feature of political parties is their participation in elections to obtain power and influence. It is for this reason that individuals within parties must occupy positions of power in order to exert influence (Dowse and Hughes 1972; Thesing and Hofmeister 1995: 13). Historically, in liberal democracies, parties have played a pivotal role in founding and consolidating democratic systems of governance. Parties aggregate diverse demands into coherent political programmes and translate these programmes into effective action once they have legitimate control of political office. To be effective, political parties need parliamentary activity to fulfil their functions, irrespective of whether parties are in the government or the opposition.

Our focus in this chapter is on opposition parties. Lipset (1967: 40) defines democracy as a system of institutionalised opposition in which people choose among alternative contenders for public office. Dahl is even clearer: '... one is inclined to regard the existence of an opposition party as very nearly the most distinctive characteristic of democracy itself, and we may take the absence of an opposition party as evidence, if not always conclusive proof, for the absence of democracy' (Dahl 1966: xi). Genuine political opposition is a necessary attribute of democracy, tolerance and trust in the ability of citizens to resolve differences by peaceful means. As a political concept, opposition refers to a conscious effort to keep those with state power from exercising it in an arbitrary way. At its broadest, it is coextensive with political conflict and dissent. At its narrowest, it is synonymous with party opposition in a legislature. In autocratic states, open, organised opposition is discouraged, if not repressed. In constitutional orders, where the government functions according to laws, opposition is accepted as a normal condition of public life and tolerated as long as it stays within legally prescribed limits. In an ideal democracy, opposition is encouraged because it makes governments defend their decisions, assures ventilation of opinions and fosters debate. An opposition party can assume the reins of government; a citizens' movement opposed to policy can see its views become law; and this happens within a legal framework that assures future oppositions that they too can win.

The focus on elections and legislatures is equally understandable. In liberal democracies, where parties dominate, only they can contest elections effectively; so without them there is no legal, constitutional way for citizens to remove an administration that no longer enjoys their support. Legislative oppositions are also crucial to democracy because, at a minimum, they formulate critiques of government policy that enable citizens to assess an administration's performance.

Three theories explain the emergence of political parties in the West. The first is a set of institutional theories focusing on the interrelationship between early parliaments and the emergence of parties. Second are the historical situation theories that focus on the historical crises or tasks which systems encountered at the moment when parties developed; and third are developmental theories that relate parties to the broader process of modernisation (La Palambora and Weiner 1969: 7). Even though all three theories have been used by scholars to explain the origin of parties globally, much of the literature traces the rise of parties to the evolution of parliament and the gradual extension of the suffrage. This rise of parties evolved through the stages of aristocratic cliques, small groups of notables and plebiscitary democracy.

In Africa, the colonial experience that introduced the Western concept of parliament envisioned political parties becoming major actors in African political systems. Due to the colonialists' newfound commitment to leave behind a semblance of democratic political institutions, the departing powers decided to export their version of liberal democracy that required the existence of several parties and an institutionalised opposition. Although the formation of parties was fast in some countries, in others it lagged behind. However, for most countries, ethnic groups were the only widespread institutional frameworks within which the majority of Africans were organised. Arising from this, most parties that would govern as well as form the opposition were formed along ethnic lines. The consequence was that conflict along ethnic lines became prevalent and most leaders, in an attempt to quell the chaos bedevilling their countries, became dictatorial and resorted to one-party states while others succumbed to military rule until the late 1980s when the move for the second liberation of the continent took root.

Although political parties and civil society groups work hand in hand, the major difference between them is that a political party's expressed and explicit objective is to control state power, as opposed to civil society groups that do not have that as a goal. It is also important to note that political parties and civil society groups have a symbiotic relationship. Civil society groups are not alternatives to political parties but rather they supplement their activities in opening up the democratic space (see Chapter 2 by Nasong'o in this volume). Although overlapping functions do exist between the two, political parties have the ultimate goal of attaining power and thus have more comprehensive programmes that cover a wide range of social, political, economic and cultural issues. Civil society groups, on the other hand, usually target certain segments of the society and address specific issues (Ouyang 2000: 6).

In Kenya, beginning in 1990, many political organisations were created to respond to the excesses of the one-party state. However, this occurred in the absence of an enabling environment conducive to the strengthening and institutionalisation of new organisations. For the most part, these organisations remained small, underfunded and often their founders also doubled up as their chief financiers and controlled them in an authoritarian way. The bottom line is that the democratisation process in Kenya and in Africa generally was chaperoned at a time when there was neither a democratic culture nor political actors of democratic persuasion. The Kenyan polity that had been accustomed to the one-party political culture found it difficult to adjust to the requirements of a multiparty political dispensation. The culture of authoritarianism reigned and still persists. This has partly contributed to Kenya's slow democratisation process.

The return to multiparty politics in Kenya was influenced by several factors. These included, first, recalcitrant incumbents who only reluctantly conceded to a multiparty framework but went ahead to obstruct, weaken, harass and divide the opposition. Second, a weak financial base limited opposition political parties' organisational capacity. This stood in contrast to the ruling party's unbridled access to state resources. Third, internal weakness as well as lack of internal democracy plagued the new parties. Fourth, the ruling party remained dominant. With the emergence of competitive politics and the establishment of many political parties, however, there is now competition for political power, yet the much-anticipated change has barely come. Even though opposition parties emerged since the early 1990s, they have miserably failed to disengage from the anti-democratic practices associated with the one-party system. One possible explanation is that most of their leaders were once part of the same dictatorial system for many decades.

One of the greatest threats to democracy in Africa has been the intense politicisation of social life, primarily because the state has traditionally dominated the distribution of national resources and every group has been seeking desperately to obtain access to or control of the national cake (Diamond 1999). Virtually all major groups, both political and civil, have been oriented to what they could get from the political system rather than to making it work fairly. This has coincided with ethnic cleavages. Put differently, the founders of political parties, which have ethnic bases, see their parties as instruments for group struggle at the national level, for access to scarce resources and for the struggle for control of the state itself (Oyugi 2003; Berman et al. 2004).

It is the ethnic combined with the charismatic character of the founders of political parties that has contributed to the mounting polarisation in the Kenyan body politic, even in a situation where a grand coalition has won power, as is the case today. The infighting within the ruling coalition – National Alliance Rainbow Coalition (NARC) – is testimony to this. Political parties remain very much the preserves of individual politicians who hold sway in their parties and who stand above the party's institutional structures. In situations where intra-party competition is intense and a contender for party control loses, party break-ups have been common. Apart from periodic electoral manifestos (many of which are uncannily similar), parties do not have any programmatic distinctions and have only one driving intention: to 'win the presidency'. The presumption is clearly that a particular party and leader hold the key to solving the country's problems. This is barely a step removed from the pretensions of authoritarian personal rule. Given the breakdown of inter-party and intra-party communication, relations with the incumbent party typically degenerate into perpetual prisoner's dilemma games in which members of the opposition make entreaties to the ruling parties to access patronage, while desperately trying to retain the respect of the masses (Ndegwa 2001: 16). The result is that the dominant mode of elite–mass relations has remained a pernicious patrimonialism and personal rule that has transcended the demise of authoritarian regimes. In essence, the nature of the political calculus has remained the same: the pursuit of personal benefit at the altar of the state. This is evident at several levels: institutional patterns within parties, discourses of electoral competition especially with regard to the presidency and volatility of party commitments, which has seen many opposition party members cross party lines to the ruling party for the most contradictory of reasons (see Bratton and Walle 1998; Throup and Hornsby 1998).

Kenya restored political pluralism in 1991 having been a de facto one-party state from 1969 to 1982 and a de jure one-party state from 1982 to 1991 (IED 1998). The history of opposition in Kenya since 1992 has been one of division, infighting and a consistent inability to co-operate to achieve common goals. Despite efforts by various individuals and pressure groups to facilitate a united opposition for the 1992 and 1997 elections – and in particular to promote the idea of a single opposition presidential candidate – no lasting alliance could be formed. It is important to note that regardless of how and by whom parties are formed, post-1991 political parties in Kenya tend to experience problems that explain their weaknesses. These include the hostile nature of the political environment; a lack of or weakness in parties' visions, missions and ideological bases; weak institutional and policy bases; limited political space within virtually all parties which are dominated by their individual founders; state intelligence destabilisation; and the availability of alternative ready-made political parties to which factions can move to (Wanjohi 2003: 249).

Opposition Politics Before 1992

Kenya's first opposition party after attaining independence, Kenya African Democratic Union (KADU), had a very short lifespan. KADU was formed from the numerically smaller ethnic groups to counter the Kenya African National Union (KANU), which comprised the numerically larger ethnic groups. KADU was, however, heavily defeated by KANU in the 1963 elections, which ushered in independence in Kenya. Through political manipulation and arm-twisting machinations by KANU in the process of consolidating its power position, KADU was forced to dissolve itself in November 1964 (see Mutoro et al. 1999; Nasong'o 2001). In essence, KADU did not play a meaningful role as an opposition in terms of its performance for the brief period of its existence. The reason its leaders gave for its dissolution was less convincing – the need to foster unity in the young nation. However, the leaders' selfish reasons for the dissolution cannot be discounted as was exemplified by the ministerial posts they were rewarded with by the KANU government.

One year after the integration of KADU into KANU, a rift between the left and the right erupted into an open ideological conflict and led to a formal split that gave birth to the Kenya People's Union (KPU). The rift was mainly the result of an internal struggle within KANU that pitted conservatives led by Jomo Kenyatta, Tom Mboya and Charles Njonjo against progressives led by Oginga Odinga and Bildad Kaggia. The formation of KPU heralded the next phase of opposition politics that took place between 1966 and 1969 with KPU as the official opposition party. The KANU government's reaction to the formation of a new opposition party was to put in place mechanisms to contain KPU. The first move was the enactment of a constitutional amendment that forced sitting MPs defecting from KANU to seek a fresh mandate from the electorate under the banner of their new party.

In the ensuing 'little general election' of 1966, there was systematic state-sponsored intimidation and massive electoral manipulation which ensured that KPU ended up with only 7 seats in parliament out of the 29 that were contested. Although the country experienced another three years of multiparty politics, there was continuous harassment of the opposition, its membership, especially in its Nyanza stronghold (see Gertzel 1974; Ochieng 1995; Ajulu 2002). KPU introduced an ideological component to the otherwise ethnically based politics of the KANU regime that was content to maintain the colonial state it had succeeded. The KPU championed a socialist agenda that sought deconstruction of the colonial state, nationalisation of the economy and fundamental agrarian reform (see Ajulu 2002; Nasong'o 2002). Nevertheless, KPU had minimal impact in parliament due to the insufficient number of seats they had in the house.

The assassination of Tom Mboya in June 1969 further worsened the relationship between the government and KPU, which was Luo-dominated. The death of Mboya, a Luo, was blamed mainly on Kenyatta's ethnic group, the Kikuyu, who, it was claimed, wanted to stop the young and ambitious Mboya from ascending to power within KANU. His death and the clash between Odinga and Kenyatta in Kisumu, barely a few months apart, sealed the fate of KPU as an opposition party. Kenyatta had gone to Kisumu, Odinga's backyard, to officially open the new Nyanza General Hospital, whose construction was funded by the Soviet Union, when chaos broke out. Odinga had led his supporters in rebuking Kenyatta. The violence that ensued led to several deaths after the presidential security reacted overzealously to the crowd's protests. KPU was subsequently banned and its leaders detained, including Odinga, who was placed under house arrest (see Gertzel 1974; Mutoro et al. 1999).

After KPU was banned, Kenya remained a de facto one-party state until 1982 when, through a constitutional amendment, the country became a de jure one-party state. The legislation of the one-party state was in reaction to an attempt by Oginga Odinga and George Anyona to form an opposition party that was to be named the Kenya African Socialist Union. The government subsequently began cracking down on all critics in a bid to stem any challenge to KANU. Among the groups that took on championing the cause of opposition politics were both university staff and students (see Chapter 2 by Nasong'o and Chapter 7 by Amutabi in this volume). Unions representing the two elite groups were all proscribed and their leaders incarcerated as others were forced into exile. In order to circumvent any opposition from trade unions, the KANU government co-opted the umbrella trade union of Kenyan workers, the Central Organisation of Trade Unions (COTU) and later also co-opted the national women's organisation Maendeleo ya Wanawake Organisation (Aubrey 1997). The void in opposition politics that was created was filled by the church and professional bodies, especially the Law Society of Kenya (LSK), both of which the Moi regime infiltrated but with little success. By 1988, the ruling party, KANU, was so arrogant with power that it massively rigged elections in which winners were declared losers and vice versa (see Ajulu 2002; Nasong'o 2002). This eventuality helped crystallise opposition and thus sowed the seeds for a return to multiparty politics.

The Return to Competitive Party Politics

By the late 1980s, domestic discontent was quite high and coincided with the sour relationship between Kenya and its financial donors (see Chapter 9 by Murunga in this volume), culminating in the *Saba Saba* riots of 1990 that led to the arrest and detention of Kenneth Matiba, Charles Rubia, Raila Odinga and several lawyers who were in the forefront of the struggle for the return to multipartyism. Heavy-handed actions by the Moi regime incensed the donor community, who started pressing the government to undertake reforms if it expected continued international support (Chege 1995). The depth of disillusionment with the Moi regime was so great that it encouraged a variety of social forces rooting for reform to temporarily set aside their particular differences – class, ethnic, regional and religious – and unite under the umbrella of one organisation to fight collectively against Moi's authoritarian state. This opposition organisation rapidly crystallised into the Forum for the Restoration of Democracy (FORD), a popular movement which brought together radical as well as moderate social forces in a common effort to get Moi and KANU out of power. Moi and KANU had become synonymous with authoritarianism, and their removal had become necessary if a democratic nation was to become a reality (Kanyinga 1998: 57). These efforts finally led to the repeal, in 1991, of Section 2(A) of the Kenyan constitution that had made Kenya a one-party state.

The return to multiparty politics had an immediate downside. Suppressed differences – class, ethnic, regional and religious – that had remained latent as the opposition fought its common enemy resurfaced. Divisions emerged within FORD that drastically fragmented the opposition. Two factions immediately emerged from the original FORD. These were FORD-Kenya (FORD-K), which revolved around Oginga Odinga and Masinde Muliro, and FORD-Asili (FORD-A), which revolved around Kenneth Matiba and Martin Shikuku. Several other opposition parties were also formed around the same time mainly by politicians who were decamping from KANU. The most formidable of these was the Democratic Party (DP) of Kenya led by former vice-president (and now current president) Mwai Kibaki. There were also other parties that failed to secure registration, the most notable being the Islamic Party of Kenya, which was denied registration on the grounds that it was espousing religious fanaticism in Kenya's secular state. Political mobilisation by nearly all the new parties was along ethnic lines.

Parties that emerged after the repeal of Section 2(A) in 1991 were formed under conditions that were quite different from those that had led to the formation of parties in the countdown to independence. Whereas nationalism was the driving force behind the formation of KANU, KADU and other nationalist parties between 1957 and 1962, the formation of post-Section 2(A) political parties was driven by different social and political forces, all united in the resolve to remove KANU from power (Wanjohi 2003). The vision of these parties, then and now, remains devoid of any cogent ideology, thus not significantly different from KANU, which they loathed. The quality of opposition parties in Kenya cannot therefore be judged on ideological or policy differences but rather from the social cleavages they draw their support from, their organisation and institutional structures as well as leadership credentials within their ranks. The ethnic tilt in these parties was evident in both the 1992 and 1997 elections in which party support followed distinct ethno-regional patterns. Candidates and parties mostly won in their home districts, basically on ethnic affiliation. Due to KANU's long stay in power and its self-prophesied claim to be the protector of minority ethnic groups, the ruling party was the only party that had votes evenly spread in most of the regions outside its Kalenjin stronghold. Yet it still found itself locked out of Kikuyuland and Luoland, the first and third largest communities in Kenya.

After the 1992 elections, new political developments began to emerge. The first was the trend of defections, which was mainly from the opposition to the ruling party. At the same time, the state began to tie development assistance to communities and districts that had voted for KANU. In effect, state patronage was now blatantly ethnically based with expenditure outlay in different parts of the country tied ever more closely to the support that different ethnic groups and regions gave to the ruling party. This domestic 'developmental conditionality' effectively meant that opposition areas could not expect government activities and projects unless their leaders switched allegiance and declared support for KANU (Kanyinga 1998). This essentially led to extensive disillusionment in the opposition strongholds as patronage-led development opportunities granted by the KANU regime and ethnic polarisation took its toll on the opposition.

Nonetheless, despite the split that occurred in FORD and the proliferation of opposition parties, numerous efforts continued to be made among the opposition to forge a common action programme in demand for political and legal reforms. Other opposition parties that came into existence were not immediately faced with the pressures of fragmentation which faced FORD. This was mainly because their support base was much smaller. These support bases were confined to well-defined cleavages or, in some cases, the parties were run by personalities who did not face any internal challenge. Such parties included the DP, the Kenya National Congress (KNC), the Kenya Social Congress (KSC), and the Social Democratic Party (SDP). Although opposition parties succeeded in some of their quests, for the most part they were derailed by their own internal inadequacies in addition to state manipulation. Among the factors that affected the performance of opposition parties were lack of institutionalisation; factionalism; absence of internal party democracy and openness; dominance of party founders and parochial interests; refusal of the state to level the playing field; lack of resources; cultural diversity; and lack of ideology.

Lack of institutionalisation

A remarkable feature of Kenyan political parties is that they have been marked by little institutionalisation. Most of them do not have proper party structures and a majority lack offices outside the major urban centres. Most of them are regional parties and lack the national outlook that is necessary for a party primed to govern a country. Indeed, this was the key item that the incumbent KANU regime capitalised on to dismiss opposition political parties as tribal parties that only served to divide the country. Former president Moi repeatedly accused the National Development Party (NDP) of being a Luo party, FORD-K of being a Bukusu party and DP of being a Kikuyu party. Whereas the respective party leaders disputed this, the results of the elections in 1992 and 1997 vindicated Moi as the parties got significant votes only from their regional or ethnic strongholds. The exception was FORD-K in 1992, which, though its presidential vote was concentrated among the Luo and the Bukusu community of the Luhyia, managed to get at least one MP from each of the country's eight provinces, a feat that eluded all other parties including the incumbent KANU, which was completely shut out of Central Province.

Parties as institutions in a representative democracy serve as vehicles for political mobilisation. In Kenya, however, one of the big threats to institutionalisation has been lack of a disciplined party membership. From 1992 to the 2002 elections, there has been a dearth in distinct party membership, coupled with very few cardholders and hence the difficulty for parties to organise. Where 'members' have cards, in most cases, the cards have been bought for them by contestants for various party posts or by candidates vying for nomination. This has led to cases of one person holding more than one party membership card for different political parties.

Party funding has been lacklustre and the few funds end up perpetuating patronage and entrepreneurial financing. Investment in political parties is by a few rich individuals who, by virtue of their financial power, single-handedly control the parties and determine their affairs. Such is the case that FORD-A took a downslide after Kenneth Matiba withdrew his patronage, which he shifted to Saba-Saba Asili. On the other hand, other parties came to life when they were taken over by financially well-endowed politicians, for example Raila's takeover of the NDP and Nyachae's takeover of the Forum for Restoration of Democracy for the People (FORD-P). The patron–client tradition that bestows upon certain individuals who own the parties the power and authority to overrule members' decisions suggests that members have no stake in their respective parties. This lack of space for membership control is clear evidence of the general lack of internal democracy in opposition parties. This creates doubt about the credibility of parties as institutions of democracy at the national level when they themselves cannot achieve internal democracy.

Membership fee is technically non-existent, further aggravating the problem of financing. A party membership fee is certainly the most acceptable means of financing political parties. This corresponds to the definition that they are associations with democratic structures and organisations that are independent of the state. A financially responsible party membership ensures that members determine the democratic structure within the party by virtue of their contributions (Schefold 1995). Conversely however, Kenyans over the years have joined political parties to receive material gains with no intentions of supporting such parties financially. Parties and candidates are therefore expected to treat voters to patronage largesse including direct payment among other inducements. Throup and Hornsby (1998: 359–82) identified this issue in the 1992 general elections where the opposition presidential hopefuls pumped millions of shillings of their own money and those of their wealthy friends into the campaigns. The DP was said to have the financial backing of big Kikuyu businessmen, while the inner circle of FORD-A reportedly included the chairman of British-American Tobacco Kenya, who had close ties with the Kenyatta family. Even FORD-K with fewer wealthy friends raised 80 per cent of its campaign funds (Kshs. 14 million) from a few large donations by 'anonymous well-wishers' (Throup and Hornsby 1998: 360).

It should be noted that although paid-up party membership is the norm in the more established democracies, it has never been a sufficient source of funds for the smooth running of party programmes even in the most developed democracies. In regard to the democratising countries, members do not fund parties because most opposition parties are personalised institutions where ordinary citizens are not welcome. It is a deliberate effort by party gatekeepers to personalise the party and exclude everybody else as a means of controlling the parties. The end result has been the absolute lack of democracy in the political parties. Currently there are 52 political parties in Kenya, most of which have no physical address. They operate on the streets, as 'Briefcase Political Parties'. These are formed not to compete for power but rather for speculation purposes as disagreements and splits arise in the major parties. Most of them end up fielding very few candidates or none at all in some election years. Some of such parties that have been taken over and revived are NDP, Liberal Democratic Party (LDP) and SDP.

The greatest impediments to institutionalisation of opposition political parties are lack of a positive political and party culture, ethnic divisions and funding. At the core of the problem is the funding for political parties. Most parties cannot finance their operations, including rent payment for their offices. The most affected are opposition parties that do not have the advantage of access to state resources for party activities.

If parties had access to adequate funding then it is plausible that they would develop the basic structural institutions to facilitate democracy. The institutionalisation of parties will certainly ensure that they operate on the basis of ideologies and policies and not at the whims of the party leaders. Further, with adequate institutional rules and regulations, multiple memberships and changing of parties by leaders can be eliminated or minimised. Lack of institutionalisation has rendered the political parties meaningless and subjected opposition parties to general weakness, vulnerability, fragmentation and dissolution. Political parties in Kenya are generally no more than vehicles for charismatic leaders attempting to achieve political ambitions. They have neither structure nor proper rules and regulations. The remedy lies in increasing the capacity of political parties by institutionalising them.

Factionalism within opposition parties

Perhaps one of the most widely publicised peculiarities of African political parties is the problem of ethnic or religious factionalism. A number of parties, both large and small, have sometimes been formed based on traditional or ethnic considerations. Oftentimes, parties originally not formed on an ethnic basis eventually gravitate towards the mobilisation of voters along ethnic lines. This is usually exacerbated by the large number of parties that have been formed, which coincides with the numerous ethnic groups that form the basic social cleavage in African societies. It is from this perspective that politicians see ethnicity as the base for political activity and ethnic sentiment as the focus of appeal. This inevitably disables them from rising above ethnic interests and puts pressure on the administration of their parties as well as the government. The result is that the government comes to be regarded as one huge cake, already baked, and it is the duty of a political leader to secure for his or her ethnic group as large a share as possible (Nwabueze 1977).

In Kenya, this has been the case for both the ruling and opposition parties. Most parties registered since 1991 have for the most part been 'briefcase parties' with no fixed abode (Oyugi 2003). No wonder that on the eve of the 2002 general elections the number of registered parties stood at 51 (as per the letter from the Registrar of Societies to the Electoral Commission of Kenya [ECK] dated 29 October 2002). Of these parties, only five were able to contest the presidential elections; another 37 managed to sponsor candidates for parliamentary contests though the majority of them only managed to do so in very few constituencies. Thirty-one fielded candidates in less than 10 per cent of the constituencies, with the actual number varying from 1 to 19 for the said individual parties.

Apart from the large number of opposition parties, the divisions within the political opposition itself also played into the hands of the Moi regime and KANU between 1992 and 1997. As a starter, when FORD emerged, it was a combination of diverse interests, and processes. The movement benefited from both external and internal forces. The external forces mainly comprised donor institutions, and foreign governments softened up the Moi regime by pegging financial assistance to both political and economic reforms that included the adoption of multiparty politics. The internal forces crystallised as they had all suffered the same fate under the authoritarian Moi regime. The leadership of FORD thus comprised both seasoned politicians representing the different ethnic, religious and sectoral interests and the 'Young Turks' drawn mainly from civil society ranks and politically minded professionals. These included Paul Muite, Raila Odinga, Gitobu Imanyara, Mukhisa Kituyi, Anyang' Nyong'o and Kiraitu Murungi.

Although ethnicity did not appear to be a major factor in the formative stages of FORD, it later turned out to be the emotive issue that finally broke up the party. Initially, it had been assumed that Oginga Odinga, by virtue of his role in the independence struggle, opposition politics, age and as interim chairman, would automatically be the presidential candidate of FORD. However the Kikuyu elite in the movement thought otherwise. They recognised that ethnicity was a dominant factor and calculated that due to the demographic advantage Kikuyus had over other Kenyan communities, they could always count on their numbers to grab the ultimate political prize. It was with this in mind that they started campaigning for Kenneth Matiba as FORD presidential candidate, who was then recuperating in London after suffering a stroke during his stint in detention. These moves were countered by the Luo elite and the Young Turks from other ethnic groups who insisted that Odinga was the natural presidential candidate.

The situation worsened as both sides settled on different electoral mechanisms for choosing the movement's presidential candidate, the Odinga faction rooting for the delegates system, the Matiba faction arguing for direct nominations. The fragmentation was hastened as both sides started operating from different offices. The Odinga faction remained rooted in the original FORD offices at AGIP House in

downtown Nairobi, while the Matiba faction opened offices in
Muthithi House in Westlands, both houses being owned by Odinga
and Matiba, respectively. The wrangling in FORD was a God-sent
opportunity to KANU, which took advantage and cajoled the
Attorney-General's office to acknowledge that both factions could be
registered as long as they had different party names and officials.
Subsequently, each faction was reluctant to lose the magic name
FORD and both factions were finally registered as FORD-K and
FORD-A, respectively.

Other opposition parties that came into existence were not immediately faced with major wrangles as in the case of FORD. However,
after the 1992 elections they too had their share of internal wars.
Between 1992 and 1997 the major opposition parties were FORD-A,
FORD-K and DP, and later in the run-up to the 1997 elections two
existing minor political parties were taken over by rebels from the
three main opposition parties. The first of the minor parties was the
NDP, which was revived by Raila Odinga after he decamped from
FORD-K following a bitter struggle with Chairman Michael Wamalwa
Kijana over the control of the party. The other one was the SDP
which was first relaunched by Peter Anyang' Nyong'o, who had technically decamped from FORD-K, and Apollo Njonjo. But the party
did not become vibrant until Charity Ngilu decamped from DP to
become its presidential candidate in the 1997 general elections.

Overall, factionalism rampant in the ranks of opposition parties
played into the hands of the incumbent party, KANU. Whereas the
combined opposition garnered the majority of votes in both the 1992
and 1997 presidential elections, KANU won both the elections with
37 per cent and 40 per cent of the votes cast, respectively.

Lack of internal party democracy

Absence of or minimal internal party democracy is yet another salient
commonality of African political parties. A well-organised party system
is expected to implement popular sovereignty by systematically putting
political leaders in touch with and making them accountable to their
citizen constituents. For a party to discharge this important responsibility, it must be democratic in its internal structures and in the way it
conducts its business. It goes without saying that a political party lacking internal democracy can be expected to subvert the democratic
process and institutions of the country if it attains power.

Amongst the vast majority of African parties, internal democracy is a rare attribute. Within the African party system, what exists generally is not democracy but some aspect of oligarchy. While parties everywhere are prone to be oligarchic in nature, those in Africa are principally so, as power tends to be concentrated in the hands of a few (Ndulo 2000). Because of this, many Kenyan parties have had difficulties in convening national congresses to hold periodic elections for their leadership. Party congresses are usually for non-party members. The entire process is usually a mere showcase or coronation of the party leader. Generally, there is an absence of openness and transparency in the conduct of party operations, including the selection of nominees to stand as candidates for elections and government positions. It is in this vein that all parties in Kenya, both in the opposition as well as in the ruling party, have faced internal wrangles, which in most cases are never resolved amicably. This has led to splits, defections, and the formations of new or revival of moribund parties. In some cases, the emergence of new parties has been encouraged by the state in order to facilitate further splits in the opposition. This has also resulted in the registration of briefcase parties that remain dormant until disgruntled dominant party stalwarts get frustrated and abandon their previous parties in order to seek power through alternative political parties.

In terms of structure and organisation, maladministration and persistent organisational problems and transparency have hampered opposition parties. Party elections are rare and even when held they have been marked by confusion, incivility, widespread charges of rigging and even violence. Party structures and lines of command often appear unclear, inefficient or haphazard. Although constitutions and manifestos spell out relatively democratic practices and progressive ideals, virtually all parties have failed to hold fully democratic elections for party offices. Party leaders and top party organs perpetually interfere with internal elections, leading to a ridiculous festival of splits, defections and violence. The nomination of party candidates is another indictment of political parties in Kenya. Party leaders and top party organs routinely control who gets nominated. Intimidation, violence, vote buying and even sidestepping the process have been seen in all the major political party nominations. The manner in which parties are currently financed also impacts negatively on internal democracy. Many parties appear to be financed mainly by their leaders. This makes the parties dependent on the whims and ambitions of these leaders and hence many of them are highly vulnerable to defections. A party that depends financially on the wealth of its leader is likely to be run as if it is the leader's personal property.

The chaotic party nomination of candidates attests to the lack of internal democracy. All political parties have, in theory, laid down procedures for identifying candidates for the various elective positions. These procedures and the rules governing them are, however, rarely adhered to. All the party nominations since 1992 have been dogged by the interference of the party leadership at every level of the contest, especially nominations for parliamentary and local council elections. There have also been cases where a contest produces a winner, only for the loser to be declared the winner and ultimately the party candidate. Likewise, there have also been cases where the winners have been ignored and direct nominations made by the party leadership. In some cases, figures are tampered with and the winner's votes are given to the losing contestant. The problem has been getting worse from one election to another. A group of local election observers from the National Council of the Churches of Kenya (NCCK), the Catholic Justice and Peace Commission and the Institute for Education in Democracy (IED) in a joint report after the 1997 elections had this to say about the situation:

> The recently concluded party nominations were marred by malpractice including autocratic behaviour of the party bosses in imposing leaders, massive bribery, violence, and administrative and structural hiccups of the electoral process. The nominations showed that democratic practices have not yet taken root and that the 'big man' syndrome continues to beleaguer Kenya's political system. (*Daily Nation*, 11 December 1997: 13)

The situation was similar in the 2002 nominations. Widespread violence was reported as aspirants sought party clearance. Violence was especially intense on the days of party nominations, the days between party nominations and the day of the electoral commission parliamentary nominations. The situation was so messy that in some cases more than two candidates would claim to have been nominated, some directly by the party's headquarters, others by provincial or district co-ordinators, in addition to those who were nominated by the voters according to the agreed formula by either secret ballot or queuing (see *People Daily*, 21–26 November 2002; *Daily Nation*, 21–22 November 2002).

Kenya's experience with party nominations and lack of internal party democracy are a manifestation of the lack of a democratic political culture. Since democratic consolidation encompasses a shift in the political culture, the shift from authoritarianism to a participatory political culture is still woefully wanting in Kenya's fledgling democracy. The use of force, fraud and other illegal means to acquire power and influence policies are thus signs of deconsolidation at the elite level (see Linz 1978: 16–18; Diamond 1999).

Dominance of the state

Whereas we recognise the adverse effect of parochial tendencies in political party formation and power contestation on the performance of multiparty politics in Kenya since 1991, we cannot ignore the attitude of the incumbent regime and the ruling party towards the opposition parties. Between 1991 and 2002, the ruling party, KANU, did all that was practically possible to circumscribe the operational areas of the opposition parties, especially those that were strong enough to pose a threat to KANU's monopolisation of power and privilege. The posture of both the Moi regime and the ruling party had the effect of weakening the operationalisation of multiparty democracy in the country. The behaviour of the KANU regime during the election period, especially during the 1992 and 1997 elections, denied the opposition parties the freedom to reach out to voters and sell their programmes. In the run-up to the 1992 elections, opposition parties' effort to meet the government and the ruling party to chart out a consensus on the changes necessary to ensure free and fair elections were outrightly resisted. The end result was that elections were held by and large on the procedures and mechanisms that had been in operation under the one-party system.

Between 1992 and 2002, the Moi government displayed a stubborn reluctance to level the playing field, and opposition parties were viewed as illegitimate entities. Moi referred to multipartyism as a foreign imposition and opposition parties as agents of ethnic conflict. In the run-up to the 1997 elections, communities associated with opposition parties became subject to sustained harassment, especially in the Rift Valley and parts of Coast Province, a situation that was reminiscent of the ethnic clashes that had characterised the run-up to the 1992 elections (Kiliku 1992; NEMU 1993; Oyugi 1997). This culminated in ethnic clashes in the Likoni constituency in Mombasa, which targeted upcountry ethnic groups, including the Kamba, the Kikuyu, the Luhyia and the Luo, perceived to be supporters of the opposition. The state under KANU also repeatedly denied opposition parties access to the publicly owned mass media and restricted opposition rallies on the pretext that they did not have permits for public meetings. In addition, the state used public resources to subsidise the governing party's campaign, permitted militias and police to intimidate supporters and agents of the opposition parties (see Chapter 3 by Gecaga in this volume), and also gave direct financial patronage to constituencies that were considered loyal to KANU.

The Moi regime also employed patron–client politics to sustain itself in power. This entailed the systematic use of state resources to circumvent and neutralise the opposition. The infrastructure of authoritarianism in place was used to ensure that there was no meaningful interaction between the opposition and the electorate (Oyugi 1998). Resource allocation was the axis of perpetuating clientelism in the pre- and post-election period. As Moi moved from one part of the country to another, he never missed an opportunity to remind his audience that only those areas that supported the ruling party, and therefore the government, stood to benefit. Opposition MPs were told before their electorate that if they wanted their constituencies to benefit from state-supported development, they had to defect to KANU. It was thus quite clear that opposition political parties were heavily dependent on the goodwill of the state if they were to make any meaningful contribution to development in Kenya. This dependence can be seen in a number of ways. State regulations concerning political parties are extensive; ranging from the rules parties must comply with in order to obtain registration, to the actual involvement of the state in regulating the substance of party competition.

KANU, through the state, also instigated ethnic clashes during both the 1992 and 1997 elections to intimidate opposition supporters. In the countdown to the 1992 elections, the clashes mainly targeted opposition supporters in the districts declared by state operatives as KANU zones. Similar clashes were again unleashed just before the 1997 registration of voters in the Rift Valley and Coast Provinces. This was calculated to lower the number of opposition voters registered in that year (Wanjohi 2003). Similarly, in both 1992 and 1997, there was a well-orchestrated policy of obstructive containment involving the restriction of movement of the opposition leaders and making sure they did not access the interior of most of the country. This meant that voters in these areas did not have an opportunity to choose from competing policies and choices. Instead voters were bombarded with KANU propaganda. This ensured the establishment of a hostile political environment for the opposition that effectively hindered their ability to market themselves and their policies amongst the electorate.

Dominance of party founders

As mentioned, a problem for opposition parties has been the dominance of founding members. Founders of political parties or their designated henchmen have used elaborate patronage mechanisms to control parties, monopolise their core functions and solely make important decisions. In the absence of openness and internal democracy, leaders through the party machine have privatised party activities, creating a disconnection between parties and the masses in periods between elections. This has made democratic practice a mirage.

Party founders have also assigned themselves the right to contest the presidency in general elections. This by itself is undemocratic unless stipulated in the party constitution. This practice has contributed immensely to party splits, evident first in the original FORD when it split into FORD-A, led by Kenneth Matiba, and FORD-K, led by Oginga Odinga. Subsequent leadership wrangles and struggles over the control of the two parties' machinery resulted in Raila Odinga leaving FORD-K to lead the NDP, while Kenneth Matiba left FORD-A to form Saba Saba-Asili. The result was that the original multi-ethnic and national-oriented FORD, which had substantial following in virtually all parts of the country, gave offshoots to at least four parties whose support was largely confined to the ethnic communities of their leaders. Another offshoot was FORD-P, which was originally meant to accommodate Matiba after he differed with Martin Shikuku in FORD-A, but later FORD-P came to be associated with Kimani wa Nyoike and, in 2002, was taken over by Simeon Nyachae.

It is commonplace for party leaders in Kenya, whether in government or opposition, not to contemplate their replacement while still politically active. The party is perceived as the property of its leader whose stewardship can only be surrendered, if at all, to a selected heir. Any open and democratic contest for party leadership is quite unlikely. The failure to nurture and adopt a democratic culture within parties has been a major drawback to the democratic efforts that began late 1980s. Yet today's political leaders, whether in government or opposition, have not fully freed themselves from the authoritarian political culture of yesteryear. This has had the effect of denying party members meaningful participation in decision making in party organs. It has also denied them the right to free contestation when there is an intra-party election. It was the single-minded decision of President Moi to anoint his own heir in KANU that contributed to the party's electoral loss in the 2002 general elections, when a sizeable portion of KANU's leading members quit in protest.

Between 1991 and 2002, the development of political parties in Kenya was conditioned largely by the ambitions of leaders and by ethnic loyalties. Most opposition parties were unable to develop national followings or distinctive policies and programmes based on coherent ideologies. Infighting based on leadership and ethnicity split the formerly united opposition movement FORD into factions, crippled their organisational capacities, and prevented them from working together on common agendas such as constitutional reform, corruption and political violence. Even with the 2002 accession to power of NARC, a coalition of the then opposition parties, there still persists a tendency to cling to the ethnic support of the key leaders of the coalition. None of the NARC leaders seem ready to go national as they risk losing the ever-binding ethnic glue. With many of the parties relying on a handful of patrons, usually their leaders or founders, for the finances to maintain party activities, parties increasingly became susceptible to building cults of personality and structures of patronage. This is not surprising as most of the opposition parties were themselves launched as vehicles for key individuals to achieve power.

Ideology and policy platform

Political parties in Kenya have also made little progress in defining party ideologies or espousing competing development policies and programmes. Though major opposition parties and some of the minor ones have unveiled manifestos in each election year, their approaches to issues have been similar and have been obscured and muddled by internal wrangles. As a result, it has been difficult for voters to tell what the different parties really stand for, as all the manifestos are different only in language but not in substance. Their ambition is to win elections and form a government. Furthermore, the frequency of defections and leadership wrangles indicates that many opposition politicians are not motivated by party principles or constructive policy commitments. Instead, they are more concerned with the quest for raw power, perceived as attainable by relying on the ethnic card.

One notable but negative similarity is that all political parties in Kenya have no discernible ideology. Party manifestos, although consistently full of lofty promises, are not based on coherent principles. In many cases there is no attempt to explain how promises will be fulfilled, as manifestos do not include a costing component. Moreover, manifestos exist but they never form the backbone of campaign strategies for political parties including the ruling party. The end result is that party ideologies, policies and programmes do not serve as the basis on which voters determine whom or which party to support. Among the currently registered political parties, ideologies are at best used for expedient posturing by party leaders. At worst, they are vague or non-existent.

The frequent defections and returns by both elected and non-elected leaders also point to the lack of an ideological base of parties in general and on the part of the defectors in particular. Although official defections have not occurred yet during the NARC regime, unofficial ones have already occurred on the political landscape. These include KANU's John Serut of Mount Elgon, who has defected to NARC through FORD-K, and Wycliffe Osundwa of Mumias, who has technically defected from FORD-K to LDP. There are also numerous new alignments from MPs allied to LDP and National Alliance (Party) of Kenya (NAK) under the ruling coalition NARC who have changed allegiance mostly in favour of NAK, which is firmly in control of state power. Among those who have openly changed allegiance from LDP to NAK are Raphael Tuju, Ali Mwakwere, Kirugi M'Mukindia, Petkay Miriti and George Saitoti. Quite a number, although not associating openly with LDP, have chosen the middle ground: Joseph Nyagah, Peter Kenneth, William Ntimama, Gideon Konchellah and Vice-President Moody Awori.

Defections have been prevalent in Kenya since the return to multi-party politics in 1992. As Nasong'o (2001) observes, the first MP to defect to KANU after the 1992 elections was DP's Protus Momanyi of Bonchari, who retained his seat on the KANU ticket and was appointed a cabinet minister. This 'positive' defection hastened the defection of the entire slate of FORD-A MPs from Kakamega, including Apili Wawire of Lugari, Nicodemus Khaniri of Hamisi, Japheth Shamalla of Shinyalu, Ben Magwaga of Ikolomani and Javan Ommani of Lurambi. Similarly, KNC's Ireri Ndwiga of Siakago and DP's Agnes Ndetei of Kibwezi also defected to KANU. All these defectors retained their seats on KANU tickets. However, Kiruhi

Kimondo, FORD-A, Starehe; Julius Njoroge, FORD-A, Makuyu; Tom Obondo, FORD-K, Ndhiwa; and Owino Likowa, FORD-K, Migori, defected but lost their seats in the ensuing by-elections (see Nasong'o 2001: 117–32). The point to note here is that those who defected and lost hailed from constituencies or areas that were dominated by the two most prominent opposition ethnic groups then, the Luo and the Kikuyu. It is also noteworthy that all aforementioned defections were from opposition parties to the ruling party. This was a clear indication that the ruling party had the carrot that was used to entice opposition parliamentarians. The only notable exception was the resignation of Raila Odinga as FORD-K Langata MP after losing the contest for chairmanship of the party to Michael Wamalwa Kijana following the death in 1994 of Oginga Odinga, Raila's father and party chairman. Raila defected to the then nondescript NDP on whose ticket he won the ensuing by-election.

If parties have no strongly held ideals, virtually anyone can join and leave without any major repercussions. The suitability of a party mainly revolves not around what it stands for but the opportunities it offers for the advancement of an individual politician's political career. Since most of the parties are formed around personalities, they pay little attention to the need to have clear visions or ideological principles. Even in cases in which such visions have been drawn out, they have mostly remained on paper and have rarely been revealed to the public in open forums. Instead, ethnicity and personality politics have remained the focus during campaigns, rather than issues. Under these circumstances, the fate of these parties has been closely tied to the vision and material support of the founder leadership; hence whenever leaders have withdrawn their support, the affected parties have gone under. This is the fate that befell FORD-A and SDP.

Resource availability

The availability of resources is undoubtedly crucial to a political party's survival. The fact that public financing for political parties in Africa is quite rare has had a negative impact on parties in general and opposition parties in particular. Ruling parties have used the advantage of incumbency to extract state resources to finance their own campaigns in election years. Lack of a stable resource base is a problem that has bedevilled opposition parties in Kenya. For two consecutive elections in 1992 and 1997, KANU took advantage of state resources to finance its election and other party activities. In addition, it solicited donations from the private sector which contributed to the KANU election kitty in return for kickbacks in the form of lucrative government contracts. Opposition parties mostly relied on their founding members and patrons for financial support and to a lesser extent on donor funding. They also relied on subscriptions from their members, which has not only been meagre but has also proved to be short-lived. This was due to voter fatigue, especially after the opposition loss in two elections. The public became reluctant to continue supporting their parties' activities.

The resource disparity between the ruling party and opposition parties has contributed to the derailment of the democratisation process in Kenya. This is because meaningful democratic elections in a multi-party electoral system can only be attained if the state is a neutral arbiter. However, where there is fusion of party and state in the interest of the ruling party, multiparty elections become a political façade. Studies of the last three multiparty elections present overwhelming evidence of how the ruling party, KANU, systematically relied on the institutions of the state (notably the public service) to gain unfair advantage over the competing opposition parties. In addition to the use of public institutions to serve its interest, KANU also used its position in the government to gain access to unlimited financial resources both in the 1992 and 1997 elections. These resources were used to disorganise opposition parties (Oyugi 2003). This greatly impaired the performance of the opposition parties and their ability to enhance the practice of democracy. It is thus imperative that an incumbent ruling party's monopoly over state funds be curtailed if a level playing field is to be realised in the conduct of elections.

Some critics have argued that the state is not obligated to help meet the financial needs of parties and that it should not relieve parties of the risk of failure and the responsibility that goes with it (see Alexander 1989). But this argument fails to take into account that an effective democracy can only be realised where there are strong political parties in and outside the government. It also fails to note that the ruling party by virtue of being in power has access to government resources, which opposition parties do not. Nevertheless, it is important to note the danger that public financing of parties can create. On the one hand, it may strengthen the position of party professionals by assuring their livelihood but, on the other hand, it may weaken parties in other ways, among them alienating the ordinary members. For example, government subsidies may create a distance between the parties and the electorate by relieving the parties of the necessity to solicit individual contributions, thus undermining the accountability of party officials to members.

The literature on funding of elections, whether in developed or developing countries, seems to suggest that political parties on their own are not capable of mobilising enough resources to enable them to compete effectively in electoral contests. This has raised the question about the need to identify reliable sources of funding for political parties to enable them compete effectively. The question that recurs is whether the state should assume the responsibility of financing all competing political parties. Arguably, the funding of political parties could be left as it is now, in the hands of parties themselves with the proviso that each party is free to get assistance from wherever it can to enable it to mount a credible campaign during election.

Concern for equitable funding of all political parties participating in elections arises from the realisation that some parties are usually better endowed than others based on their ethno-regional bases of support. Since 2001 there has been a concerted initiative by a few NGOs to influence the enactment of a political parties (financial) law under which the state will assume the responsibility of financing political parties represented in parliament. In fact the NGOs in question went as far as drafting the Bill wherein it was proposed that an annual figure of 1 per cent of the total budget (about Kshs. 2.8 billion or US$ 36,845,105) be spent annually to fund political parties. They further suggest that the finances be allocated on a quarterly basis based on the number of votes each party garners in the previous elections and that the ECK be responsible for the administration of political parties (Transparency International-Kenya 2002). This is intended to level the playing field between the opposition parties and the ruling party.

In the meantime, Kenya operates an open-door policy according to which there is no limit on how much a candidate or a party can spend in an election. Nor is there any restriction as to the sources of funding. Whereas the state is fully responsible for financing the ECK activities, it has left the political parties to fend for themselves. The experience in the 1992, 1997 and 2002 elections has revealed that without a strong financial base, a political party cannot mount a credible campaign, and therefore cannot expect to win even a single seat in parliament. This explains why a number of fringe presidential candidates in the past three multiparty elections failed to be elected as MPs for their constituencies.

According to the electoral laws of Kenya, one has to be an elected MP in order to qualify to be a president.

Indeed, a fallout in the opposition party FORD-K after the 1992 elections was occasioned partly by allegations that key individuals, among them the then Young Turks in the party, had received a lot of money in the name of the party but had opted to keep it for their own personal use, thereby denying the party the opportunity to support candidates who were in greater need of financial assistance. The resignation of Paul Muite as the first vice-chairman of FORD-K in 1994 as well as the departure of several other Young Turks from the party was occasioned by revelations that the party chairman, Oginga Odinga, had received Kshs. 20 million from Kamlesh Pattni of the infamous Goldenberg scandal to finance the Migori and Ndhiwa by-elections, thereby compromising the party's stated stand against corruption. The matter was worsened by the fact that when confronted, Odinga acknowledged having received only Kshs. 2 million from a seemingly well-meaning young man whom he did not recognise as the Kamlesh Pattni of the Goldenberg ignominy. In the same vein, in the 2002 elections, newspapers were full of reports of senior members of the NARC coalition travelling abroad for the sole purpose of raising funds for the party. But instead of the funds being surrendered to the party, it remained in the pockets of the individual recipients, to be disposed of in the manner that best served the personal interests of those that mobilised the funds. This clearly shows that lack of resources undermines the performance of an opposition party and critically compromises its candidates (Oyugi 2003).

Furthermore, the private sector, the only potential source of funding for opposition parties, has been forced to resort to covert funding of opposition parties rather than risk punitive actions by the government such as loss of government contracts and harassment by tax authorities. Because of the constraints that limited funding imposes on opposition parties, the opposition is forced to become antagonistic to the ruling party, hence they oppose every initiative that emanates from the government. Consequently, the opposition comes to see its role in governance as the need to bring the incumbent government down by whatever means possible. This has a negative impact on the democratisation process.

The introduction of public funding for political parties, if the pending political parties fund bill is passed, would be a big step towards alleviating the problems of lack of resources, inequitable access to resources or appropriation of state resources for use by the ruling party to the disadvantage of the opposition parties who are denied similar access. A similar provision also existed in the draft constitution that was rejected in the referendum in November 2005; therefore, either way the funding of political parties seems to have received the needed attention of appreciating its necessity for the development of multiparty democracy. It is imperative that constitutional and statutory means be put in place to entrench the institutionalisation of political parties and enhance their transparency and internal democracy. This would help safeguard various political parties against undue influence from private and foreign sponsors who often threaten their freedom and ability to represent the interest and will of the people. Further, it would ensure that opposition parties survive and overcome any moves towards single-party authoritarianism through the use of financial muscle to obliterate parties that do not have rich financiers. In addition to promoting competitiveness, it would also discourage utilisation of other state resources by the party in power.

Alliance Building, Opposition Parties and Parliament

After losing the general elections twice to the ruling party, the opposition finally accepted the reality that their only chance of securing victory over the KANU regime was the unity of the myriad opposition parties. But KANU, true to its machinations, was the first off the block to counter this new opposition strategy. Immediately after the 1997 elections, the ruling party realised that the country had a hung parliament and it was therefore prudent to reach out to some opposition parties without necessarily entering a formal coalition government. To this end, KANU reached out to the now defunct NDP and FORD-K. The former stayed put with the relationship being transformed from 'co-operation' to 'partnership' and finally NDP was dissolved and its members merged into KANU. For its part, FORD-K back-pedalled from the relationship after a few months of warming up to KANU's courting. The merger between KANU and NDP stung the main opposition parties into action. The three main opposition parties, DP, FORD-K and the National Party of Kenya (NPK), began to engage in unity talks that finally led to the creation of the NAK as the umbrella body for the three parties. NAK was later transformed into NARC after LDP joined forces with NAK. It was this unity and the disarray in KANU after the Rainbow group decamped that made it possible for the opposition to finally dislodge KANU from power in the December 2002 general elections. Other alliances that sprouted at the time were the People's Coalition for Change, fronted by FORD-P, and Safina. These developments signified that the age of coalition politics in Kenya had arrived.

With regard to opposition parties and parliamentary business, the return of multiparty elections in 1992 reinvented the national assembly by facilitating an eminently strong opposition representation hitherto not witnessed in the single party parliaments. This emboldened some of parliament's organs, which had been dormant over the years during the one-party regime. Consequently, opposition MPs began to vigorously question and challenge the policies of the executive and the government in general with little or no fear of reprisal. Subsequently, parliament began conducting hearings on reports of the Comptroller and Auditor-General in which it summoned senior civil servants to appear before it. Furthermore, parliament also started questioning the expenditure patterns of some ministries.

Overall, the presence of opposition parties in parliament led to some gains on the democratic front, though not very substantial. First, non-governing parties have been able to question the government's activities in parliament and also chair the two parliamentary watchdog committees, the Public Accounts Committee (PAC) and the Public Investments Committee (PIC), which audit government accounts and public investment portfolios respectively. The constant exposure of government misdeeds and shortcomings keeps the public aware of what the government is doing and this has gone a distance towards keeping the government of the day on its toes. Second, the fact that the opposition chairs these committees has also made them worthy watchdogs over government expenditure. Third, opposition parties have successfully tabled a number of bills over the short period of multiparty politics. Examples include the all-important Parliamentary Service Commission Bill that has strengthened parliament vis-à-vis the executive and the Political Parties Funding Bill, which, although not yet passed, will certainly level the playing field in terms of resources during elections. Other bills that were brought by the opposition include the Gender Equality Bill and the Donde Bill that sought to regulate banks in Kenya (see Chapter 9 by Murunga in this volume).

Despite the positive developments cited above, parliament still faces a lot of shortcomings. These include the lack of basic facilities such as a good reference library for MPs and reluctance on the part of senior bureaucrats to provide relevant information to the parliamentarians. This has been compounded by the fact that the executive still dominates the calendar and direction of parliamentary affairs. The executive also has an advantage over parliament in terms of information access and this deprives the opposition of the opportunity effectively to deliberate on national issues in the House. There is also the self-interest of MPs, which has to be considered in any analysis of the performance of the opposition in enhancing democracy. For some MPs, their parliamentary seats are their only source of income. Any decision that might bring their parliamentary career to an abrupt end is naturally dreaded. The fear of facing an election whose outcome they are unsure of is literally overwhelming and is a risk that none would want to take.

The constitution gives the president the power to summon, prorogue and dissolve parliament. This power touches directly on the life and integrity of parliament as a decision-making institution. Since independence this power has more often than not been the subject of abuse by the executive. The dissolution and proroguing of parliament was used by the previous regime as an election weapon to disorganise and scatter the opposition.

The post-2002 election scenario

Since NARC won state power and KANU became the opposition, it appears that not only have roles changed but behaviour too seems to have changed, raising the question as to whether NARC will substantially behave differently from the tyrannical KANU. In a liberal democracy, the government of the day is constantly supervised and made accountable to the people by both the opposition parties and civil society, as they are essential prerequisites for democratic governance. Ironically, the aftermath of the 2002 general election, which was supposed to herald the collapse of an autocratic state, has seen a flow of key civil society organisations and individuals who had been part of the second liberalisation absorbed into government. This, it can be argued, set a new fertile ground for the germination of a new seed of autocracy. It is not surprising that the coalition government under the NARC has been behaving as if it is headed towards the restoration of the KANU culture of manipulation. Further, the by-elections that have largely been occasioned by the death of incumbent parliamentarians clearly show that NARC, like KANU in past years, has undue advantage by virtue of being the party in power and hence having at its disposal resources of the state.

The co-optation of KANU and FORD-P into the government in the 30 June 2004 cabinet reshuffle left many in doubt as to the continued existence of opposition parties. The justification by the NAK wing of NARC has been that the persistent wrangles with their erstwhile partner, the LDP, demanded that the country have a government of 'national unity' if stability and credibility of the government was to be restored. However, the constitutional and parliamentary conditions that would warrant the formation of a government of national unity did not exist. This explains why many, including members of the so-called 'government of national unity', are deeply divided as to the nature of the government in place. The logic was the need by the NAK faction of the NARC government to stem growing opposition from within and marshal enough MPs to ensure the passing of crucial government bills. This was especially highlighted in the wake of numerous defeats of bills, such as the Forest Bill, defeated by the joint opposition from the LDP faction of the NARC coalition and KANU. One therefore sees a concerted effort by the NAK faction of the government to cripple the opposition by co-opting KANU and FORD-P MPs into the government.

These moves are not unique to the NARC regime. Indeed the past regimes used similar tactics and strategies to stem opposition. What remains to be seen is whether KANU can effectively counter this move by the government and still retain its role as the official opposition party. KANU argues that those who were co-opted by the NARC government did so as individuals and the party was not consulted as would be expected in the formation of a government of national unity. KANU has consequently filed a case in court challenging the inclusion of its party members in government without the party's approval, arguing that the said action was unconstitutional. However, in an environment devoid of a democratic culture and proper party disciplinary machinery for dealing with errant members, NARC has the advantage of being able to immobilise the opposition parties and get away with it just as its predecessors did.

One unique aspect of opposition politics in the post-2002 election scenario is the increasing salience of opposition from within the ruling party. Such has emanated from the bad blood between the two factions in NARC, NAK and LDP, over disagreements on the now contentious memorandum of understanding (MoU) that brought the two together in 2002 to form the winning combination, NARC. Indeed at one point observers started wondering whether KANU was really the opposition, as LDP seemed to have usurped its role. The loose nature of the coalition of parties forming NARC is likely to persist as NAK makes moves to consolidate its position, while LDP embarks on its party activities in readiness for the 2007 general elections.

Opposition politics in the post-2002 period has therefore taken two distinct dimensions, that is, internal opposition emanating from the ruling party itself and the traditional opposition from the parties out of government. Ostensibly, the complications that this two-pronged opposition scenario presented warranted the formation of the 'government of national unity' to ensure the Kibaki regime's security and survival. Co-optation and blatant disregard of party politics protocol were used to achieve this goal. The danger that it portends if not checked is political monolithism, decay of party politics and the risk of reverting to a single-party outfit or a dominant party system in the South African style.

Conclusion

There is no doubt that the electoral system that Kenya uses, namely the single-member-district first-past-the-post winner-takes-all model, worked to the detriment of the opposition in 1992 and 1997. The number of seats the opposition won in both the 1992 and 1997 elections was not proportionate to its share of the popular national vote. The two multiparty KANU regimes therefore lacked the popular mandate of the people. In terms of governance, the ruling party, in spite of this anomaly, continued to govern without any input from the opposition. Instead, it employed two main instruments concurrently to guarantee its survival in power. On the one hand, it sought to isolate and intimidate opposition MPs and, on the other hand, it attempted to lure the opposition with the carrot of state patronage. Pressure on the opposition was also exerted by the ruling party through the freezing of all public development projects in the constituencies that voted for opposition politicians. These acts of desperation were more evident during by-elections, with the Kipipiri by-election being a case in point. During the by-election campaigns, the KANU regime ordered the immediate electrification of the constituency, and electricity poles were hurriedly transported to the constituency only to be withdrawn in haste after KANU lost the seat. Since voting under multipartyism has often taken on distinct ethno-regional patterns corresponding to the perceived ethno-regional character of the parties, such punitive measures implemented by the ruling group acted, at one level, to reinforce popular ethnic and religious identities and, at another level, to pressure individual opposition politicians to make peace with the party forming the government. In this environment, the quality of the public political discourse did little to enhance the popular interest in the struggle for meaningful political change (see Olukoshi 1998).

The opposition was also derailed by the lack of a level playing field. But the opposition should shoulder the blame here. In articulating their demands for multiparty politics, the opposition elements in Kenya were too quick in allowing themselves to be hurried by the KANU regime into elections without first insisting on the implementation of far-reaching constitutional changes that were necessary for governing post-electoral political activities. The opposition appeared content that multipartyism had been introduced, a contentment that was partly reflective of the confidence that some of them had in the chances of defeating the incumbent party in spite of their regionally limited support. Thus, the crucial questions regarding the manner in which transition to multiparty politics would be managed, and by whom, were ignored. The fate of opposition parties was further worsened by individual rivalries, which were reinforced by lingering or resuscitated ethno-regional competition and suspicion. In this context, internal party democracy was hardly given priority by the main opposition elements except as an instrument in their struggle for individual and group advantage. In addition, factionalism took hold and the prospects for electoral success of opposition parties dimmed. Arising from the internal wrangles, prominent opposition figures moved from one party to another with the majority tracing their roots back to the ruling party from where they had defected in the first place. This demoralised the opposition and weakened popular interest in democratic politics.

Opposition political activity also came to depend on donor funding for sustenance. On the whole, this aspect fed into the elitism that was a defining feature of parties. Very few retained the mass appeal they had elicited when they were first formed. To this end, opposition parties were very effective in the urban areas but not so much in the rural areas where the majority of Kenyans live. The ruling party had a more formidable grassroots structure and used its long stay in power as the only known political party to maximum advantage. The ruling party thus sought to justify the assertion that multipartyism, in the way in which it had unfolded, meant little for the practice of governance and for the ordinary Kenyan. Although Kenya's opposition parties have faced a lot of frustrations propelled by the state, some of the problems are basically internal. This is mainly because most of them have attracted the bulk of their support from cleavages of ethnicity, kinship and, to a lesser extent, religion. Unable to win power in the first two multiparty elections, many of the opposition parties splintered into factions and/or faded into irrelevance; others became victims of short-term goals.

Parties have also been formed with the sole purpose of speculation. Small opposition parties have, on several occasions, been offered for sale to the highest bidder especially when splits occur in major parties in an election year. It is thus imperative to note that not all parties have been formed to organise around specific political agendas. This again hinges on institutionalisation. Entrepreneurial party founders have known that every successive election year will be good for business, since people will want to give their political careers a fresh outfit. Accordingly, founders of parties such as the Labour Party of Kenya (LPK), the Kenya National Democratic Alliance (KENDA), the Party of Independent Candidates of Kenya (PICK), the KSC, and the KNC, among others, are not likely to dissolve their parties any time soon, even though they have performed dismally in three consecutive elections and there is no indication that they can do any better in the future. Others have not participated in two elections in a row and still remain political parties. This is because the founders still hope that these parties will one day catch the eye of politicians with clout, which would change their fortunes. Sale of parties is not just in monetary terms; most founders of these small parties also hope to ride on the popularity of the new 'big man' in the party to enhance their own political fortunes.

Whereas we recognise that public funding, highlighted earlier, may not be the quick-fix solution to the woes of opposition parties and multi-party democracy in Kenya, it is one important step that can remedy some of the problems bedevilling party politics in Kenya. Apart from the general lack of a democratic culture, resources have been one of the key baits that have been used to capture the people and retard the development of democracy in Kenya and therefore require major attention and remedy.

References

Ajulu, R. (2000), 'Thinking through the crisis of Democratization in Kenya: A Response to Adar and Murunga', *African Sociological Review*, vol. 4, no. 2.

Ajulu, R. (2002) 'Politicised Ethnicity, Competitive Politics and Conflict in Kenya: A Historical Perspective', *African Studies*, vol. 61, no. 2.

Alexander, H.E. (1989) 'Money and Politics: Rethinking a Conceptual Framework', in H.E. Alexander (ed.), *Comparative Political Finance in the 1980s*, Cambridge, UK: Cambridge University Press.

Aubrey, L. (1997) *The Politics of Development Cooperation: NGOs, Gender, and Partnership in Kenya*, London: Routledge.

Berman, B. et al. (2004) *Ethnicity & Democracy in Africa*, Oxford: James Currey.

Bratton, M. and N. Van De Walle (1998) *Democratic Experiments in Africa: Regime Transitions in Comparative Perspective*, New York, NY: Cambridge University Press.

Chege, M. (1995) 'The Return of Multi-party Politics', in J.D. Barkan (ed.), *Beyond Capitalism vs. Socialism in Kenya and Tanzania*, Nairobi: East African Educational Publishers.

Dahl, R. (1966) 'Preface', in R.A. Dahl (ed.), *Political Oppositions in Western Democracies*, New Haven, CT: Yale University Press.

Diamond, L. (1999) 'Developing Democracy in Africa: Africa and International Imperatives', *Cambridge Review of International Affairs*, vol. XIV, no. 1.

Dowse, R.E. and J.A. Hughes (1972) *Political Sociology*, New York, NY: John Wiley & Sons.

Gertzel, C. (1974) *The Politics of Independent Kenya*, Nairobi: East African Publishing House.

Institute for Education in Democracy (IED) (1998) *Political Party Organization and Management in Kenya: An Audit*, Nairobi: IED.

Kanyinga, K. (1998) 'The Land Question in Kenya: Struggles, Accumulation and Changing Politics', unpublished PhD Dissertation, Roskilde University, Denmark.

Kiliku, K. (1992) *Report of Parliamentary Select Committee on Ethnic Clashes in the Rift Valley*, Nairobi: Government Printer.

La Palambora, J. and M. Weiner (eds) (1969) *Political Parties and Political Development*, Princeton, NJ: Princeton University Press.

Linz, J. (1978) *The Breakdown of Democratic Regimes: Crisis, Breakdown, and Reequilibration*, Baltimore, MD: The John Hopkins University Press.

Lipset, S. (1967) *The First New Nation*, Garden City, NY: Doubleday.

Mutoro, H. et al. (1999) 'Political Leadership and the Crisis of Development in Africa: Lessons from Kenya', in R. Gosh et al. (eds), *Good Governance and Sustainable Development: The Indian Ocean Region*, New Delhi: Atlantic Publishers.

Nasong'o, S.W. (2001) 'The Illusion of Democratic Governance in Kenya', in R. Dibie (ed.), *The Politics and Policies of Sub-Saharan Africa*, Lanham, MD: University Press of America.

Nasong'o, S.W. (2002) 'Political Consolidation and the Betrayal of Nationalism in Kenya: The Dynamics of External Linkages', Paper Presented at the SORAC Conference on 'Internalist vs. Externalist Interpretations of African History and Culture', Montclair State University, Upper Montclair, NJ, September.

Ndegwa, S.N. (2001) 'A Decade of Democracy in Africa', *Journal of Asian & African Studies*, vol. 36, no. 1.

Ndulo, M. (2000) 'Political Parties and Democracy in Zambia', International IDEA Conference – Towards Sustainable Democratic Institutions in Southern Africa.

NEMU (1993) *The Multiparty General Elections in Kenya: 29th December 1992*, Nairobi: NEMU.

Nwabueze, B.O. (1977) *Judicialism in Commonwealth Africa: The Role of Courts in Government*, New York, NY: St. Martin's Press.

Ochieng, W.R. (1995) 'Structural and Political Changes', in B.A. Ogot and W.R. Ochieng (eds), *Decolonization and Independence in Kenya, 1940–93*, London: James Currey.

Olukoshi, A.O. (1998) 'Economic Crisis, Multipartyism, and Opposition Politics in Contemporary Africa', in A. Olukoshi (ed.), *The Politics of Opposition in Contemporary Africa*, Uppsala: Nordiska Afrikainstitutet.

Ouyang, Hongwu, (2000) 'Political Parties and Consolidation of Democracy: The Case of Russia', *Perspective*, vol. 1. no. 6.

Oyugi, W.O. (1997) 'Ethnicity and the Electoral Process: The 1992 General Elections in Kenya', *African Journal of Political Science*, June, New Series, vol. 2, no. 1.

———— (1998) 'Ethnic Politics in Kenya', in O. Nnoli (ed.), *Ethnic Conflicts in Africa*, Dakar: CODESRIA.

———— (2003) 'The Politics of Transition in Kenya, 1992–2003: Democratic Consolidation or Deconsolidation', in W.O. Oyugi et al. (eds), *The Politics of Transition in Kenya: From KANU to NARC*, Nairobi: Heinrich Boll Foundation.

Schefold, D. (1995) 'Background and Basic Principles of Financing of Political Parties', in Josef Thesing and Wilhelm Hofmeister (eds), *Political Parties in Democracy*, Sankt Augustin: Konrad-Adenauer Stiftung.

Thesing, J. and W. Hofmeister (1995) *Political Parties in Democracy*, Sankt Augustin: Konrad-Adenauer Stiftung.

Throup, D. and C. Hornsby (1998) *Multi-party Politics in Kenya: The Kenyatta and Moi States and the Triumph of the System in the 1992 Election*, Oxford: James Currey.

Transparency International-Kenya (2002) 'Funding Political Parties: A Look at Political Parties Finance bill', *Adhili*, no. 6, 25 March.

Wanjohi, N.G. (2003) 'Sustainability of political parties in Kenya', in M.A. Mohamed Salih and Abdel Ghaffar Mohamed Ahmed (eds), *African Political Parties: Post-1990s Perspectives*, London: Pluto Press.

PART III

Major Constituencies in the Democratisation Process

5

Leaders of Tomorrow? The Youth and Democratisation in Kenya

Mshaï S. Mwangola

The youth are leaders of tomorrow

Leo ni leo! Asemaye kesho ni mwongo!
(Today is the day! Whoever says tomorrow is a liar!)

Popular Swahili saying

Introduction

The opening quotation is a cliché that is characteristic of speeches of Kenyan leaders with regard to the nation's youth. This is especially so in politics where, until recently, youthfulness was considered a negative attribute for aspiring leaders. Kenya has an established trend that requires one to make a name elsewhere before plunging into politics. A flood of resignations from the civil service and corporate world in the final few months before the poll marks the five-year election cycle in Kenya. Retirees, usually male, seek to crown their careers of several decades by successfully contesting parliamentary seats in general elections. For most of the first four decades of the post-colonial period,[1] one could be forgiven for assuming that for youth the present functions purely as a transitory period to a future in which they can actually begin to participate in society. Thus, the challenge of understanding Kenyan youth as active participants in society, especially as significant players in politics, is one that has been largely ignored or superficially treated in reflections on Kenya.

Youth have tended to feature in political analyses as societal burdens of some kind, who have to be carefully 'handled'. There has been little change in attitude since cabinet minister Tom Mboya qualified the statement '[y]outh are ... important to the nation' with the observation, '[t]heir energies must be channelled to useful and productive purposes' (Mboya 1986: 54). Forty years after independence, the government admits: 'The youth have remained on the periphery of the country's affairs and their needs and aspirations have not been accorded due recognition. They have been excluded from designing, planning and implementing programmes and policies that affect them and the country at large' (NYPSC 2003: 25). This situation is, however, beginning to change. The period 1990–2005 has brought to the fore an aggressive youth discourse that has rejected prevailing perceptions of youth and demanded a reconfiguring of the social roles and responsibilities of this category. This chapter traces the evolution of this discourse, locating its genesis in indigenous political cultures that have continued to evolve in the creation of an endogenous understanding of democracy in Kenya.

Two terms, democracy and youth, are central to this discussion and are therefore worth exploring further at this stage. The chapter prioritises Kenyan understandings of these terms as manifested in everyday discourse in the public sphere. We recognise that their use within the present Kenyan society has been influenced by both a socio-cultural history encapsulating different perspectives and influences and an ongoing experience of lived reality shaped by the local and global contexts of related discourses. The majority of studies on either democracy or youth within the Kenyan context tend to privilege definitions occurring within academic and global discourses on these issues, most of which focus on anarchy, chaos, violence and war (see Kagwanja 2006). We will concentrate on the local, especially taking into consideration endogenous cultural influences (see Hountondji 1997).

A Cultural Foundation

The concept of democracy and the generational principle

As elaborated in Chapter 1, democracy is a difficult term to authoritatively define. Kenyans tend to use the term to refer to the ideal of universal enfranchisement, placing emphasis on the political, social and economic realms. Democracy is seen as something to aspire to, rather than something that is practically and realistically attainable. It seems more useful therefore if one is dealing with lived experience to discuss democracy as a verb rather than a noun, as a process of transition occurring over time. This discussion of Kenyan youth, therefore, focuses on democratic transition and is undergirded by several assumptions.[2]

First, the present 'era of democratic transition' is merely one among a series of many other developments. The phrase 'an era of democratic transition' is used herein to refer to any peak period of political activity climaxing in major democratic gains. The discussion of successive eras takes into consideration the interregnums, where the focus is on the incubation and consolidation of the principles undergirding the changes in the status quo. The foundational period preceding the intensity of actual transition is a time of motivation and preparation in which a critical examination of the status quo leads to a demand for an alternative. The aftermath often seems rather flat in comparison to the intensity of the peak period of activity, but it is a necessary time of rest, reflection and consolidation, which gradually gives way to another cycle. It is often difficult to determine precisely when any of these three stages begins or ends, since they tend to flow into each other. The process of transition is determined by the movement of a critical mass of people into and through each particular stage. Nasong'o's discussion of the three stages of social movements (in Chapter 2) is relevant here, although his emphasis is on the leadership of these movements. Caution should also be exercised here since these cycles do not always constitute progress in the move towards democratisation. Rok Ajulu (2001) has shown how the democratisation process in Kenya takes one step forward and three steps backwards.

Secondly, while attention these days is often paid to elections as a marker of 'true' democracy, other issues, such as the right and ability to participate in decision-making forums in other ways beyond voting, must also be taken into account.[3] The phrase 'democratic transition' has generally referred to the process of enabling the interests of all Kenyans to be fairly represented in the governance of the nation. However, representation is only the beginning. Beyond it are issues of participation, which are at the heart of an internal drive for inclusion in social movements agitating for democratic transition. Third, and finally, different ideas of democracy and experiences of democratic transition have existed in the Kenyan past, all of which continue to influence and contribute to the present understandings of the challenge of democratic transition. There is a tendency to view democracy as a new thing, a Western political tradition revolutionising the African way of life. Indigenous political systems are still sometimes portrayed as being limited to two extremes: either authoritarian systems of governance revolving around absolute monarchs, or undeveloped networks of loose alliances in constant danger of lapsing into anarchy. Such generalised descriptions are inaccurate in casting indigenous political systems as primitive frameworks with little relationship to contemporary ideals entailing democratic principles of governance. These political systems are, in contrast, foundational to the lived experience of Kenyans today and, as Simiyu (1987) ably demonstrates, the basis of home-grown democracy.

While present understandings of democracy have been influenced by new ideas coming from elsewhere, they have been equally shaped by indigenous practices existing before the colonial period. Focusing particularly on the legacy of the latter, we argue the importance of taking into account indigenous influences in the present discourses of democracy. As Kenyatta (1978) argues, many indigenous political systems, particularly those of decentralised states, were organised around principles of democratic governance. In his discussion of the political celebration *itwĩka*, Kenyatta emphasises its beginnings as a revolutionary replacement of despotic dictatorship with 'a new order where every section of the community would have a practical part to play in the people's government' (Kenyatta 1978: 198). Fundamental to the 'spirit of *itwĩka*' was what would later be recognised as the manifested guarantor of democracy in Kenya – the 'changing of government in rotation through a peaceful constitutional revolution' (Kenyatta 1978: 196).

Itwĩka could therefore be described as a celebration of the concept of democracy that was instrumental in enabling the regular inauguration of a new generation of political leadership in the Gĩkũyũ community.[4] Kenyatta traces the root of the word '*itwĩka*' to '*twĩka*' which means 'to break away from'. The first *itwĩka* was a revolution culminating in the installation of a new government after the nation 'broke away' from autocracy to institute a system of democracy (Kenyatta 1978: 187). Following this revolution, successive generations took over the responsibilities of political leadership, being inaugurated at each new *itwĩka* ceremony which occurred regularly every quarter century or so. Each new generation took over the leadership of the nation after enacting a constitution that served as a covenant with the rest of the society. Although only a select number of individuals, generally males of a particular generation and social status, were members of the council working out the details of the constitution, they were expected to take care of the interests of the entire community fairly. Only after the transitional ceremony was completed could the governance of the nation pass on to devolved levels of government. The devolution of power transferred authority over specific sections of the community to a series of governing councils. Youth were represented at the senior levels of government by the *njama ya ita* (the council of war) whose members were expected to ensure that the interests of young people were taken into consideration in deliberations.

Two main reasons underlie the use of *itwīka*, as described by Kenyatta (1978), as an example of the performance of pre-colonial forms of democratic governance. First, many Kenyans, no matter their ethnicity or race, have some understanding of this particular political tradition.[5] Secondly, it provides an example of enduring principles that make manifest political traditions as the past recurring with appropriate revision in the present; what Drewal (1991) calls 'repetition with a significant difference'.[6] One such principle of political tradition as a 'changing same' is that of generational politics, common to many indigenous communities preferring decentralised systems of government. Generational groupings make it possible to organise society on the basis of social responsibilities and rights. Each generation, in itself made up of several age groups, passes through four phases: childhood, youth, adulthood and elderhood. In childhood, a generation has negligible influence on policy making, while in youth it is prepared for the responsibilities of leadership through the supervised performance of selected duties. In adulthood, it assumes the leadership of the nation through the performance of delegated authority, finally taking on in elderhood the ultimate socio-political authority, overseeing the smooth running of the nation. Comparatively few individuals ever attain the ultimate levels of elderhood and socio-political authority. Those who do, even when they appear to exercise such authority only sparingly, hold a moral legitimacy beyond any military or other might. It is expected that those who live long enough to do so will have learned to balance the accruing rights of such power with a sense of responsibility to the nation.

By mandating a regular transfer of power from one generation to another at appropriate intervals, nations that used this political system made it difficult for socially irresponsible individuals or groups of people to accumulate too much power or entrench themselves in positions of political power. Generally, generations were offered the incentive of different and socially superior levels of authority and responsibility to motivate them to cede power when the time came to move on. They also had to ensure that they had adequately mentored those who replaced them, since the latter were the ones they had to work most closely with. Religious and moral authority was considered superior to political leadership; thus those in political positions had to be careful to both respect those holding such authority and perform ably so as to ensure their own graduation to religious and moral authority at the appropriate time. Another important feature of this kind of politics was the elevation of the group above the individual. This distributed the responsibilities of governance amongst all those being entrusted with leadership, who were collectively accountable to and for the nation during the tenure of the term they were granted. Individuals could certainly attain positions of 'first among equals' in formulating, articulating, influencing or enforcing policy; they were, however, still expected to conform to an agreed vision.

This generational principle continues to be an important aspect of Kenya's post-colonial period. As shall be demonstrated below, it has influenced the role of youth in contemporary Kenyan politics. It is manifest today in the three generations that have been most politically active in the post-colonial era. These are the Lancaster House Generation, the Lost Generation and the Uhuru Generation. Herein, age remains secondary as a factor in the determination of generational affiliation. Of more significance is the manifest commitment of an individual to the historical mission of a particular generation. Fanon (1963: 169) argues the importance of the identification of a specific historical mission for different generations within the post-colonial context. There has to be significant and practical commitment to a specific vision before it is possible to articulate a historical mission for any generation. As has been observed above, while certain individuals can be instrumental in proposing, articulating and leading each peer group in carrying out the agenda that successfully fulfils the generation's historical mission, it is however the commitment of a critical mass of people to that agenda that determines its success as a generational mission.

The first three decades of Kenyan post-colonial politics were dominated by the generation just emerging on to the political scene in the decade leading up to independence. While Jomo Kenyatta might have been the face of Kenyan independence, he represented an older generation of politicians generally associated with the colonial period who found themselves supplanted by a new generation of political leadership in the decade immediately preceding independence. It was this latter group – those most associated with the deliberations of the Lancaster House conference, thereby earning themselves the identity of the Lancaster House Generation (LHG) – that took on the ultimate responsibility of the consolidation and definition of the newly independent state. The historical mission that the LHG is associated with is the consolidation of the gains of independence as negotiated at the Lancaster House constitutional conferences.[7]

The crown heirs to the LHG have been dubbed 'the Lost Generation' (LG). To some, the adjective 'lost' is an apt description of a generation defined by the loss of the original vision of 'uhuru', which Oginga Odinga memorably articulated as full political, economic and cultural independence beyond the limited political achievements of legal independence (Oruka 1992: 50; Odinga 1966). To others, it connotes the lost opportunities – all that this generation has been prevented from achieving by the greediness of those in the LHG who have effectively maintained their grip on power through most of the first four decades of Kenyan independence. To yet others, it represents the inability of this generation to find or concentrate on its own historical mission. The generation is portrayed as 'lost' since it has focused its energies on completing the historical mission that ought to have been completed by the LHG.

The Uhuru Generation (UG) has only emerged as a distinct entity within Kenyan society in the last few years of the multiparty era, and is therefore yet to make an impact on the nation. It would seem, however, that the UG is anxious to avoid the fate suffered by its predecessor. Rather than wait for definition by default, there has been a concerted effort by its members to identify, articulate and map out a definite mission encompassing a broad-based agenda that competently responds to the present historical context. In contrast to the LG whose members were old enough at the time of independence to have experiential understanding of the colonial period, the UG has no personal engagement with colonialism and interprets itself through the lens of its post-colonial reality. Both the LG and UG are focused on the vision of an ideal: uhuru. Their historical missions are, however, different: whereas the LG is fixated on the recovery of the lost promises of uhuru, the UG looks forward to implementing its unrealised potential.

The idea of youth

Youth is a concept whose use is heavily dependent on context. Many people understand this term in relation to age, which is generally accepted as the most important characteristic in formal delineation of this category (see Barkan 2003, 2004). The confusion that the emphasis on age creates in discourses of youth in Kenya is evident in the discrepancies in statistical information testifying to the inability of those with vested interest in youth issues to set universally acceptable age boundaries. Estimates of the number of Kenyan youth, depending on the age boundaries under consideration, range from as high as 50 per cent of the Kenyan population to somewhere around the 25 per cent mark. Some consider 13-year-olds as 'youth', especially when all those who should be in secondary school or have graduated through rites of initiation from childhood are included in this constituency. Others base their classification on purely pragmatic grounds. Youth Agenda, for example, a leading NGO focusing on making 'youth issues part of the national agenda', considers all those falling between 15 and 40 years of age as youth.[8]

The Kenyan government is also caught up in the challenges of working with age, with differing definitions setting up the potential for conflict in the formulation of youth-specific initiatives. Several government ministries and departments, especially those offering social services such as health and education, have had long-standing youth-specific initiatives. These however are yet to be harmonised. They offer differing definitions, perspectives and understandings of youth and youth issues, reflecting the confusion that attends to state programmes to define, guide, and control youth. This is evident in definitions of this category articulated in the drafts of two important documents slated to become foundational to policy formulation. One of these is the draft of the National Youth Policy, as prepared by the National Youth Policy Steering Committee (NYPSC 2003). Its definition, which 'takes into account the physical, psychological, cultural, social, biological and political definitions of the term', describes a Kenyan youth simply as 'one aged between fifteen and thirty' (NYPSC 2003: 24).[9] This is in contrast to the definition included in the Kenyan draft constitution adopted at the final session of the National Constitution of Kenya Review Commission (CKRC) conference in March 2004 (CKRC 2004). According to Chapter 20 article 307 (30) of that document, youth means the collectivity of all individuals in the republic each of whom: (1) has attained the age of 18 years and (2) has not attained the age of 35 years. It is noteworthy that these definitions were arrived at within the same period with the input of a fairly homogeneous set of stakeholders.

The NYPSC recognition of diverse definitions, especially those emphasising cultural and political understandings, is useful in delineating the role of youth within the political realm. But their commendable intentions are not implemented in this definition in which the social, cultural and even psychological dimensions of the term 'youth' have been largely ignored in favour of biological and physical dimensions. As elsewhere, this leads to the danger of the term 'youth' being unwittingly conflated with terms such as 'adolescent' or 'teenager'. Ultimately this could result in the misrepresentation of the lived experience of this social category. As adolescents, youth are often considered as being too immature to have anything significant to contribute to present discourses of national importance. On this basis, they are therefore marginalised in significant decision-making forums. This is precisely the misperception that youth organisations sought to correct in multiple representations to the CKRC. Their effort led to the inclusion in the draft constitution's bill of rights the provision of adequate opportunities for youth in the social, political, economic and other spheres of national life, including the right of participation in governance. It is important then to seek out alternative ways of conceptualising youth that displace the emphasis on physical immaturity, making it possible for those in this social category to be recognised as partners in, and active contributors to, national development.

The term 'youth' in this chapter is used to denote the transitional stage of life between childhood and adulthood characterised by the transfer of societal responsibilities affirming the change of status from the former to the latter. Youth in this sense bears only incidental relationship to age. Hence the use of such terms as 'Young Turks' and 'party youth wingers' in reference to people over 50 years of age need not raise any eyebrows. The term denotes a social category characterised by pressure to demonstrate allegiance to legitimate authority and to perform capably in service to the wider society. We therefore distinguish between 'young people' – which we use to specifically emphasise age – and 'youth' defined as a social category. We do recognise, however, that these terms are often conflated in public discourse.

Note that this term is often used in the socio-cultural realm to refer not only to individuals but also to generations. It is generally recognised that individuals may graduate into or out of this social category ahead of or after the critical mass of their age group. There have been cases where those with exceptional leadership ability have been allowed to take on the responsibilities of the social category senior to that of their peers. Paul Mboya (1967) observes, for example, that among the Luo, while community leadership was usually the preserve of the elderly, young people who had proven themselves as ready for such responsibility could be appointed to the appropriate positions of authority. This is another reason for arguing against age as the sole definer of this category. As will be seen below, political leadership – especially in times of societal crisis – may be conferred on young people who have demonstrated the ability to take on such responsibilities. They remain young people from a biological or physical consideration, but are no longer considered as youth by society.

The commemoration of the commencement and cessation of youth as a stage of life differs in timing and orientation from one community to another. Specific rites of passage may mark the entry into and out of this period. Some of these important rites of initiation are celebrated accordingly as public occasions emphasising the individual's membership of a community, such as is seen in the annual *basinde* rites among the Isukha. Celebrations of the corresponding *kekebo* rites among the Maragoli mark the transition from childhood of a new age group every decade. On the other hand, emphasis can also be placed on the less visible occasions where privacy gives an initiate the opportunity to reflect on the newly acquired status. This is indeed the hallmark of *kuaikwa*, the period of seclusion enabling the rite of passage from girlhood among the Wadawida. What is common amongst the different expressions of exit out of childhood and into youth is the deliberate taking on of responsibilities by the individual initiate or peer group. Children may be expected to carry out certain duties but are not expected to bear responsibility on behalf of society. Youth, on the other hand, are entrusted with responsibilities on behalf of society, albeit under strict supervision. The transition into full adulthood can only take place after youth have proven themselves as capable of being entrusted with responsibility. Adults are expected to need little, if any, supervision as they undertake such social responsibilities integral to the functioning of the community, such as the nurturing of the human and material resources indispensable to the survival of the society. Adulthood is itself divided into a series of life stages leading to elderhood. Just as cultural understandings of 'youth' can be said to have only incidental correspondence to the number of years, so too is the term 'elder' given to an individual as the recognition of more than the appearance of grey hair as a consequence of a relatively long life.[10]

Two alternatives dominate youth performances of their readiness to 'graduate'. The first is a demonstration of allegiance to legitimate authority in the performance of specific duties associated with the nurture, expansion or protection of the community. Among the Wadawida, for example, newly wedded wives and new mothers, considered *waka* (women), were often assisted in their responsibilities by *wai*, maidens, who, having recently graduated from childhood, were keen to prove their expertise as homemakers or economic entrepreneurs. Similarly, junior ranks of warriors were drawn from young unmarried men who organised themselves under their own leaders, *vishingila*, although they still remained under the authority of *mandu gha waghosi* (councils of elders). These young people were only expected to go through the next rites of passage – in this case, marriage and the establishment of a new home – after successfully demonstrating to society their ability to take on the communal responsibilities that would accompany their rights as adults.

Second, youth demonstrated their readiness for responsibility by taking initiative without waiting to be assigned tasks to carry out. An analysis of many oral narratives specifically directed to youth revolves around a test where the hero, whether female or male, is faced with a choice of some kind. The protagonists in such cases find themselves in a situation where the security of the society or their family is threatened by some outside force, for example some natural disaster or enemy, who could be supernatural or human. This is indeed the catalyst for the unfolding of the conventional plot of the 'ogre' or 'monster' genre of narratives. Those who try to resolve the situation using the 'normal' way of doing so are doomed to fail. In many cases, the elders and adults in the community give in to despair as a result of such failures, forcing youth to take on the challenge of restoring peace in whatever sense it is missing. The 'right' course of action might seem at first glance to be unconventional, but is always guided by principles upholding community values.[11] In many cases, these heroines/heroes have to challenge some kind of illegitimate authority, such as that imposed by brute strength, in their successful pursuit of their objectives. Those who display characteristics such as generosity, kindness, selflessness, thrift and courage are almost always rewarded with graduation to the ranks of adulthood at the end of the narrative. This could explain the common ending of many Kenyan folk tales, which end by 'rewarding' youth protagonists with wealth and marriage. The real value of such an ending is the graduation into womanhood or manhood, societal approval of the protagonist's capability to fulfil her or his role and successfully balance the rights of adulthood with the attendant responsibilities as a woman or man within the community.

Thus, while youth are usually understood to carry out tasks but not bear responsibility on behalf of society, in exceptional circumstances youth take the initiative and fulfil the role of 'saviour' for the ultimate good of the community. Such cases demonstrate that the line between youth as 'social juniors' and adults was constantly susceptible to negotiation and bargaining and is hardly a new development as some analysts suppose (see Diouf 2003: 6). Although rare, periods of extreme societal crisis could actually climax in the early graduation of a generation into the next stage of political life. This happens when those in either 'adulthood' or 'elderhood' stages prove to be unable or unwilling legitimately to discharge their responsibilities to the nation, thereby forcing the following generation to step into the vacuum. A generational transition of power of this nature should not be confused with the otherwise natural elevation of specific precocious individuals into positions of leadership in which they serve as apprentices to those in power, thus preparing the way for their own generation's transition into this stage in due time.

Overall, studies on politics tend to ignore or downplay the contribution of youth who are seen either as purveyors of violence or as victims of poverty (see O'Brien 1996; Honwana 1999; Kaplan 2000; Sharp 2002). According to Diouf (2003: 3), the construction of African youth as a threat or as a problem is symptomatic of a changing society where the status quo is being challenged in important arenas. He identifies in particular the changing relationship between identity and citizenship, the emergence of new forms of inequality, and the transformation of the nature of chronological and psychological passage from youth to adulthood as important phenomena worthy of academic attention. While acknowledging violence as a feature of youth participation in politics, we concentrate on less spectacular performances of youth investment in the political arena. Similarly, the chapter considers the social and economic realities and challenges that youth face not as debilitating impediments to their active participation in society but rather as factors motivating and influencing their engagement in the political arena. This discussion of youth involvement in Kenyan politics with regard to democratic transition privileges their agency, emphasising a dialectical relationship with dominant forces that may appear to control them.

The Makings of a Kenyan Political Tradition

The imposition of colonial rule in Kenya resulted in the systematic erosion of all existing forms of democracy. The colonial authorities operated from the assumption that all African forms of governance were primitive at best and non-existent at worst. They made every effort to replace such political systems with what they thought of as 'civilised rule'. Thus, the first couple of decades following the imposition of colonial rule in Kenya were dominated by a final wave of localised resistance to the new British administration, which was also in effect a battle to retain existing political systems. A couple of decades passed before the majority of indigenous people became aware that they now belonged to a new political entity first established in 1895 and whose boundaries were adjusted in 1902 to their current status. The first era of democratic transition – the initial tangible attempts to institute a measure of democracy in Kenya – could not even begin in earnest until a foundation for a shared identity had been established. It would be inaccurate therefore to talk about Kenyan politics until the majority of its people – those now bearing the identity of Kenyan Africans – began to develop this larger notion of a shared community that transcended ethnic boundaries. This period is significant because it established a foundation for an endogenous political culture.

Since imposition of colonial rule, Kenya's political history has been marked by successive cycles of political transition, each marked by some expansion of democratic space. Each cycle has facilitated the inclusion of hitherto marginalised voices in political forums. Advances are never fully realised in the sense that a hundred per cent participation, even of the focus group, is never achieved. This inevitably leads to the next cycle. Youth have always featured in such periods of transition as active participants, even though their identity as youth has often been subsumed by their allegiance to particular ethnic, racial or social communities.

The first attempt at pushing for the opening of political space occurred in the early 1920s. At this time, a national sense of identity had begun to coalesce amongst the African majority in the country.

This was most manifest in urban centres amongst youth that had acquired some Western education. Elsewhere, ethnic-based organisations like the Young Nyika Association, the Young Kavirondo Association (YKA-a) and the Young Kikuyu Association (YKA-b) were launched among young people, as dissatisfaction with colonial rule gave birth to the beginnings of the nationalist struggle for independence. While these organisations may not have had a long-term perspective in their agenda at the time, they did evolve out of a determination to influence a different kind of relationship with the colonial authority, with consequent benefits to themselves and their communities.

YKA-a grew out of *Piny Owacho*, a grassroots movement among the Luo. *Piny Owacho* can be translated into English as 'the country (or land) says'. *Piny Owacho* represented an alternative moral authority whose social legitimacy enabled the questioning of the might of the colonial regime. YKA-a could therefore be said to have been faithful to the traditional mandate justifying youth resistance to illegitimate authority. Its potential as a serious threat to British rule in this area was only quenched by the intervention of the Christian Missionary Society's resident Archdeacon, Rev. Owens, who was instrumental in its transformation into the relatively harmless Kavirondo Taxpayers Welfare Association (KTPWA). On the other hand, the YKA-b evolved into the East African Association (EAA) under the leadership of Harry Thuku in recognition of the pan-ethnic agenda of its constituents. This was evident in 1922, when the arrest of Harry Thuku resulted in a spontaneous strike by Africans from different ethnic communities working in Nairobi, who gathered outside the Kingsway (now Nairobi Central) Police Station where he was being held, to demand his release. The peaceful demonstration turned violent when police shot at the crowd. The official death toll of 21 Africans was widely disputed by independent observers at the scene, who counted over 200 victims (Thuku 1970; see Chapter 8 by Gimode in this volume).

The political tensions of the 1920s were exacerbated by the publication of the Devonshire White Paper, intended as a comprehensive statement of British intent in Kenya. Although it set out clearly the fundamental principle that 'Kenya is an African territory and that the interests of the indigenous people should be paramount', in reality, it was not designed with the interests of the Africans in mind but rather to forestall the increasing agitation among the Asian communities for equal rights with European settlers. Sir Charles Eliot, the first British Commissioner of the protectorate, puts it best, conceding, '[I]t is mere hypocrisy not to admit that white interests must be paramount, and that the main object of our policy and legislation should be to found a white colony' (cited in Mboya 1986: 47). The European settlers on their part were developing bigger ambitions, dreaming of the establishment of a 'White Man's country' along the lines of independent dominions like Australia and Canada, or even republics like the United States of America.

These years of revolutionary advance represent an era of political transition in Kenya. At this stage of Kenyan politics, different ethnic and racial communities all desired inclusion in the governance of the country, but were less focused on an all-inclusive policy. They understood that inclusion in the political realm would impact in the socio-economic sphere. The colonial government represented an outside authority that even the most influential of the local communities, the European settlers, could not claim to control. Thus, this era is characterised by a jostling for influence among different racial groups, each pushing a reformative agenda, with political activists concentrating on demanding only limited change in governance. While representing the majority in terms of numbers, Africans remained marginalised throughout this era, with no representation and negligible influence in official political forums such as the Legislative Council (Legco) (see Berman 1984). They used alternative spaces as sites for political struggle, most manifest during this period in the socio-economic realm. Here, youth participation was guaranteed since indigenous systems of governance privileging generational structures of authority were generally no longer viable, especially in urban spaces where they did not exist, or in places where the colonial authority had altered or erased traditional structures of governance. Where traditional leadership still held sway having adjusted to the new reality, youth sought alternatives that ranged from direct challenge to the status quo to a quiet assault on its underlying structure. Asians achieved limited success in forcing the opening up of the Legco, although they never did attain equality of numbers or influence therein. Legco remained closed to Africans until 1944 when Eliud Mathu became the first nominated member. It would take over a decade before it admitted its first elected African members, who remained a minority in the House from 1957 until 1960.

Away from the attention-grabbing political activities in urban centres, other important developments were taking place that would greatly impact the coming years. These included the establishment of independent churches and schools that challenged the mission establishments that had been the vanguard of the colonial assault on indigenous social and religious institutions. The Kikuyu Central Association, for example, supported two school groups: the Kenya Independent Schools Association and the Karinga Schools Association, which set up a number of schools that were influential in instilling a revolutionary agenda in a new generation (see Chapter 3 by Gecaga in this volume). So successful was this programme that a teachers' training college was set up at Githunguri in 1939, to fulfil a demand for trained teachers whose pedagogical philosophy supported the political and socio-cultural agenda of the independent schools movement.

These activities built up to the next era of transition that was associated with the State of Emergency, which commenced in 1952. The era itself commenced earlier in a growing swell of unrest manifest in a number of strikes, protests and other forms of resistance to colonial policies. The divide between rural- and urban-based populations became increasingly irrelevant as was demonstrated by the 1938 Ukamba Members Association protest, organised in Nairobi to draw attention to the livestock crisis among the Akamba. The 1939 Taita Hills Association protest organised among the Wadawida spread as far as Mombasa. These climaxed in the devastating general workers' strikes organised by trade unions in Mombasa in 1947 and Nairobi in 1950. The focus on youth involvement in this period is almost always on the violence of the emergency period, which the government blamed on 'the Mau Mau fighters ... ignorant, gullible young people who had been led astray by ruthless African demagogues' (Maloba 1989: 189–90). It is important to note however that

> Mau Mau was the child of economic and social problems which had accumulated over the years and which had not found any solution through constitutional channels ... They were nearly all problems of discrimination against Africans in different forms; discrimination in employment and salaries ... refusal by Government to let Africans grow cash crops ... discrimination in post offices, hotels and restaurants ... discrimination by Government in giving aid to schools and hospitals established on a racial basis; the absence of African representation in the Legislature or of any voice at all in the government; the indirect rule of the African people through chiefs and administrative officers who did not reflect any local African opinion. All these irritations went together to create frustrations which accumulated over the years. There was also the sensitive problem of land. (Mboya 1986: 47)

Underneath the violence that stole media headlines in the fifties, there was steady progress towards a democratic society in the expansion of alternative spaces enabling greater participation on the part of the disenfranchised majority. These included the trade union movement and later Legco, which became instrumental in developing the new generation of leaders who inherited the state in 1963. Among the 'young men in a hurry' (see Mboya 1986; Zeleza 1989) to change the course of the nation as the first elected African representatives to Legco was Tom Mboya, who embodied these two spaces. A leader within the trade union movement at the age of 22 years, Mboya went on to chair the 1958 All Africans People's Conference in Ghana only six years later, challenging misconceptions of African obsession with old age as the defining characteristic of leadership.

The Legco of the fifties was an exciting site, highlighting a generational transition of power whose significance would only become apparent later. What would become known as the LHG was thrust into the political limelight well before its time; forced to fill the vacuum of leadership created in the crisis years of the fifties. The preceding era of democratic transition had been successful in forcing state recognition of Africans as stakeholders in the political realm. However, although the Legco had opened up to African membership in 1944, this was limited to a single nominee. It soon became clear, therefore, that very little had really changed with regard to African participation in influencing state policy. Few Africans regarded the new political elite that was being created with the support of the state as their true leaders.[12] Instead, it was the leadership of the trade union movement and political entities such as the Kenya African Union (KAU) who retained grassroots support. Originally formed as the Kenya African Study Union (KASU) to support the nominated African member of Legco, KAU soon evolved a more radical agenda as its members became frustrated with the impotence of this largely symbolic concession.

Sweeping changes were soon to impact these arenas, bringing with them new leadership. In 1950, the arrests of trade union leaders Fred Kubai and Makhan Singh paved the way for younger leaders such as Mboya. Meanwhile, the moderate leadership of KAU was being replaced or strategically undermined by militants whose advocacy of the more radical agenda of 'uhuru now' involved putting in place measures to support their dream (Anderson 2005). Things came to a head with the imposition of the State of Emergency. 'Almost overnight Kenya's African political leadership (then dominated by the "adult generation" that was leading the political challenge to colonial rule) was put behind bars' (Odinga 1968: 113). Those who survived were paralysed or largely subdued by the draconian measures that followed. In the vacuum that ensued, youth of the LHG emerged to take over the leadership of the economic and political fronts. By the time the Mau Mau war of independence and the State of Emergency were over, the LHG had replaced its predecessor at the helm of the nation. Kenyatta emerged from detention to lead his generation in the performance of their duties as 'elders'. Youth who had begun this period as a generation-in-waiting were now the effective 'adults' in governance. In the coming decades, the authority traditionally associated with eldership would also be gradually transferred to the LHG without a corresponding transfer of status, thus setting the stage for a generational power struggle in the post-colonial era.

Post-Colonial Generational Politics

Just as colonialism occasioned major constraints to people's political participation, independence brought new challenges for youth. The new political context changed some fundamental elements about Kenyan politics, but this had little impact on the political role of youth. Despite several serious political crises, the urgency of a major social upheaval equivalent to that catapulting the LHG into power was not repeated in the post-colonial era. Not only was there no major transition of generational power, but the LHG also refused to transfer power to its juniors in the following years and worked steadfastly to deny the following generation the opportunity to graduate. Part of its strategy became an obsessive 'seek-and-destroy' mission against precocious young individuals who threatened to lead a generational transfer of power. Thus, while a number of young people did distinguish themselves in the political realm in the first three decades of the post-colonial period, youth were relegated to footnote status in political analyses of the Kenyan experience. These politics of exclusion were most glaringly performed in the Ninth Constitutional Amendment of 1968, which in imposing a minimum age of 35 years for the presidency, reinforced the false association of young people with immaturity. Youth became associated in the public imagination with one role: that of *watu wa mkono* (handymen), to be used to actualise the purposes of others.

Tom Mboya's identification of youth as an important human resource to be exploited for 'productive' purposes was a government strategy that was not only articulated in official statements, but also in public policy, as illustrated by the formation of the National Youth Service (see Mboya 1970: 54–5, 106–7). The government saw youth as a vehicle to help propagate its ideas and policies and the philosophy of a new society (Mboya 1963: 58). The new Kenyan government did little to change the oppressive power dynamics and administrative structure that it inherited from the colonial government (Maloba, 1989: 63). In the end, '[d]ecolonisation was essentially about the re-arrangement (and not the total overhaul) of the political structure' (Chazan et al. 1992: 43). Youth were immediately officially relegated to the *watu wa mkono* role that had served the colonial government so well through forced labour. The most visible manifestation of 'youth as *watu wa mkono*' in Kenyan politics during the first three decades of independence was the ubiquitous presence of the party 'youth wings'. These existed on both sides of the political divide and were basically charged with carrying out instructions 'from above'. One of the most interesting facts of these youth wings was their total disregard for age as a determining characteristic for membership. It was not rare to find men over the age of 50 taking an active role in youth wing activities. Older women, on the other hand, tended to join women's party wings.

The Kenya African National Union (KANU) ruled virtually as the sole political party for most of the first four decades of independence. Therefore, it was the KANU youth wing that was most notoriously associated with the abuse of power, which confirmed local associations of youth with violence when it came to political issues.[13] It operated as the de facto police in many parts of the country during its peak, at the climax of President Moi's leadership, with the power to mete out instant (in)justice to anyone who crossed its path (see Amoko 1999). KANU youth wingers were almost never identified as individuals in the public realm. Their red uniforms gave them a faceless identity affirming their marginal role in decision-making forums. While those challenging the status quo may not always have had officially recognised 'youth wings' since they themselves operated underground for most of this period, they did have youth cells that operated on a similar basis. Indeed, it was the advent of multiparty politics that heralded the highest incidences of politically motivated youth violence (Mwagiru et al. 2002: 7). Additionally, there were also unofficial youth wings aligned to different political factions in both ruling and opposition parties. Thus, while the 1991 newspapers are littered with reports of numerous incidents of KANU youth wingers harassing, intimidating or meting out violence against actual or suspected multiparty advocates, those of 1992 focus on battles between rival youth wing factions of different parties. The acrimonious split of the original FORD into the rival FORD–K and FORD–A parties was especially notable in this regard (Mwagiru et al. 2002: 6–7). Ostensibly, each of these youth wings existed to give direction to young people, providing purpose, resources and support so as to harness their energies 'productively'. In reality, they served to protect and consolidate political power bases 'by any means necessary'. While youth may have had limited authority within these wings, they were powerful influences on the Kenyan political scene, since few people dared confront those who controlled them.

From youth wings to private armies

With the arrival of a measure of political accountability in the era of multiparty politics, party youth wings became unfashionable although they did not wholly disappear (see Onyango 2004). As their power and visibility waned, they reconstituted themselves into two categories. On the one hand, there were many vigilante groups bearing names such as *Jeshi la Mzee* (Elder's Army), Kaya Bombo Youth and Baghdad Boys. These names encouraged public association of youth with political violence and in particular with such violence being perpetrated in the service of 'elders'. Each of these groups was generally associated with a political faction or individual, and a significant number were known to be criminal gangs. Anderson (2002: 549–51) gives as examples: *Jeshi la Mzee* (Fred Gumo), *Jeshi la Embakasi* (David Mwenje), *Jeshi la Mbela* (Darius Mbela) and Runyenjes Football Club (Njeru Kathangu). While some were specifically started as political 'support' groups for particular politicians, others either took advantage of the political context to offer their services to particular factions or emerged in response to insecurity, poverty or other needs. These categories are by no means clear-cut or fixed, as is demonstrated by the most well-known of these groups, mungiki, which has been identified with each of these different agendas during its history (see Anderson 2002: 539; Chapter 3 by Gecaga in this volume).

The other heir to the youth wing legacy was the phalanx of sophisticated 'lobby groups' that first emerged in the run-up to the 1992 elections. If the vigilante groups had favoured the stick as their modus operandi, the lobby groups preferred to dangle the carrot. In contrast to the 'goon squad image' of the vigilante groups, the lobby groups presented a highly articulate, well educated and most of all, relatively moneyed face, designed to impress, attract and ultimately motivate Kenyans into voting for their sponsors. Instead of brute force, groups like Youth for KANU '92 (YK '92) refined the culture of 'buying' public support. YK '92 became a conduit for so much (newly minted) money during this election period that the newly issued banknote for Kshs. 500 became informally known as 'Jirongo', the name of the YK '92 chairman. YK '92 was widely credited with KANU's success in the 1992 general elections, becoming the inspiration for myriad other youth groups on both sides of the political divide. Some of the founders and members of such groups may have been motivated by ideological commitment to the particular political philosophies of the parties or individuals they supported. For most, however, it was the flashy personal success of some members of the 'inner circle' of YK '92 that provided the inspiration for their political activities. While not all of the YK '92 members had political ambitions, over ten went on to become government ministers within the next decade, including Cyrus Jirongo and William Ruto, who would play kingpin roles in the final months of the Moi regime.

Emergence of 'Young Turks'

The most influential alternative for youth actors in the post-colonial period was taking up direct apprenticeship to the political heavy-weights of the preceding generations. 'Political sons' such as Katana Ngala, Michael Wamalwa, Musalia Mudavadi, Vincent M'Maitsi, Uhuru Kenyatta, George Khaniri and the brother-duo of Oburu Odinga and Raila Odinga inherited precious capital from their biological fathers in terms of reputation and power base.[14] They joined those who had been crafted into the political bloodline by virtue of ideological commitment, being carefully cultivated, sometimes covertly, as 'leaders of tomorrow'. They were sometimes encouraged to take initiatives in carrying out the broad mandate with which they were associated, but this was always subject to the ultimate approval of their mentors. Those in this category would spend years building a career, patiently working on agendas associated with others already in the national political limelight, thus establishing their own credibility as politicians in their own right. This is the background of those who emerged on to the national political scene as the 'Young Turks' of the Kenyan opposition, including Raila Odinga, Wamalwa 'Kijana', Peter

Anyang' Nyong'o, Mukhisa Kituyi, James Orengo, Gitobu Imanyara and Paul Muite. These politicians who would go on to define the political arena during the multiparty era of democratic transition first made their mark supporting the political agendas of elder statesmen like Jaramogi Oginga Odinga, Masinde Muliro, Kenneth Matiba, Martin Shikuku and Daniel arap Moi. The not-so-young 'Young' Turks ranged between 40 and 50 years at the onset of the multiparty era, but were considered 'youth' in a cultural hierarchy recognising them as the continuation of a political tradition, which clearly defined their status as the legitimate heirs of those with whom they were associated.

The above categories represent the diverse ways in which youth have participated in Kenyan politics as defenders, supporters and messengers of 'elders'. These youth are by no means entirely gullible or mindless followers of hypnotic leaders. Their participation in the political activities of the organisations to which they belong is often a deliberate and well thought out response to the political, social and economic contexts in which they live. Their actions, for better or worse, perform a determined refusal of 'victim' status on the part of both individuals and groups.

One of the interesting twists to emerge in the multiparty era has been the reversal of the 'invisible youth' policy. This was best demonstrated during the 2002 election period where 'youthfulness' became a positive quality for aspiring candidates to flaunt. Whereas youthfulness in post-colonial Kenyan politics had hitherto been equated with political naivety and thus glossed over wherever possible, it now became equated with the push for a new moral order. KANU used the presidential candidature of political novice Uhuru Kenyatta, backed by the best known of YK '92's success stories, to launch its 'Kizazi Kipya, Mwongozo Mpya' (New Generation, New Leadership) campaign. Meanwhile, the 'elders' of the opposition began to highlight their association with their own 'youth brigade'. Candidates who a decade earlier would have attracted only minimal interest in media coverage, such as Yvonne Khamati, Najib Balala, Jackson Mwalulu, Cecily Mbarire and Danson Mungatana, suddenly became the focus of public attention. It is important to note, however, that the apparent integration of youth into the top echelons of the powers that be was, for the most part, largely cosmetic. The visibility of the party youth in the front row of the party line-ups and official policy statements was ultimately revealed to be just another strategy through which youth were used to support the agenda of the party 'elders'. As Yvonne Khamati, who at 22 attracted much attention when she entered the political fray as a parliamentary candidate for Makadara constituency in Nairobi in 2002, was later to observe ruefully, 'When National Alliance Rainbow Council (NARC) came into power, it did not take me long to realise there was little space in the new leadership for the young (to actively participate)' (Onyango 2004: 6).

The overwhelming prevalence of this political tradition where youth in all their diversity serve others has pushed their own alternative agenda to the periphery of public attention. Youth pursuing independent political initiatives have tended to achieve very limited success. Attention, when paid to them, tends to focus on initiatives that have some association with violence. Sharp (2002: 20) observes rightly that non-violent and less spectacular youth initiatives tend to attract minimal attention. It is important, however, to acknowledge such alternative initiatives for two reasons. First, they provide tangible evidence of a political tradition that is becoming more and more visible in the aftermath of the gains of the multiparty transition: the potential of youth to provide legitimate political leadership. Secondly, they offer models for viable non-violent and youth-centric alternatives that could be used to engage situations characterised by the 'violent or victim' reaction to the socio-economic and political realities of particular contexts.

Student political activism

Given the past out of which the present has emerged, it is perhaps inevitable that educational institutions have provided the optimum environment for the imagining of alternatives in the initial stages of the era of multiparty democratic transition. Apart from the historical precedence of such social institutions as nurturing environments for the formation of political positions, they provided ideal spaces within their contemporaneous contexts for the nurturing of alternative ideas that challenge the hegemony of prevailing ideologies. Not only were such institutions dominated by young people, they were also relatively free from the overt policing of political discourse. While the licence for free speech within educational institutions during this period was by no means a blanket endorsement of the right to free public discussion on socio-political issues, the university in particular nurtured provocative intellectual discussion on issues that would have been considered seditious in practically all other public spaces. Universities also provided willing and able mentors in the form of politically committed faculty, many not much older than the students they taught, who fostered lively and vibrant academic debates that provoked young Kenyans into a critical examination of society (see Amutabi 2003; Klopp and Orina 2003; Munene 2003).

The arena of student politics was perhaps the only overt arena of genuine political debate throughout this period. Even during the most repressive years of KANU rule, the government was unable to totally 'destroy the university as a site of potential rebellion', although the state was able to limit its influence to its confines (Murunga 2003: 13–14). University student politics is generally associated in the public imagination with oppositional positions. This was largely the result of government efforts to define those espousing alternative policies like socialism as radical leftists who were unrealistic dreamers in danger of degenerating into national traitors. However, pro-government positions were also always represented and often vigorously defended on campus by articulate student leaders, enabling these sites to offer both theoretical discussions and practical illustrations of the ideas, consequences and practicalities of the ideals of democracy. After all, it would be simplistic to assume that all university students would automatically support progressive processes such as the drive to democracy as defined within a particular era, since university student activism and its popular expression also manifests all the streaks of conformity, treachery, opportunism, cynicism, survival and appropriations of the very instruments of domination for ends that are often personal (see Outa 2004).

The university therefore existed as the location of a complicated political contest pitting pro-government positions against pro-opposition ones, even during the most repressive years of both the Kenyatta and Moi regimes. Take for example the response of the university administration to theatrical performances in 1990 by the Literature Students Association (LSA) at the University of Nairobi (UoN). Following a particularly charged Poetry Night in which student responses to the assassination of foreign minister Dr. Robert Ouko featured prominently, much to the chagrin of the university administration, not only was an immediate ban pronounced on the activities of the LSA but the Literature Department Chair also approached the vice-chancellor of the institution to seek the expulsion of its leadership. The vice-chancellor, however, responded by setting out to recruit these students to the 'other' side, offering them a generous amount of 'slush funds' to persuade them to transfer their loyalties (Outa 2004). This incident reiterates two important facts. First, it shows that even at the end of a decade widely acknowledged to be the most politically repressive of the post-colonial period, alternative sites of political discussion existed that allowed youth of differing perspectives to engage each other while carrying out a dialectical relationship with the regime. Secondly, while this relationship was not one of equals, it is clear that Kenyan youth, even in this period, demonstrated a determined refusal to fall into the 'victim or violent' trap. Instead, the potential for individual decisions to be taken to support or oppose the government demonstrates these students to be significant political players who could not, for better or worse, be ignored by the government.

Although less prominent in the public eye, secondary school students were also active in the risky business of engaging and provoking public debate on national issues. Even more than their older counterparts in universities, secondary school students have tended to be associated with the immaturity of teenage adolescence and childish naughtiness, and are therefore assumed to have little understanding of national politics. Evidence of the investment of young people of this age in national politics has been regularly provided at the annual Kenya National Schools and Colleges Drama Festivals (KNSCDF), part of the national school calendar since its inception in the early fifties. Students have taken advantage of the platform provided through the festivals to articulate their concerns on national issues. A careful examination of the Kenyan society has become the hallmark of the festival. Political issues tend to dominate the festivals, enabling festival observers to use each annual festival to gauge grassroots opinion on the most volatile issues of the day. Popular themes of the last couple of decades include the land/ethnic clashes, worsening economic situation, abuse of political office, and numerous presidential commissions on issues such as the constitution, land, devil worship and political assassinations. Attempted government censorship of the content of the festival entries, especially in the latter part of the eighties, was difficult to enforce as most schools simply opted to translate much of the most provocative interventions into non-verbal language.

Religious institutions also provided the environment for youth to imagine alternatives to the political realities of the day. The government found it difficult to harass religious leaders and institutions, especially those affiliated with powerful organisations such as the National Council of the Churches of Kenya (NCCK) and the Kenya Episcopal

Conference (KEC), creating a kind of safe haven for religio-political expression. But even 'illegal' religious movements such as Mungiki and the unregistered Islamic Party of Kenya commanded a moral legitimacy in the eyes of their followers, even conferring on them, at least for a period of time, some public sympathy. Anglican Bishop Alexander Muge, Sheikh Balala and other outspoken spiritual leaders became heroes to younger Kenyans looking for role models. Indigenous religious organisations such as the Akorino and *Hema ya Ngai wi Mwoyo* (Tent of the Living God) also thrived as forums where youth questioned state injustice. While youth were not always in the lime-light in these forums, they found in them the space for the formulation of revolutionary agenda that was supported by a moral legitimacy overriding that offered by the status quo.

The above social institutions continued the radical political tradi-tion, nurturing the development of positions that would influence the future, even as they made important interventions in the present. Both individuals and groups emerged from the educational and religious institutions with political positions and experience that would radically influence the nation. For example, Kenyans first heard of (Philomena) Chelegat Mutai as the editor of the UoN student paper *University Platform*, which in 1972 vigorously protested police brutality against students. Two years later, Mutai was elected to parliament as its youngest female member, making it clear from the onset that she was not there to serve anyone else's interest apart from those of the people she represented. Until a politically engineered imprisonment in 1976, Mutai fought an increasingly lonely battle as one of the few isolated 'voices of reason' in the third parliament (Murunga 2003: 15; see Chapter 6 by Nasong'o and Ayot in this volume).

The case of religio-cultural movements like *Hema ya Ngai wi Mwoyo* and Mungiki is discussed in this volume (Chapter 3) by Gecaga. Two other sites of intervention particularly worth mention-ing in this regard despite the KANU government's ultimate success in containing them are the print media and the junior ranks of the mili-tary. Among activities both the Kenyatta and the Moi governments labelled as 'seditious' was the publication and circulation of political literature in the alternative press tradition of colonial period youth. Then, Jomo Kenyatta, Achieng' Oneko and Oginga Odinga, and Paul Ngei had used their publications *Mūigwithania*, *Ramogi* and *Uhuru Wa'Afrika*, respectively, to provoke discussion of pressing political issues and court support for a radical political agenda. Similarly, underground publications emerged in independent Kenya to provide a site for questioning the status quo. Publications such as *Pambana* and *Mpatanishi* introduced Kenyans in the eighties to the revolutionary agendas of the December Twelve Movement, *Mwakenya*, the February Eighteenth Revolutionary Movement and other underground organisations, some of which espoused change by any means necessary. Youth provided the overwhelming membership for these radical groups, which despaired of ever changing Kenyan society through conventional means as it became increasingly clear in the post-independence years that the ideal of democracy had not been achieved with the attainment of majority rule.

A New Era, A New Focus? The LHG, LG and UG Struggles

The pressing need for change is primarily articulated in most analyses of the transition period as the drive towards 'true' multiparty democracy. Arguably however, the multiparty era of transition was equally a struggle for generational transfer of political responsibility. The 1992 multiparty elections heralded the possibility of true multiparty democracy, but the LHG was as firmly ensconced in power as it had been during the historic 1961 elections. The leading presidential candidates of that election – Daniel arap Moi, Oginga Odinga, Kenneth Matiba and Mwai Kibaki – were all members of the LHG and had all served at cabinet levels in previous governments. All but Matiba had held the vice-presidency. As argued above, the LHG used the first years of independence to consolidate its hold on power by gradually shifting the ultimate socio-political authority, traditionally the domain of elderhood, to adulthood. It thus effectively sidelined the generation that had preceded it within the first decade of independence, so that Kenyatta and his peers were effectively little more than figureheads by the end of their first decade in power. Over the years as its members age physically, the LHG has attempted to resurrect the division between the social categories of 'elderhood' and 'adulthood' to facilitate the retention of the moral authority to societal leadership even as it reluctantly cedes the governance of the nation to the LG. Under the leadership of Mwai Kibaki, the original submission of the Democratic Party of Kenya to the Ufungamano Initiative (the 'People's Commission') with regard to the review of the Kenyan constitution advocated the inauguration of a Council of Elders, slated to become the ultimate moral authority over the nation. This particular proposal was overturned by those who argued that to institute such a Council of Elders would in effect return to power 'by the back door' the very leaders Kenyans were doing their best to get rid of. Unsure that it can successfully manage a transition while holding on to ultimate social authority, the LHG has remained reluctant to consign itself to political irrelevancy and thus resists handing over the leadership of the nation to the LG. This in turn has precipitated an increasingly hostile generational battle for power.

From this perspective, the transition of power from Moi to his peer Kibaki was not really the transfer of political responsibility that many had hoped for; the LHG successfully maintained the status quo. It did not pass unnoticed in political circles that while the LG was able by sheer force of numbers to take over national leadership by dominating political positions in both the ruling coalition and opposition parties, the LHG retained control of the presidency and other influential positions that oversaw crucial sectors such as the economy. Kibaki's first government retained the powerful finance portfolio in the hands of the LHG in the appointments of both minister and permanent secretary as well as other important civil service positions, such as the offices of the auditor general and the comptroller of State House, even though civil servants such as Auditor General Daniel Njoroge and Permanent Secretary Francis Muthaura had already passed the age of mandatory retirement. The appointment of LHG's 76-year-old Moody Awori to the post of national vice-president following the death of Michael Wamalwa in 2003 was a further setback for the LG. Similarly, the inclusion of several LHG stalwarts in the cabinet in the first NARC cabinet reshuffle in June 2004 was greeted in the LG ranks with consternation. In naming what he styled 'a government of national unity' Kibaki dropped all pretence to coalition loyalties, naming generational compatriots such as Njenga Karume and Simeon Nyachae to the cabinet despite the fact that they were opposition members of parliament. In turn, these LHG leaders ignored the dismay of their parties who loudly protested these appointments on the grounds that their members, vocal government critics only days before their appointments, had not as much as consulted with the rest of their party leadership before accepting the posts.[15]

At the same time, Kibaki demoted or significantly watered down the responsibilities of some of the more militant cabinet members of the LG, promoting in their place those of their peers widely perceived as amenable to the *watu wa mkono* tradition of deference to those they perceived as their elders. For example, Labour Minister Ali Makwere, who had demonstrated his loyalty to Kibaki (and the LHG) by opposing his own party's (the Liberal Democratic Party) policy on the explosive issues of internal coalition politics, was rewarded with the plum Foreign Affairs position at the expense of party mate Kalonzo Musyoka, who had emerged as a direct alternative to Kibaki's candidacy for the presidency. Musyoka was moved from Foreign Affairs to the less prestigious Environment portfolio. Raila Odinga, widely regarded as the LG's most prominent politician, was stripped of responsibility for Housing and left with the reduced portfolio of Roads and Public Works. The cabinet reshuffle was no aberration; it became just another example of the Kibaki administration's broken promises with regard to the radical aims of generational transfer of power.

The question of who holds ultimate political power in Kenya is not merely a concern of the present, a battle between the two generations now in the political limelight. This inter-generational struggle for social legitimacy also has implications for those currently on the sidelines. Sooner or later the political future of the UG will be determined by the outcome of this present tussle. The strategy it chooses could well be instrumental in deciding when it attains socio-political legitimacy in its own right. So how will the UG respond to the challenge facing it? It could, of course, do nothing, leaving the LHG and LG to resolve the situation. However, doing nothing, whether as a deliberate choice or not, leaves the UG in the most vulnerable of positions, since it would then remain at the mercy of whoever wins the generational war, thereby running the very real risk of becoming the next 'lost' generation.

Conversely, the UG could choose to support the agenda of the LG in the hope that doing so would hasten its own graduation into a position of socio-political responsibility. It can be argued that unless it positions itself strategically as significant allies to the LG in this crucial battle, it might as well resign itself to remaining a generation-in-waiting for at least another 20 years. After all, after so many years in limbo, the LG is hardly likely to be in any hurry to cede power to anyone, unless it can be encouraged to do so by the obligation of coalition responsibilities. The UG could alternatively choose to enter into partnership with the LHG and actively support a return of historical understandings of the roles of 'elders', 'adults' and 'youth'. This option would allow the LHG to retain ultimate socio-political authority over the nation even as it cedes to the LG the daily administration of government, while legitimising the UG as heirs to be mentored and entrusted with forms of apprenticeship allowing a measure of responsibility.

These two options, however, do not necessarily guarantee an expansion of the political space for youth. Without a clear understanding of the inherent right of youth to participate actively and at all times in the political realm, there is a danger that the UG would find itself relying on the goodwill of others, which may only grant youth a limited measure of political expression whose boundaries are strictly delineated. It must be remembered too that the history of post-independence coalition agreements in Kenya, ranging from watering down the *Majimbo* (regional) constitution to the ill-fated NARC Memorandum of Understanding is scarcely one that builds confidence in covenants guaranteed purely by honour and good faith.

There is yet another alternative that allows the UG proactively to negotiate alliances with both the LHG and the LG, placing itself and its own needs at the centre of the debate. It is significant that UG discourses of the last five years have emphasised the possibility of a new socio-political landscape. This discourse engages the logic of a strict delineation of roles that limits social categories to the performance of specific duties. It specifically re-examines classifications of youth, which rely solely on age as the defining determiner of this category, and acknowledges the relationship between the physical, social, cultural and political dimensions that complicates attempts at definition. The discourse notes that youth, who are otherwise today recognised to be mature enough to undertake other responsibilities associated with democracy such as voting and membership of political parties, have been denied full rights of participation by effective if not legal exclusion in the realm of political leadership. It therefore insists on a full recognition of the right of youth to participate fully as youth in all aspects of political life. This is in line with other youth discourses in the continent that 'present a challenge to the construction of youth as a period of "life on hold" … the conception of a life that must be prepared and supervised by adults' (Diouf 2003: 6). It is in fact, an illustration of Diouf's (2003: 6) argument of youth at the vanguard of a

> new trajectory [that] could be summed up as a radical transformation of the idea of citizenship, together with the conflation of the domestic and public spheres, the production of new forms of identification which appeals to multiple resources, and a refashioning of the indices and signs of autochthony and membership, of inclusion and exclusion.

Rather than throw its weight behind the agenda of either the LG or the LHG, it appears that the discourse of the UG imagines a new political landscape where the nation's 'youth' are now recognised as participants with equal rights to all others in the practice of democracy.

This alternative seeks to challenge the insistence of either the LHG or the LG on retaining ultimate political leadership of the nation, by offering the UG as credible participants in the political leadership of the nation (Mue 2000). While one might expect the UG to challenge the very existence of the social categories such as 'youth', 'elder' or 'adult' in this political discussion, it is interesting that instead, this generation has been associated with the affirmation of these social categories. In other words, the actions of the UG challenge the belief that the present struggles of African youth against the status quo perform a 'refusal to be embedded in the memory of the state and the nation … [and] a rejection of communitarian … and family memory' (Diouf 2003: 6). Indeed, while youth in Kenya reject the conception of their life as 'on hold', waiting for a tomorrow that never seems to come, they are conscious of and seek to build on the positive dimensions of the past, even if that past was misused by the rhetoric of the nationalist and first-generation leaders. One finds therefore a critical engagement that pushes for a re-examination of this social category, affirming its value as a conceptual tool enabling different levels of political engagement for Kenyan youth.

Conclusion

Given the gerontocratic nature of Kenyan politics, youth as a social category has traditionally been viewed as a burdensome category that needs to be 'carefully handled' and whose energies need be channelled to 'productive' endeavours ostensibly by elders and more 'responsible' members of society. As the foregoing analysis amply illustrates, however, this situation is beginning to change. The period 1990–2005 has brought to the fore an aggressive youth discourse that has rejected prevailing perceptions of youth and demanded a reconfiguring of the social roles and responsibilities of this category especially as pertains to the political realm. This chapter has traced the evolution of this discourse, locating its genesis in indigenous political cultures that have continued to evolve in the creation of an endogenous understanding of democracy in Kenya.

Challenging existing definitions that exclude youth from the possibility of leadership has opened up a new front in the push towards democratic transition. In insisting on retaining the category 'youth' while expanding the possibilities of the role to include leadership in the sense hitherto reserved for the social categories of 'adult' and 'elders', the youth have entered into alliance with other marginalised communities such as women and pastoralists. Accordingly, identities that were once highlighted for the purposes of exclusion are today being celebrated as reasons for inclusion and sometimes are even fronted in demands for affirmative action that seeks to redress historical and other injustices. Instead of automatic 'graduation' into honorary 'adulthood', 'male' or 'settled' identities, Kenyans from these categories are now claiming social legitimacy as significant political players in their own right. Clearly, this signifies yet another transition period between eras of democratic transition. We look forward to seeing what new levels of political participation this new era will enable.

Notes

1. 'Post-colonial' serves in this chapter purely as a chronological indicator. Similarly, the term 'independence' is used solely in relation to the political event of legal political independence achieved in 1963.
2. In Africa, the two scholars who have emphasised that democracy is a process rather than an event are Claude Ake (1996) and Ernest Wamba-dia-Wamba (1992).
3. For a critical look at elections, see Said Adejumobi (2000). In fact, Claude Ake (1996) goes further by arguing that elections in the multiparty era have disempowered the masses since the conditions under which they vote force them to vote without choosing. The result, as Ihonvbere (1996) argues, is the creation of democratic dictators whose 'legitimacy' is periodically endorsed by election monitors.
4. *Itwīka* was last celebrated among the Gīkūyū in the second-last decade of the nineteenth century. In 1925, the colonial government brought the ceremonies that were only just commencing to an end by labelling the artistic performances at the centre of this rite of generational transition as seditious activities, thus effectively cancelling the inauguration of the new generation.
5. *Facing Mount Kenya*, first published in 1938, was the first internationally acclaimed and academically recognised 'insider' perspective or auto-ethnography from the perspective of a Kenyan scholar. It has remained a landmark text in post-independence school and tertiary curricula in several disciplines, ensuring its availability and wide circulation among Kenyans of all ethnic and racial backgrounds.
6. 'Tradition' is neither static nor a phenomenon of the past (in contrast to the present). It is a constantly evolving continuity linking the past to the future, what Paulin Hountondji (2002) refers to as a 'transmission from the past to the present'.
7. These conferences resulted in the compromise independence constitution that would be constantly renegotiated in the coming years, reflecting the continuing disagreements as to what these gains actually were.

8. Interview with Danny Irungu, Youth Agenda Programme Co-ordinator, 2002. Youth Agenda focuses their activities on the 18–35-year-old bracket as this is the optimum target age range for its priorities.

9. According to the NYPSC, this translates to 9.2 million Kenyans, constituting 32 per cent of the population and 60 per cent of the workforce.

10. The Kiswahili term often translated into English as elder, '*mzee*', is often used today as a term of respect for one recognised as having 'achieved' success – whether this be in terms of wealth or political power. It is not uncommon to find older people referring to their much younger employer as *mzee*. An equation of 'elder' with 'old one' may therefore be inaccurate, depending on the context.

11. For example, in one such tale from the Wadawida, the protagonist, an adolescent, becomes the latest of a greedy ogre's abductees. As it makes the long journey back to its lair where it intends to eat her, she apologises for being so heavy, suggesting that the ogre might want to take rest since it must be very tiring to have to carry her all the way. When it agrees and stops for a while, she offers to groom its hair while it rests. The ogre accepts, because unlike all its other victims, she is unfailingly polite and seems to have resigned herself to her fate. Her gentle ministrations accompanied by the lullaby she sings as she tends to its tangled and dirty hair lulls the ogre to sleep. In the meantime, she plaits the hair firmly to the tough *kinya-ng'ombe* grass on which they are resting. The ogre awakens to find itself captive, unable to move while she makes a sharp stake which she then uses to kill it.

12. As Odinga (1968: 156) reminded other members of Legco, those in detention or jail 'before they were arrested, were the political leaders of the Africans in the country and Africans respected them as their political leaders, and even at this moment, in the hearts of the Africans, they are still the political leaders'.

13. Ironically, the party's Secretary General Tom Mboya had argued even in the euphoria of independence that the party had to take the responsibility of ensuring that the youth in its youth wing remained disciplined citizens who were well looked after and not exploited by 'quarrelling leaders' to carry out 'jobs that are not necessarily in the party's [or country's] interests' (1986: 91, 93).

14. Apart from Margaret Kenyatta, who served as Nairobi's mayor in the sixties, no other 'political daughter' has emerged as a household name on the same scale, although there have been a handful of other female politicians also associated with political families. In order to differentiate offspring from parent, political sons tend to be referred to by their first names instead of the family surnames associated with their fathers. Hence, Kenyans generally refer to Uhuru, Raila or Musalia instead of Kenyatta, Odinga or Mudavadi.

15. At the time of his appointment to the cabinet as a member of Kibaki's new 'government of national unity', for example, Simeon Nyachae was still – on paper at least – the leader of the Coalition of National Unity, the opposition coalition formed the previous year with KANU.

References

Adejumobi, S. (2000) 'Elections in Africa: A Fading Shadow of Democracy', *International Political Science Review*, vol. 21, no. 1.

Ajulu, R. (2001) 'Kenya: One Step Forward, Three Steps Back: The Succession Dilemma', *Review of African Political Economy*, no. 88.

Ake, C. (1996) *Democracy and Development in Africa*, Washington, DC: The Brookings Institution.

Amoko, A. (1999) 'The Missionary Gene in the Kenyan Polity: Representations of Contemporary Kenya in the British media', *Callaloo*, vol. 22, no. 1.

Amutabi, M. (2003) 'Crisis and Student Protest in Universities in Kenya: Examining the Role of Students in National Leadership and the Democratisation Process', *African Studies Review*, vol. 45, no. 2: 157–78.

Anderson, D.M. (2002) 'Vigilantes, Violence and the Politics of Public Order in Kenya', *African Affairs*, vol. 101, no. 405: 531–55.

_____ (2005) *Histories of the Hanged: The Dirty War in Kenya and the End of Empire*, New York, NY: W.W. Norton.

Barkan, J.D. (2003) 'New Forces Shaping Kenyan Politics', *Africa Notes*, no. 18.

_____ (2004) 'Kenya after Moi', *Foreign Affairs*, vol. 83, no. 1.

Berman, B. (1984) 'Structure and Process in the Bureaucratic States of Colonial Africa', *Development and Change*, vol. 15.

Chazan, N. et al. (1992) *Politics and Society in Contemporary Africa*, Boulder, CO: Lynne Rienner.

CKRC (2004) *Draft Constitution*, Nairobi: CKRC.

Diouf, M. (2003) 'Engaging Postcolonial Cultures: African Youth and Public Space', *African Studies Review*, vol. 6, no. 2: 1–12.

Drewal, M.T. (1991) *Yoruba Ritual: Performers, Play, Agency*, Bloomington, IN: Indiana University Press.

Fanon, F. (1963) *The Wretched of the Earth*, Hammondsworth: Penguin.

Honwana, A. (1999) 'Negotiating Post-War Identities: Child Soldiers in Mozambique and Angola', *CODESRIA Bulletin*, nos 1–2.

Hountondji, P. (ed.) (1997) *Endogenous Knowledge: Research Trails*, Dakar: CODESRIA.

_____ (2002) *The Struggle for Meaning: Reflections on Philosophy, Culture, and Democracy in Africa*, Athens: Ohio University for International Studies.

Ihonvbere, J. (1996) 'Where is the Third Wave? A Critical Evaluation of Africa's Non-transition to Democracy', *Africa Today*, vol. 43, no. 4.

Kagwanja, P.M. (2006) '"Power to *Uhuru*": Youth and Generational Politics in Kenya's 2002 Elections', in *African Affairs*, vol. 105, no. 418: 51–75.

Kaplan, R.D. (2000) *The Coming Anarchy: Shattering the Dreams of the Post Cold War*, New York, NY: Random House.

Kenyatta, J. (1978 [1938]) *Facing Mount Kenya*, Nairobi: Kenway Publications.

Klopp, J.M., and J.R. Orina (2003) 'University Crisis, Student Activism, and the Contemporary Struggle for Democracy in Kenya', *African Studies Review*, vol. 45, no. 1: 43–76.

Maloba, W. (1989) 'Nationalism and Decolonisation', in W.R. Ochieng' (ed.), *A Modern History of Kenya 1895–1980: In Honour of B.A. Ogot*, Nairobi: Evans Brothers.

Mboya, P. (1967) *Kitgi gi timbegi: A Hand book of Luo Customs.* Nairobi: Equatorial Publishers.

Mboya, T. (1963) *Freedom and After*, Nairobi: East African Educational Publishers.

———— (1970) *The Challenge of Nationhood: A Collection of Speeches and Writings*, Nairobi: East African Educational Publishers.

Mue, N. (2000) 'The Uhuru Generation: Taking a Stand on High Ground!', in *2000 Kenya Community Abroad Conference*, St Paul, July.

Munene, I. (2003) 'Student Activism in African Higher Education', in D. Teferra and P.G. Altbach (eds.), *African Higher Education: An International Reference Handbook*, Bloomington, IN: Indiana University Press.

Murunga, G. (2003) 'Thinking Through the Crisis of Radicalism', in *CODESRIA East Africa Sub-Regional Conference*, Addis Ababa, October.

Mwagiru, M., et al. (2002) *Facts About Majeshi ya Wazee*, Nairobi: Freidrich Ebert Stitfung.

National Youth Policy Steering Committee (NYPSC) (2003) 'Draft of the National Youth Policy', *East African Standard*, 21 November: 24–5.

O'Brien, C. (1996) 'A Lost Generation: Youth Identity and State Decay in West Africa', in Richard Werbner and Terence Ranger (eds), *Postcolonial Identities in Africa*, London: Zed Books.

Odinga, O. (1968 [1966]) *Not Yet Uhuru*, London: Heinemann.

Onyango, D. (2004) 'Driven by ambition', *East African Standard*, 3 July.

Oruka, Odera H. (1992) *Oginga Odinga: His Philosophy and Beliefs*, Nairobi: Initiatives Publishers.

Outa, O.G. (2004) 'Telling the Story: Two Decades of Theatre at the University of Nairobi', in *Popular Theatre in Modern Kenya's Lecture Series*, Nairobi, August.

Thuku, H. (1970) *Harry Thuku; An Autobiography*, Nairobi: Oxford University Press.

Sharp, L.A. (2002) *The Sacrificed Generation: Youth and the Colonized Mind in Madagascar*, Berkeley, CA: University of California Press.

Simiyu, V. (1987) 'Democratic Practice in Traditional African Societies' in W.O. Oyugi, et al. (eds), *Democratic Theory and Practice in Africa*, Nairobi: Heinemann.

Wamba-dia-Wamba, E. (1992) 'Beyond Elite Politics of Democracy in Africa', *Quest*, vol. 6, no. 1.

Zeleza, T. (1989) 'The Establishment of Colonial Rule', in W.R. Ochieng' (ed.), *A Modern History of Kenya 1895–1980: In Honour of B.A. Ogot*, Nairobi: Evans Brothers.

6

Women in Kenya's Politics of Transition and Democratisation

Shadrack Wanjala Nasong'o and Theodora O. Ayot

Introduction

This chapter focuses on women in the politics of transition and demo-cratisation in Kenya. It argues that while the participation of women in Kenya's political arena and decision-making processes goes back to the period prior to colonisation, their systematic political marginalisation has roots in the colonial legacy that is actively perpetuated by the post-colonial political elite. Indeed, after the achievement of independence in 1963, the establishment of a political system based on authoritarian and over-centralised state structures engendered male dominance in all aspects of Kenyan society. These structures of leadership denied women the chance to develop strategic initiatives and blocked all channels that would have given women a visible political voice. They prevented them from mainstreaming their own political agendas through politi-cal negotiations and procedures that would have enabled them to enhance their bargaining power in the national political process.

Beginning with a theoretical conceptualisation of the key terms, the chapter identifies five major political transitions in Kenya, all of which have had serious implications for the role of women in politics. The chapter proceeds from the premise that the establishment of colo-nial rule in Kenya, as elsewhere in Africa, was carried out through force and intimidation, which in turn produced a culture of violence. It is this culture that reinforced the authority of the colonisers over the

colonised people and, in the process of its application, further reinforced the authority of African men to the disadvantage of African
women. Though the struggle for independence in Kenya witnessed
equal participation of women and men, the emerging post-colonial
authoritarian political system relegated women to the back seat of
political life. But despite the existing obstacles and challenges, some
women continued to struggle to highlight women's and gender issues,
and to penetrate the male-dominated political arena.

This chapter also argues that although the process of democratisation
of the 1990s and Kenya's transition from the entrenched Kenya African
National Union (KANU) regime to the National Alliance Rainbow
Coalition (NARC) government following the December 2002 elections
has expanded the space and opportunities for women's political participation, women still face gigantic obstacles associated with the social
division of labour in the country and the construction of the political
arena as a male domain. In the final section of the chapter, we identify
and analyse these obstacles in the light of the theoretical assumptions.
Overall, the gist of this chapter's thesis is that given their demographic
superiority, women's effective participation in the political process,
especially in the policy-making institutions of governance, is critical
to the prospects for a truly democratic political dispensation and
meaningful socio-economic transformation in Kenya.

Theoretical and Conceptual Issues

National legislatures are the basic institutions within which laws governing contemporary societies are made as well as the site where national
priorities on public revenue expenditure, development funding and
allocation of national resources, both material and symbolic, are determined. Accordingly, representation of the various diversities of any
given state in this institution is critical to a wholesome policy-making
process and, ipso facto, to democratic practice. Yet a glance at available statistics on women's representation in national legislatures
around the world presents a dismal picture. In terms of regional aver-
ages, the Americas lead the world in women's representation as of 31
January 2006 with an average of 20.1 per cent, followed by Europe,
18.4 per cent; Sub-Saharan Africa, 16.6 per cent; Asia, 15.9 per cent;
the Pacific, 13.9 per cent; with the Arab states coming in last at 6.8 per
cent (IPU 2006). According to the Inter-Parliamentary Union (IPU)

2006 ranking of 187 countries in terms of women's representation in parliament, five African countries rank among the top twenty. These are Rwanda, the world's first, with 48.8 per cent, Mozambique in the 10th position with 34.8 per cent, South Africa in the 14th position with 32.8 per cent, Burundi in the 18th position with 30.5 per cent and Tanzania in the 19th position with 30.4 per cent. These countries are closely followed by Namibia in the 25th position with 26.9 per cent and Uganda in the 33rd position with 23.9 per cent. Kenya is placed 114th in the world and 44th in Africa with a paltry 7.6 per cent women's representation in parliament.

The above reality raises a fundamental question as to the impact of the wave of the 1990s democratisation in Africa. What difference has it made to gender dynamics and women's representation in political processes in the democratising countries? To answer this question, we conceptually premise the chapter on a very simple argument: 'When the composition of decision-making assemblies is so markedly at odds with the gender make-up of the society they represent, this is clear evidence that certain voices are being silenced and suppressed' (Phillips 1992: 88). Given the above statistics and the key role of parliament as the principal policy-making institution of any given state, this innocuous observation calls for a re-examination of mainstream political thought and practice. For the purposes of this study, two key concepts, 'gender' and 'state', need to be conceptualised and theorised, especially in their relation to gender dynamics and political processes.

Conceptualising gender

The need for a theoretical framework that integrates gender dynamics into the analysis of female and male political actors cannot be gainsaid. As Phillips (1992) warns, under the seemingly innocent guise of gender neutrality, masculinity defines the terms of political theory and practice. One perspective that seeks to theorise the differential roles of men and women in society proceeds from the premise that gender is a social construct. In this view, cultural socialisation experiences transmitted through parents, schools, peers and the media orient girls towards 'feminine' mothering and wifely roles while encouraging boys into 'masculine' roles that include being aggressive and ambitious and venturing into the world beyond the domestic arena. Such stereotypical expectations of the sexes, which are held by men and internalised by women, help to perpetuate gender inequalities in society (Hunt 1990; Walker 1990; Hansen 1992). These role socialisation theorists hold that notions of patriarchal gender ideologies that emphasise maternal altruism and wifely duties for women and men's right to women's service and nurturance as well as to control over their reproductive capacities would all predict the performance of women and men who decide to participate in politics.

The second conceptual approach that seeks to go beyond the role socialisation theory is the institutional perspective. Taking cognisance of the great effect that gender exerts on individual lives and social interactions, some feminist theorists view it as a social institution in and of itself. West and Zimmerman (1987: 137), for example, perceive gender as an institutional and interactional enterprise whose 'idiom is drawn from the institutional arena in which [social] relationships are enacted'. They define gender as 'the activity of managing situated conduct in light of normative conceptions of attitudes and activities appropriate for one's sex category'. Thus West and Zimmerman conceptualise gender as a 'routine, methodical, recurring accomplishment', which is produced through interpersonal interactions. In other words, individual women and men 'do gender' largely on account of being hostages to its production. Whereas earlier theories locate gender in the individual, the institutional/macrostructural perspective locates it in the integral dynamic of social order, outside the individual. As Lorber (1994: 6) writes: 'The gendered microstructure and the gendered macrostructure reproduce and reinforce each other. The social reproduction of gender in individuals reproduces the gendered societal structure; as individuals act out gender norms and expectations in face-to-face interaction, they are constructing gendered systems of dominance and power.'

Whilst the above conceptualisation is rooted in Western gender epistemologies that view gender theory as explaining the universal oppression of women, some theorists argue that what females in one society think, act and live can differ enormously from what females in another society learn. In fact, '... there can be very significant differences within a given society' (Fouche 1994: 79). Attention must therefore be paid to the nuances of gender relations, which manifest variable factors in different societies and may in turn inform gender discourse in different contexts. Most African theorists of gender concur, for instance, that even the tag 'women' as it has been deployed by Western feminism to imply universal unity and similarity of female experience is misleading.

The idea of women having a common enemy in men passes under the notion of sisterhood, but as contributors to Oyewùmí's (2003) study show, there is no universal sisterhood of women. They go on to question the analytical value of the notion of gender for African realities, seeking instead to replace it with the more culturally relevant idea of motherhood. They contend that though Western feminism has taken remarkable strides in dealing with patriarchy and sexism, it has failed to transcend its own internal forms of exclusion along racial and class lines. As a result, differences along class and racial lines have been perpetuated and reinforced even when Western feminists seek support for their political agenda on the basis of a unified gender category of biological females (see Amadiume 1987; Oyewùmí 1997; Nzegwu 2001; Lung'aho 2002; Murunga 2002).

For purposes of this analysis, we conceptualise gender as a socially constructed reality whose maintenance and practice manifests in personal identities and in interactions in the social realm. It is, as Lorber (1994) notes, an institution that establishes patterns of expectations for individuals, orders the social processes of everyday life and is built into the major social organisations of society. The implications of theorising gender from this institutional perspective are significant. First, the institutional character of gender and the gendered character of the institutions facilitate our analysis in understanding its pervasiveness and the power relations in any given social setting. Second, because such conceptualisation takes into account the micro as well as the macro aspects of gender relations, it allows for a comprehensive and perspicacious examination of the material forces at work in the process of women's quest for empowerment and their capacity to organise in a male-dominated world.

Unlike much of Western feminism, however, our task is not to simply delineate and bemoan the 'subordination and marginalisation' of women, but to highlight and assess their contribution in the pre-colonial societies, their role in the struggles for decolonisation, and their ardent participation in the push for democratisation, before analysing the ways in which they have not shared equally in the fruits of their struggles. We recognise women do not constitute a homogeneous group as there are many women who have provided the female face of a largely patriarchal order. Women are diverse and range from the educated (in the modern Western sense) to the uneducated, the urban to the rural, the professional working women to those working in informal employment or self-employment, the married to the single, and the young to the old. The experiences, interests and actions of all these groups differ markedly. While the collective value of women's activism cannot be underestimated, it is clear that there is no homogeneity in women's actions and responses to institutional authoritarianism in Kenya; an eventuality that has serious implications for their role in the country's political process.

The state and its gendered character

The concept of state has both a legal and a structural–functional definition. The legal conception of state is a relatively modern one, based on the idea that a state is 'a territorially bound sovereign entity' (Danziger 2005: 110). The notion of sovereignty, which emerged in the sixteenth century, is the premise that each state has complete authority and is the ultimate source of law within its own boundaries. More relevant for purposes of this analysis is the structural–functional perspective, which conceptualises the state as 'the organized machinery for making and carrying out political decisions and for enforcing the laws and rules of the government' (Danziger 2005: 113). From this standpoint, as Danziger rightly points out, states have existed since ancient times in the sense that a state exists when there are distinctive leadership roles, rules for social interaction, and a set of organisational arrangements to identify and serve collective needs.

In defining the true nature of the modern state, Rothchild and Olurunsola (1983: 25) delineate two major functions of state. First, the state's central role is to manage and mediate social resources. In this context, the state is 'the political organization of the society' that provides the framework of institutional relationships, and the body of customs and conventions. It articulates the needs of the dominant political class in efforts to reconcile issues, which impact on ethnicity, the mediation of competition between groups, and the recruitment of elites into the existent economic and political systems. Second, the state is a control agency whose most important function is to control society. Thus, a dominant group of the population, whether based on variables of ethnicity, class, region, ideology or other factors, utilises the power of state institutions in order to force others to comply (Rothchild and Olurunsola 1983: 2; Nzongola-Ntalaja 1989).

The perspective of state as controller is espoused by Marxists and neo-Marxists, who postulate that the state is controlled by the dominant class in a system of exploitation (Leonard 1974; Marx and

Engels 1992 [1848]). According to Lemarchand (1983: 47), the major weakness of this view is that it places undue emphasis on the importance of class as the primary determiner of status. Other factors are equally germane, such as the differences of meaning between the social, political and ruling classes. Conversely, the view that regards the state as manager is decidedly a liberal perspective. Liberal theorists, in contrast to neo-Marxists, postulate that states are really 'neutral umpires' (Parpart and Staudt 1989: 3). In recent years, however, 'the analysis has been more complex – a connecting thread is apparent; claims to neutrality on the part of the state and its agencies are dismissed and the search for trans-class consensus is regarded as inappropriate' (Lemarchand 1983: 46). Thus, the state is characterised as resting on group advantage and power, and its instrumentalities are defined as being supportive of the economic interests of the controlling elements (see Shivji 1991; Ake 1996: 3).

According to Nzomo (1998), the reality of women's exclusion from formal politics and power, in general, reflects the gendered nature of the post-colonial state. State power in Africa remains conspicuously male power, ingrained with predominantly male values, ideology and vision of the world. This male-constructed machinery codifies, institutionalises and legitimises patriarchy, a system that manifests itself not only in social and economic life but also in the low and biased political and legal statuses of women (see Mucai-Kathambo 1993; Mukabi-Kabira 1993; Aubrey 1997; Kameri-Mbote and Kiai 1999). The gendered quality of the state is clearly seen in its institutions such as the cabinet, the parliament, the judiciary, the army and the civil service. Male authority in the state is so ubiquitous that for a very long time it has been taken for granted.

While the male-dominated state in Africa has been the prime instrument for acquisition and distribution of power and status, it has virtually blocked the majority of women from entering the ruling class. In this connection, it has been noted that women's past quest for status and wealth heavily depended on aligning themselves with powerful men, what Mama (1997; 1998) calls 'femocracy'. In so doing, they accept the male vision of the world and the patterns and processes of their own subordination. In the absence of such alignments, women have tended to withdraw from the public to build their own parallel and independent spheres of survival. There are also cases in which women's political actions create the impression that they sometimes undermine rather than promote their own advancement and autonomy.

Women's contribution to their own subordination and oppression can be attributed, in part, to the patriarchal socio-cultural 'conditioning' that pervades gender relations in African societies and that has created what Amadiume calls daughters of imperialism (Amadiume 2000). As Fatton (1989: 54) points out:

> In Africa, where patriarchal traditions are so ingrained in the fabric of society, women's struggle for emancipation is replete with contradictions, ambivalence, and silence. This is not to say that women fail to resist and protest, but that their resistance and protest are easily co-opted or suppressed by the structural, political, and ideological powers of male supremacy.

Overall, scholars have argued that women's representation in state institutions must reach a critical mass of at least one-third of the total membership for them to achieve substantive influence in any institution (Kanter 1977; Dahlerup 1988; Miguda 2002).

In analysing how gender shapes the character of contemporary Kenyan politics, we perceive state institutions as a reflection of their location in particular historical junctures and cultural milieus, with their power sites always shifting. Even though most aspects of the patriarchal character of national politics may remain intact over time, that character is amenable to change. It is the analysis of such change, born of the struggles for democratisation in Kenya, that the rest of this chapter focuses on. The idea is to extrapolate the extent to which the various transitions in the country have opened up and expanded space for women's representation in politics.

Women and Kenyan Transition Politics

From the pre-colonial to the post-colonial times, Kenya has undergone several political transitions. These include pre-colonial to colonial transition; colonial to independence transition of the early 1960s; multiparty to de facto single party in the 1960s, then to de jure single party in the early 1980s; and from the one party to a formal multiparty in 1991. Kibwana (2002: 204) contends further that 'political contestation during the periods of transition is dominated and driven by the elite who bar genuine involvement in politics by the mass of the people'. In such a political context, gender disparities become increasingly glaring. A close examination of the political periods engendered by some of the major political transitions in Kenya illustrates this reality.

Sexual dualism and equity

In pre-colonial Kenyan societies, clusters of patrilineal clans lived in clan villages, which provided a framework for territorial organisation. They had their own systems of government, religion, education and culture, which were all an integral part of life (see Chapter 3 by Gecaga in this volume). Although male domination in the ideological structure existed, this was mitigated by sexual dualism. There was flexibility and balance in the sexual division of labour. Women had areas of social life in which they predominated. They had their own political, economic and cultural institutions whose very existence was unknown to external observers (Likimani 1985: 15). Women enjoyed a status of respect and dignity and exercised a certain amount of social control in their capacity as mothers, co-wives, daughters, aunts, political leaders, as well as members of the extended lineage (Stamp 1986; Ayot 1994; Ogundipe-Leslie 1994; Gordon 1995).

Women's status was enhanced further by their multiple social and economic roles as food producers and distributors, reproducers, guardians of the hearth, fire, water and land as well as healers, creators and disseminators of indigenous knowledge (Kamau 1994; Nasong'o 2005). Moreover, production was for utility value and the household was an important unit of production. If food provision is regarded as the primary role of the breadwinner, women were, and continue to be, the major breadwinners in Africa. As subsistence farmers, women had usufruct (use or access) rights to the land, which was communally owned. Women controlled and distributed what they produced and as such had more power, more resources and more control over their own lives than they do today (Okeyo 1980; Newman 1984; Likimani 1985).

To an alien observer, politics in pre-colonial Kenya appeared to be the exclusive realm of men. This was partly because of the male dominance that prevailed in largely patriarchal societies. However, the intimate inner workings of the different cultures and historically distinct arrangements between the sexes allowed for women to participate in politics, both on a formal and informal basis (Kandiyoti 1988). The common misconception about women's political participation at this time is confounded by two important factors. The first is a misunderstanding of the meaning of 'public' and 'private' life in pre-colonial Kenya, which leads to oversimplified cultural evaluations of the sexes based on the domestic–public divide. Due to the fluidity and interconnectedness of the two spheres, employing the public–private (or political–domestic) dichotomy as an analytic tool for conceptualising gender relations in Kenya, as in the rest of Africa, would be mis-leading (Sudarkasa 1986). In pre-colonial Kenya, women had never been confined to the private or domestic sphere. Rather, roles in society were socially constructed and multiple responsibilities between and across spheres shaped their political history, and the political/juridical spheres depended heavily on personal relationships that women could, and often did, influence.

The development of sexual division of labour in Kenya, as in many other African societies, preceded the colonial period. However, the dynamics of such sexual division of labour at this time were somewhat different from what they became with the introduction of capitalism. Gender relations at this time took on a form that was more comple-mentary than hierarchical. Men generally built houses, hunted, herded and milked, fished, and fought. Women cultivated, processed and marketed crops; collected fuel and water; cared for the children, the sick and the elderly; made pottery, cooked, cleaned and washed. There was no negative evaluation attached to these different roles. As Driberg (1932) explains, a woman carrying out her duty was held in just as high esteem as a man carrying out his, and the nature of the occupation was of no moment. This characteristic of pre-colonial African societies' socio-political structure is aptly captured by Nyerere (1968) who observed that the traditional African family lived according to the basic prin-ciples of *Ujamaa* (communalism). Its members did this unconsciously and without any conception of what they were doing in political terms. The results of their joint effort were divided unequally between them, but according to well-understood custom. They lived together and they worked together; and the result of their joint labour was the property of the family as a whole.

Roots of women's subordination

The colonial enterprise introduced capitalism in Kenya and its concomi-tant attributes of a cash economy and wage employment. Consequently, women's roles were increasingly subordinated to those of men. While women were confined to the subsistence economy and domesticity, men were simultaneously socialised into capitalism (as wage earners, cash crop producers, taxpayers, etc.) and political leadership as local chiefs and assistants to colonial officials. Women's exclusion from wage employment denied them the power that comes with a pocket-book for the man at the end of each month. As a result, men steadily acquired new sources of power and prestige. Women's hitherto valu-able roles were undervalued within the capitalist context. Roberts offers a succinct summary of the reasons why capitalism increased the subordination of women in the non-capitalist sector:

> The intensification of female labor in peasant economies released male labor for the production of cash crops ... Their [women's] productive labor was intensified to ensure the subsistence basis of labor reserve areas while their reproductive labor ensured the maintenance and reproduction of labor power at no cost to the capitalist wage. (Roberts 1984: 176)

The British colonial government introduced cash crop farming and a policy of taxation, which had profound consequences on gender relations. African men reigned in the new economy based on cash crop production and wage labour as they were compelled to work harder in order to meet their tax obligations to the colonial govern-ment. In a number of cases, women's labour actually supplemented male labour for such obligations on top of women also producing for subsistence. Furthermore, men were forced to leave the rural areas in search of wage-earning opportunities in urban areas and European-owned cash crop plantations (Jalang'o-Ndeda 1991). As primary actors in the new cash economy, African men not only learned new farming techniques, but also obtained the necessary exposure in monetary issues and schooling. These opportunities were, however, not made available to women. Women stayed at home, raised children, conti-nued subsistence farming and took care of the homestead. Hence, Western capitalism enhanced the status of men, undermined that of women and helped to solidify the traditional gender roles.

As cultivators of both food and cash crops on a subsistence level, Kenyan women became the primary producers, constituting 60 per cent of the labour force in the agricultural sector and accounting for 80 per cent in food production. The fact that women were (and still are) not paid for their productive and reproductive labour means that they provide the chief subsidy to capitalist production. Such exploitation of women's labour markedly lowered their status relative to that of men.

Clearly, therefore, the development of colonial capitalism pushed women into low-status jobs. In a world structured around the needs and priorities of men, employers were happy to use women as a source of cheap labour. Moreover, capitalism and industrialism took from women the traditional skills such as brewing, medicine making, spinning and weaving, which were learnt at home, and formed a means of gaining social standing and respect in the community. Furthermore, the British transplanted their own ethnocentric version of male-dominated politics into colonial Kenya and completely ignored women's political roles. As observed by Smock (1977: 181):

> Colonial policies had a rather important influence on sex role definitions and opportunities for women. Christian missionaries and colonial administrators brought with them Victorian conceptions concerning the place of women in society. Generally, they did not appreciate the significant contribution frequently made by women and their sense of independence.

Where there had been a blurred distinction between private and public life in Kenya, British structures and policies focused on delineating a clear distinction guided by an ideology that perceived men as public actors and women as private, domestic performers. Colonialists worked hand in hand with African patriarchs to develop inflexible customary laws, which evolved into new structures and forms of domination (Schmidt 1991). Colonial policy on education was among the most potent factors adversely affecting the relative position of women in Kenya. As in Victorian Europe, educational opportunities were disproportionately provided to men. Missionary education for women was primarily geared towards providing educated men with good wives and homemakers.

The pressure and demands of Kenyan nationalists, coupled with those of multilateral imperialism in the post-war period, made it increasingly difficult and unprofitable for Britain to cling to its colonial empire. The Mau Mau uprising taught the colonial establishment that the African quest for freedom was unstoppable. During this struggle for Kenya's independence from colonialism, women fought hard alongside men. Many women, such as Me Katilili and Mary Muthoni Nyanjiru, were instrumental in Kenya's fight for freedom as well as in advancing women's rights and interests (Morgan 1984; Kanogo 1987a, 1987b; Presley 1988; Oduol 1993). Former Mau Mau freedom fighters argued that independence would not have been achieved were it not for the rebellion and especially the active role of women (Kinyatti 1997: 125–6). Indeed, the colonial government recognised women's fervour and resilience remarking that female freedom fighters were 'far more rabid than the males' (Presley 1988: 504). But Kenyan women's efforts and sacrifices did not translate into their greater political participation after independence. Indeed, all negotiations for

Kenya's independence took place between the colonisers and elite male politicians.

'Not yet uhuru': the Kenyatta state

Though actively involved in the nationalist struggle for independence, Kenya's women were sidelined during the negotiations for independence and in the early politics of post-colonial Kenya. It is instructive to note that there was only one woman out of about 70 or so Kenyan delegates at the Lancaster House conference in London, where Kenya's independence constitution was negotiated. Moreover, the fact that Kenya's independence constitution was a product of a male-dominated discourse, negotiated and drafted in a foreign country, ensured that women's perspectives and unique gender experiences were not taken into consideration. Furthermore, the British largely influenced the recruitment of the 70 or so Kenyan delegates who negotiated for the independence constitution, some with wanting intellectual aptitude and necessary alertness to fully comprehend the complexities inherent in constitution-making. Critically, again, these indigenous leaders did not consult the Kenyan people in a bid to establish a representative understanding as related to the future of independent Kenya's politics and governance. Not surprisingly, Kenya's independence constitution was premised on the Westminster constitutional model and was not subjected to popular debate and approval. According to James Orengo (2000):

> The constitution of Kenya was deliberately designed to fail. We borrowed the worst features of other people's constitutions. The result is a machine without rhythm or reason. We have borrowed the American presidential system but ignored the checks and balances that make the president accountable to the Americans. We have borrowed the parliamentary system from Britain but none of the parliamentary practices that makes the British parliament effective. We borrowed the Bill of Rights from the Universal Declaration of Human Rights but added in all the exceptions to rights that were common in Stalinist countries. In short, we now have a presidency without checks, a parliament without teeth, and a Bill of Rights that reads more like a Bill of Exceptions rather than Rights.

Thus, the independence constitution provided the ideal framework for autocratic leadership. Kenyatta enthusiastically embraced the republican constitution as the most appropriate for the 'young' country and its people. In reality, according to Munene (2001: 6):

> the republican constitution that Kenyatta talked about rolled the powers of the governor-general and those of the prime minister into one in the name

of the president and enabled him to enjoy those powers unfettered by the British government, any party opposition, or constitutional position that he did not like … the governor-general and the prime minister became, in 1965, the absolute president.

Essentially, the Kenyatta government did not fundamentally alter the colonial system and its structures. Kenyatta's vision of the future was conservative. This led to an authoritarian system of government, which in many cases simply re-baptised the former colonial structure with new terminology. According to Munene (2001: 5), '[i]ndependent Kenya became a republic but not a democracy. It had a republican constitution that bordered on turning Kenya into some kind of monarchy with a lot of power concentrated in the hands of the president'. He elaborates further that Kenyatta was not a democrat; he was an autocrat who did not hide his inclinations. It was mainly on account of this that Kenyatta fell out with his more progressive vice-president, Oginga Odinga, who, writing in the late 1960s, declared that Kenya was 'not yet uhuru'.

The constitution of Kenya, as drafted at independence, was glaringly insensitive to gender. Whilst Chapter 5 provides the fundamental rights and freedoms of the individual, both men and women, whose enjoyment is guaranteed by Section 70, one finds that Section 82 of the Constitution, which is concerned with discrimination, affects women more than men. Section 82(1–2) provides that no law shall make provision that is discriminatory 'either of itself or in the effects' and neither should a person be treated in a 'discriminatory manner by a person acting by virtue of any written law or in the performance of the function of a public office or public authority'. Discrimination for purposes of Section 82(3) means giving preferential treatment to different persons on the basis of race, tribe, place of origin or residence, other local connection, political opinion, colour or creed. One's gender as a basis for discrimination is not provided for. A number of laws are exempted in Section 82(4) from the provisions against discrimination. These include laws of adoption, marriage, divorce, burial, devolution of property on death and personal law matters. Yet, these laws are in areas that affect women. Coupled with Section 82(3), which omits 'sex' as a basis of discrimination, one finds that women's enjoyment of the fundamental freedom guaranteed by the constitution is severely restricted (see Republic of Kenya 1998). The omission of 'sex' has generated arguments for and against the omission. Kibwana (1991: 2–3) points out that:

> Significantly, the constitution does not ban discrimination based on grounds of sex, given that in section 70 'sex' is included as one of the categories which must not be used to disenable a citizen from enjoyment of human

rights, it becomes clear that constitutional language deliberately excluded 'sex' as a category for purposes of barring discrimination. The oft-advanced argument that sex discrimination was thought to be so objectionable that it was so assumed without explicit constitutional provision is a weak argument ... Existing constitutional silence on whether sex discrimination is not allowed ensures that where such discrimination occurs there is no clear-cut existing operative law which can be relied on to challenge the discrimination.

In most patriarchal states, there is a fear that illegalisation of sex discrimination may lead to countless court suits by women. This fear has therefore meant that women, who are most likely to be affected by such provisions, are denied constitutional protection from sex-based discrimination. The so-called liberal school of thought justifies the omission on the grounds that provision of sex as a basis for discrimination was unnecessary since both men and women have the same rights and privileges and thus ought to be treated equally. For the conservative school of thought, failing to refer to sex implies that affording different treatment on grounds of sex is not considered discrimination in law. Whatever the argument, women are the majority of victims of sex-based discrimination, by virtue of being women. In this case, Section 82(3) denies women protection outside their homes (e.g. in the work place) whilst Section 82(4) and (6) further denies them protection in their homes (see Republic of Kenya 1998). The effect is that at no time are women guaranteed protection from sex-based discrimination.

In view of the foregoing, it is clear that Kenya's women had little to celebrate other than the fact that a common enemy, the British colonists, had been dislodged from the land. The new era did not deliver democracy. Women's issues were not part of the national agenda. Violence, intimidation, detention and police harassment constituted the political culture that characterised Kenya's politics during the Kenyatta era of the 1960s and 1970s. Women were scared stiff and kept off politics. Relationships of political domination and control developed quickly as men dominated Kenya's political scene and women retreated home. The die of the public–private divide, indelibly cast during the colonial era, was thriving. Social and political structures were in place; law, religion and the educational system ensured that this ideology remained embedded not only in the socio-political stratum but also within the consciousness of independent Kenya. Though women were granted full suffrage at independence, it meant little in reality. Not only had they been completely sidelined in all negotiations leading to independence, they had also been systematically alienated from the redefined political structure. Women played only marginal roles in decision-making processes and in the designation of political priorities.

The situation was exacerbated by gender inequality in access to education. The priority given to girls' future roles as mothers and wives has a negative impact on their participation in formal education and politics. Women are socialised around kitchen chores, and learn how to be submissive and accept male power as a norm. They do not challenge authority, a factor that plays a role in their marginalisation. The school curriculum structure undervalues the role of women as compared to men. As Wanja, the barmaid in Ngugi's *Petals of Blood* reveals: 'But boys were always more confident about the future than us girls. They seemed to know what they wanted to become later in life: whereas with us girls the future seemed vague … it was as if we knew that no matter what efforts we put into our studies, our road led to the kitchen and the bedroom' (Thiong'o 1977: 37).

There is a strong African belief that once a girl gets married she belongs to her husband's family, and so it is not worth investing in her education. The family considers it a waste of funds to invest in her education, which has no immediate returns to the family. Usually, female education is at its lowest in the rural and marginal areas where poverty exists and where there are limited opportunities for income generation. This lack of intellectual nourishment among female children in their early years takes its toll in their later years. Women come to face social pressures that discourage them from active participation in electoral politics. Those who make it to elective positions before they are married rarely get partners. The general perception is that they are 'acting manly'; they are unconventionally tough and rude, uncooperative, and feminists who cannot stay at home and cook, and are hence unfit for marriage. Lisa Aubrey sums up the situation thus:

> The patriarchal disposition of the state disempowers women as it empowers men, the spillover of which creates a gender hierarchy that subordinates women, as gender group, to men. This is also a global phenomenon … Specific to the African context, gender hierarchies are resultant of both internal processes and external contact. That is, the genderedness of public life and the subordination of women (1) are embedded in African traditional cultures, (2) were exacerbated in the periods of Islamic expansion and European colonialism, (3) are stringently enforced by post-colonial state policy and practices, and (4) are reproduced by the gendered cultures of politics. (Aubrey 2001: 89)

Accordingly, by the time Kenya's founding president, Jomo Kenyatta, died on 22 August 1978, only a handful of women had been elected to parliament. Those elected in the 1960s included Ruth Habwe from Western Kenya (1964) and Grace Onyango from Luo Nyanza (1969). The 1970s women parliamentarians included Winfred Nyiva Mwendwa, Julia Ojiambo, Eddah Gachukia, Jemima Gecaga and Philomena Chelagat Mutai. Moreover, for his entire rule (1963–78), Kenyatta never appointed even a single woman to a full cabinet position.

Continuity from Kenyatta to *nyayo*

President Daniel arap Moi was a devout 'disciple' of Kenyatta, whose *nyayo* (footsteps) he vowed to follow. Moi's immediate challenge came from an entrenched political elite from the Gikuyu, Embu and Meru Association (GEMA), an association that brought together the culturally related Kikuyu, Embu and Meru ethnic groups ostensibly for cultural and economic interests. The group became immensely powerful during Kenyatta's presidency, held more political sway and influence than any other group in the country, and its members benefited from the regime in terms of political appointments and economic opportunities. To contain the group's power, Moi forged a political ideology, which embraced terror, violence, fear, detention, intimidation, corruption, electoral abuse and political ethnicity. Not surprisingly, his 24-year rule established a new political paradigm marked by further alienation of women from Kenya's political mainstream. Marked out as Moi's enemy number one, the GEMA leadership was put in disarray as the president mobilised other ethnic elites on a strong anti-GEMA platform. Notably, Moi systematically replaced GEMA senior personnel in corporations and government with individuals drawn largely from his Kalenjin ethnic group.

Meanwhile, a cult of personality was taking shape around Moi. Suddenly he became Baba Moi, *Baba wa Taifa* (Father of the Nation). Politicians hailed him, mass choirs sang and danced in his praise, and some declared him number one in every known profession. Opposition to, or criticism of, Moi's government was outlawed. Defiant and persistent critics of the system were publicly ostracised, terrorised, tortured, harassed or branded enemies of the state. Under these circumstances, a culture of political persecution, fear and violence was gradually established with the consequence of discouraging and scaring women from participating in politics. Anyang' Nyong'o (1993: 9) articulates this disturbing development thus: 'When people in public office espouse no

principles, aspire to no ideals, excel in nothing but immorality and maintain power by repression and not popular consent, one must expect some
sheep-like behavior from the oppressed and dehumanized.'

Women who ventured into politics were not spared the psychological impact of the culture of physical and verbal violence that in turn
generated a culture of fear and silence (Aubrey 1997: 89). The psychological impact of the culture of violence affected not just women
politicians but also other ordinary women citizens. This is captured in
the work of Gumbonzvanda et al. They explain:

> The struggle for multiparty politics in Kenya came at the height of KANU's
> intolerance in the late 1980s and early 1990s. People with dissenting voices
> were simply detained without trial or charged and convicted of sedition.
> Many women watched helplessly as their sons and husbands were brought
> to court on trumped-up charges and sent to jail. Their anger, frustration
> and agony found expression in 1991 when mothers, wives, and daughters
> of political detainees stripped naked at Nairobi's Uhuru Park to put a curse
> on the Government for refusing to release their kin. The women kept vigil at
> the park despite beatings and tear gas from the police and, eventually, their
> husbands, sons and fathers were released. (Gumbonzvanda et al. 2004: 11)

Jael Mbogo, a perennial parliamentary candidate and political activist,
not only witnessed but also lived through the culture of violence during
the period she contested a parliamentary seat. She advocates the reform
of the electoral laws, stating that in Kenya:

> The electoral laws must be reviewed with a view to making election
> violence a crime … Women do not organize thugs to fight for them [as
> many politicians do] so they always end up as victims. There is also the
> threat of being raped, which is dreadful. If somebody is threatened with
> rape if you are a candidate, imagine where you will be … We need a level
> ground for all … Economically, they [women] are very weak … The cul-
> ture of violence, the culture of money, corruption during elections, and
> vote rigging, all those should be stamped out. In the last general elections,
> altogether we had 47 women candidates. Of those who I was working
> with very closely, I remember there were three who had to drop out. One
> was rescued from death. One was kidnapped. For the whole nomination
> period, we did not know where she was. When she came back, all her
> vehicles had been vandalized; they poured salt in all her vehicles so that
> engines wouldn't work. She was completely traumatized. There is one
> whom they threatened and blocked from presenting her papers.
> (http.www.peacelink.it/wajibu/17-issue/p2.html)

Even Kenya's first female assistant minister, Julia Ojiambo, was not
spared from the culture of violence and abuse. She recalls her experience

and that of her female colleague, Grace Onyango, Kenya's first woman member of parliament, and their response:

> I recall when Grace Onyango and I were in Parliament we never abused anybody we talked about policy matters affecting all Kenyans. I insisted on my manifesto, talked about water, education, health and economic activities etc. This is what we want done to our girls. Inferiority of women must end soon. Women need to co-operate as women in terms of respecting one another. Politics is survival for the fittest. (Nzomo 1997b: 12–13)

Throughout the 1990s, political violence and gender biases/stereotypes remained women's greatest obstacles in political participation. A survey conducted by the League of Kenya Women Voters in 2002 indicated that insecurity was ranked, together with financial ability, as the most significant factor considered by women when making the decision to run for political seats. In addition, there was widespread liberal use of sexist and derogatory language against women candidates, aimed at undermining their public image and social standing. The electoral campaign experience of Edna Sang, a female parliamentary candidate in a by-election occasioned by the sudden death of Kwanza constituency's Member of Parliament George Kapten, was revealing. She endured gender-specific forms of violence and at one point desperately cried out to the press: 'They blocked my exit from the meeting area. In the ensuing struggle to leave the meeting ground, they attacked my husband. When I rushed to assist him, they attacked me and undressed me' (Kiai 2002). It is apparent that had Edna Sang been a man, she would not have been undressed by her tormentors. Indeed, her husband was not. Yet, due to her sexuality, she was forcibly stripped naked. The reason for this is clear: not only to scar her physically, but also to traumatise her psychologically.

The female/male and private/public dichotomous relationships emanating from the colonial period left indelible impressions on the African psychology. President Moi succinctly demonstrated this mentality when he addressed a Conference of East African Women Parliamentarians in Nairobi, Kenya on 6 March 2001. Staring the delegates in their faces from his elevated presidential dais, the president charged, 'You can achieve more, can get more, but because of your little minds, you cannot get what you are expecting to get' (*East African Standard* and *The Daily Nation*, 7 March 2001). Similarly, when Wangari Maathai, the 2004 Nobel Peace Prize Laureate, successfully campaigned against the allocation of Uhuru Park in Nairobi to the Kenya Times Media Trust (that runs KANU's mouthpiece, *Kenya Times*) for a commercial development project in 1989, her humanity and person-hood came under severe attack from Moi's henchmen and members of parliament (Nzomo 1997a). The significance of the issue and its national value were sacrificed at the altar of male chauvinism. The Maathai issue became extremely personal as facts were shelved. Being a divorcee, her marital status was questioned and ridiculed. It mattered pretty little that President Moi too was a divorcee!

Maendeleo Ya Wanawake Organization (MYWO), whose existence dates back to the colonial times (see Aubrey 1997: 45–88) was increasingly viewed suspiciously by male politicians on account of its potential to mobilise women for electoral politics. As such, a policy of divide and rule was adopted and perfected as KANU forged an alliance with the women's national organisation, which became KANU-MYWO. It was within this context that the KANU leadership manipulated women to the extent that 'some women groups affiliated with the KANU-MYWO held demonstrations to condemn Maathai's actions and to dissociate themselves from her' (Nzomo 1997a: 240). Whereas during Kenyatta's time MYWO for long remained under the leadership of Jane Kiano, wife of cabinet minister Dr Gikonyo Kiano, by the turn of the 1990s, the KANU government incorporated MYWO within the ruling party as its female wing. Within this conjuncture, only pro-KANU women were cleared to lead the organisation. During the multiparty period for instance, the organisation was under the leadership of Zipporah Kittony, a cousin to President Moi, who viewed her chief mission as mobilising women to support KANU and the president.

Women and the Transition of the 1990s

The women's movement of the 1990s greatly benefited from the emergence of a number of new feminist lobby groups and civic associations, notably the League of Kenya Women Voters (LKWV), the National Commission on the Status of Women (NCSW), the Education Centre for Women in Democracy (ECWD) and the Collaborative Centre for Gender and Development (CCGD) among others. These organisations initiated civic education on gender sensitisation for men and women, and training curriculum aimed at political empowerment and capacity building especially for women political candidates and voters. All these various women's organisations are a living testimony of the active involvement of Kenyan women in their desire to bring about democratic change in their society. Unlike the more than 23,000 groups already in existence, the new lobby groups were much more political in their orientation and more assertive and willing to take political risks in pursuit of the women's agenda. At the same time, many of the existing groups and organisations, such as the International Federation of Women Lawyers-Kenya (FIDA-K), the National Council of the Women of Kenya (NCWK) and the Young Women's Christian Association (YWCA), which had never before articulated a political agenda, also became vocally critical of the undemocratic status quo. Jointly with the new lobby groups, they vigorously lobbied all political parties to integrate gender issues within the context of their democratic agendas. This unity of purpose in the organisations provided leadership that greatly facilitated gender activism in Kenya's first multiparty elections in December 1992.

Kenya's women's lobby groups drew immense inspiration from the ideals and goals espoused by women's worldwide movements, articulated in a series of United Nations World Conferences on Women held in Mexico, Denmark, Kenya and China in 1975, 1980, 1985 and 1995, respectively. Building on the gains from the last three world conferences, the United Nations Fourth World Conference on Women that was held in Beijing, China, in 1995, became one of the highlights of women's movements. One of the key resolutions at this conference that is of great relevance to the question of women in politics was the setting of targets for a critical mass of women's representation of at least 35 per cent in key policy-making institutions by the turn of the millennium. Towards this end, the restoration of a multiparty system in Kenya in December 1991 created some political space for civil society groups, including women's groups, to participate actively in the multiparty democratic struggles of the 1990s (Nzomo 1998: 548). In the process, the women's movement demonstrated its potential as a formidable political force capable of seeking and influencing change in the oppressive state autocracy and patriarchy. Political empowerment became the number one priority for women, notwithstanding the equally great concern for redressing economic and social injustices that underlie female subordination to men. Women activists argued that if women attained key political decision-making positions in large enough numbers – at least 30 per cent of the total – they could ensure the removal or repeal of laws that discriminate against women at the social and economic levels. They would also participate in designing policies that would bring women into the political mainstream.

While the December 1992 general elections did not result in a critical mass of women elected to decision-making bodies, it did reflect the enormous efforts of the women's movement to empower female voters and candidates. According to an assessment report of the condition and the status of women in Kenya presented at the East African Regional Conference on Women in Kampala, Uganda, the multiparty system contributed to a larger representation by women at the local government level and the National Assembly. It noted, 'Over 40 women were elected councillors in 1992 as compared to 20 in 1983 while six were elected to parliament compared to two in 1983' (Weru 1995: viii–ix). The report further noted that despite the increased number of women in Kenya's 222-member parliament, they have not been effective in the male-dominated House. And the ruling party, KANU, did not honour its promise to include women in the 12 nominated MPs. However, one of the 40 elected councillors was later elected mayor of the town of Embu, the capital of Eastern Province, becoming the fourth female mayor since independence. Furthermore, in May 1995, the first female cabinet minister in independent Kenya, Winfred Nyiva Mwendwa, was appointed to head the Ministry of Culture and Social Services.

Overall, the performance of women in the multiparty elections of 1992, 1997 and 2002 was below expectations. The projected critical mass of 30 per cent representation was not attained. In 1997, only four women were elected of the country's 210 elected legislators. But, in an encouraging note, five were nominated out of a total of 12 slots for nominated legislators. This constituted only 4.0 per cent representation, a far cry from the projected target. This is notwithstanding the intensive civic education campaigns that had been launched. Many factors, however, have been cited as causes for women's poor performance. These include party affiliation, culture, religion, education, and resources in terms of time and money. Yet, these factors are very closely interrelated and make the problem of women's political participation very complex. In Kenya's politics, party affiliation is accompanied by two major elements: ethnicity and clanism. Most of the women candidates had hoped that gender block voting would beat tribal block voting, but the results showed the reverse. Most Kenyans, including women, are inclined to ethnicity rather than any other social category, including gender.

Even of more critical concern is the marginalisation of women by fellow women. As the leader of the MYWO organisation, for instance, Zipporah Kittony campaigned for President Moi and mobilised her organisation to support KANU in the 1997 elections in spite of the fact that a woman (Charity Ngilu) was contesting the presidency for the first time in the country's history. Kittony's support for the established order earned her a place in parliament as nominated legislator. Subsequently, a glaring pointer to the division among the nine female parliamentarians over issues of women's empowerment emerged in December 2001. The KANU government introduced a motion in parliament aimed at reducing the number of women nominated to the East African Legislative Assembly. Quite interestingly, Zipporah Kittony and Grace Mwewa (both KANU-nominated members) and Maryam Matano (NDP-nominated) absented themselves from the vote in parliament for the purposes of playing it safe vis-à-vis their respective parties. On the other hand, Marere wa Mwachai (elected KANU member and assistant minister) voted for the motion to lock out more women nominees to the East African legislative assembly (Nasong'o 2005). Clearly, women who align themselves with men in order to find space in the political mainstream are victims of femocracy and are thus a hindrance to the promotion of gender equity.

Through the coordinative and collaborative efforts of the various women's organisations under the rubric of Engendering the Political Process Programme (see EPPP 2003), the number of women who managed to be elected and nominated to parliament improved significantly over all other previous elections since independence. A total of nine women were elected in the December 2002 general elections compared to only four in the 1997 elections. In addition, of the 12 nominated legislators, eight slots (66.7 per cent) went to women, compared to only five (41.7 per cent) in 1997 (see Table 6.1). Accordingly, the number of women parliamentarians following the 2002 elections stood at 17, representing 7.6 per cent of the 222-member parliament, a marked improvement on the 4.0 per cent women's representation after the 1997 elections, and, as already mentioned, the best women's representation in the country's history. This improvement was further enhanced by the appointment of three women to full cabinet positions – Charity Ngilu for Health, Martha Karua for Water Resources and Lina Kilimo for Immigration – and three women assistant ministers – Beth Mugo for education, Betty Tett for Local Government, and Wangari Maathai for Environment and Natural Resources. The presenece of women in the cabinet was further enhanced by the appointment of four women permanent secretaries, Esther Tolle for Foreign Affairs; Rebecca Nabutola for Gender, Sports, Culture, and Social Services; Rachel Arunga for

Table 6.1 Women in Kenya's ninth parliament, 2002–2007

Name	Party	Status
Beth Mugo	NARC	Elected
Christine Mango	NARC	Elected
Charity Ngilu	NARC	Elected
Alicen Chelaite	NARC	Elected
Wangari Maathai	NARC	Elected
Naomi Shaban	KANU	Elected
Winfred Mwendwa	NARC	Elected
Martha Karua	NARC	Elected
Lina Kilimo	NARC	Elected
Betty Tett	NARC	Nominated
Julia Ojiambo	NARC	Nominated
Ruth Oniang'o	KANU	Nominated
Cecily Mbarire	NARC	Nominated
Adelina Mwau	NARC	Nominated
Amina Abdalla	KANU	Nominated
Njoki Ndung'u	NARC	Nominated
Esther Keino	KANU	Nominated

Source: Compiled by authors.

Environment and Natural Resources; and Nancy Kirui for Labour and Human Resource Development. More women were also appointed to leading positions in the country's Foreign Service, including Maria Nzomo as High Commissioner to Zimbabwe and Raychelle Omamo as Ambassador to France, among others.

Clearly, therefore, the democratisation crusade of the 1990s, especially the 2002 transition from the entrenched KANU regime to the NARC government, has yielded for women the best results so far of all the political transitions in Kenya. This eventuality illustrates that with time, women's movements are increasingly able to have an impact on the creation of democracy and a role within the subsequent post-transition phase. These positive developments are a result of deliberate efforts of national-level women's movements and the synergy created between them and initiatives of the global women's movement for political representation. Nevertheless, it should be noted that women's representation in politics and in policy-making institutions remain far below the critical mass required to make an impact. The 17 women legislators constitute only 7.6 per cent of the total legislators, a far cry from the targeted 30 per cent. The figure is also far below the Sub-Saharan

Africa average figure of 16.6 per cent women's representation in parliament as of January 2006. Furthermore, the three full women cabinet ministers constitute a mere 9.7 per cent of the total cabinet members. The complexity of this problem is illustrated by the fact that whereas the number of women political candidates has grown almost 100 per cent between 1992 and 2002, an infinitesimally small number of them emerge victorious. This is a pointer to the reality that in spite of the opening up of political space, women still face serious impediments in their quest for political office, obstacles that must be addressed if the political process is to become fairer.

Challenges and Constraints

The fact that 7.6 per cent women's representation in the Kenyan parliament following the 2002 elections is the best representation for women in the country's history speaks volumes as to the kind of challenges Kenyan women face in their quest to participate effectively in the political process in Kenya. Based on the foregoing analysis, these challenges can be categorised into socio-cultural, economic and political constraints.

Socio-cultural constraints

Culture encompasses particular lifestyles derived from history and perceived traditions. It is both a product of and engine for contemporary social and political dynamics. Although by no means static and impervious to change, culture plays a certain role in determining the way we behave at any given moment in time. It defines and is also defined by events happening at the local, national, regional and international levels. Karam (1999) rightly notes that because of its vastness, culture is often used as a tool to validate all manner of actions, not all of which may be acceptable to all concerned. It is often intimately connected to issues of identity. Although not always imposed, cultural frameworks are open to manipulation and interpretation from many angles and sources for both positive, benign purposes as well as for selfish, egotistical ones. In regard to gender and politics, there are three socio-cultural constraints that women face in their quest for political representation.

First is the social division of labour leading to the cultural perception that women's primary responsibilities are as wives and mothers. Yet in many cases, either as a result of a quest for personal development or out of sheer economic necessity, women also go out to work in the labour market. Hence a political career may well come, in these cases, either as a second or a third job. Juggling these different occupations and their consequent triple responsibilities is no easy task for anyone, whether man or woman (see Karam 1999). The situation is further compounded by the increased dichotomisation of social space between the public and the private spheres, where women are meant to belong to the latter. These notions are remarkably persistent, and are the basis of much of the difficulties women face not only in attempts at entering the political sphere but also in gaining credibility and impacting from within it. It is this cultural perception that explains the derogatory remarks against Wangari Maathai in 1989 when she stood against the rapacious established order that was set to take over the only open green space in Nairobi to construct a high-rise building. Bereft of any logical arguments against Wangari's eloquent stance that riveted national and international attention, the men simply resorted to denouncing Maathai as a divorcee. The implication is that, as a woman, she should have been married and preoccupied with tending her husband and family, not raising fundamental issues against the powers that be.

The second socio-cultural constraint is the widespread perception of politics as a dirty game. Indeed, the kind of violence that attends political campaigns in Kenya are such that many women intent on running for political office are often forced to withdraw and leave the dirty game of politics for men to fight out (see Kagwanja 1997; Murunga 1999). The third and final constraint is illiteracy, which affects women differentially in comparison to men globally. In Kenya, illiteracy among women stands at 30 per cent compared to only 14 per cent for men (Nasong'o 2005). This reality is a major challenge to some of the women in that they are not able to benefit from the dissemination of knowledge about the universal principles of human rights and the advantages of their inalienable rights as human beings (see Kameri–Mbote 2001: 2). It is this illiteracy level that serves to divide the educated, professional and urban Kenyan women from the less educated and informally employed majority in the rural areas, who continue to vote in ways that disadvantage women's presence in the political arena.

Economic constraints

Economic statistics reveal that a sizeable number of women are differentially affected by the level of poverty in Kenya compared to men. Of the active female population in Kenya 69 per cent work as subsistence farmers compared to 43 per cent of men (Nasong'o 2005).

Granted subsistence farmers are among the very poor, this relatively high dependence of women on subsistence farming explains their extreme vulnerability. The effects of economic liberalisation and monetisation of the economy, which have had the effect of further peripheralising the majority of the Kenyan women economically, compound their vulnerability. Given their economically disempowered position, women are unable to participate effectively in electoral politics, which requires enormous resources, with men who excel in it having made their money elsewhere before venturing into politics (see Chapter 5 by Mwangola in this volume).

The feminisation of poverty means that women become more concerned with struggling for their daily bread than following any specific political development. Women are thus unable to find time and resources to participate actively in the political process (see Karam 1999). This plays into the second economic constraint for women, which is lack of access to adequate financial resources. This has a major limiting impact in terms of campaign financing on the part of women who seek elective office as well as their ability to undertake initiatives that are critical for building their individual profiles necessary to gain name recognition. Karam (1999) notes that a major recommendation of many international gatherings is that both political parties as well as governments attempt to provide and set up various funds especially destined for women, yet women in many parts of the world still end up with less, if any, access to resources. Indeed, with regard to Kenya, political party funding from public resources has not been implemented. The parties thus remain dominated by their founders, largely male politicians who are their chief financiers (see Chapter 4 by Oloo in this volume).

Political constraints

Two major political constraints to women's political participation can be identified. The first has to do with electoral system design. Available evidence indicates that the type of electoral system plays an important role in determining women's representation. Generally, proportional representation (PR) systems, in which the electorate vote for party lists and parliamentary seats are allocated on the basis of the proportion of votes a party garners, are most conducive to women's legislative presence. In such PR systems, there is a greater incentive for political parties to draw up diversified lists of candidates that include women for purposes of appealing to the widest base of voters possible. Conversely, plurality electoral systems are based on single-member districts with the candidate securing a plurality of the votes winning the seat. With only one seat available for each constituency, parties are less likely to nominate women in this system in which incumbents, usually men, tend to have an added advantage. It is thus by no accident that African countries that use a variant of the PR system such as Rwanda, South Africa and Mozambique rank highest in terms of women's representation in politics. Most African countries use the plurality single-member district system, hence the negligible presence of women in electoral politics in most of these countries.

The second political constraint is related to the structures and agendas of political parties. Many political parties, reflecting the general conditions in the rest of society, do not easily accept or promote many women into their echelons, let alone women's occupation of important positions within these parties. Yet it is the party leaders that largely determine who gets to be nominated to run for political office. As Amutabi shows in this volume, it was the intellectual leaders in the Social Democratic Party (SDP) who decided to nominate Charity Ngilu to run for president in 1997 on account of her strong credentials as an advocate of social issues since entering parliament in 1992. In the run-up to the 2002 elections, however, the SDP leaders decided they would not nominate Ngilu to contest the presidency on account of her weak academic credentials (she has no university education). Ngilu, in an act of political prudence, decamped from the SDP, registered her own party, National Party of Kenya (NPK) and subsequently regained her bargaining power within opposition circles at the national level, emerging as the only woman in the eight-member NARC Summit, the top decision-making organ of the opposition coalition that eventually swept KANU out of power. But for her party leadership, Ngilu would never have been one of the leading lights of the opposition forces that oversaw the transition from KANU to NARC.

Conclusion

The limited, almost negligible participation of women in the Kenyan political process is a function of the social division of labour, the rigid dichotomisation of the public and private spheres, the social construction of the political realm as a man's domain, and the general perception of politics as a dirty game. Nevertheless, we have also demonstrated that the gendered nature of political institutions and processes is a function of the historical junctures and cultural milieus within which they are located. Accordingly, they are amenable to change over time through political activism and deliberate public policy. Indeed, as elaborated above, the political activism of the Kenyan women's movement in the 1990s yielded an almost 100 per cent improvement in women's representation in parliament following the 2002 election, as well as the greatest number ever of women appointments to the cabinet and to high positions in the foreign service. Though women's representation in parliament in Kenya is less than half the continental average, the prospects are quite positive, given the gender activism and the increased awareness of women's issues.

To help enhance the prospects for equity in women's representation, it is critical that the constraints identified above be addressed. Even more importantly, it is imperative that the various advocacy groups within the gender movement in the country find common ground in terms of a clearly stated unity of purpose, organisational capacity and vision for the future. They need to seek to bridge the divide between rural and urban women, educated professionals and uneducated non-professional ones, and to overcome their own divisions along ethnic, religious and class lines in order to advance their collective interests within the complex, multilayered and dialectical process of democratisation in the country. For, at the end of the day, women's presence in key policy-making institutions in critical numbers enhances and strengthens the political agenda on social issues such as health care, education and environmental protection. Their increased participation in politics is thus important for a more balanced, wholesome and equitable socio-economic development.

References

Ake, C. (1996) *Democracy and Development in Africa*, Washington, DC: Brookings Institution.

Amadiume, I. (1987) *Male Daughters, Female Husbands: Gender and Sex in an African Society*, London: Zed Books.

——— (2000) *Daughters of the Goddess, Daughters of Imperialism: African Women Struggle for Culture, Power and Democracy*, London: Zed Books.

Anyang' Nyong'o, P. (1993) *The Challenge of National Leadership and Democratic Changes in Kenya*, Nairobi: Shirikon Publishers.

Aubrey, L.M. (1997) *Politics of Development Cooperation: NGOs, Gender and Partnership in Kenya*, New York, NY: Routledge.

———— (2001) 'Gender, Development, and Democratisation in Africa', in Stephen Ndegwa (ed.), *A Decade of Democracy in Africa*, Leiden: Brill.

Ayot, T. (1994) *Women and Political Leadership in Pre-colonial Period: Case Study of Chief Mangana of Kadem in Western Kenya*, Nairobi: Kaswanga Press.

Dahlerup, D. (1988) 'From a Small to a Large Minority', *Scandinavian Political Studies*, 11.

Danziger, J.N. (2005) *Understanding the Political World*, New York, NY: Pearsons Education.

Driberg, J.H. (1932) 'The Status of Women Among the Nilotics and Nilo-Hamitics', *Africa*, vol. 5, no. 4: 404–21.

Engendering the Political Process Programme (EPPP) (2003) Proceedings of the Learning Platform Workshop Held at Naro Moru River Lodge, 10–13 March.

Fatton , R. (1989) 'Gender, Class, and State in Africa', in J.L. Parpart and K. Staudt (eds), *Women, the State and Development*, Albany, NY: State University of New York Press.

Fouche, F. (1994) 'Overcoming The Sisterhood Myth', *Transformations*, vol. 23.

Gordon, A. (1995) 'Gender, Ethnicity, and Class in Kenya: Burying Otieno Revisited', *Signs: Journal of Women and Culture*, vol. 20, no. 4.

Gumbonzvanda, N., et al. (2004) *A Journey of Courage: Kenyan Women's Experiences of the 2002 General Elections*, Nairobi: Kenya Literature Bureau.

Hansen, T.K. (ed.) (1992) *African Encounters with Domesticity*, New Brunswick, NJ: Rutgers University Press.

Hunt, N. (1990) 'Domesticity and Colonialism in Belgian Africa: Usumbura's Foyer social, 1946–1960', *Signs: Journal of Women in Culture and Society*, vol. 15, no. 3.

Inter-Parliamentary Union (IPU) (2006) *Women in National Parliaments: Status as of 31 January 2006*, archived at: www.ipu.org.

Jalang'o-Ndeda, M.A. (1991) 'The Impact of Male Labour Migration on Rural Women: A Case Study of Siaya district, 1894–1963', PhD Thesis, Kenyatta University.

Kagwanja, P. (1997) 'Politics of Marionettes: Extra-Legal Violence and the 1997 Elections in Kenya', in M. Ruttem et al. (eds), *Out for the Count: The 1997 General Elections and Prospects for Democracy in Kenya*, Kampala: Fountain Publishers.

Kamau, M.N. (1994) 'African Indigenous Education: Providing a Space for Women's Empowerment', in National Association of African American Studies Association Conference, Petersburg, Virginia State University, February.

Kameri-Mbote, P. (2001) 'Gender Consideration in Constitution-Making: Engendering Women's Rights in the Legal Process', *University of Nairobi Law Journal*, 12 July.

———— and W. Kiai (1999) 'The Women's Movement in Kenya: An Overview', in S.A. Khasiani and E.I. Njiro (eds), *The Women's Movement in Kenya*, Nairobi: Association of African Women for Research and Development.

Kandiyoti, D. (1988) 'Bargaining with Patriarchy', *Gender and Society*, vol. 2, no. 3.

Kanogo, T. (1987a) *Squatters and the Roots of Mau Mau*, Athens, OH: Ohio University Press.

———— (1987b) 'Kikuyu Women and the Politics of Protest', in S. Macdonald et al. (eds), *Images of Women in Peace and War: Cross-Cultural and Historical Perspectives*, Madison, WI: University of Wisconsin Press.

Kanter, R. (1977) *Men and Women of the Corporation*, New York, NY: Basic Books.

Karam, A.M. (1999) *Beijing + 5: Women's Political Participation: Review of Strategies and Trends*, New York, NY: UNDP.

Kiai, M. (2002) 'Poll Violence Harms Women Most', *Daily Nation on the Web*, 1 July 2002.

Kibwana, K. (1991) *Women and Autonomy in Kenya: Policy and Legal Framework*, Nairobi: Claripress.

———— (2002) 'Constitution-Making and the Potential for a Democratic Transition in Kenya', in L.M. Mute et al. (eds), *Building an Open Society: The Politics of Transition in Kenya*, Nairobi: Claripress.

Kinyatti, M. Wa (1997) *Kenya's Freedom Struggle: The Dedan Kimathi Papers*, London: Zed Books.

Lemarchand, R. (1983) 'The State and Society in Africa: Ethnic Stratification and Restratification in Historical and Comparative Perspective', in D. Rothchild and V. Olurunsola (eds), *State Versus Ethnic Claims: African Policy Dilemmas*, Boulder, CO: Westview.

Leonard, W. (1974) *The Three Faces of Marxism*, New York, NY: Holt, Rinehart & Winston.

Likimani, M. (1985) *Passbook Number F. 47927: Women and Mau Mau in Kenya*, London: Macmillan.

Lorber, J. (1994) *Paradoxes of Gender*, New Haven, CT: Yale University Press.

Lung'aho, R.H. (2002) 'In Search of Ideology for the Women's Movement in Kenya', in 8th International Interdisciplinary Congress on Women, Kampala, July.

Mama, A. (1997) 'Feminism or Femocracy: State Feminism and Democratisation', in J. Ibrahim (ed.), *Expanding Democratic Space in Nigeria*, Dakar: CODESRIA.

———— (1998) 'Khaki in the Family: Gender Discourses and Militarism in Nigeria, *African Studies Review*, vol. 41, no. 2.

Marx, K., and F. Engels (1992 [1848]) *The Communist Manifesto*, New York, NY: Bantam Books.

Miguda, E. (2002) 'Engendering Democracy in Kenya: Effects of Multiparty Electoral System on Women Participation in Politics', in L. Chweya (ed.), *Electoral Politics in Kenya*, Nairobi: Claripress.

Morgan, R. (1984) *Sisterhood is Global: The International Women's Movement Anthology*, Garden City, NY: Anchor Books.

Mucai-Kathambo, V.W., et al. (1993) 'Law and Status of Women in Kenya', in W. Mukabi-Kabira et al. (eds), *Democratic Change in Africa: Women's Perspective*, Nairobi: African Centre for Technology Studies.

Mukabi-Kabira, W. (1993) 'Gender and Ideology: The Cultural Context', in W. Mukabi-Kabira et al. (eds), *Democratic Change in Africa: Women's Perspective*, Nairobi: African Centre for Technology.

Munene, M. (2001) *The Politics of Transition in Kenya 1995–1998*, Nairobi: Friends of the Book Foundation/Quest and Insight Publishers.

Murunga, G.R. (1999) 'Urban Violence in Kenya's Transition to Pluralist Politics, 1982–1992', *Africa Development*, vol. XXIII, nos 1–2.

——— (2002) 'African Women in the Academy and Beyond: Review Essay', *Jenda: A Journal of Culture and African Women Studies*, vol. 2, no. 1.

Nasong'o, S.W. (2005) 'Women and Economic Liberalization in Kenya: The Impact and Challenges of Globalization', in S.H. Boko et al. (eds), *Women in African Development: The Challenges of Globalization and Liberalization in the 21st Century*, Trenton, NJ: Africa World Press.

Newman, J.S. (1984) *Women of the World: Sub-Saharan Africa*, Washington, DC: USAID.

Nyerere, J.K. (1968) *Ujamaa: Essays on Socialism*, New York, NY: Oxford University Press.

Nzegwu, N. (2001) 'The Politics of Gender in African Studies in the North', in C. Veney and P. Zeleza (eds), *Women in African Studies Scholarly Publishing*, Trenton, NJ: Africa World Press.

Nzomo, M. (1997a) 'Kenyan Women in Politics and Public Decision-Making', in M. Gwendolyn (ed.), *African Feminism: The Politics of Survival in Sub-Saharan Africa*, Philadelphia, PA: University of Pennsylvania Press.

——— (1997b) *The Gender Dimension of Electoral Politics in Kenya: Capacity Building of Women Candidates for 1997 and Beyond*, Nairobi: Friedrich Ebert Foundation.

——— (1998) 'Women in East Africa', in N.P. Stromquist (ed.), *Women in the Third World: An Encyclopedia of Contemporary Issues*, New York, NY: Garland Publishing.

Nzongola-Ntalaja, G. (1989) 'The African Crisis: The Way Out', *African Studies Review*, vol. 32, no. 1.

Oduol, W. (1993) 'Kenyan Women in Politics: An Analysis of Past and Present Trends', *Transafrican Journal of History*, vol. 22.

Ogundipe-Leslie, M. (1994) *Re-creating Ourselves: African Women and Critical Transformations*, Trenton, NJ: Africa World Press.

Okeyo, A. (1980) 'Daughters of the Lakes and Rivers: Colonization and the Land Rights of Luo Women', in M. Etienne and E. Leacock (eds), *Women and Colonization: Anthropological Perspectives*, New York, NY: Praeger.

Orengo, J. (2000) 'Constitution and the Crisis of Governance in Kenya', Address Given to the Kenya Community Abroad Conference, Concordia University, Minnesota, 30 June–3 July.

Oyewùmí, O. (ed.) (1997) *The Invention of Women: Making an African Sense of Western Gender Discourses*, Minneapolis, MN: University of Minnesota Press.

——— (2003) *African Women and Feminism: Reflecting on the Politics of Sisterhood*, Trenton, NJ: Africa World Press.

Parpart, J.L., and K. Staudt (eds) (1989) *Women, the State and Development*, Albany, NY: State University of New York Press.

Phillips, A. (1992) 'Democracy and Difference: Some Problems for Feminist Theory', *The Political Quarterly*, vol. 63, no. 1.

Presley, A.C. (1988) 'Kikuyu women, the Mau Mau rebellion, and social change in Kenya', *Canadian Journal of African Studies*, vol. 22, no. 3.

Republic of Kenya (1998) *Constitution of Kenya*, Nairobi: Government Printer.

Roberts, P. (1984) 'Feminism in Africa: Feminism and Africa', *Review of African Political Economy*, vol. 10, nos 27–28.

Rothchild, D., and V.A. Olurunsola (1983) 'Managing State and Ethnic Claims', in D. Rothchild and V. Olurunsola (eds), *State Versus Ethnic Claims: African Policy Dilemmas*, Boulder, CO: Westview.

Schmidt, E. (1991) 'Patriarchy, Capitalism, and the Colonial State in Zimbabwe', *Signs: Journal of Women in Culture and Society*, vol. 16, no. 4.

Shivji, I.G. (1991) *State and Constitutionalism: An African Debate on Democracy*, Harare: SAPES.

Smock, A. (1977) 'Ghana: From Autonomy to Subordination', in J. Giele and A. Smock (eds), *Women: Roles and Status in Eight Countries*, New York, NY: John Wiley.

Stamp, P. (1986) 'Kikuyu Women's Self-Help Groups: Toward an Understanding of the Relation between Sex-Gender System and Mode of Production in Africa', in C. Robertson and I. Berger (eds), *Women and Class in Africa*, New York, NY: Africana.

Sudarkasa, N. (1986) 'The Status of Women in Indigenous African Studies', *Feminist Studies* vol. 12, no. 1.

Thiong'o, N. wa (1977) *Petals of Blood*, Nairobi: Heinemann.

Walker, C. (ed.) (1990) *Women and Gender in Southern Africa*, London: James Currey.

Weru, G. (1995) 'Special Report', *Daily Nation*, Nairobi, 23 August.

West, C., and D. Zimmerman (1987) 'Doing Gender', *Gender and Society*, vol. 1, no. 2.

7

Intellectuals and the Democratisation Process in Kenya

Maurice N. Amutabi

... all men are intellectuals, one could therefore say: but not all men have in society the function of intellectuals. (Gramsci 1971: 9)

... the challenge of the intellectual life is to be found in dissent against the status quo at a time when the struggle on behalf of underrepresented and disadvantaged groups seems so unfairly weighted against them. (Said 1994: xvii)

Introduction

The aim of this chapter is twofold. First, it interrogates the role of intellectuals in Kenya's political transition and their contribution to the democratisation process. Second, it examines the collaboration between the intellectuals and the masses in the expansion or constriction of political space. The chapter addresses the role of intellectuals in Kenya not only as agents of social change and continuity but also as sources of ideas and revolution, as role models whose demonstration of leadership capabilities and potential for mass mobilisation entice emulation. It thus seeks to unravel the role of intellectuals in influencing political action and practices in Kenya. Intellectuals are often considered to be the engines of transformation, continuity and change in any society. Ali Mazrui (1978: 352) has noted that 'Many of the great movements of change have been initiated or led by intellectuals'. Further, Said (1994: xi) has affirmed that 'one task of the intellectual is the effort to break down the stereotypes and reductive categories that are so limiting to human thought and communication'. Intellectuals constitute the core of Kenya's intelligentsia. They are supposed to be the formulators and vehicles of ideological dissemination, representatives of the majority and sympathetic to the cause of the ordinary people. The chapter is based on research carried out on Kenya's public intellectuals over a period of two years and covers the years from 1964 to 2004. The discussion engages the body of evidence from different historical and contemporary sources in Kenya, drawing upon primary and secondary sources of data to explore the significance of the role of Kenyan intellectuals in political transition.

Generally, Kenyan intellectuals and the state have never been bedfellows. Many have been detained, sent to jail or ostracised for taking on the government in the past. In presenting this oppositional binary of the relationship of the intellectual to the state in Kenya, we discern intense tensions that are inevitable for the intellectual in social and political life in Kenya. These tensions remain submerged within much of the remnants of the left and radical scholarship in Kenya. We also see these tensions between progressive and reactionary intellectuals. The chapter advances a taxonomic typology of Kenyan intellectuals and examines how they relate among and between themselves and with the government in influencing Kenya's political development.

The Dilemma of Defining Intellectuals

Ali Mazrui (1978: 347) defines an intellectual as 'a person who has the capacity to be fascinated by ideas, and has acquired the skill to handle some of those ideas effectively'. Mazrui's definition is problematic in two ways. First, he assumes that all intellectuals are or must be 'fascinated' by ideas. There are many who are not. Second, lacking a gauge to measure effectiveness, the means of determining if a scholar has handled an idea 'effectively' is imprecise at best. To Edward Said (1994: 23), an intellectual is

> … not always a matter of being a critic of government policy, but rather of thinking of the intellectual vocation as maintaining a state of constant alertness, of a perpetual willingness not to let half-truths or received ideas steer one along. That this involves a steady realism, an almost athletic rational energy, and a complicated struggle to balance the problems of one's own selfhood against the demands of publishing and speaking out in the public sphere …

Of course intellectuals must not always disagree with the positions of governments, but they must also not agree with whatever governments say or do. They should be able to interpret what the government stands for or its position towards ordinary people. They are not expected to believe half-truths but at the same time they need not justify and belabour justification of everything including that which is too obvious (see Mafeje 1995; Mkandawire 1996).

Ideally, an intellectual is a highly informed, opinionated individual in public life who is capable of generating ideas for society, shaping social change and development positively or negatively through public action, speeches, writings and dissemination. Such individuals are self-motivated, highly regarded public spokespersons, who often speak for certain interests of society, especially for the marginalised, the voiceless, the weak and those without representation. On this, Said says, '… intellectuals are individuals with vocation for the art of representing, whether that is talking, writing, teaching, appearing on television. And that vocation is important to the extent that it is publicly recognizable and involves commitment and risk, boldness and vulnerability' (Said 1994: 12–13). An intellectual should be able to contribute to finding solutions to societal problems, especially as far as the weak are concerned, as the intellectual belongs or ought to belong on the same side as the weak and the unrepresented.

The intellectual represents the voice of the people and is often used to legitimate a new nationalist conscience and thinking. An intellectual is not simply an academic or an expert ensconced in the safety of the ivory tower, but a person whose ideas are useful and whose solutions to societal problems should be clearly articulated, ideas that can be animated and galvanised into political programmes and action. As Said notes:

> The intellectual's representations, his or her articulations of a cause or idea to society, are not meant primarily to fortify ego or celebrate status. Nor are they principally intended for service within powerful bureaucracies … Intellectual representations are the *activity itself* [emphasis original], dependent on a kind of consciousness that is sceptical, engaged, unremittingly devoted to rational investigation and moral judgment; and this puts the individual on record and on the line. Knowing how to use language well and knowing when to intervene in language are two essential features of intellectual action. (Said 1994: 20)

Thus, the intellectual is neither a pacifier, an arbitrator, a reconciler nor a consensus builder, but a person whose entire being is staked on a critical realisation, a realisation of being unwilling to accept easy answers or formulas or ready-made clichés, or slogans of what the powerful have to say. It is tough to be an intellectual. That is why in the past, intellectuals such as Karl Marx, Frederick Engels, Che Guevara and Walter Rodney had to flee their home countries (see Lamming 1960; Zeleza 1994; Anyidoho 1997; Sand 1997; Said 2000; Nyamnjoh and Jua 2002; Zeleza and Olukoshi 2004). Some of Kenya's intellectuals such as Ngugi wa Thiong'o, Ali Mazrui and Alamin Mazrui have been forced to flee into exile for dear life. There are many others who underwent similar tribulations under Kenya African National Union (KANU) in Kenya. Others withdrew into convenient cocoons or conformed to the mundane, pedestrian, systemic and ethnic pandering prevalent in Kenya's intellectual arena.

An intellectual is also a respected opinion leader; a paragon of social, economic and political engineering; a transformative social agent committed to particular articulation of the interests of the economically and politically dominated, sectionalised, classed and raced, and gendered interests, needs, desires and aspirations of embattled social groups. '... the intellectual always stands between loneliness and alignment' (Said 1994: 22). Such an individual is supposed to be a projection, a representation, a mirror or even an 'emanation', to use the language of Robinson (1983), of particular group interests and historical and cultural realities. The intellectual straddles the contradictory world of the private, solitary practice of scholarship and the public world of the embattled masses, their popular imagination and their popular will.

The role of intellectuals in Africa cannot be gainsaid. As Mazrui (1978: 352) has noted, 'The effect of intellectuals on the modern face of Africa's history has been enormous. The twentieth century might indeed be called the golden age of intellectuals in Africa's history. Many of the great movements of change have been initiated or led by intellectuals'. Ochieng' (1984) foregrounds the existential contradictions of the production of Kenyan intellectuals and links these processes to the vital role in Kenya's political space. Here intellectuals have been leaders of ideas. They have contributed through newspaper columns, workshops and seminars, through works of fiction such as novels and plays among other ways. Others have contributed by participating in public action such as demonstrations and protest rallies. It was, however, from the 1980s culminating in the 1990s that Kenya's organic/activist and academic intellectuals galvanised the people in bringing about profound and tremendous changes in the political and social arena. In this endeavour, Kenyan intellectuals were helped by changes taking place at the global level, where dictatorships were collapsing. It was just a matter of time before the Kenyan dictatorship under KANU would also capitulate.

Typologies of Intellectuals

Antonio Gramsci identified two types of intellectuals, traditional and organic. Traditional intellectuals included teachers, priests and administrators. Organic intellectuals included industrial technicians and specialists in political economy among other specialists. Gramsci believed that organic intellectuals were dynamic and active. They were actively involved in societal development in many ways, and they struggled to change minds and expand opportunities such as markets, unlike priests and teachers who seemed to remain in one place doing the same jobs year in and year out (Gramsci 1971: 9). But no fine line prevents one individual from straddling these categories of intellectuals. In Kenya, there have been traditional intellectuals, especially teachers and priests, who went beyond what Gramsci imagined of them. The leaders in the immediate post-independence Kenya, such as Oginga Odinga, Joseph Otiende and Jeremiah Nyagah among others, were mainly teachers before they became politicians. Accordingly, in his discussion of elites, Kipkorir (1972: 259) has noted that the interaction between the elite's social aspirations and African societies' politico-economic exigencies, in general, created the climate of hope both for the solution of the masses' problems and for the attainment of the elite's own political objectives. Its basis was the mass societies' belief in education as the primary qualification for leadership. Priests and other clergy have also been vocal in Kenya's public space, and names such as Henry Okullu, Alexander Muge, Timothy Njoya, Ndingi Mwana Nzeki and Mutava Musyimi come to mind immediately due to the role they have played in the democratisation process in Kenya.

Ali Mazrui (1978) has identified four types of intellectuals. These include academic intellectuals, literary intellectuals, political intellectuals and general intellectuals. He says that academic intellectuals are the category that relates intellectual pursuits to higher learning and commits its mental resources to the arts of teaching and research and are found at university campuses. Literary intellectuals, according to Mazrui, need not be attached to the university, but they could be. They are engaged in a significant way in writing either as a full-time profession or as a serious pastime. Many eminent journalists belong to this class of intellectuals. So do poets, novelists and playwrights, who may or may not be involved in higher education. Political intellectuals are the most ideologically engaged of all intellectuals, though they by no means hold a monopoly of ideological commitment. Finally, general intellectuals are a residual category that caters to people who do not fall under the former three categories.

Mazrui's categorisation is problematic in several ways. First, in the Kenyan context, there are many academics who are also writers and politicians at the same time, such as Kivutha Kibwana, Grace Ogot and Anyang' Nyong'o. There are also academics such as George Saitoti, Christine Mango, Kilemi Mwiria and Ruth Oniang'o, among others, who also happen to be politicians. Mazrui's typology can be misleading and confusing. As an alternative, I propose four types of intellectuals in Kenya, including organic or activist intellectuals, bourgeois or authoritarian intellectuals, academic or philosophical intellectuals and generic or general intellectuals.

Organic or activist intellectuals

Organic or activist intellectuals need not be politicians or clergy or academics. They can be two of the above, or all. They are the most known. The majority in this category constitute the political martyrs. They are often the societal vanguards and live poor miserable lives as they are usually married to the struggle. Unfortunately, it is from the ranks of this category that ruling elites often recruit their followers, owing to the success of this group of intellectuals in bringing about change. Recruiting them often makes them mellow. In Kenya, almost the entire organic and activist group of intellectuals has been incorporated and absorbed into the ranks of the National Alliance Rainbow Coalition (NARC) government. There is a completely new set of organic or activist intellectuals that is emerging and joining ranks with the former bourgeoisie and authoritarian intellectuals.

Organic or activist intellectuals are in many ways populist in their pursuits. They pursue political and people-centred objectives, which by and large get them into direct confrontation with the state. They are always at the centre of action and directly involved. The work of the organic intellectual is always linked to a larger dynamic than a particular locality or moment in history. This is in realisation of the fact that the best way of influencing the masses is an organic bonding in which the intellectual draws directly from the collective power of the embattled and oppressed sections of society, such as the case of the urban poor and the unemployed who were effectively utilised by the National Convention Executive Council (NCEC) in 1997 under Kivutha Kibwana and Willy Mutunga (see Mutunga 1999). However, this type of vanguardism should not be taken for granted. When this type of vanguardism occurs, as Freire (1970) and Harris (1989) have warned, society must be aware of those with 'egocentric imaginations' who are otherwise opportunistic. Though presenting themselves in contemporary impressionistic language of 'people-centred', 'grassroots-oriented', 'people-driven', these mask their real intentions. Usually, they operate within the broader projection of the transformation of society that argues for rights, for ordinary peoples' access to basic needs and wants, and the desire for a good life. Although without any pretence to Marxist or socialist ideals, this category of intellectuals certainly contains elements of vanguardism.

Since they are mainly populist in their pursuits and will stop at nothing to satisfy their followers, organic or activist intellectuals often encounter violence on issues where the state is against their intervention or where the state wants to have its way and perceives their actions as interference. Their actions and concerns range from human rights, public land, political grievances and education for the marginalised to environmental issues, and include in their agenda anything that requires intervention on the side of the masses. These individuals cannot avoid the police and they often spend a reasonable amount of time in litigation against the state and in police cells, such as Ngugi wa Thiong'o, Wangari Maathai, James Orengo, Nicholas Nyangira, Odegi-Awuondo, Katama Mkangi, Kivutha Kibwana, Willy Mutunga and Alamin Mazrui (see Amutabi 2002). They often suffer tribulations as Alamin Mazrui recollects:

> As you may be aware, my decision to take up a job and establish residence in the USA can be traced back to June 1982 when I and a few other colleagues at Kenyatta University and the University of Nairobi – Willy Mutunga, Kamoji Wacira, Edward Oyugi, Maina Kinyatti – were arrested and (with the exception of Maina) detained (under the Preservation of Public Security Act). By all indication, our fate seemed connected to our role in the University Academic Staff Association that had been critical of certain government policies. I believe that at that time we had just reacted to a statement by Joseph Kamotho – the then Minster of Higher Education – that the government would seek to control what we teach at the university. In my own case, there was an added factor of my newly released Kiswahili

play, *Kilio cha Haki*, which at that time and for some unclear reason was considered subversive. (Personal interview, 17 May 2002)

Subsequent to his arrest, Alamin Mazrui spent 18 months in detention at Kamiti Maximum Security Prison. After his release from detention, he could not secure a job at any Kenyan institution and was forced to flee into exile, first in Nigeria at the University of Port Harcourt, then later in the United States. Thus, the differential consciousness of the organic and activist intellectual is often generated across a plurality of sites and contexts, such as the academic rights that Mazrui and colleagues were pursuing in the 1980s and 1990s and the constitutional court battles that James Orengo, Gibson Kamau Kuria and others mounted against Moi's regime before 2002. Therefore, the defining dimension of people like Ngugi wa Thiong'o or Alamin Mazrui as organic or activist intellectuals is in their striking ingenuity in interpreting Kenya's politics, tensions, similarities and differences in class through works of drama and fiction and the art of dialogue and deconstruction.

Bourgeois or authoritarian intellectuals

Authoritarian intellectuals are the types that were used for generation of propaganda materials in Eastern Europe by communist dictators such as Nicolai Ceausescu in Romania and Erich Honecker in East Germany. In the former Soviet Union, the Politburo had a litany of propaganda specialists that were respected by ordinary people. The capitalist counterparts of the authoritarian intellectuals are the bourgeois intellectuals. Many dictatorial regimes in Africa recruited such intellectuals who often acted in cahoots with the state while pretending to espouse their own views. In Kenya, Dr Nick Wanjohi and Prof. Henry Mwanzi played such a role for KANU, when they served in the party's Directorate of Research and Development and as the party's Executive Officer, respectively. The extreme case of such a crop of intellectuals was observed in Rwanda during the genocide (see Chege 1996; Mamdani 2001).

The bourgeois/authoritarian intellectuals are often committed to status quo issues. They are converts to the ideals and projects of the system of production favoured by the status quo. They are never ashamed of their actions (or pretend not to be) so long as they are compensated for their services to the system. Bourgeois intellectuals in particular are at home with capitalism. They are fascinated by and in agreement with capitalism's organisation, so-called efficiency, planning and its means-ends pretended rationality even as it radically reduces and subordinates Africans' creativity and imagination, turning them into commodities for production and profit-making. For the bourgeois intellectuals, any project, even within the academy, is just part of an instrumental infrastructure where capitalist and state interests are to be allowed to function freely so long as their interests are also catered for. Here, the bourgeois/authoritarian intellectuals are on hire and receive spillover effects within the system where they strategically embed themselves as gatekeepers to the feasts inside. They often constitute the nucleus of national institutional think tanks that more often than not act as conduits of reward more than any meaningful solution-seeking programmes to development problems.

Freire (1970) warns that the bourgeois or authoritarian intellectual is a vanguardist class that leads by commands, edicts and pronouncements without consultation with the popular will, and which ultimately cuts itself off from the humanising processes associated with the masses. In the most extreme form, such an intellectual is what Nietzsche (1967) calls a resentment type. That is, they define their identity through the negation and resentment of others, through chicanery and lies. Such intellectuals exist in real or imaginary isolation from society's working poor and are driven by a dangerously narrow-minded programme of retributive morality and personal gain, expedience and survival. We live in the times of the ascendancy of this intellectual type in Kenya in more pronounced ways than before. But the most vivid embodiments of this bourgeois/authoritarian type of intellectual are the veiled ethnic chauvinists who rail against the government and against the corruption at City Hall in Nairobi so long as a member of their own ethnic group is not one of the fat cats under scrutiny. They are hopelessly hooked on *Majimboism* and addicted to the idea of rotating the presidency. They often speak of the interests of minority ethnic groups as permanent features in their writings to attract attention.

In this category of bourgeois/authoritarian intellectuals are also writers of political commentaries that were often aired on state-owned radio and television, and conformists and supporters of the KANU system. Some writers of status quo commentaries in national newspapers could be included even if they were not on the payroll of the establishment. These types can be disruptive in as much as they push their own agenda. Their best mode is a distorted propaganda approach that often undermines the progressive elements of society.

They derive a lot of pleasure from labelling and misrepresenting. They are often hired by authoritarian governments to do the dirty political jobs and at times participate in authenticating and justifying state schemes through pseudo-journalistic analyses veiled in some pedestrian, commonplace jargon. Such intellectuals are described in Achebe's *Anthills of the Savannah* (1987).

Academic or philosophical intellectuals

Academic and philosophical intellectuals are interested in issues of discourse and knowledge production. They are excited about new ideas and pushing the academic and scholarly projects to new logics and horizons. They are not activists but they make their ideas known through recognisable dissemination. They might occasionally write in the media and even appear on television or radio. They love the university and other academic forums. In Kenya, the late Odera Oruka would be the best example. Others would include Daniel Mbiti, Jay Kitsao, Katete Orwa and Eric Masinde Aseka (after he quit YK '92) among others.

The academic or philosophical intellectuals are widespread and found mainly in learning institutions besides other areas. They draw on the peculiarities of knowledge that exists in society and pursue specific objectives pertinent to societal good. They often focus on such issues as development models and paradigms, cultural revivalism and nationalism, and historical memories of such issues as language and customs, their recuperation and restoration, and preservation for posterity. They ask new questions, whose answers help society. They often seek answers to national questions and issues that cannot be solved by society in general. Academic/philosophical intellectuals are often concerned with remedying and correcting previous ills beyond the kind of stifling essentialism, philistinism and absolutism that accompany dictatorial regimes and which can too often damage the sense of vision and perception of what is useful for the national good. They are also concerned with the interconnections and linkages among differently arranged groups and ethnic groups in a nation, establishing ways through which positive energies can be cultivated, and minimising tensions and conflict situations.

The academic/philosophical intellectual insists on the interdependent relations between national interest groups and the societies they create and inhabit, and not on exploitative pursuits such as those pursued by bourgeois/authoritarian intellectuals. The academic or philosophical intellectuals and bourgeois or authoritarian intellectuals do not often agree and most of the time they do not like each other, as they tend to belong to different camps in the same state. Oruka's discourse on sage philosophy and the place of widow guardianship among the Luo, for example, belongs to academic/philosophical intellectual discourse. His views were widely embraced because of his simplicity and interaction with ordinary people who easily identified with his ideas. His contribution democratised and humanised widow guardianship among the Luo while faulting its demonisation by activist groups and religious extremists.

But perhaps the most consuming theoretical object of academic or philosophical intellectuals' work in Kenya has been their effort to understand the relationship between the intellectual as professional mediator in the violent confrontation between capitalism and its materialistic power on one hand and the masses' struggle to overcome impositions of state comprador authority on the other. The academic/philosophical intellectuals have ceaselessly been preoccupied with attacks on the KANU regime, de-emphasising ethnic isolationism, separation and bifurcation of the individual and nation, and opposing *majimboism* (regionalism) as promulgated by snobbish KANU politicians. They instead presented well-articulated arguments as a counterpoise to majimboism, presenting democracy as a panacea to development problems afflicting Kenya besides eradication of regime rigidities and poor leadership.

These intellectuals have exposed the vices of the KANU regime, especially theft, human rights and abuse of office, particularly in the post-1992 period when the state spiralled into more decay and development quagmire. In the process the intellectuals won the confidence of the international community, even the conservative British. A struggle ensued between articulate academic and philosophical intellectuals such as Peter Anyang' Nyong'o and randy establishment politicians rallying ethnic masses to their side. This occurred widely and at all levels in the then ethnicised Kenyan society. For Nyong'o, for example, democracy was best articulated and organised around institutions and was much more than just removing KANU from power. To him, as to many academic as well as organic and activist intellectuals, ethnicity was a negation, as ethnic logic rode on the underside of the rapid democratisation of modern Kenyan society.

Nyong'o and Apollo Njonjo's experimentation in building Charity Kaluki Ngilu as a formidable presidential candidate under the Social Democratic Party (SDP) in the 1997 presidential elections was a great success even if she did not make it to State House. Planning and careful strategising were clearly deployed and it was apparent that these were identified as strong ingredients in electioneering in Kenya for the first time, a lesson that would prove useful in 2002 when the opposition united under NARC. Many intellectuals were in agreement that ethnic logic was the product of the colonisation of Kenya, which the Kenyatta and Moi regimes had used successfully to insulate their own regimes, and would be pursued by whoever removed KANU. What they did not agree with was that this was an obstacle to unity. Of course, ethnicity was subsequently deployed by NARC in ways similar to KANU. On this fact, Eric Aseka has been vindicated in his re-Kikuyunisation of Kenyan bureaucracy thesis. In his public conversations, debates and utterances, Aseka had warned about this happening in the event that KANU capitulated. Kenyans have seen this come to pass under the NARC government.

Generic or general intellectuals

These intellectuals are generic in the sense that they are derived from other types and general because they cannot easily fit in any of the other categories of intellectuals. Generic/general intellectuals are not easy to discern as a category and are best suited to the cocktail of all kinds of public protests that have impacted society in one way or another. Even reaching a conclusion on whether a contribution by a public functionary qualifies as an intellectual pursuit is also not easy to pinpoint as there are usually no agreed-upon intellectual conjectures. Of course in the past, much of the discussion about intellectuals in public life was heavily influenced by Marxist revolutionary thought and framed in the language of oppositional discourse, so that any opposing or dissenting voices often found recognition in the intellectualist discourse as 'other' voices. Thus, all kinds of voices that are oppositional and have strong dogmatic and persuasive ideological articulation could pass as intellectual pursuits within this realm.

We can include in the rubric of generic/general intellectuals the work of artists, writers, poets, teachers, singers, journalists, clergy, the petite bourgeoisie and other professionals involved in shaping society's behaviour. Works of fiction such as novels and other types of creative writings belong to this category. What comes to mind as a useful example is the *Whispers* column by Wahome Mutahi, which appeared alternately in the *Sunday Nation* and the *Sunday Standard*. Wahome allows us to see the complexity of the generic intellectual through the eyes of *Whispers*, a middle-class protagonist struggling to survive capitalism. Visible in all the accounts is a ceaseless struggle 'to arrive'. There are tensions between the characters and those around them and a certain will to survive the ravages of capitalism and expectations of the ordinary people represented by *Whispers*' wife (Thatcher), children (son Junior and daughter Pajero), mother (Appep) and uncle (Jethro), and how they all fail to master a terrain ingrained and dominated by capitalist structures, but which bourgeois intellectuals celebrate. Wahome Mutahi also churned out some plays, mostly in Gikuyu which were by entirely Kikuyu casts to Kikuyu audiences in mainly Kikuyu dominated places. It is very clear that Whispers was a space for expressing political frustration by calling politicians names. Equally, many Kikuyus who watched Wahome's plays said that they received political messages in coded language and in rich Kikuyu metaphors. But how successful this was in helping transform Kenya's political space is a tough call to make. Hence Wahome's contribution falls in the realm of generic/general intellectual pursuit. Included in this category are the work and activities of religious leaders such as Henry Okullu, Alexander Muge, Timothy Njoya, Ndingi Mwana Nzeki and Mutava Musyimi.

Many generic intellectuals have no institutional basis, are sporadic and unpredictable in what they state and have often styled themselves as freelance newspaper columnists, social and political commentators and political pundits, who at times serve atavistic, sectarian and ethnic interests. However, the important thing to note in this categorisation is that all these typologies are not cast in iron but dynamically overlap. They nevertheless help us in appreciating the complexity inherent in the actions of intellectuals in Kenya. It is apparent in these typologies that in order to be a fully rounded actor who optimises on this critical role in society, the intellectual has often been made to think beyond the particularity of his or her individual interests, ethnic allegiance, personal needs and desires. From the available evidence, this has not always been successful. We should interrogate the work of the public intellectual in Kenya more carefully and critically, taking into consideration the pitfalls of abandonment and even betrayal of the collective course of unravelling and correcting KANU excesses. Even as we examine intellectuals through the four typologies, we must be reminded that part of the brief for all intellectuals is to ensure societal equity and egalitarianism. That is, to pay close attention to the dialectic between oppression and rebellion, and unravel the uneasiness in the relations between the exploiters and the exploited with a view to proposing ways of bridging the gap.

Kenya's Intellectuals in Action

The 1970s are often remembered in East Africa as the most productive for the intellectuals. This is the time when East Africa was a significant player in the global arena of ideas. In all this, organic/activist intellectuals were the most effective vehicles of interest articulation and political mobilisation. The political course in Kenya would not be the same today without organic/activist intellectuals especially from the 1970s to the 1990s. If anything, there seems to be a decline in the role of intellectuals in Kenya since the 1990s compared to the earlier period. Ochieng' notes:

> There was a time, immediately after independence, when the Kenyan politician worth his salt was never happy until he had been given an opportunity to address university audiences. In the mid-sixties major policy statements were addressed to the gathered academicians and red-gowned students at the University's Taifa Hall. I can still remember the endless debates, which Kenyan leaders like Tom Mboya, Gikonyo Kiano, and Ronald Ngala held with us. (Ochieng' 1984: 48)

Referring to those days, Ochieng' says, 'Those were the days when our celebrated scholars like Okot P'Bitek, Allan Ogot, Ali Mazrui and Taban Lo Liyong would write incessantly on African culture, literature and political thought. The pages of the now defunct *East African Journal* were littered with insightful ... dialogues between academicians and members of parliament on our social, economic and political aspirations' (Ochieng' 1984: 48).

But the vibrancy of the intellectual climate was not confined to Kenya. At the University of Dar es Salaam, Walter Rodney, Dani Nabudere, Issa Shivji and Grant Kamenju among others were articulating socialist ideas in the wake of the dependency, underdevelopment and neo-colonialism debates. At Makerere University, Mahmood Mamdani, Ali Mazrui, Semakula Kiwanuka, Edward Rugumayo and Apollo Nsibambi were also very active in bipolar debates. Thus, Shivji (2002) has cynically dismissed the new fascination with post-modernism and donor-inspired praises at Dar es Salaam, arguing that the main reason why it was a renowned centre of excellence was because the discourses there paid keen attention to the plight of the majority working classes and peasants of Africa. In Uganda, Apollo Nsibambi has been disarmed, as many others, through political rewards and serves as prime minister. Semakula Kiwanuka is minister in charge of the Luwero Triangle and Edward Rugumayo the minister for Trade and Industry. As Nabudere put it during the 10th CODESRIA General Assembly in Kampala, these intellectuals led by Museveni have become 'revolutionaries of the World Bank'.

The plight of intellectuals in Kenya had a lot to do with the nature of the state and the perceptions of intellectuals and intellectual work among Kenya's leaders. Presidents Jomo Kenyatta and Daniel Moi had no thick skin to entertain critics and intellectualism in their terrain. They were not very intellectual themselves. Compared to Julius Nyerere of Tanzania who often engaged intellectuals at the University of Dar es Salaam in debates on politics and development, Kenyatta and Moi were intellectual pariahs. They instead assumed a gerontocratic stance and regarded themselves as untainted *wazee*, without blemish. They eliminated, detained or co-opted political critics and intellectuals critical of the excesses of their regimes. Argwings Kodhek, Pio Gama Pinto and Josiah Mwangi Kariuki were all victims of political elimination during Kenyatta's regime. Robert Ouko was the most prominent victim of Moi's regime, although the cover-up scheme snowballed to claim many more lives of those directly or indirectly involved. Because of the murderous nature of these regimes, intellectuals ran scared from the late 1970s to the late 1990s in Kenya. Of course, there are some who worked for these regimes as conformists, composing patriotic songs, praising and 'philosophising' on 'Harambee', 'Nyayo' and so forth.

Thus, even as the university in Kenya was at its zenith with regard to influencing events and thinking at the national level, its infiltration with special branch spies undermined intellectual creativity and its ability to influence national trends. The presence at the university of perceived leftist luminaries or radical lecturers like Ngugi wa Thiong'o, Okot P'Bitek, E.S. Atieno-Odhiambo, Maina wa Kinyatti, Willy Mutunga, Alamin Mazrui, Kamoji Wachira, Edward Oyugi, Mukaru Ng'ang'a, Peter Anyang' Nyong'o, Gibson Kamau Kuria, Shadrack Gutto, Nicholas Nyangira, Katama Mkangi and Ngotho Kariuki among others caused a lot of excitement nationwide but also opened them to state interference that limited the space for free expression and innovative thinking. But in the final analysis, and for a sustained period of time, the university remained academically vibrant and tumultuous and a hub of political activism, active theoretical formulation, debates and Marxist sloganeering. Popular and political literature, public speeches and pamphleteering became widespread. In articulating the democratic initiative, national leaders were invited to the university to give talks on different aspects of national development. In these exchanges, the university communities helped in shaping or influencing policy as some important decisions were made in such meetings. Overall, however, despite the respect and place of honour for dons, there was increasing suspicion from the secret police (special branch) and the politicians. The picture that one therefore obtains of the university is one where alternating struggles for vibrancy and freedom co-existed with authoritarianism and mismanagement.

Contrasting examples of intellectuals in action

The heroic narrative on the role of intellectuals discussed in the previous section is based on the inspiring work of the gadfly Kenyan historian William Ochieng', who until the end of the 1980s had little experience as a bourgeois intellectual. In 1990, Ochieng' was appointed Principal of Maseno University College before being promoted to become Permanent Secretary (PS) in the Office of the President based at State House. Using Ochieng's own case of co-optation, one can hazard a response to a set of questions that he ironically posed. Regarding the apparent political inactivity of intellectuals in the 1980s compared to the 1960s and 1970s, Ochieng' asks:

> What went wrong? Did our academicians lose interest in the political issues of the state? Or have they been scared into silence? Or can we assume that our current academicians are incapable of reflecting on fundamental political issues that affect us? How come that we never get, from time to time, authoritative discussions and reflections by our political scientists on our political performance? How come that none of our political scientists ever discuss African and international political developments in the magazines that one comes across everywhere in the streets of Nairobi? (Ochieng' 1984: 48)

There are no straight answers to these questions. But a clear reality is that many are the intellectuals whose formerly admirable careers as proponents of the disempowered majority have been co-opted to join the state propaganda machine that has in turn been deployed to defeat any serious intellectual work and innovative research. Ochieng', who was once admired as a voice of reason, became conformist himself from 1990 upon appointment as Principal and later as PS in charge of Research and Policy (actually propaganda). His commitment to the course of the ordinary people disappeared. He turned against the very peasants that educated him. In 1998, Ochieng' shocked the academic world that knew his advocacy for the peasants when he told a Nyanza leaders' symposium on education at the Kisumu Tom Mboya Labour College that there was need for a deliberate policy to be put in place to have land among the peasants in Nyanza shifted to the educated middle class with resources to exploit it commercially. He said more than 90 per cent of the land in Luoland was owned by impoverished peasants who, in his opinion, could not put it to economic use. He said, 'You see huge embarrassing bushes everywhere, even during the planting season. They are owned by old men and women who cannot afford to make economic use out of it' (quoted in Onditi 1998: 1). Ochieng' had come full cycle to become a bourgeois/authoritarian intellectual of the KANU think-tank mode.

As a bourgeois intellectual doing KANU's bidding, Ochieng' defended the dictatorial Moi system to the hilt in newspaper articles, especially through the KANU mouthpiece, the *Kenya Times* news-paper, and at workshops and conferences. A personal experience will suffice to illustrate this. One time in 1995, a departmental seminar in which I was to present a paper entitled 'Beyond Nyayo: Some Reflections on the Post Moi Era in Kenya' was cancelled at the eleventh hour at Moi University. The university authorities asked me if I knew that I was risking sedition and treason for imagining Kenya without Moi. I was taken to the local CID offices in Eldoret where I recorded a statement. Three months later at a UNESCO conference in Kericho, Ochieng' requested to meet me over lunch to give me 'some fatherly advice'. It turned out that he knew everything about my so-called radicalism at Moi University. He asked me to slow down. He said that he was once like that – in a hurry – but changed when he saw no sense in it. He did not tell me when he stopped see-ing sense, but when he became PS, I figured that it would take him a while to rediscover the sense. He did in 2002. In a piece published in the *Sunday Standard* newspaper of 26 October 2003, Ochieng' lamented about how the Kibaki administration had kicked him out of State House without caring about how he would pay his rent and what his children would eat! Ochieng's own words, before he converted to bourgeois/authoritarian intellectualism, explain what went wrong with some Kenyan intellectuals: '… majority of our academics are capitalists who, in their quiet way, support the rampant rat-race of our time. Many of them dream of huge cars, professorial chairs, fantastic bungalows and brimming bank accounts. All these they hope to acquire without any tangible work. The welfare of the people and the conduct of public affairs is hardly their concern' (Ochieng' 1984: 51).

During the KANU reign, surveillance was the order of the day. It was an open secret that some lecturers spied on fellow lecturers on behalf of the government. Radical lecturers could not hope to get promoted but those that were committed to the struggle for democratisation were not bothered by this tokenism sometimes advanced through promotions or appointment as chairs of departments. In those days, universities were under the control of the Office of the President (OP) in everything but name, and one required clearance from the OP to visit even a neighbouring country. It was a reign of terror particularly after the 1982 attempted coup, around the period when Alamin Mazrui became a victim of the terror and security surveillance. It was because of this grip of the OP on universities that universities could not hire perceived radical lecturers. Vice-chancellors became gatekeepers of the state and ranking members of KANU.

Ngugi wa Thiong'o is one of Kenya's foremost organic and even academic/philosophical intellectuals. He provides a contrasting example to Ochieng's described above. His forte has been knowledge production and generation and dissemination of ideas. There is no doubt that the person and ideas of Ngugi have been at the centre of democratic action for a while in Kenya. Ngugi is the first Kenyan organic intellectual to use writing and fiction to successfully take on the postcolonial state in Kenya. Simon Gikandi has pointed out that Ngugi's novels and essays provide a framework for understanding politics in Kenya, arguing that indeed 'fiction can be a conduit of understanding and a means of confronting the past… [in Kenya]' (Gikandi 2000a: 3). A true revolutionary, Ngugi has been bothered by the fact that just like the colonial state, the post-colonial Kenyan state had developed elaborate structures of domination, control and manipulation which he has always sought to change. In *Devil on the Cross*, he examines the power dynamics in Kenya, revealing that the hold of the African capitalist class in Kenya is stronger than before, but is even more visibly a satellite or derivative power, given or withheld by the international capitalist system. Ngugi is unhappy with the undemocratic arrogance of Kenyan capitalists towards their own people, which is matched only by their grovelling to their foreign masters (the Kenyan master of ceremonies at the Feast at Ilmorog declaring that they are the willing slaves of foreign capitalists).

However, it is with *I Will Marry When I Want* that Ngugi achieved his greatest democratic appeal, as an organic/activist, and academic/philosophical intellectual. Gikandi (2000a: 185) says that 'With the writing and performance of *I Will Marry When I Want* in 1978 Ngugi was finally able to achieve his aesthetic ambition – to overcome the gap that separates his art and his politics'. Ngugi sought a revolutionary way of speaking to the peasants through a village theatre at Kamirithu near Limuru. Here, villagers intermingled with university students and lecturers as they enjoyed political satire and caricaturing of political leaders. The valorisation of the village theatre was itself revolutionary in two ways. First Ngugi was able to access the peasants and engage them in unmediated dialogue in his own language. Second, he did not need a government permit, as was the case then, to hold the meeting as it was educational, hence circumventing the dictatorial Kenyatta and Moi regimes. In 1980, the government banned and demolished the theatre because of its increasing popularity, which the government feared would lead to widespread disaffection. In *I Will Marry When I Want*, Ngugi (with Ngugi wa Mirii) menacingly engaged the Kenya government in an indirect manner, as it considered the peasants its preserve. Indeed Ngugi was arrested and detained in December 1977 for this onslaught on what the government considered its terrain, an act that was meant to stop production and publication of *I Will Marry When I Want*. Many were surprised that Ngugi was detained for a work that did not contain anything he had not stated in *Petals of Blood*, which had been published only the year before. Perhaps the concern of the State was Ngugi's direct engagement with *hoi polloi* at Kamirithu (Gikandi 2000b).

The play *I Will Marry When I Want* was as political as Ngugi's other plays, but it was the way that the play was performed that played more politics on stage than the words. A seminal scene in Act 1 of the play opens with a bold declaration of its political message through Kiguunda's invectives against the post-colonial condition. The audience was made to admire the violence of the peasant Kiguunda. It was very clear that Ngugi's discourse was about the haves and have-nots. Through the play, Ngugi was concerned with the recovery of memory and its recuperation. He was concerned about the dissemination of facts and enlightenment of the peasants. The past returns to Kiguunda in the form of songs and dances that were banished throughout the colonial project. The dialogic tone ranges from memory to action, nostalgia to defiance, in two emotional binary oppositions that connect the actors and the audience to a time that many in Kenya would prefer to forget. Thus, 'the remembrance of things past' is a marker of the relevance of the past in the present. It is the defiance of memory against the amnesia and silence that the state wants to promote (Thiong'o and Mirii 1982: 26).

To Ngugi, the culture of suppression and silencing through issuing of permits is bad and should be opposed. There is a need for the people to know the truth and circumvent the state. His project is one of 'de-silencing' or giving voice to the masses. It is one of memorialising great moments in the history of ordinary people whether they are supported by the state or not. As well as offering a model of intellectual practice in his radical oppositional approach to history, Ngugi stands out as someone who, despite all the vagaries of politics and vicissitudes of history in Kenya, retains a clear-sighted belief in left-wing politics and the possibility that ordinary people can create a fundamentally better world for themselves. A true intellectual, he has not wavered and has remained committed to his radical position over the years, and this has earned him admirers and followers not only in Kenya but globally as well. His liberation literature has been very fulfilling and empowering to Kenyans who read his books. Ngugi has been criticised for having decided to write in his native language Gikuyu. Whereas many have seen this as retrogressive for someone with such a large national and international following, one commentator has pointed out that this was not only a significant intellectual decision but a democratic one as well. The change, Williams (1999: 13) argues, convinced Ngugi of the importance of communicating with his people without foreign interference.

Following Kamirithu, the use of theatre for civic education and fostering of democratic ideals were taken up more fervently by literary scholars and other playwrights in Kenya, such as Francis Imbuga. Francis Imbuga's *Man of Kafira*, a play based on a political plot that re-enacted Kenya's political happenings in comical satire, became the prototype of the kind of plays that were performed in many theatres. In fact, *Man of Kafira* among other plays did not have it smooth. It was initially banned as being 'too political'. Imbuga's *Betrayal in the City* and

Kivutha Kibwana's *Kanzala* are other examples of the role of theatre in democratisation, as they both carried political messages.

Intellectuals and Kenya's Second Liberation

The second liberation in Kenya owes a lot to intellectuals. It was the result of careful planning, calculation, organisation and strategy on the part of all those opposed to KANU. For instance, intellectuals worked hard in 1992 to create the Forum for Restoration of Democracy (FORD) but their scheme was nipped in the bud when FORD was destroyed by KANU machinations and the alter egos of individual politicians. The originators of the idea to form FORD were Anyang' Nyong'o, Wamalwa Kijana, Mukhisa Kituyi and James Orengo who handed over to Oginga Odinga, Masinde Muliro and Martin Shikuku among others. FORD almost succeeded in forming the government in 1992. But it was not until 2002 that they succeeded in forming NARC, an alliance that cut across political and class divides.

Apart from Ngugi wa Thiong'o, there were many other intellectuals whose role in the democratisation process in the 1990s was instrumental. One such prominent organic and activist intellectual who has played a formidable role in the second liberation was Wangari Maathai. Maathai was often at the receiving end of the KANU regime from the 1980s, attacks she faced with single-minded determination and vigour as she spearheaded the struggle for the respect of democratic values and the environment. Maathai's Green Belt Movement (GBM) was instrumental in forcing change from wrong and unpopular KANU government policy pursuits.

Maathai relinquished her academic position at the University of Nairobi in the 1970s and devoted herself to work in defence of the environment. Such was the route that led her to confrontation with KANU in 1986. This was the controversy that started on 19 July 1989 when KANU blocked off a section of Uhuru Park (the only significant public park in Nairobi) with the intention of building what was billed to be the tallest building in Africa, with 80 floors. The gigantic building complex was to be KANU headquarters. Newspapers and the grapevine were awash with stories that the building's upper 20 floors were to be shaped in the likeness of President Moi's head or his favourite club (*rungu*). Initially supported overwhelmingly by KANU hawks, it appeared at first that the party would have its way on the acquisition of this public land. But Maathai led opposition against the project and mounted campaigns against it. Opponents of the construction rallied countrywide, made presentations at local and international conferences challenging the project, and mobilised and brought local and international pressure to bear on KANU. Eventually, KANU called off the project. After only two years, the major financier for the construction pulled out citing the unfeasibility and environmental risks of the project. On 17 November 1991, KANU pulled down the remaining part of the fence. This triumph raised Maathai's standing in society as a crusader for the environment. Ten years later, Maathai achieved yet another victory by successfully stopping the dismemberment and sharing out of Karura Forest among KANU bigwigs.

Wangari's fight against the obstinate KANU regime did not end with the Uhuru Park construction affair. On 4 March 1992, police beat and tear-gassed innocent and unarmed women who had stripped naked in protest against the unjust detention of political prisoners. Most of them were mothers and sisters of political prisoners. The sight of nude women at Uhuru Park being clobbered mercilessly by police was scary and many predicted doom for KANU since, as someone pointed out, 'traditionally, when a woman bares herself, you run away, you do not beat her'. All this happened amidst a hunger strike in Uhuru Park, organised by Wangari Maathai. Maathai and fellow activists were pressing for the release of political prisoners. A confrontation ensued in which Maathai was clubbed unconscious by the police and was hospitalised in a critical condition at a Nairobi hospital. The country expected the worst. However, contrary to expectations, Maathai not only recovered but was even able to travel to Rio de Janeiro, Brazil, for the June 1992 Earth Summit, where she gave the keynote address for non-governmental organisations dealing with the environment. Freedom Square (the place where women protesters were beaten by police) was born as a separate space at Uhuru Park where people plant trees in commemorating significant developments. Eventually, Maathai was elected in December 2002 to become MP for Tetu in Nyeri District and appointed an Assistant Minister for Environment and Natural Resources in the NARC government. But her efforts were crowned with the award of the Nobel Peace Prize of 2004 beating a range of icons on the nomination list. Above all else, Maathai's nomination has gone a long way to refocus attention on the role of African and Third World women in making the world a better place.

The high point for Kenyan intellectuals came towards the end of 1997, when the country seemed on the verge of a serious meltdown due to street demonstrations in many towns in Kenya (Mutunga 1999). The National Convention Assembly and its executive arm, the NCEC, were sailing on the crest of unprecedented popularity with Nairobi and urban crowds throughout Kenya backing the demonstrations. It all began with a group of organic/activist intellectuals led by lawyers and academics such as Kivutha Kibwana, Willy Mutunga, Davinder Lamba, Kathurima M'Inoti, Korwa Adar, Onyango Omar, Kiraitu Murungi, Katama Mkangi and Gibson Kamau Kuria, and clergy such as Timothy Njoya and Mutava Musyimi resolved to fight for a new constitution following the Limuru and Ufungamano initiatives (see Chapter 2 by Nasong'o in this volume). Then the campaign moved from the Limuru Conference Centre and Ufungamano House to the streets of Nairobi in the form of mass action for minimal constitutional reforms before the 1997 elections. These people had started an initiative to force through constitutional reforms under the auspices of NCEC. As the initiative gathered momentum, the mainstream opposition leaders, Mwai Kibaki, Michael Wamalwa, Raila Odinga, James Orengo and others joined the mass action, which was now euphoric and had reached fever pitch. It was obvious that the police were losing the battle to the crowds and some were slowly joining in. Matters were not helped when it became obvious that there were goons and hoodlums who were taking advantage of the demonstrations and were looting and robbing. Shops in downtown Nairobi closed as the city became deserted. Some people stopped going to work. Owners of public service vehicles withdrew them from service in the city and Nairobi slowly crawled to a halt. There was talk of a grand march to State House. The government tried to use the media to win the war, but in vain.

When the demonstrations and brutal clashes with police threatened general disorder, President Moi moved to State House, Nakuru, from where he issued stern warnings and press statements through the Presidential Press Service. He warned NCEC and other leaders of the consequences of their actions. While NCEC stayed put, the police slowly lost ground in other areas of Kenya to the movement. The government had to negotiate to remain in power. But in a strike of shrewdness, Moi refused to negotiate with the NCEC, claiming that doing so implied recognising a movement they had declared illegal. Thus, even as Moi capitulated and sought dialogue with religious leaders, his aim was not only to resolve the crisis but also calm things down. In the end, the government was forced to concede minimum constitutional and legal changes necessary to facilitate freer and fairer elections. Following the victory of mass action and the threat of it, the Constitution of Kenya Review Commission Act of 1997 was passed to provide a framework for constitutional review. The victory for intellectuals was that they had not only forced Moi to the negotiating table but that there was going to be a review of the constitution before the next elections in 1997. Not many people had given NCEC a chance for pushing it that far but the intellectuals had read the mood of the country, as people wanted change and wanted it urgently. They were only waiting for a vanguard, some ostensible leadership, which the organic/activist intellectuals gave them.

Nevertheless, Moi's broader strategy was to create a schism within the NCEC by emphasising that the government could only talk to elected leaders, not unelected and unrepresentative civil society activists. He made sure that the discussions were conducted in the framework of parliament. The intellectual wing of NCEC fell for the bait and Moi moved the initiative to parliament as soon as the intellectuals gave in to dialogue. When parliament took over the reform agenda, Kenyans expected little, as many of the MPs (both KANU and opposition) were on the payroll of KANU and were ready to do KANU's bidding. The result was the formation of the Inter-Parties Parliamentary Group (IPPG), with Jilo Falana, MP for Fafi, as chairman and George Anyona as secretary. In rapid succession as the 1997 elections approached, parliament enacted many of the constitutional and legislative measures demanded by NCEC intellectuals and activists. Jilo Falana and George Anyona took full advantage of their positions at IPPG and Anyona's mastery of parliamentary procedure to push through outrageous amendments that even Moi would not have envisaged. Anyona, a former firebrand and radical politician, had lost his old fire and had become a fence sitter, easily compromised on many issues in parliament. After the 'minimal' constitutional reforms of 1997 followed by peaceful elections, the opposition was again badly divided, with many opposition leading lights such as Mwai Kibaki, Michael Wamalwa, Raila Odinga, Charity Ngilu and George Anyona gunning for the presidency and losing it to Moi very easily. Maathai had unsuccessfully tried to unite the opposition just before the elections. Although the opposition leaders all retained their seats in the new parliament, Moi won.

After the elections, KANU reneged on many promises it had made at the IPPG meetings. It was obvious that KANU had short-changed the intellectuals through greedy parliamentarians and vocal supporters of IPPG such as Kiraitu Murungi and Mukhisa Kituyi. Other IPPG supporters such as Jilo Falana and Joseph Misoi were locked out, having lost their seats in the elections. Thus the IPPG was used to steal the thunder from intellectuals such as Kibwana, Mutunga and others and from that point it became very difficult for them to recapture the reform and leadership initiative from the Eighth Parliament. But why were the opposition MPs in a hurry to embrace KANU proposals and lock out intellectuals from the negotiating table? First, most MPs feared the popularity that the NCEC had earned for the intellectuals. Second, the NCEC had appeared to blame both KANU and the opposition for the problems afflicting Kenya, and some MPs were not happy. Third, some opposition leaders wrongly thought that the success of the NCEC mass action was a litmus test, which had confirmed that KANU was unpopular and was going to be routed in the polls with or without a new constitution. Finally, it was thought that KANU bought some of the opposition MPs and used them to silence the intellectuals.

Finally, following their high profile participation in the politics of democratisation, some of the intellectuals were eventually elected to the Ninth Parliament following the 2002 General Elections, including Kivutha Kibwana of NCEC fame, Kilemi Mwiria of UASU fame, and Wangari Maathai of the GBM, among other generic intellectuals such as Mirugi Kariuki, the human rights activist, and Koigi wa Wamwere, the perennial rabble-rouser. The problem, however, is that most of these organic and activist intellectuals of the pre-2002 Kenya, except perhaps Maathai, have exploited their relationship with the masses to install themselves as legitimate actors in sites and spaces of change, situating themselves in positions of influence, authority and prestige while simultaneously abandoning the struggle midway. Much of what this new crop of co-opted intellectuals evince reminds one of the heydays of Moi's authoritarianism, when reasoned dissent was frowned upon and dismissed as a harbinger of chaos. For instance, in 1997 Moi referred to Kivutha Kibwana and Willy Mutunga's NCEC as a subversive group. He described the two as proxy intermediaries financed by foreigners to cause chaos in Kenya. It is ironical that today Kibwana, the former organic intellectual, has become conformist first as Assistant Minister in the Office of the President in charge of internal security, whose antics in the constitution review process would be laughable if they did not have the serious consequence of delaying the enactment of a new and viable constitution, and second as Minister for Environment, and chief proponent of the interests of the ruling class. Not only is he now instrumental in issuing threatening orders to organisers of popular public rallies and civic education campaigns on behalf of an increasingly unpopular and corrupt NARC government, but he does this without a trace of shame or an iota of embarrassment.

During the public rally organized by Katiba Watch (which Kibwana claimed was a Liberal Democratic Party of Kenya proxy lobby), he described the rally as an exercise in bad faith that would not promote peaceful and speedy constitution making. Many were surprised at outbursts from Kibwana at a press conference in 2003 in full glare of television cameras and rolling tape recorders. Many wondered if it was really the former respected University of Nairobi Law Professor and organic intellectual of the 1990s reading such an outrageous and undemocratic statement. This instance showed that the activist intellectual had come full circle. With Kibwana, an erstwhile organic intellectual, speaking on behalf of the new government, his credentials bestow an air of legitimacy to what the government holds. But in fact, this sense of legitimacy betrays the fact that the state in Kenya has not learned its lessons. What should be clear to the government is that the more one threatens political opponents, as Kibwana has done, the more these opponents get popular and therefore emboldened. This kind of betrayal is fathomable only in the context of the history of the radical left in Kenya's politics. According to Ajulu, '[t]he idea of a political left in Kenya is rather problematic ... the so called left has not existed as an organized political force. If it exists at all, it has been characterized by organizational weakness and numerical insignificance' (Ajulu 1995: 229–35). In supporting Ajulu's view, Murunga (2003) has argued that one explanation of this is that the state has retained the initiative of identifying radicals (the left) in Kenya and influencing their agenda. The same can be said of the right in Kenya, which is equally confused in its rush to attract the eye of the ruling elite. The right is by and large also defined by its relationship to the state. Thus, the right in Kenya is even more difficult to isolate, as it is constituted by a bunch of wealth-seeking academic crowds, motivated by nothing more than opportunism.

The effect of state co-optation of intellectuals has also had intriguing reverberations within the university, especially in connection with faculty unionisation. This was clearly demonstrated with the altercations involving the registration and operations of the UASU. During the Moi years, the vexing question was on the role of intellectuals in Moi's disbandment of UASU in 1980. For obvious xenophobic reasons, the Moi government was uncompromisingly opposed to the idea of an academic union in Kenya. Mazrui and Mutunga have pointed out that 'the Moi government has treated the idea of an academic union as an anathema to Kenya's body politic' (Mazrui and Mutunga 1995: 257). Moi disbanded UASU because of the union's demand for reinstatement of Ngugi wa Thiong'o to his former position at the University of Nairobi after his release from detention. UASU also condemned the way the government and the university administration handled student unrest besides calling for improvement of the terms of service for academics. But what was very intriguing was the way the government relied on a small group of pro-establishment bourgeois/ authoritarian intellectuals to argue against unionisation.

In this regard, Henry Mwanzi, Professor of History at Kenyatta University, who later became KANU's executive officer, argued that university academics were not fit for trade unions which were, he believed, for ordinary trades such as tailoring, mechanics, plumbing, hotel and sugar plantation workers (*The Weekly Review*, 21 January 1994, p. 8). Mwanzi is no longer in the establishment 'think tank', having lost favour when KANU was voted out of power. But a former organic intellectual, Kilemi Mwiria, is now on the side that Mwanzi occupied a few years ago. A former Secretary General of UASU, Mwiria is now an Assistant Minister in the Ministry of Education in charge of higher education and his views on UASU have also changed. During the 2003–04 public university lecturers' strike, Mwiria pitched tent on the government side invoking the dubious principle of collective responsibility to undermine the very UASU ideals and needs that he fronted in the 1990s. When matters suited him, Mwiria remained aloof during the UASU national strike. That the strike was called to pressurise the government to improve the terms of service and working conditions of dons in Kenya did not bother Mwiria to take the pro-UASU stand he had always fronted until he was fired from Kenyatta University.

Despite the modest success that UASU had during the protracted strike, it was very clear that Mwiria and other former organic intellectuals in the government, such as Kiraitu Murungi, Kivutha Kibwana and Peter Anyang' Nyong'o, among others, were not concerned, and neither were they moved into supportive action. In fact, at the time the strike was on, the government moved to suspend some officials of UASU in

Maseno University and to reintroduce the requirement that lecturers clear it with the government before travelling abroad. Few of these intellectuals in NARC could be heard rallying against such punitive measures that they had opposed during the Moi years. Thus, former organic/activist intellectuals such as Kivutha Kibwana and Kilemi Mwiria have become conformists, and now talk from the privileged position of government. One ought therefore to be sympathetic to the likes of Mukaru Ng'ang'a and Nicholas Nyangira, who died under the genuine rallying call of *a luta continua* (the struggle continues).

Conclusion

If, as noted at the beginning of this chapter, the challenge of intellectual life is to be found in dissent against the status quo at a time when the struggle on behalf of underrepresented and disadvantaged groups seems so unfairly weighted against them, then intellectuals who take pride of place in meeting this challenge in Kenya are the organic/activist intellectuals. At the opposite end of the spectrum are the bourgeois/authoritarian intellectuals who are conservative, rooted in the status quo and exercise their intellectualism in defence of the establishment. In between the two groups are located the academic/ philosophical intellectuals and the generic/general intellectuals. Whereas the former tend to be left of centre, members of the latter group tend to straddle the political spectrum, with some espousing radical views in support of progressive forces, while others choose to align with the powers that be.

Nevertheless, as demonstrated in this chapter, not all organic/activist intellectuals who serve a vanguard role in the struggles for democracy are firmly committed to such popular struggles for social change. Whilst some have remained focused and committed to the cause even with the allure of materialism, others have foregrounded their egotistical and egocentric interests. The disconnection between what these intellectuals espouse while in the struggle and what they practise after assuming state office reveals three major contradictions. First, once in office, the intellectuals become less instrumental in pushing for the cause of the ordinary person. Second, they become the 'organisation men' of the constricted field of state capitalism practised in Kenya. Third, they become impersonal, interested only in their own gratification, and all of a sudden assume the role of defenders of the same status quo they had hitherto fought against. The fact that some of the intellectuals behind the struggles for democracy appear to have been more interested in personal glory and gain rather than in the ideals of democracy and good governance exposes the danger inherent in vanguard intellectual leadership and its malleability when it comes to alliance with the masses.

References

Achebe, C. (1987) *Anthills of the Savannah*, New York, NY: Anchor Books.

Ajulu, R. (1995) 'The Left and the Question of Democratic Transition in Kenya: A Reply to Mwakenya', *Review of African Political Economy*, vol. 22, no. 64.

Amutabi, M. (2002) 'Crisis and Student Protest in Universities in Kenya', *African Studies Review*, vol. 45, no. 2.

Anyidoho, K. (ed.) (1997) *The Word Behind Bars and the Paradox of Exile*, Evanston, IL: Northwestern University Press.

Chege, M. (1996) 'Africa's Murderous Professors', *The National Interest*, no. 46.

Freire, P. (1970) *Pedagogy of the Oppressed*, New York, NY: Herder and Herder.

Gikandi, S. (2000a) *Ngugi wa Thiong'o*, New York, NY: Cambridge University Press.

_____ (2000b) 'Travelling Theory: Ngugi's Return to English', *Research in African Literatures*, vol. 31, no. 2.

Gramsci, A. (1971) *The Prison Notebooks: Selections*, New York, NY: International Publishers.

Harris, W. (1989) 'Literacy and the Imagination', in M. Gilkes (ed.), *The Literate Imagination*, London: Macmillan.

Kipkorir, B. (1972) 'The Education Elite and Local Society: The Basis for Mass Representation', in B.A. Ogot (ed.), *Politics and Nationalism in Colonial Kenya*, Nairobi: East African Publishing House.

Lamming, G. (1960) *The Pleasures of Exile*, London: Allison & Busby.

Mafeje, A. (1995) 'African Intellectuals: An Inquiry into Their Genesis and Social Options', in M. Diouf and M. Mamdani (eds), *Academic Freedom in Africa*, Dakar: CODESRIA.

Mamdani, M. (2001) *When Victims Become Killers: Colonialism, Nativism, and the Genocide in Rwanda*, Princeton, NJ: Princeton University Press.

Mazrui, Ali (1978) *Political Values and the Educated Class in Africa*, Berkeley, CA: University of California Press.

_____ and W. Mutunga (1995) 'The State vs. the Academic Unions in Post-Colonial Kenya', *Review of African Political Economy*, vol. 22, no. 64.

Mkandawire, T. (1996) 'The State, Human Rights and Academic Freedom', in J.D. Turner (ed.), *The State and the School: An International Perspective*, London: Falmer Press.

Murunga, G. (2003) 'Democratization in Kenya: Thinking Through the Crisis of Radicalism', in CODESRIA 30th Anniversary Celebrations, East African Sub-Regional Conference, Addis Ababa, 30–31 October.

Mutunga, W. (1999) *Constitution Making from the Middle: Civil Society and Transition Politics in Kenya*, Nairobi and Harare: SAREAT/MWENGO.

Nietzsche, F. (1967) *On the Genealogy of Morals*, New York, NY: Vintage.

Nyamnjoh, F., and N. Jua (2002) 'African Universities in Crisis: The Political Economy of Violence in African Educational Systems', *African Studies Review*, vol. 45, no. 2.

Ochieng', W.R. (1984) *The Third Word*, Nairobi: Kenya Literature Bureau.

Onditi, A. (1998) 'Don Cites Hitches in Education', *Daily Nation*, 23 June.

Robinson, C. (1983) *Black Marxism*, London: Zed Books.

Said, E. (1994) *Representations of the Intellectual*, New York, NY: Pantheon Books.

——— (2000) *Reflections on Exile and Other Essays*, Cambridge, MA: Harvard University Press.

Sand, S. (1997) 'Between the Word and the Land: Intellectuals and the State in Israel', in J. Jennings and A. Kemp-Welch (eds), *Intellectuals in Politics: From the Dreyfus Affair to Salman Rushdie*, London: Routledge.

Shivji, I. (2002) 'Globalisation and Popular Resistance,' in J. Sembja, et al. (eds), *Local Perspectives on Globalisation: The African Case*, Dar es Salaam: Mkuki na Nyota.

Thiong'o, N. wa, and N. wa Mirii (1982) *I Will Marry When I Want*, London: Heinemann.

Williams, P. (1999) *Ngugi wa Thiong'o*, Manchester: Manchester University Press.

Zeleza, P.T. (1994) *The Joys of Exile*, Concord: Anansi.

——— and A. Olukoshi (2004) *African Universities in the Twenty-First Century: Volumes 1 and 2*, Dakar: CODESRIA.

8

The Role of the Police in Kenya's Democratisation Process

Edwin A. Gimode

Introduction

This chapter examines the role of the police in the struggle for democracy in Kenya. It proceeds from the premise that the role played by the police institution in the Kenyan political system has its roots in the colonial state. Colonial rule in Kenya, as elsewhere in Africa, was illegitimate, and being so, it relied on oppression, repression and brutal force to sustain itself. It is the police force that was used in this regard acquiring, in the process, an oppressive modus operandi that has characterised its operations to this day. The chapter demonstrates how the Kenyatta and Moi regimes, just like the colonial state, manipulated the police institution into an instrument of regime protection instead of citizen security. Both regimes eschewed all pretence to democratic governance by banning and outlawing political opposition respectively, then using the police routinely to harass, torture, jail and even kill regime opponents. The chapter concludes that the global movement for democracy after the end of the cold war was received by the long suppressed Kenyan opposition as a great window of opportunity to initiate democracy. This turned into a massive popular movement for democracy, which was unstoppable in spite of the harassment of the combined law enforcement organs of the police, the judiciary and the prison system.

Democracy, The State and the Police Institution

Different paradigms emphasise different conceptualisations of the notion of democracy. What is not in question is the overwhelming general tendency of societies to want to be categorised as democratic. This is because of the appeal and approval that the notion bequeaths the claimants. But democratic governance must ultimately entail the idea of government by consent of the governed. It is a system whereby the state is governed by representatives of the people. The type of governance that is generally opposite to the democratic is statist governance where the state takes precedence over individual rights. Post-colonial states in Africa largely belonged to this category before the global movement for democracy of the 1990s. Most of these states subsumed individual rights and liberties under the notion of national or state security. The African state was a heritage of the colonial state. It largely represented a change of power from whites to Africans. The ruling elite emphasised order, stability, efficiency and growth. The state visualised its mission as that of facilitating 'development'.

Whatever form of state one may consider, the institution of the police is a critical instrument of its survival. The police constitute the primary state institution responsible for internal security. The key function of the state is to create public safety. This is done through the police, the chief law enforcement organ of the state. The mandate of the police is the prevention and combating of crime, enforcing law and order, and generally ensuring a climate of security. Unlike any other state organ, the police have access and recourse to the use of force in the task of maintaining law and order. Yet it is not just social ordering that is the concern of the police. Ideally, the police should combine humane policing and hard policing depending on the material circumstances. According to Bayley (1996: 123), the police '... stand at the fulcrum between liberty and order but they tend to lean on the right'. The police force is the most apparent manifestation of the state (Marks 1999: 234). They can serve as an index of change (or lack of it) in a state. Most Western countries can be said to have moved to the level of policing that engenders human rights or 'democratised policing'. A democratised police force provides a fairly wide range of services to the citizenry. These include security for all, resolving conflict, protection of various freedoms and prevention of crime. This puts the police in constant contact with the citizens. The latter are ready to identify and to support the police because the institution has both attained legitimacy in the eyes of the public and won its confidence.

The history of policing in Africa is the story of the statist form of governance. The state and the police force were almost inextricably yoked together from the dawn of colonial rule. All over the continent, the modern police was first created to meet the aspirations of the colonisers from conquest to the maintenance of subjugation. From an army of conquest, it slowly grew into an instrument of maintaining colonialism. The police owed their loyalty to colonial masters, whom they protected together with their property. They were used to alienate Africans from their land, to force them to provide labour on white estates and to exact taxes from them. The force was trained to quell riots and protests by the indigenes. Hence the police were a 'foreign tissue' in the midst of African communities. They represented the '… most visible public symbol of colonial rule …' (Anderson and Killingray 1991: 2). Their operations were characterised by the use of brute force to impose and maintain the colonial social order of exploitation. Thus, the modern police lacked legitimacy in the eyes of Africans. As a result, the first police officers were expatriates either from outside the continent or from other African regions.

The post-colonial governments in Africa inherited the police institution without democratising it. Like the army, the police remained one of the most colonial of colonial legacies. Because they had dictatorial tendencies couched in terms such as 'development' and 'national security', they perpetuated the modus operandi of the colonial police. The main function of the police became protection of the ruling elite. During the decades of independence, policing was chaotic, diffuse, excessively repressive and unaccountable. With the onset of the 1990s, however, the police force in contemporary Africa has had to face the challenge of changing and democratising. The benchmark in this challenge against statist governance and policing was the collapse of the Soviet Union and the 'triumph' of liberal democracy. Many Third World states were forced to espouse multipartyism. The police institution has found itself in a major dilemma – whether to retain the historic usage of brutal force or to reinvent itself by democratising and helping to entrench democracy.

Colonial Origins of Kenya Police's Modus Operandi

Of the three major law enforcement organs, namely the police, the judiciary and the prison system, the most pronounced in colonial Kenya was the police force. In the modern state, the police force is the institution responsible for internal security. The police force was first instituted in Kenya by Sir William Mackinnon of the Imperial British

East African Company (IBEACO) in 1887. It consisted of Indian units set up to oversee security on the trade route to the interior of modern Kenya and Uganda. The force was necessary so that '... the wheels of commerce might revolve smoothly and not subjected to constant hindrance or attacks from savage tribes along the trade route' (Foran 1962: 3). In 1895 the British Foreign Office took over the responsibility of administering the British East African Protectorate (modern Kenya). In 1897 Sir Arthur Hardinge, the first commissioner, appointed Mr R.H. Ewait to become the first European Police Officer of the protectorate. The latter was charged with the responsibility of starting a 'proper' police unit for purposes of extending British control into the interior and guarding emerging local administrative centres known as *bomas*.[1] In the initial decades of colonialism the force mainly consisted of the Somali and the Nubians, and a smattering of Africans. The number of the latter, however, would grow with time. Therefore, in terms of jurisdiction, police power focused on privileged areas of European settlement.

The defining element of this police was its exercise of brutal force. It was a semi-military outfit and was often on active service with the Kenya African Rifles (KAR). At the very start of the colonial presence, it was primarily involved in the crushing of protests and rebellions by African people whose democratic right of self-determination was violated by the establishment of colonialism. After the forceful imposition of colonialism, the force would mainly ensure that Africans provided the labour and other resources required to fuel the settler economy. Hence an investigation of the role of the police in post-colonial Africa and in the democratisation process of the late twentieth century necessarily calls for an overview of the colonial origins of the institution together with its style of operation. This is because a cursory glance at the police force seems to highlight the birthmarks of this colonial origin. In principle, the Kenya police were expected to demonstrate exemplary behaviour and service. Indeed, the force adopted the motto: *Salus Populi*, meaning *Service to All*, or in Kiswahili, *Utumishi Kwa Wote*. The motto appeared for the first time under the badge of cover of the police journal in 1929 (Foran 1962: 79). The subsequent history of the force proved to be a constant negation of this principle.

Colonial repression was legitimised by a corpus of oppressive laws that created an all-powerful executive, while leaving little room for dissent. In 1897 the East African Order-in-Council instituted the office of the Commissioner of the East African Protectorate, with vast powers to legislate, establish courts and to deport anyone deemed undesirable in order to maintain colonial law and order (KHRC 1998: 116). These immense powers by the executive effectively served to muzzle dissent in the colony, and set the stage for the manipulation of the law enforcement organs in the post-colony. Especially prone to this manipulation would be the police force. This marked the start of the politicisation of the police, whose duties of maintaining law and order would be invoked by the executive in silencing alternative political opinions. The first casualties of the politicised colonial police in the democratic struggle in Kenya were the leaders of the first stirrings of the nationalist movement in the 1920s like Harry Thuku. Thuku organised Africans to fight for their rights, starting with the fight against the carrying of the *kipande*.[2] He demanded a degree of representation in the governing structures. All these activities were undertaken through the East African Association (EAA). On 14 March 1922 Thuku was arrested by the police, which led to massive demonstrations in the streets of Nairobi demanding his unconditional release. The response of the government was a display of mounted troops with guns at the ready. The persistence of the crowds led to a massacre as police fired shots into the masses outside the Norfolk Hotel. Thuku was taken away to detention in different camps at Kismayu, Lamu and Marsabit for nine years. His lasting contribution was that he had expressed the democratic aspirations of his day and met the full force of the security forces acting in the name of law and order.

In the 1940s, a new brand of African leadership emerged to replace the Thuku generation. The group led to the formation of the Kenya African Union (KAU). The democratic ideals and aspirations of this group were informed by the knowledge of the World War II returnees, who increasingly made political demands on the colonial regime. The colonial state responded by promulgating the Public Order Ordinance in 1950, which provided for the preservation of public order and mandated District Commissioners to vet public meetings and grant permits to those deemed to meet the requirements for public order. The police force was at the centre of this new political order of guaranteeing security. If the local administration thought there were sufficient grounds to fear risk, the permit would be denied or, if it had already been given, cancelled. Protests were silenced by the police. But time for this repressive approach to containing dissent was running out. Some colonial officials saw need for change, but they were in the minority.

One such was a senior police officer, Foran. According to him, 1949 '... marked the beginning of a great change in the mentality and outlook of the African in the colony, a rapidly growing consciousness of his social status, his political rights, his education, limitations and other circumstances as they affect him' (Foran 1962: 160). Consequently he needed 'very different handling', a better system of policing that was commensurate with these changing circumstances. The overall edifice of the colonial structure ignored this observation. The outcome was the Mau Mau nationalist struggle.

The Mau Mau movement started in the 1940s. It was active by 1947 (Foran 1962; Anderson 2005). By 1950 the movement called for police action. Its message was radical, namely to rid Kenya of foreign occupation and to reclaim African land. To contain this momentum for self-determination, Governor Evalyn Baring declared a State of Emergency in October 1952. This was done by invoking the Emergency Powers of the Colonial Defence Order-in-Council of 1939 (promulgated at the onset of World War II). These emergency powers had actually enhanced the 1897 Native Courts Regulations by increasing the arbitrary powers of the governor and reducing accountability by manipulating the most poignant symbol of state security, the police. New laws were enacted which at the core involved exercise of brutal force to obtain denunciation of the struggle by Africans. These emergency regulations turned Kenya into a police state. Administration and law enforcement organs were given powers to arrest anyone without a warrant, to declare quarantine status over certain areas and to shoot on sight anyone who 'trespassed' (KHRC 1998: 120). The actual exercise of these powers turned the 1950s into one of the bloodiest decades in Kenya's history. The powers brought into clear light the deadly consequences of the combination of law enforcement organs in a dictatorship.

In October 1952, Kenyan political and labour leaders, led by Jomo Kenyatta, were arrested. Many were incarcerated in concentration or detention camps without trial. In instances where there were trials, these were at best a travesty of justice perpetrated by an oppressive regime manipulating the prosecution (police) and the magistracy. The main camps for detention were usually deliberately chosen for their hardship in order to break the inmates' fighting spirit. The major ones were Mackinnon Road, Manyani, Lang'ata, Hola, Mageta, Lodwar, Lokitaung and Marsabit. There were a total of about 100,000 detainees held in these camps who were brutally treated by representatives of another sub-organ of law enforcement, namely the prison warders. Inside and outside the detention camps, some 1,000 people were executed under Emergency Powers. Many more went missing. Then there was the forced relocation of whole villages, under police supervision, into the so-called 'Emergency Villages', that were supposedly protected from Mau Mau contagion. The lesson of what absolute power and manipulation of security organs can make humankind do to fellow humankind was unfortunately not learned during Mau Mau. The subsequent history of Kenya demonstrates this.

Law Enforcement and Political Dissent under Kenyatta

The release of Jomo Kenyatta and his colleagues from detention, and the subsequent formation of the first independent government, ushered in the hope of a new era founded on democratic principles and practices. The manifesto of the Kenya African National Union (KANU), the party that won the first general election, amplified this aspiration. It was apparently clear that the 77 or so years of colonial police repression were over. However, the actual unfolding of political events during the Kenyatta era proved to be antithetical to these hopes. By the time Kenyatta died in August 1978, Kenyan institutions could hardly be identified with democratic principles, least of all the law enforcement organs.

In the run-up to independence, KANU had emerged as the primary organ of addressing the aspirations of Kenyans. The KANU manifesto pledged to redress the wrongs of the colonial regime and to establish true democracy by immediately dealing with the colonial detention laws, regulations and rules as a priority. Of special note among those were the Preservation of Public Security Ordinance, and the Detained and Restricted Persons Ordinance. The implications were that the police force would be reinvented to shed its colonial repressive role and to get on with the business of genuine policing to enhance security for all. Yet amendments by parliament carried out between 1963 and 1966 increasingly granted the presidency more powers and broke down the checks and balances enshrined in the independence constitution, betraying the pro-people democratic ideals in the KANU constitution. These powers would ultimately enable Kenyatta to control the law-enforcement agencies and to use them ruthlessly to undermine human rights, especially the right to challenge the incumbent for the control of power.

The first constitutional amendment established the Republic of Kenya, while assigning the presidency the former powers of the governor as well as those of the prime minister. This created a presidency that overshadowed parliament as an effective watchdog. The Emergency Powers Order-in-Council (1939), used to justify terror against Mau Mau in the 1950s, was adopted by parliament in 1966, encapsulated in the Public Security Act, which gave the president Emergency Powers, ostensibly in order to handle the *shifta*[3] menace. According to the newly repackaged powers, the president would exercise his discretion in detaining a person without trial. He would limit freedom of movement, association, expression and assembly. At the centre of the execution of these powers were the police. These powers would be used in the 1960s, 1970s and thereafter to muzzle political dissent, in the process negating claims by the KANU government to democracy.

By 1966 Kenyatta's power enabled him to take total control and to manipulate the coercive forces of the state especially against political opposition. He had at his disposal various sub-departments of the police force, which had earlier been created to deal specifically with maintenance of the repressive colonial law and order. Of these, the regular uniformed police were the more visible but less frequently used compared to the Criminal Investigations Department (CID) and the Special Branch (later called Directorate of Security Intelligence [DSI] and later still, National Security Intelligence Services). In 1926 the colonial government had established skeletal staff for the two units in Nairobi. By 1953 they had expanded into the provinces and districts for purposes of gathering intelligence especially for the war against Mau Mau (Foran 1962: 62). When the Kenyatta administration came to power, it refined the network into one of the most efficient in Africa. Unfortunately, the efficiency was in no small measure for purposes of undermining the realisation of democratic ideals.

This came out clearly in the ideological war that emerged in Kenya in the 1960s. The more capitalist-orientated group led by Kenyatta himself and his lieutenants such as Njoroge Mungai, Mbiyu Koinange, Tom Mboya and James Gichuru favoured close partnership with Western multinationals. Others with a leftist orientation led by Jaramogi Oginga Odinga, Pio Gama Pinto and Bildad Kaggia considered the policies espoused by Kenyatta's government as neo-colonialist and exploitative. These differences in ideological positions coalesced into a major crisis that came to be characterised by harassment of political dissent by the regime using law enforcement agencies. In the 1960s and 1970s, this harassment entailed complete silencing by assassination, proscription of alternative political organisations and detention without trial. Assassination is the most extreme measure to deal with political dissent. During Kenyatta's rule, three clearly state-linked assassinations took place, namely that of Pio Gama Pinto, Tom Mboya and J.M. Kariuki. In all of them, the state intelligence system was implicated by both omission and commission. This was easily discerned in the way the suspects were arrested, prosecuted and convicted. In the case of one of these murders, not a single suspect has been arrested to date.

Pinto was a Goan politician and nationalist who had participated effectively in the struggle for independence. He was the main strategist of the leftist wing in the immediate post-independence era and a close ally of Oginga Odinga. Pinto was a nominated MP when he was gunned down outside the entrance to his home on Lower Kabete Road on the morning of 24 February 1965. He had won nomination to parliament as a candidate of the parliamentary left wing at a time when the 12 nominated members of parliament were nominated by parliament sitting as an electoral college. Pinto's assassination was meant to throw the budding opposition to Kenyatta into disarray. What was most disturbing in this respect was the fact that a nationalist had been murdered in cold blood in independent Kenya. All possibilities seemed to point to the government, meaning the security system and its machinery.

Two youths were arrested and charged with the murder, namely Kisilu Mutua (21 years old) and Chege Thuo (19 years old). After a protracted trial Chege was released, while the court found Mutua guilty and sentenced him to death. Mutua argued that he did not know Pinto and pleaded innocent. He languished in jail for 37 years, being shuttled between Kamiti and Naivasha maximum security prisons. He was released only on 4 July 2001, having earned the distinction of being Kenya's longest serving prisoner. What is important here is that a security intelligence system with a near unparalleled record in Africa arrested Mutua on apparently shaky evidence. It seems that Mutua was set up by the Special Branch. What is intriguing is that several convicted murderers in Kenya were released after serving shorter terms. Mutua was not released, despite numerous positive recommendations by the prisons review board.

Tom Mboya suffered a more or less similar fate to that of Pinto. After being used by Kenyatta to throw Oginga Odinga's political career into disarray,[4] Mboya was assassinated on 5 July 1969. One Nahashon Isaac Njenga Njoroge had pulled the trigger and was arrested. But his pleas of having been sent by the 'big man' did not seem to prompt the investigating officers to get to the bottom of the matter (see Ajulu 2000). Njenga was sentenced to death, leaving question marks on the credibility of the police force and the judiciary. Mboya's funeral became a rallying point against Kenyatta and his so-called Kikuyu allies. The only Kikuyu leader present during the burial was one Josiah Mwangi Kariuki.

Perhaps it is the assassination of Josiah Mwangi Kariuki in March 1975 which best illustrates how the Kenyatta regime abused the police mandate by turning the security forces into an army fighting partisan political battles. Kariuki was the MP for Nyandarua North and was vocal in criticising Kenyatta's regime for corruption and impoverishment of Kenyans. On 2 March 1975, JM, as he was popularly known, was last seen alive leaving Nairobi's Hilton Hotel in the company of General Service Unit (GSU) (a para-military police force) Commandant Ben Gethi. The following day, a Maasai herdsman found a body in the Ngong' Forest on the outskirts of the city. It was taken to the City Mortuary by the police. After several days, JM's family reported him missing. Many of his friends immediately thought that he might have been taken into detention by security forces on the orders of the government. But Kariuki's wife, Terry, discovered and identified JM's body at the City Mortuary. This sent the nation into mourning while many 'openly' implicated the government in his grisly murder. Why had Daniel Moi, the Vice-President and Minister for Home Affairs, assured parliament that JM was in Zambia?

The government, with all the security instruments, was not able to come up with any plausible explanation. A Parliamentary Select Committee under Elijah Mwangale found the government and its security machinery culpable. State culpability was further manifested in the decision by then Attorney-General Charles Njonjo to move a motion seeking to 'note' the committee's findings rather than to adopt it, which would have meant implementing the committee's recommendations by way of investigating and prosecuting the suspects. Further, before the report was submitted to parliament, Kenyatta ordered the chairman, Elijah Mwangale, to delete the names of his close allies implicated in the murder, including Mbiyu Koinange. In response, cabinet minister Masinde Muliro, and assistant ministers Peter Kibisu and John Keen jettisoned the principle of collective responsibility to vote against the government motion, with Muliro arguing that his conscience could not allow him to observe collective responsibility in a murder case he had no hand in. Needless to say, the three were promptly relieved of their ministerial positions.

Later private investigations revealed that when JM left the Hilton, Ben Gethi accompanied him to Kingsway House, the headquarters of the Special Branch. He found waiting for him Ignatius Nderi (Director of CID), Wanyoike Thungu (Kenyatta's Security Chief) and Patrick Shaw (the Irish police reservist dreaded for his ruthlessness with violent criminals). JM was tortured and shot. Two different guns were used to shoot him. Probably he was shot twice at two different times and in different places. When his body was discovered, the face indicated corrosion by acid, probably to destroy identity. JM had survived colonial detention only to be silenced permanently in independent Kenya. Not a single person has ever been arrested in more than 30 years since his assassination (*Daily Nation*, 3 March 2004).

The detention of political opponents in post-colonial Kenya is an abuse by incumbent regimes of not only the police force but also other law enforcement organs such as the judiciary and the prison system. Detention laws, rules and regulations were an instrument of colonial domination. They were the main reference point of the activities of the colonial police in muzzling free expression perceived to be anti-establishment. Kenyatta had retained these regulations under the cover of the Public Security Act. The key actors in this drama were the Special Branch, CID and the prison system. It all began in 1969 when, after a bitter verbal exchange with Odinga in Kisumu, Kenyatta went ahead to detain (without trial) Odinga and his associates in the Kenya Peoples Union (KPU). These included Achieng' Oneko, Wasonga Sijeyo, Dennis Akumu and V. Wachira, among others. This initial opening of the floodgates to detention was to remain a characteristic method of dealing with political opposition not only during Kenyatta's era, but even more so during Moi's.

Virtually all the detainees in the 1970s and the 1980s were associated with opposition to the regime. In August 1975 Koigi wa Wamwere, the young and vocal MP for Nakuru North, was detained without trial. He was accosted in a Nakuru street, blindfolded and bundled into a van that took him to Kamiti Maximum Security Prison (Onyango 2003). On 15 October 1975, Deputy Speaker of Parliament

Jean Marie Seroney and the MP for Butere, Martin Shikuku, were picked up from the precincts of parliament by plainclothes police-men. This was in total contravention of the privileges and immunities conferred by the National Assembly Act (*Daily Nation*, 4 September 2003). During the previous week Shikuku had stated, probably in jest, that any member who branded others rogues was '… trying to kill parliament the way KANU was killed'. When a member demanded that the statement be substantiated, Seroney (in the chair of the House) quipped that there was no need to substantiate the obvi-ous. Moi, then vice-president, led a walkout by the front bench. Before being taken, Shikuku had had time to tell colleagues: 'The more you think of it, the more frightened you get and you are likely to get bogged down. If they want to take me, there is nothing I can do or else they make you shaken up' (*Daily Nation*, 4 September 2003).

In 1977, George Moseti Anyona (MP for Kitutu Chache) joined the pool of detainees. He was arrested and sent to detention at Shimo-La-Tewa in Mombasa. Anyona had quickly come to be known as the 'one man back-bench' after Wamwere, Shikuku and Seroney had been incarcerated. He had attacked corruption and inefficiency in high places. On 30 December 1977 the first academic joined the queue to detention. Professor Ngugi wa Thiong'o was Chairman of the Department of Literature, University of Nairobi. His Marxist orientation had made him critical of the Kenyatta regime. His novel, *Petals of Blood*, was a statement about political repression, exploitation of the poor and the abetting of neo-colonialism in Kenya. In the mid-dle of the night, Ngugi's house at Kamirithu village in Limuru area was invaded by a platoon of armed policemen. He was woken up and his house searched. He was carried away together with a number of publications on Marxist literature. He began the year 1978 at Kamiti prison as a political detainee (Thiong'o 1981).

By the time Kenyatta died in August 1978, there were a total of 26 political detainees in Kenyan prisons. The detention papers were signed by Daniel arap Moi, Minister for Home Affairs, under whose portfolio fell the police. It was the same Moi who, as second president of the Republic of Kenya, decreed the release of all detainees on 12 December 1978. His decree was accompanied by an apology for the vice of detention. He said that detention was always a last resort (*Daily Nation*, 18 September 2003). This had a sinister ring to it. It was not a thing of the past, and it would come in full force under Moi beginning 1981.

Moi and the Remaking of a Police State

The passing away of Kenyatta promised to usher in greater freedom and liberty. The mood was perhaps best captured by Martin Shikuku after his release from prison in December 1978: 'My release and that of other detainees is a clear example to the world that Kenyans are mature. It has also demonstrated that they believe in leadership by a capable man, irrespective of his ethnic origin' (*Daily Nation*, 18 September 2003). In apparent fulfilment of these hopes, Moi embarked on a vigorous campaign of populism to earn the respect and acceptance of Kenyans (Ogot 1995). With a rare display of energy, he traversed the country to the chanting crowds: *Moi Juu, Nyayo Juu*, (Up With Moi, Up With Footprints).[5] This turned out to be correct especially in the area of dealing with dissent. Instead of a new democratic dawn for the decade ahead, the 1980s turned out to be a study in extreme repression, where authoritarianism became the established mode of governance.

Unlike Kenyatta, who had a high level of modern education, a booming voice and the gift for demagoguery, Moi had limited education and a rather permanently hoarse, unappealing and rasping voice. He was not as good a public speaker as Kenyatta. These qualities seemed to instil in him a kind of inferiority complex which he made up for by a contradictory combination of apparent piety and love for everybody on the one hand, and, on the other hand, a rather deep resentment for the educated, the politically critical and those who were ready to challenge him to be accountable, transparent and democratic in his execution of public duties. This resentment translated into a deadly war of attrition against the advocacy of democratic practices in the 1980s, turning the decade into the darkest period after independence. Among those advocates who attempted to stand up to Moi were courageous politicians, university lecturers and students, and lawyers and journalists who dismissed Moi's so-called philosophy of peace, love and unity as a sham.

Moi's approach was to create conditions that led to a culture of crippling fear, which tended to turn many into 'silent and passive spectators' due to 'oppression, repression and marginalisation' (Akivaga 2002: 27). Moi governed through violence, harassment, intimidation and increased use of organs of state security for self-preservation. In the process, he destroyed the last vestiges of civil liberties, concentrating power in his own hands, and virtually outdoing Kenyatta in the process (KHRC 1998: 132). This was accomplished by instituting far-reaching constitutional amendments so that he easily manipulated the law which allowed him to resort to extralegal strong-arm measures. This he did directly by manipulating the police force, and indirectly through the judicial and prison systems. The first blow for political pluralism in the *Nyayo* era was struck by Odinga. In the run-up to the April 1981 Bondo by-election, Odinga was barred from running. The incumbent had actually resigned from parliament to make way for Odinga to be eased back into the mainstream of national politics, since his fallout with Kenyatta more than a decade earlier. No reasons were given by the KANU headquarters for barring Odinga. Many Kenyans were critical of this unexpected move of political intolerance, and university students expressed their resentment by demonstrating against KANU (*Daily Nation*, 19 April 1981). There were veiled threats from the government to the effect that Kenyans were peace loving, and that the police were closely monitoring those inciting students trying to disturb public order.

One year after this, Odinga travelled to Britain and held a meeting with British Labour MPs. This alarmed Moi and his KANU sycophants who alleged that he had solicited for money to form a socialist party with former detainee George Anyona (*Daily Nation*, 21 May 1982). Odinga had described Kenya as a democratic country '… with a constitution that embodies human rights and provides for a multi-party system' (*Daily Nation*, 21 May 1982). He therefore pointed out that criticism of government was in good faith and should not necessarily be viewed as being anti-government. For these views, Odinga was completely expelled from KANU. In response to Odinga's speech, Moi came out fighting with bare knuckles. On 1 June 1982, he warned against any political dissension saying 'that we shall not allow a number of individuals who regard themselves as revolutionaries promoting foreign ideologies to be disrupting our education and training programmes' (*Daily Nation*, 2 June 1982). His main concern was not so much the disruption of education as the emergence of a democratically conscious political culture in the country.

Soon after, the Leader of Government Business in parliament, Vice-President Mwai Kibaki, led the House through the motions of introducing the notorious Section 2A of the Kenyan constitution. On 9 June 1982, Kenya became a de jure one-party state. There was no debate. The bill was passed unanimously. From 1969 when KPU was proscribed, Kenya had been a de facto one-party state. The sudden courage of Odinga and Anyona to challenge this had made Moi go a step further than Kenyatta had done. He got the constitution amended to give him a legal basis for muzzling dissent. His close associate, Charles Njonjo, the Minister for Constitutional Affairs, summed up what was happening in a most cynical manner. He argued that Kenya was a sovereign state and that it could amend the constitution at will; and if anyone wanted to see an example of democracy, Kenya was one (*Daily Nation*, 10 June 1982).

As Amutabi shows in greater detail in this study, the University of Nairobi had increasingly become the seat of democratic discourse. This led to the DSI's infiltration of student ranks, surveillance of lecturers, banning of the students' representative body, the Nairobi University Student Association, and suspension and expulsions of student leaders including John Munuhe, Mukhisa Kituyi, Odindo Opiata and Saul Busolo. Because of constant surveillance and threats from the police, some students escaped to Tanzania, where they found sanctuary at the University of Dar es Salaam (Kihuria 2003). With time there developed a growing diaspora of Kenyan intellectuals who escaped Moi's deadly security operations. It was in this general mood of belligerence that Moi rediscovered detention without trial as a deterrent to free expression. In this way, Moi manipulated into deadly combination the three arms of law enforcement – the police, the magistracy and the prison system. If dissidents escaped police harassment, they would be caught by an increasingly corrupt judiciary and ultimately subjected to an equally harsh prison system.

Moi used a bizarre analogy to justify his detention of opposition. He argued that it was not his wish to detain anybody, but '... if one puts a finger into your nose you are bound to react' (*Daily Nation*, 12 November 1982). Apart from a number of university lecturers (see Chapter 7 by Amutabi in this volume), in May and June 1982, Anyona and his lawyer John Khaminwa were detained. Anyona had protested against the introduction of Section 2A while Mukaru Ng'ang'a had warned that Section 2A and a crackdown on pro-democracy activists would only drive opposition underground. For this he was detained, with KANU operatives warning that the government was capable of also going underground against dissenters (M'Inoti 1998: 540). On 2 June 1982, armed plainclothes police officers invaded Maina wa Kinyatti's house at Kenyatta University College and confiscated literature on Mau Mau and Marxism as exhibits of subversion. They also got a pamphlet entitled: 'Moi's Divisive Tactics Exposed'. He was taken to DSI headquarters, subjected to intimidation by the CID and the Special Branch officers and ultimately jailed for five years on what were essentially fabricated sedition charges. Released in 1988, Kinyatti took off in 1989 in order to escape a second arrest. Also, Katama Mkangi of the Department of Sociology was arrested and jailed in 1982. He was released later only to be detained again in 1986.

The attempted coup d'état of 1 August 1982 was a major turning point in Moi's rule. Organised by junior officers of the Kenya Air Force, the coup was the most overt expression of growing disillusionment with Moi's leadership. When news of the overthrow of Moi was announced, university students joined the rest of the Nairobians in demonstrating in the streets in support of the Kenya Air Force takeover of the government. Yet the coup attempt aborted after eight hours of fierce fighting between the loyal armed forces and the rebels. It left many people dead, half of whom were students who had been caught up in the crossfire (*Daily Nation*, 2 November 1982). The net result of the failure of the coup was to grant Moi a fresh opportunity to justify and intensify his war of attrition against political dissent. The KANU government embarked on a programme of perpetuating political control and repression by heightened manipulation of all law enforcement instruments. This gradually turned Kenya into a virtual police state in all but name.

The academy immediately bore the brunt of repression. The university was closed for a year, and when it was reopened, Moi was categorical that any student suspected of having participated in the coup attempt would not be readmitted. Meanwhile, the security system hunted down and arrested scores of students who were hauled to courtrooms and tried on sedition charges and sentenced to lengthy jail terms. Some 63 students were held in custody for six months and were not released until February 1983 when Moi decreed clemency for them. Quite a number of others, however, were sentenced. Mwandawiro Mghanga was detained without trial at the GSU Training School, Embakasi. Peter Oginga Ogego was sentenced to ten years in prison on sedition charges. He had initially been given six years, but justice Muli reconsidered the sentence '... due to lack of remorse' on the part of the student (*Daily Nation*, 12 November 1982).

David Onyango Oloo was arrested in a train to Mombasa two days after the coup attempt. Among his books was found a handwritten document on the role of students and youth in the struggle for democracy (*Sunday Nation*, 16 November 2003). The document condemned the harassment and arrest of lecturers. It urged the university students to be firm in the quest for wider democratic space. Oloo was charged with one count of being in possession of subversive literature and two counts of subversion. His two advocates had in succession urged him to plead guilty. They abandoned him when he refused. This again reflects the generally despondent mood of lawyers. Before being sentenced on 1 November 1982, Oloo asked the magistrate: 'Where is the line between constructive criticism and sedition?' (Ibid). This was considered an irrelevant side issue by the court. He was sentenced to a total of 15 years in prison, five on each count to run concurrently. At Kamiti he met many lecturers and other students, all political prisoners. Amnesty International took up his case in 1986 and he was released in May 1987 with token compensation. But he learned of his imminent rearrest in 1988, at which point he fled to exile in Canada, where he has settled to date.

And of course, there is the tragic case of Titus Adungosi that is discussed by Nasong'o and by Amutabi in Chapters 2 and 7, respectively, of this volume. What is intriguing about Adungosi is that he was not anti-government as such. He kept a giant portrait of Moi in his room. According to fellow political prisoner Peter Oloo, Adungosi '... just happened to be in the wrong place when the rebels were being pursued' (*Sunday Nation*, 16 November 2003). The court took him through the motions of a trial for sedition. Counsel, relatives and the state intelligence system put him under pressure to plead guilty. The relatives were made to believe that such a plea would earn him clemency. But in fact, the law enforcement machinery used the plea to prove that the government was justified and fair. After pleading guilty as charged for sedition, he was given a maximum sentence on 1 September 1982. In December 1988, he died as a result of hostile prison conditions including denial of access to medical facilities.

Repression was not limited to the university. It was directed at any person or people who dared to stand up to Moi and the KANU policies. These included journalists, lawyers and uncompromising politicians. In October 1982 a Nairobi journalist, Wang'ondu Kariuki, was jailed for being in possession of a 'seditious' document. Other journalists Onyango Ndenga, Jimmy Akara and Musa Jeffa, who were associated with critical commentaries, were also rounded up (*Daily Nation*, 11 November 1982). In April 1983, the government gazetted the detention of 38-year-old Raila Amolo Odinga, son of Oginga Odinga. Together with him were Professor Alfred Otieno of the University of Nairobi and Otieno Mak'Onyango, Assistant Managing

Editor of the *Sunday Standard* (*Daily Nation*, 16 April 1983). Earlier the trio had been arrested and charged with treason and failure to report the planning of the coup of 1982 of which they were supposedly aware. They had then been committed to the High Court but refused to plead guilty. When the government failed to convict them, it resorted to the arbitrary use of the colonial detention laws. The Attorney General entered a *nolle prosequi* whereupon they were released, only to be rearrested by armed plainclothes policemen in the precincts of the High Court and spirited away to detention. Raila was destined to become the person most frequently detained under the Moi regime. But before Raila's detention was Koigi wa Wamwere's. He had remained outspoken since his release from detention in 1978. He criticised the performance of Moi's regime in regard to social and economic policies. Hence he was arrested and became the first detainee after the failed coup. He was to be released in 1986, upon which he fled into exile in Norway.

Opposition forces go underground

The harsh manner in which the Moi regime dealt with dissent ultimately drove opposition underground. Several clandestine movements sprang up, but the most prominent by the mid-1980s was *Mwakenya* (acronym for *Mungano wa Wazalendo wa Kukomboa Kenya* or Nationalists' Union for the Liberation of Kenya). Though it was not until 1985 that *Mwakenya* became a household name in Kenya's political discourse, the movement had had its first stirrings in early 1982, finding expression in the activism of the university lecturers and students, journalists, lawyers, and known political dissidents who pushed for political pluralism. All the same, the nerve centre was not easily discernible. In actual fact, Mwakenya was a later name for the movement previously known as the December Twelve Movement (DTM). An author-cum-publisher, Gakara Wanjau, was arrested and confessed to the police that *Mwakenya* was the same thing as DTM, and that it comprised many intellectuals and politicians who were either in jail or in detention without trial or overseas in 'voluntary' exile. However, he argued, those at the forefront were university lecturers and students, including Ngugi wa Thiong'o, who had been involved since 1980. This account finds corroboration in Mwandawiro Mghanga's account 20 years later. Mghanga was an active student leader who was among the first to join *Mwakenya* and to organise cells

(Kahuria 2003). As DTM, the movement published a newsletter called *Mpatanishi* (Reconciler). Later, as *Mwakenya*, the movement's newsletter was called *Pambana* (Struggle).

By the mid-1980s leaflets critical of Moi's regime regularly appeared on the streets of major towns, but especially in Nairobi and Nakuru. They appeared under several names, the major one of which was *Mwakenya*. So serious had the movement become that there was panic in the government, which in turn led to a new round of crackdowns on democratic forces by the combined onslaught of the law enforcement organs – police, courts and prisons. The panic in the government came out clearly in Moi's speech on 1 June 1986. He attacked *Mwakenya* as a threat to national security and the foreign diplomats and international journalists in Nairobi for encouraging internal dissent against his eight-year rule (*Daily Nation*, 16 October 2003). He warned that he would not brook opposition. With this Moi embarked on containing *Mwakenya*. The police tracked down and arrested an ever-increasing number of suspects for political crimes. The secretive nature of the movement added to the heightening of the anxiety and fear in the country. In 1985, Mghanga, who had gone back to the university, led students in demonstrating against the jailing of their leader Adungosi. The police descended and dispersed the students. Mghanga was arrested and charged with being a member of *Mwakenya*, and was jailed for five years.

Several other people were detained around this time. In fact the government no longer bothered to gazette all detained prisoners. It was no longer possible to know all the people who were in detention. Because of the negative publicity of political prisoners in Kenya by Amnesty International, Moi's government slackened the pace on detention. Instead, it adopted the strategy of fabricating and charging opponents in the court and then getting them jailed for long terms. The magistracy became a willing accomplice in the state strategy to subvert democracy. Court cases were hurriedly prepared. It was in this general state of the magistracy that two democracy activists, D.K.L. Mzrai and C.N. Onyango, were convicted. This spread a debilitating mood of fear of security forces and the courts that continued for the rest of the decade. It is against this background that the crusade for multipartyism that started in earnest in 1990 has to be analysed. This particular case demonstrates the resolve Kenyans were developing to fight authoritarianism and to establish democratic governance.

The Crisis of Authoritarian Governance

With the collapse of the Iron Curtain in August 1989, the West stopped its unconditional partnership with Kenya. Instead, some Western powers asked Moi to take initiatives to introduce multiparty democracy in Kenya as a condition for continued financial support. Pro-democracy forces in Kenya also seized the opportunity to enlist this international goodwill to initiate change. Moi ultimately acquiesced to multiparty politics in 1991, and to greater constitutional reforms in 1997.

Nevertheless, the 1990s were not easy for pro-democracy forces. The law enforcement agencies, loyal to Moi and used to repression, were major obstacles on the road to democracy, leaving many of the proponents wounded. After all, Kenya was ushered into the 1990s with the murder of Dr Robert Ouko, Moi's Minister for Foreign Affairs and International Cooperation. Ouko had vigorously defended the Moi government against negative publicity of abuse of human rights in the international media. Yet on the night of 12 February 1990, Ouko was brutally murdered. He was shot, his limbs broken and his body set on fire. The charred remains of the body were found on a hill – Got Alila – a few kilometres from his home at Koru in the Kisumu District. Shock, tension and anger gripped the country as details of the grisly murder emerged. Particularly offensive to Kenyans was the theory by the government security instruments that Ouko committed suicide. The theory did not measure up in explaining how a man could break his own limbs, shoot himself and finally set himself on fire. The violent demonstrations by university students across the country expressed the public's belief that the death of Ouko was the work of security forces. This view was held even more strongly when the government pathologist, Jason Kaviti, repeated the same suicide theory before a commission appointed to inquire into the death (*Sunday Nation*, 20 March 2003). Suprintendent John Troon of Scotland Yard had also been called in to help resolve the murder. After nine months he came up with a 2,000-page document, which should have formed the basis of investigation. But the government never made it public, further implicating the state machinery.

Twelve years after Ouko's death, and a year after Moi left power, a Parliamentary Select Committee reopened the Ouko case, with witnesses increasingly suggesting state complicity. A former police officer, David Mukhwana, who had worked in Kisumu, told the committee sitting in February 2004 that 100 police officers had been dispatched to Got Alila to search for any items belonging to Ouko, only for them 'to stumble on Dr Ouko's body' (*East African Standard*, 28 February 2004). David Mukhwana believed that this exercise was a set-up to confuse the public and that the intelligence system knew the perpetrators.

The Ouko assassination was a harbinger for a greater clamour for democracy. As Oloo shows in Chapter 4 of this volume, Kenneth Matiba and Charles Rubia began the crusade to repeal Section 2A of the constitution and to restore political pluralism. Their application for a licence in June 1990 to hold a political rally at the historic Kamukunji grounds in Nairobi received strong support from most Western ambassadors in Nairobi, especially US Ambassador Smith Hempstone. Since no one had dared confront Moi in this manner since he had assumed power in 1978, his response was swift. He deployed state security to deter those who would support the duo. Journalists and lawyers were equally closely monitored, and Matiba's house in Nairobi was broken into by people who physically injured and traumatised his wife and threatened her with dire consequences.

In addition, the government started vicious propaganda using the government-owned Kenya Broadcasting Corporation (KBC) radio and television to demonise activists and to criminalise political dissent. Moi argued that his primary duty as head of state was to ensure security and the maintenance of law and order. These were not negotiable, and those found undermining them would be dealt with severely (Murunga 1999: 190–1). He alleged a secret meeting of the 'agents of anarchy' (democracy activists) and reminded Kenyans of the legal position of the police in using force against dissent. He warned that those who '… carry out acts of violence or hooliganism against any citizen, no matter what his/her station in life or stance on public affairs, will be dealt with by the full might of the law. The constitution of this country', he warned, 'gives wide-ranging powers to the police for precisely this reason' (*Weekly Review*, 6 July 1990). Such a statement was hardly surprising coming from Moi, for whom the mainstay of political supremacy throughout the 1980s had been the use of police while invoking the law. Hence he detained Matiba and Rubia two days before the rally. But instead of subduing the tension, this move heightened anxiety and anticipation for 7 July.

The day turned out to be historic in the struggle for democracy. Kenyans turned out in large numbers in major towns to mark what came to be known as *Saba Saba*.[6] Platoons of the no-nonsense GSU and regular police went to the venue of the rally at dawn, ostensibly to intimidate those who would be daring enough to venture to the venue of the outlawed meeting. Yet for the following three days, the scenario that unfolded was of violent confrontation between the security forces and the citizens. The violence was mostly concentrated in the streets and suburbs of Nairobi, and in Nakuru, Kisumu and other towns. While 63 people died, over 1,000 were arraigned in court on riot-related charges, a majority of whom had obviously visible bruises and yet were without legal representation. On the other hand, the arrest and detention of Matiba and Rubia without trial marked a new start of the crackdown on advocates of multipartyism. Shortly after the detention of Matiba and Rubia came the detention of Raila Odinga and lawyers John Khaminwa, Mohammed Ibrahim and Gitobu Imanyara. Then came the arrest of Anyona, Ngotho Kariuki, Edward Oyugi and Njeru Kathangu at an unpretentious Mutugi bar in a Nairobi suburb. They were picked up by armed special branch officers and charged with plotting to overthrow Moi's government, holding a meeting with seditious intentions and being in possession of a pro-scribed publication (Gaitho 2003). The proscribed publication was the draft manifesto of a proposed party, Kenya Social Congress. Another document allegedly found on them and presented as evidence in court was a list of cabinet ministers in a new government to be headed by Matiba. Assistant Minister John Keen of the Office of the President explained to parliament the arrest of the four and read the list in the House. Later, after joining the opposition, Keen confessed that the list was a fabrication of the security forces.

The prosecution of the 'Anyona Four' came to be one of Kenya's most closely followed political trials and a big test for the police pro-secution and the judiciary. They were sentenced to four years each, but served less than a year before being released on bail pending appeal. When the appeal came, the state surprisingly did not oppose it and the four were set free. This inconsistency demonstrated the lack of independence in the magistracy. In this case the quartet were released because the government had come to the realisation that political pluralism was a fait accompli.

In October 1990, Koigi wa Wamwere, together with Mirugi Kariuki, Geoffrey Kariuki and Rumba Kinuthia, was arrested and charged with treason. After his release from detention in 1985, Wamwere had fled into exile to avoid a possible third detention. From Norway, he propagated the *Mwakenya* agenda. Occasionally he came to East Africa to give material support to colleagues inside Kenya, but operating from across the border in Uganda or Tanzania. In 1990 the police arrested Wamwere, allegedly inside Kenya 'with an assortment of arms'. Wamwere insisted that he had been kidnapped from across the border in Uganda by the Kenyan security forces and brought to Kenya before fabricated treason charges were preferred against him. On these charges, Wamwere and three others were held until January 1993, after the first multiparty elections, when the charges were dropped by the police. As Amutabi shows in Chapter 7 of this volume, this came after mothers of the prisoners were brutalised by police when, under the auspices of the 'release political prisoners' lobby group, they staged a hunger strike in March 1992 at a corner in Uhuru Park, christened the 'freedom corner'. This became a public spectacle that greatly embarrassed the government (*Daily Nation*, 6 November 1992).

In the heat of the crackdown, however, a new round of flight into exile, reminiscent of 1982, began. Gibson Kamau Kuria and Kiraitu Murungi fled to the US. Mukaru Ng'ang'a's rural home in Murang'a was invaded by 35 policemen in March 1990 for commenting on the possibility of linking the murder of Ouko to the government. He refused to be arrested without the production of a warrant (M'Inoti 1998: 540). The presence of many villagers led to the withdrawal of the contingent. Fearing further attempts to arrest him, however, he applied to the court for protection from arbitrary arrest. The court refused to grant his wish. Moi publicly commented on the matter to the effect that Ng'ang'a did not need special protection. Upon this he quietly slipped out of the country until after the repeal of Section 2A of the constitution.

Section 74 of the Kenyan constitution provides that a suspect '… may not be subjected to torture or degrading treatment'. Similarly, the Evidence Act, Section 2(6) provides guidelines on what constitutes a valid confession: 'No confession made by a person while he is in custody of a police officer should be proved as against such a person unless it is made in the immediate presence of: (a) a magistrate, (b) a police officer of or above the rank or equivalent to Inspector'. In total contradiction of these provisions, the Kenyan police became so politicised, especially during the Moi regime, that being in custody of the police on suspicion of political crimes meant extreme torture in the name of interrogation for purposes of procuring a confession. The most notorious torture chambers were at *Nyati House* (then national headquarters of the Special Branch), and *Nyayo* House. It was at Nyati that Professor Micere Mugo was taken, a few months before the 1982 coup attempt. For two days she was interrogated by menacing officers as to why University of Nairobi students of the Faculty of Arts and Social Sciences, of which she was Dean, were the most vocal against the government of President Moi. Her head was repeatedly banged on the table and threats of rape issued. It was shortly after her release from these chambers that she made up her mind to go into exile. She quickly slipped out of the country to Zimbabwe and the US (Mugo 1997).

It was also to Nyati House that Maina wa Kinyatti of the Department of History, Kenyatta University College, was taken in the middle of the night after his arrest in early 1982. On being stubborn and refusing to confess to criminal activities, Kinyatti was told:

> Since you have refused to cooperate, there will be no food, no water, and no blankets for you. You will remain naked and chained until you coop-erate ... Professor we know that Marxists are tough men, and in order to confess they must be put against the wall and have their testicles burned with fire until they confess. We will be back at 8:00 a.m. to receive your confession. Think it over ... we are not playing. We take our work seriously. (Onyango 2003)

The most dreaded torture chambers for political opponents to Moi in the 1980s and early 1990s were, however, not at Nyati but at Nyayo House. Nyayo House (after Moi's Nyayo philosophy) was opened in 1983 as the Provincial Headquarters of Nairobi. Its base-ment was designed to have 12 strong rooms, '... intended for the safe storage of classified government documents' (*Daily Nation*, December 1983). This was also the provincial headquarters of the Special Branch. It was here that the torture of most of the *Mwakenya* suspects took place. Suspects held on grounds of their political stand would be stripped naked in the interrogation room. Such rooms had stains of blood, fresh as well as dried, as a message to the suspects. There were pieces of furniture on the floor. The interrogators were menacing and brutal, with unrevealed identity but apparently led by one James Opiyo. At the inquest of Peter Njenga Karanja who died from torture injuries, magistrate Mango had this to say of Opiyo: '... Mr. Opiyo has not been willing to tell who the other interrogators were for what he calls reasons of "state security"' (*Nairobi Law Monthly*, no. 14, February 1989). The state thus approved of the activities of the officers and actually protected them from prosecution.

Raila encountered this squad in 1988. He spent ten days standing in water before facing '... a row of five or six well-dressed men sitting on a raised platform' (Onyango and Mburu 2003). Israel Agina, Raila's close associate, was in the chambers for 96 days, of which five a week were spent standing in cold water. In 1986, lawyer Ng'ang'a Thiongo was tortured using hot cigarette butts. The list is long, but undoubtedly the case of lawyer Wanyiri Kihoro merits special mention. He was arrested in Mombasa in July 1986. His house was invaded by armed police officers in the middle of the night. He was brought to Nairobi and locked up in a cell in the Nyayo House basement, where he was physically and mentally tortured. He spent 74 days here, 24 of them in water. He was forced to undress before a panel of police officers who beat him up. He was starved for most of the time he was there. He could not sleep and his feet developed blisters. He was consequently detained at various prisons: Naivasha, Kamiti, Manyani and Shimo-la-Tewa.

It was only after Moi left power that the torture chambers at Nyayo House were exposed to the public, which had not known much of the real activities that had been undertaken there. Meanwhile, in 2000, DSI was transformed into the National Security Intelligence Services (NSIS) in order to disassociate it from its previous preoccupation and reputation of hunting down political dissenters. It was totally delinked from the police and its mandate redefined. It now focuses on matters of national interest: security, anti-terrorism, campaigns against corruption, narcotic trafficking, the proliferation of illicit arms and money laundering (*Sunday Nation*, 27 September 2003). NSIS officers have no powers to arrest or detain anybody. On detecting a security threat they would pass the information to the police for action.

Judicial and Prison System Complicity in Police Repression

Much as the focus of this study has been on the hurdles put in the way of democratisation in Kenya by the police system, the latter could not have been successful in repression for so long without the complicity of their sister organs, namely the judiciary and the prison systems. In a democratic context, the judiciary is the institution mandated to mediate justice by fairly interpreting the constitution and safeguarding the freedoms and liberties of the individual. The judiciary is the constitutional arbiter of disputes between citizens and the government, and

between citizens themselves (M'Inoti 1998: 337). This role is especially important when dealing with suspects on the road to trial or
already undergoing trial. A suspect has his rights and freedoms enshrined
in the Bill of Rights. It is correct to say that the treatment of suspects,
especially those charged with political crimes, is a gauge of how deeply
entrenched democracy is in a society.

The history of the Kenyan judiciary in handling cases relating to
political dissent amounts to a tale of miscarriage of justice. It is understandable that the ideology and powers of the colonial government did
not allow for dissent from the Africans. Yet post-colonial Kenya,
under Kenyatta and increasingly under Moi, witnessed a systematic
breakdown of the constitutional checks and balances and the independence of key organs like the judiciary. In 1988 Moi got the constitution amended so that the Attorney General lost security of tenure,
while judges could be fired at his discretion. With time, the judiciary
became a virtual appendage of the executive, which overwhelmed it
with the duty of containing and frustrating regime opponents by putting its legal *imprimatur* on the repressive actions of the police. Many
perceived the courts as interpreting public interest to favour law and
order interests of the state as against the rights of the individual (Mulei
1998: 289). The magistrates became so suffused with the interests of
the executive that the inescapable result was judicial surrender and
executive excesses. A few examples will suffice.

In virtually all the *Mwakenya* related trials of the 1980s, conviction
was based on the accused person's own confession. It never seemed to
bother the magistrates that there was the possibility of violation of
the rights of the suspect including the right not to be tortured. This
happened to be the time of Matthew Guy Muli as AG, who was wont
to make cynical comments on the political opposition of the day. For
instance, on entering *nolle prosequi* to treason charges against Raila,
Mak'Onyango and Professor Otieno in April 1983, the AG commented that it did not mean that 'the accused cannot be charged with
the same offence' (*Daily Nation*, 15 April 1983). And true to his word,
as the trio left the magistrate's court, they were rearrested and detained
without trial. Perhaps the most dreaded person at the courts in these
cases was the then Deputy Public Prosecutor, Bernard Chunga. He
prosecuted all of them in what came to be dubbed as the '*Mwakenya*
inquisition'. Almost all his known public life Chunga worked at the
AG's chambers. He acquired a reputation for being ruthless. In what
appeared to be hurriedly prepared cases, Chunga prosecuted political

suspects at odd hours, always in the night; the charges preferred being either sedition or treason. The outcome was always a foregone conclusion. In remembering these trials, Ngotho Kariuki said that many were '… jailed as *Mwakenya* members in fake trials conducted at night and prosecuted by Deputy Public Prosecutor, Bernard Chunga' (*Sunday Standard*, 26 January 2003).

At the peak of the clamour for multiparty democracy at the start of the 1990s, the judiciary displayed a partisan streak in the cases of the pro-democracy proponents who appeared before the courts. M'Inoti (1998: 535) rightly observes, 'While the government's response was decidedly hostile, the judicial response, to a large extent, mirrored that attitude.' The judiciary sought to and actually jailed those brought before it. The case of Lawford Imunde, a Minister of the Presbyterian Church of East Africa, clearly illustrates this point. He was arrested in March 1990 without a warrant and held for a week. When his lawyer sought to institute a habeas corpus, he was hurriedly produced in court and charged with 'possessing and printing a seditious publication'. The said publication was his personal diary, where he had made comments criticising the government's suicide theory on the death of Ouko earlier in the month. In sentencing him to six years in prison, the judge stated: 'As a warning to others who may still be in the dreamland of the accused thinking of destabilising the solid, just and fair government of the land, a custodial sentence commensurate with the times is called for' (M'Inoti 1998: 538).

In another instance, Paul Muite contested the Law Society of Kenya (LSK) chairmanship in 1991 and won. In his acceptance speech he, among other issues, called on the government to allow political pluralism and to release political detainees. A few of the colleagues opposed to him sought a court injunction to restrain him from making what they considered political statements. In granting their plea, the magistrate's statement displayed ineptitude, partisanship and a lack of understanding of the basics in human rights requisite of any legal arbiter. He judged:

> It is unreasonable for those agitating for the release of political detainees to assume that they know the reasons for their detention in the first place. The government has all the machinery for gathering reports and information from whatever source, which those agitating are not likely to have and, as we know, even the detainees themselves may not know how much the government knows about them. The Act doesn't provide as one of the objects of the Society to make such unreasonable demands on the government. (M'Inoti 1998: 542)

Such was the mood of the courts at the time of democratic transition in the early 1990s. The courts condoned and even abetted the torture of suspects. In law, a suspect may not be subjected to torture or inhuman or degrading treatment while under interrogation (Mbaya 1998: 298). In contravention of this convention, virtually all suspects in custody on politically stated grounds bore signs of recent torture, but feared risking more torture if they talked about it. Whenever the issue arose in court, the magistrates absolved the government. Hence the characteristic plea of 'guilt' before these *Nyayo* courts.

The police and the courts acted together in an effort to kill free media, which is a significant marker of a democratic society. The status of the press in the 1980s and 1990s remained firmly determined by the government. Print media that were perceived to be critical of the system and supportive of free expression came to be increasingly targeted for police harassment. Staff of such media would be beaten and arraigned in court for law breaking. The magazine *Beyond*, published by the National Council of the Churches of Kenya (NCCK), was the first publication to take on Moi in the second half of the 1980s. It came under severe criticism from the government and was proscribed on the flimsy grounds that the editor failed to comply with the regulation of submitting a copy to the authorities. Hence Bedan Mbugua, the editor, was arrested, charged and jailed under the Books and Newspapers Act. Possession of past, present and future issues became a criminal offence. Mbugua appealed against the sentence and the banning. This took a long time. Ultimately his conviction was overturned, but only after he had served the full sentence.

The same fate awaited the *Society* magazine, which had become very critical of police repression in the early 1990s. The government levelled charges of sedition against Pius and Loise Nyamora, proprietor and publisher. In this case the court was used to cripple the operations of the publication by ensuring that the hearings would proceed at an extremely slow pace. Furthermore, court hearings were taken to Mombasa and not Nairobi (the base of the defendants). The couple was expected to travel to Mombasa some 500 kilometres away every other week to attend court. The obvious idea was simply to tire them out so that ultimately they would give up. Indeed, the government achieved its objective when the finances of the publication became disorganised leading to closure of the publication. Then, and only then, did the prosecution drop the charges.

Perhaps the worst example of the government policy against free press was that of the proscription of the *Finance* magazine and *People Daily*. These were highly critical of the government and were associated with Matiba. In February 1993, police confiscated thousands of copies of *Finance* and *People* from the streets of Nairobi. The papers were printed by Fotoform, owned by Dominic Martin. The printer was dismantled and vital parts confiscated by police. Martin was charged with sedition. The printing could not go on while the case lasted because of the missing components (which were described by prosecutors as being crucial exhibits for the prosecution). Later the court dropped the charges, having made sure that the press could not easily be restarted.

In the early 1990s, the state preferred sedition charges to stifle a particularly new medium of political expression. Following the government's refusal to license the Matiba and Rubia proposed *Saba Saba* rally, many music composers in Nairobi released cassettes with songs whose theme was democracy versus dictatorship. The compositions were subtle but hard-hitting against the regime. The police targeted them for suppression. The Attorney General declared the compositions seditious. The police moved in to carry out swoops on the production stations and the vendors. Both cassettes and production materials were destroyed (Murunga 1999: 147). This was meant to deter the train of democracy. It did not succeed.

The exit of Moi from the Kenyan political scene at the start of 2003 proved to be the lifting of a dark cloud that had hung over the prison system of the country. Under Kenyatta, Moi had been the Minister for Home Affairs, under whom prisons fell. As president in the 1980s and 1990s, he had a hand in what went on in the prisons, especially in relation to political prisoners. Prison conditions were inhuman during the Kenyatta and Moi eras. The case was worse for people jailed or detained for political crimes. Prison life was meant to break an inmate. This was especially the case for those detained without trial. Ngugi wa Thiong'o (1981) gives a graphic picture of these conditions in the 1970s. They did not change for the better in the 1980s and early 1990s. The prison system was an extension of the police system. It was a 'repressive weapon' in the hands of the ruling elite. The system was nothing more than '… an account of oppressive measures in varying degrees of intensity and one's individual or collective response to them' (wa Thiong'o 1981: 100). Especially dehumanising was detention without trial, which was a means of physical removal of dissenters from the arena of active politics, with the express objective of making them recant their political beliefs. Unlike regular imprisonment, the detainees never knew when they would be released. This suspense was in itself a torture.

The detainees were subject to beatings from prison warders. They would occasionally be made to sleep on cold or wet floors without blankets, making the body weak and prone to disease. They were denied access to news media. Detention was meant to weaken the spirit of the prisoner so that he pleaded for release. Life was monotonous in its repetitive rhythm of eating and sleeping. The prison atmosphere was perpetually polluted, with a permanent stench of urine and human waste. The detainees were held in a block where they were identified by specific numbers rather than names. They were subjected to confinement in a room for 23 out of 24 hours in a day with only one hour to go out. The rest of the time was spent under a bulb of light, day and night. The prison diet was pathetic and calculated to weaken the body. The food was often deliberately uncooked and, according to Wamwere, one had to psych oneself up for long hours to bring oneself to eat the food. In his particular case, Wamwere would engage in a lot of physical exercises in order to induce appetite (Onyango 2003).

Disease was the condition most dreaded while in detention. It was conveniently used by the prison system to humiliate and degrade prisoners. When one reported that he was sick, the administration took time to allow the disease to soak into the system of the prisoner before treatment commenced. Oftentimes diagnosis by the prison doctor was given as depression. For this the routine treatment was Valium, an anti-depressant. The case of Martin Shikuku was the most pathetic in the late 1970s. He contracted a disease at Kamiti and virtually became a cripple. He was hardly given any meaningful treatment until after his release. The prison commandant of Kamiti in the 1970s, Edward Lokopoyit, introduced new measures that further dehumanised the prisoners. He introduced the practice of chaining ailing prisoners as a condition for being taken to hospital for further treatment. At Kenyatta National Hospital, a patient would be chained to a bed and heavily guarded by armed policemen and warders.

In the early 1990s, while in detention, Matiba was denied access to a commissioner of oaths for purposes of swearing an affidavit to enable him challenge the legality of his detention (M'Inoti 1998: 544). He was denied access to proper medical facilities. Ultimately he suffered a near-fatal stroke that left him partially paralysed. His health would never be the same again. His close associate, Rubia, came out of detention in bad health. He lost his voice as the harsh prison conditions worsened his thyroid gland problems (Onyango and Mburu 2003). Adungosi, as was mentioned above, died in detention in 1988 and the government never carried out an inquest to ascertain what caused the death. Professors Edward Oyugi and Ngotho Kariuki were detained in the 1980s and rearrested in 1990. When they came out they were sick people. Oyugi had developed diabetes. Ngotho had to travel to the US '… for treatment of my spine which had been damaged when I was tortured at the Nyayo House dungeons' (Kihuria 2003).

At the end of the day, the greatest challenge to democratising the Kenya police force has consisted of having to change with the times to reflect the global reorientation in policing style. A series of steps have been taken to grapple with the challenge of democratising the force. Change in policing seriously began after the end of the 40-year rule of KANU and the ascension to power of NARC at the end of 2002. Brigadier Mohammed Ali of the Kenya Army was appointed to the position of Police Commissioner in early 2004. It was argued that the Kenya Police needed someone from outside it in order to reinvent it. The NARC government is investing heavily in this project of redefining the role of the police and repackaging its image. This commitment is reflected in the decisive moves to review the terms of service of the force, to retrain the officers, and in the submission by the officers to the Constitutional Review Commission to rename the institution as 'The Kenya Police Service'. Beginning April 2004, Brigadier Ali began a programme of reorienting senior police officers to the essentials of community policing. The strategy has been to hold seminars where facilitators are invited from different professional areas to give lectures to the officers. Kenyatta University faculty have played a big role in these seminars. Following these refresher courses, it is hoped that the senior officers will then have a positive impact on the force that will have trickle-down effect to their juniors in the stations.

Conclusion

This chapter has demonstrated that the story of the struggle for democracy in Kenya is incomplete without an analysis of the negative role of the law enforcement organs. It has argued that the struggle starts with the establishment of colonial rule in Kenya at the close of the nineteenth century. The resistance to the police force of the time was a fight for the democratic ideal of self-government. The origins of repressive policing are traced from these early decades of the twentieth century and throughout the colonial period. The formation of political associations in the 1920s and 1930s was a stage in the development of a democratic consciousness. This ushered in the activities of KAU in the 1940s and the option of militancy by the Mau Mau movement in the 1950s. The colonial police played a leading role in hunting down and hounding to detention the political leaders of the day instead of executing their ideal mandate, namely security and order for the public. The promise of a democratic order with independence under Kenyatta proved a false dawn as Kenyatta accumulated power under the executive and manipulated the police institution to silence his opponents. The security forces were implicated in the assassination of Pinto, Mboya and Kariuki by way of covering up the truth or by directly executing the murders. At the same time, Kenyatta invoked the constitution to detain without trial his opponents under barbaric conditions.

The ascendancy of Moi as president began a 24-year reign of autocracy that came down hard against democratic opposition by manipulating the security forces, the courts and the prison system. The arrests, torture and detention of the *Mwakenya* democracy proponents marked the darkest decade in independent Kenya. But the subsequent democratising wind of change across the globe at the end of the 1980s signalled a new dawn of democratic dispensation. The joint pressure from the forces of democracy at home and help from the international community precipitated the adoption of multiparty politics. Accompanying this has been the effort by the government to retrain the police and to review their terms of service so that their modus operandi reflects the needs and wishes of *wananchi* (citizens). What impact these efforts will have in reshaping the operational code of the police force for the better, only time will tell.

Notes

1. *Boma* is a Kiswahili term simply meaning residence. In this respect *centres* where either traders or colonial administrators set up camp became nuclei of public activities, and ultimately administrative centres. They retained the term *boma*, which took the new meaning of administrative headquarters.
2. *Kipande* is Kiswahili for identity card. It was in the form of a numbered piece of metal, secured by a string, which the natives were required to wear around the neck.

3. *Shifta* were Somali terror militias that operated in Northern Kenya especially in the 1960s and 1970s. Their dream was the creation of what they called 'Great Somalia'. The Northern Frontier District of Kenya (covering most of today's North-Eastern Province) was part of Somaliland. Hence they waged a kind of war of liberation by visiting terror on the government presence in Northern Kenya.

4. Mboya was used by Kenyatta's kitchen cabinet of politicians mainly from the Kiambu District to fight Odinga and marginalise the latter from the centre of power.

5. Moi had declared from the beginning of his ascension to power that he would follow the footprints (Nyayo) of his predecessor, Mzee Jomo Kenyatta.

6. *Saba* means seven in Kiswahili. Hence *Saba Saba* referred to the seventh day of the seventh month.

References

Ajulu, R. (2000) 'Thinking Through the Crisis of Democratization in Kenya: A Response to Adar and Murunga', *African Sociological Review*, vol. 4, no. 2.

Akivaga, S.K., et al. (2002) *Multipartyism Without Democracy: Challenge to the Voter*, Nairobi: Ecumenical Centre for Justice and Peace.

Anderson, D. (2005) *Histories of the Hanged: The Dirty War in Kenya and the End of Empire*, New York, NY: W.W. Norton.

Anderson, D., and D. Killingray (1991) 'Consent, Coercion and Colonial Control: Policing the Empire, 1830–1940', in D. Anderson and D. Killingray (eds), *Policing the Empire: Government, Authority and Control, 1830–1940*, Manchester: Manchester University Press.

Bayley, D. (1996) *Police for the Future*, New York, NY: Oxford University Press.

Foran, W.R. (1962) *The Kenya Police, 1887–1960*, London: Robert State.

Gaitho, M. (2003) 'Anyona's Chequered political Career' *Daily Nation*, 6 November.

Kenya Human Rights Commission (KHRC) (1998) 'Independence Without Freedom: The Legitimisation of Repressive Laws and Practices in Kenya', in K. Kibwana (ed.), *Readings in Constitutional Law and Politics in Africa: A Case Study of Kenya*, Nairobi: Claripress.

Kihuria, N. (2003) 'The Return of the Exiles: What Next?' *Sunday Standard*, 26 January.

Marks, M. (1999) 'Policing for Democracy? The Case of the Public Order Police Unit in Durban', *Africa Development*, vol. XXIV, nos 1–2.

Mbaya, W. (1998) 'Criminal Justice in Kenya: Role of the Judiciary in Safeguarding the Pre-trial Rights of Suspects', in K. Kibwana (ed.), *Readings in Constitutional Law and Politics in Africa: A Case Study of Kenya*, Nairobi: Claripress.

M'Inoti, K. (1998) 'The Judiciary in Multi-Party Politics in Kenya: 1990–1992', in K. Kibwana (ed.), *Readings in Constitutional Law and Politics in Africa: A Case of Kenya*, Nairobi: Claripress.

Mugo, M. (1997) 'Exile and Creativity: A Prolonged Writer's Block', in K. Anyidoho (ed.), *The Word Behind Bars and the Paradox of Exile*, Evanston, IL: Northwestern University Press.

Mulei, C. (1998) 'Human Rights, Democracy and the Rule of Law', in K. Kibwana (ed.), *Readings in Constitution and Law and Politics in Africa: A Case of Kenya*, Nairobi: Claripress.

Murunga, G.R. (1999) 'Urban Violence in Kenya's Transition to Pluralist Politics', Africa *Development*, vol. XXIV, nos 1–2.

Ogot, B.A. (1995) 'The Politics of Populism', in B.A. Ogot and W.R. Ochieng' (eds), *Decolonization and Independence in Kenya, 1940–93*, London: James Currey.

Onyango, D. (2003) 'Locked Away From the Real World', *The Daily Nation*, 18 September.

_____ and S. Mburu (2003) 'We Want the Bitter Truth, Say Four Exiles, Torture Victims', *The Sunday Nation*, 26 January.

Thiongo, N. wa (1981) *Detained: A Writer's Prison Diary*, London: Heinemann.

PART IV

Donors and the Politics of Structural Adjustment

9

Governance and the Politics of Structural Adjustment in Kenya

Godwin R. Murunga

Introduction

Generally, Africa experienced declining economic fortunes in the last two decades of the 21st century. The period saw many countries slide into the list of the poorest countries in the world. Some of them ran very high balance of payment deficits and high rates of inflation, and began to rely very much on donor aid to meet their budgetary deficits and to fund basic programmes at home (Ake 1996). Others lost the ability to provide basic welfare needs to their citizenry, while some degenerated into authoritarianism, anarchy and war. With increased levels of indebtedness, state sovereignty was compromised as many states were compelled to adopt externally designed remedies. The shock therapies administered were collectively called the structural adjustment programmes (SAPs). Designed largely by the World Bank (WB) and the International Monetary Fund (IMF), the SAPs were a set of policy and fiscal austerity measures designed to stabilise African economies in the short term, reverse their declining economic performance and, in the long run, re-engineer and ensure sustained economic development. This goal remains elusive to date.

Conceptualised as the best and, at times, the only means to Africa's recovery (World Bank 1994), the designers of SAPs constructed Africa as an ailing and helpless patient that had run out of ideas on economic recovery and development. They ignored local input in these remedial policies and championed neo-liberal alternatives that focused almost exclusively on market-based reforms. The reform packages were presented as sacrosanct as opposed to the irrational local policies dominated by neo-patrimonialism and rent seeking – habits that, it was argued, inhibited growth and created 'dysfunctional' economies. Thus African development problems were associated with the nature of the African post-colonial state that promoted neo-patrimonial tendencies and limited the efficacy of the rational bureaucratic system of management (Sandbrook 1986; Chabal and Daloz 1999; van de Walle 2001). On the whole, analysts blamed Africa's ailing economic situation on state interventionism, a failure that was traced to the putative moment of *uhuru*, when local development policies encouraged the concentration of wealth in a tiny urban coalition that controlled state power and promoted urban-biased policies even though the key to productive enterprises, it was alleged, rested with the largely agricultural-based sectors in rural areas (Bates 1981).

This reading of African development challenges has been critiqued on theoretical and empirical grounds (Gibbon 1992, 1996; Olukoshi 1998; Mkandawire 2001b, 2004; Mkandawire and Soludo 2003). The assumption that Africa has been in 'permanent crisis', to use van de Walle's (2001) obviously exaggerated characterisation, is empirically inaccurate. This chapter argues that, like most other African countries, Kenya maintained a mixed record of economic development in the 1960s and early 1970s. It locates Kenya's governance problems in the centralisation of power in the presidency, showing how this centralisation encouraged forms of state intervention in the economy that benefited a few political actors while gradually eliminating political and economic competition. The concentration of power and elimination of competition took place at the instigation or with the active connivance of most bilateral and multilateral lenders. The inability of lenders to implement reforms or to enforce compliance on agreed reforms after 1990 was ultimately because of the nature of the relations that Kenya's leadership had forged with lenders during the cold war. In a nutshell, at the centre of Kenya's poor economic performance and its failure to effect a speedy economic adjustment are governance issues whose manifestations have internal and external dynamics.

The concept of governance

Governance refers to the management of public affairs. It involves rules and norms of policy making and implementation (Hyden 2000: 9).

Studies of governance stress the importance of predictability in the relations between the rulers and the ruled (Barkan 1994: 27). But governance must be contextualised in the terrain of politics where the institutions that make and implement policy are located. This terrain includes the institutional frameworks of policy making, implementation and validation. Since this is a contested terrain, governance necessarily involves struggles on how to tip gains in favour of particular actors, sectors and constituencies. The struggle to maximise on rewards in favour of any sector, so maligned in Africanist political science, is not unique to Africa, and stigmatising such struggles simply substitutes labels for analysis, thereby perpetuating a 'tropicalised' reading of African politics (Olukoshi 1999).

Governance is not a neutral term that can be measured with the 'objective' finesse of a scientific experiment. Its practice is based on subjective perceptions and judgements. The line between good and bad governance is not permanent; it is constantly negotiated depending on the balance between the effectiveness of policies and their effects on the citizenry. The virtues of governance reside with democratic participation rather than the technocratic-managerial inclination of the Bretton Woods Institutions' (BWIs) neo-liberalism. The advantages of governance accrue only with reference to the needs, values and interests of the citizens of a country. Thus, it is true that the Kenyan leadership failed in their governance responsibilities, yet donors also failed to consider the impact of the SAPs on state legitimacy. Their policies led to endless altercations between the Kenyan government and the BWIs that constituted the politics of adjustment in Kenya (Herbst 1990). Politics is nested in legitimacy. Ideally, political decisions ought always to seek to attain a balance between efficient management for sustained development and effectiveness of reform judged on the basis of rewards to the generality of citizens. The post-colonial leadership in Kenya anchored their political rhetoric in the guise of popular legitimacy and exercised this to frustrate donor and opposition pressure for reform. Thus, the idea of politics of the SAPs in this chapter signals the contested nature of the process and practice of governance and stresses the centrality of political rhetoric to understanding the success or failure of reforms. To understand this rhetoric, one must question the donor logic that effectiveness of economic policies could only be measured in terms of getting the prices right and on the basis of profitable returns to investment. This logic subordinated state legitimacy to markets and ignored the fact that the politics of economic reform required a hegemonic state. In a nutshell, the logic failed to focus on the people to whom returns on investment were expected to accrue.

The Ruse of a Model Economy under Kenyatta

The WB/IMF conceived the SAPs on the assumption that Africa's post-colonial development record was a total failure. They assumed that most African economies were dysfunctional. This assumption had a self-serving caveat that presented some few countries as star performers and models to be emulated. In the 1970s and early 1980s, Kenya and Cote d'Ivoire were examples of model economies in Africa. But their star status served a neo-colonial purpose. Kenya was presented as a good model of what adoption of a capitalist development path heralded. For the US, Kenya's status as a bastion of capitalism made it a useful bulwark against communism in the region, especially because the US wished to keep a watchful eye on communist infiltration into the country (Okoth 1992). To bolster their interests and cordon off Kenya, the US guaranteed foreign assistance to Kenya as long as the local leadership maintained their support for the West and kept a capitalist outlook (Attwood 1967). This 'agreement' between the local elite and foreign interests, maintained until 1989, stalked the reform agenda with devastating consequences. When economic decline set in and pressure for political reform earnestly ensued, most donors found it difficult to pressure the Kenyan government into reform for fear of losing a strategic cold war ally. But Kenya's star status, like that of Ghana and Uganda in the adjustment era, was short-lived. Kenya's economic performance during this era should be judged against the propaganda designs and interests of the bilateral and multilateral donors during the cold war era.

The first development strategy in Kenya adopted a market-based vision of development with an emphasis on individual rights and protection of private property. Clothed in the garb of African socialism, the Sessional Paper No. 10 of 1965 balanced between market-based policies and state interventionism. State intervention in social welfare provision was in vogue. It was under this development regime that Kenya attained a mixed record of economic growth between 1963 when it gained independence and 1978 when President Jomo Kenyatta died. The economy maintained a GDP growth rate of over 6 per cent per annum in the 1960s. This rate was backed up by fiscal balance, low inflation rates and a stable exchange rate. The terms of trade were favourable and export volume was high until it began to stagnate in the 1970s and to decline in the 1980s. With the oil shocks of 1973, GDP growth declined to 2.8 per cent in 1975 before the real GDP growth rate that averaged 6.8 per cent was realized between 1976 and 1978. The GDP growth rate was 8.2 per cent in 1977 before it dropped to 5 per cent in 1979 and 3.9 per cent in 1980. The impressive growth rate in 1977 was associated with the coffee boom in Kenya, a temporary gain following the frost affecting Brazilian coffee. But this temporary boom was accompanied by increased government expenditure that was not scaled down as the boom ended. From 1979, especially with the second oil shock, Kenya experienced high inflation rates and a fiscal deficit. Government revenue could not sufficiently finance its expenditure (Bigsten and Ndung'u 1992: 48–50). The budgetary deficit reached a peak of 10.0 per cent in 1980 and kept a high of over 5.0 per cent from then on except in 1983 when it was 3.4 per cent. In 1987, the deficit stood at 9.5 per cent (Bigsten and Ndung'u 1992: 51; Maxon and Ndege 1995). As these statistics suggest, there was need for decisive reform action in the mid-1970s to ameliorate the effects of this decline but Kenyatta procrastinated.

The budgetary deficit came at a time when Kenya enjoyed donor confidence on account of its cold war role. The government did not act to stem economic decline. Instead, a series of management failures that exacerbated the decline set in. No decisive action was taken to halt the rising government expenditure in the 1970s so as to balance it with government revenue. Employment within the public service continued to swell and government expenditure on wages alone increased exponentially in the 1960s and 1970s. While the logic of such increases in the workforce and its justification neatly fit within the developmentalist logic of most independent countries, there is no doubt that rationalising the wage bill against government revenue was required. But analysts and lenders were seduced by the states' pro-Western record into procrastinating on this rationalisation. After all, the state was favourably disposed to foreign capital. It promoted policies that allowed entrenchment of foreign capital in Kenya to a scale never witnessed before. Thus, foreign capital came to control key sectors of the economy including the main productive arteries in agriculture, manufacturing and the service sectors (Langdon 1975; Leys 1975, 1980; Kaplinsky 1978, 1980).

The economic growth characteristic of the 1960s and 1970s in Kenya was, to a considerable extent, a reflection of investments undertaken by foreign capital in alliance with a local petit bourgeoisie who assumed the reins of state power at independence. This bourgeoisie used independence to take control of the state and used foreign capital to gain a foothold into the key business and productive sectors of the economy for purposes of personal wealth accumulation. By the mid-1970s, some felt confident enough to stand on their feet alongside foreign capital. They created an enabling environment for foreign exploitation of local resources. Using their political power, they whittled down the worker unions and maintained unrealistically low wages for the workers whose wrath was slowly building up as their purchasing power was eroded. This process of class differentiation was later reflected in the political cleavages in the country. For instance, political discussion in parliament reflected a mounting concern about inequality in the distribution of wealth. The elite, on the other hand, had gained economic wealth that was necessary to back up their hold on power. They strategically positioned themselves in alliance with foreigners. Together, the elite and their Western backers constituted a formidable bulwark against potential local opposition. Thus, when economic decline hit in the late 1970s, the local leadership in alliance with foreign capital did not act to correct the causes of the decline.

State-led development and political authoritarianism

The literature on Kenya has carefully documented the nature of the country's elite and their link to foreign capital. But until the mid-1980s, it had failed to study how the elite controlled and used state power (see Ajulu 2000: 134). This failure served very well the perception of Kenya as a success story of post-colonial development. By 1982, Kenya was still lauded as a model economy with a fast growth rate that was 'compatible with an improvement in the living standards of the mass of people' (Mosley 1982: 271; Barkan and Holmquist 1989: 359). Though it is debatable whether the rates of growth were compatible with improvement in living standards of the mass of people, there is no doubt that the growth record achieved at the time was spurred through state interventionism (Olukoshi 1998: 16; Mkandawire 2001a, 2001b; Olukoshi 2001). The logic of the state-led model of accumulation was to enable the state to correct previous imbalances and begin an era of nation building based on local needs. In Kenya, it involved government control of the development process through the entrenchment of parastatals and marketing boards to oversee the management of agriculture and industry, the strengthening of district and provincial offices to ensure state oversight over policy design and implementation processes, and state provision or subsidy in the health, education, energy, infrastructure and water services. The state regulated the distorting effects of uncontrolled marketisation by licensing businesses and trade, controlled agriculture, regulated taxation, imposed tariff barriers, and controlled foreign exchange systems and prices. The state was also expected to provide gainful employment. It was indeed the main employer. In other words, state interventionism was responsible for Kenya's successes in the 1960s and 1970s. But at the political level, it interpreted its role to mean a virtual monopoly of dos and don'ts (Atieno-Odhiambo 1987).

The state-led model of accumulation allowed Kenyatta to establish a system of rule characterised in the literature as 'presidential authoritarianism' (Anyang Nyong'o 1989; van de Walle 2003: 310). The political problems that affected Kenya's economic performance in the 1980s must be located in this history of personalised rule initiated by the Kenyatta and inherited by the Moi regime (see Ochieng' 1989, 1995). This system concentrated power in the presidency at the expense of countervailing institutions. Kenyatta and his allies developed this system by dismantling the nationalist coalition of the 1950s and 1960s (see Anyang Nyong'o 1989), amending the constitution to serve private and indefensible political goals (Okoth-Ogendo 1972) and, in its place, installing a system that vested power in the president. The president was above the law; he appointed and fired the cabinet, top civil servants and the provincial administration at will, reigned over the bureaucracy, and determined judicial tenure and the parliamentary calendar. Kenyatta put in place a domineering network of loyal provincial and district officials who represented him at various local levels. With power centralised and intensely personalised, the idea of a one-party system came into vogue.

Presidential authoritarianism entailed presidential control over state finance which was exercised with little, if any, accountability. The president appointed loyalists to top positions in lucrative public enterprises including the major parastatals. As Amutabi and Gimode show in Chapters 7 and 8, respectively, in this volume, Kenyatta controlled the armed forces, the police, the civil service, the provincial administration and the academy. His hold on key levers of governance put him in control over patronage resources and gave him unparalleled hold over key sectors of the economy and politics. As a result,

Kenyatta grew hostile to political dissent, established Kenya as a de facto one-party state in 1969 and earnestly began to eliminate the potential foci of organised opposition through assassinations, detention without trial or by rigging elections as in the case of the KPU in the 1966 'little general election' (Tamarkin 1978, 1979; Mueller 1984).

Kenya's mixed economic performance reflected the instability of the system Kenyatta built. There is no doubt that state interventionism to stabilise the economy contributed to the overall positive performance of the Kenyan economy in the 1960s. But in the absence of presidential accountability to the public and constructive engagement with broader national constituencies, negative tendencies emanating from centralisation of power set in. For instance, foreign capital dominated the economy and wealth was concentrated in a small group of local elite around Kenyatta. Using state power, the elite used the legal and institutional framework that had underpinned white settler dominance in the agricultural sector to further concentrate wealth among themselves. In their conceited mission of accumulation, these elite whittled the workers' rights to benefit from both their primitive accumulation interests and those of the foreign capital and exacerbated income inequalities between the rich and the poor.

The elite's misuse of the state for conspicuous consumption was clearly highlighted in a tariff incident in 1976. Pointing to the increasing dominance of luxurious foreign commodities in the local market, a local newsmagazine underscored the major loopholes that centralisation without accountability had generated. It highlighted licensing rackets and corruption in the ministry of commerce and industry that allowed non-essential items to be imported at the expense of local ones thereby affecting the foreign exchange situation in the country (see *Weekly Review*, 22 March 1976, pp. 14–19). The paper accused the ministry of ruining the economy through misdirection in its trade licensing policy. Such leaks in tariff barriers, it added, would explain the entry into the Kenyan market of items whose quality was lower than those produced locally or items that merely served the luxurious appetite of the elite. Against this background, the newspaper went on to highlight the continued large deficit in balance of payments on current accounts that could explain the slowing down in the rate of economic expansion, unemployment and income inequalities. It is within this context that J.M. Kariuki accused 'a small but powerful group of greedy, self-seeking elite in the form of politician, Civil Servants and businessmen, [of] steadily but surely monopoliz[ing] the fruits of independence to the exclusion of the majority of the people' and warned that 'we do not want a Kenya of ten millionaires and ten million beggars' (quoted in Ochieng' 1995: 103).

By the end of Kenyatta's rule, Kenya faced serious political and economic problems. As economic performance worsened, the political leadership sent mixed signals regarding their commitment to stabilise the economy, to institute measures to ensure growth, and to guarantee democracy and basic rights to citizens. The leadership legitimately blamed the economic decline on the world economic crisis of the 1970s, the oil shocks of 1973 and 1979, the droughts that affected Kenya in 1979–80 and 1984, and on the high population growth rates. These explanations prevented close analysis of the governance failures of the Kenyatta regime with regard to regulating government expenditure and restructuring the economy. Yet by 1976, it was obvious that government overexpenditure was a major problem contributing to the slow growth rates. While the minister for finance, Mwai Kibaki, exuded confidence on the performance of the economy, the Central Bank of Kenya released statistics that questioned such confidence (see a series of reports in the *Weekly Review*, 5 April 1976, pp. 22–6; 26 April 1976, p. 6; and 3 May 1976, p. 19). Ignoring these early warning signs, analysts continued to praise the Kenyatta regime as a 'great success', lauding it as 'more accountable' and 'more legitimate' to its citizens (Barkan and Holmquist 1989; Widner 1992; Throup 1993 and critical reviews by Gibbon 1995; Ajulu 2000).

Stagnation under Moi, 1978–88

Upon assuming the presidency, Moi acknowledged the management failures of the Kenyatta era. He agreed that inefficiency, financial mismanagement, waste and corruption plagued the public sector and appointed committees to investigate and recommend ways of solving the problems. A Committee on Review of Statutory Boards was set up in 1979 to review and make recommendations with regard to urgent financial, administrative and operational problems facing important boards. It confirmed widespread inefficiency, financial mismanagement, waste and malpractices in many parastatals and recommended, among other things, firm government regulation of this sector (Grosh 1991: 16–17). The 1982 Working Party on Government Expenditure also identified serious public sector inefficiencies. Placing the onus of poor financial performance with the central government, the committee found that the treasury was unable to exercise adequate financial control. It recommended against 'overextension of public enterprise into sectors that were strictly commercial' and called for a programme of divestiture in order to ensure that public enterprises with important social mandates do not overlap with those of a strictly commercial nature (Grosh 1991: 18). Further review of government policies came with Sessional Paper No. 4 of 1980 on Economic Prospects and Policies, which scaled down development programmes in response to the oil shocks, Sessional Paper No. 4 of 1981 on National Food Policy which sought to establish policies to attain self-sufficiency in food production following the food shortages of the previous two years and Sessional Paper No. 4 of 1982 on Development Prospects and Policies which outlined the adjustments to be made in response to the severe financial crisis of the time. This culminated in the Sessional Paper No. 1 of 1986 on Economic Management for Renewed Growth which was a comprehensive policy document meant to reorient national development priorities.

These policy papers confirmed, at least in writing, the government's intentions to deal with emerging challenges. That the government, on its own volition, identified key areas needing reforms and committed to implementing them was a chief smokescreen in the eyes of the donors. Most of these reforms identified by the government were not implemented. In fact, most of these policy papers were reactive; they documented government responses, or intended responses, to problems after they had visited their negative consequences on the people. At times, the government issued such papers in anticipation of donor aid or conditionality and used them to disarm donors who were getting impatient with the government's failure to implement agreed-upon conditions. The Sessional Paper No. 1 of 1986 served this purpose. This strategy became Moi's trademark, leading Mosley (1991: 270) to admit that 'few country ... experiences have given the Bank so much cause for frustration'.

Misguided and ill-timed reform policy

Gurushri Swamy (1996) accurately describes Kenya's reform record under Moi as 'patchy and intermittent'. Though he places the blame on lethargy in Kenya, it is obvious that bilateral and multilateral donors significantly aided this lethargy. For instance, Kenya signed its first IMF extended facility loan in 1975. It received a second IMF standby loan in 1978. These two loans were part of the IMF medium-term lending designed to provide balance-of-payment support. They had a ceiling on government borrowing and on total domestic credit. The second loan also included a wage restraint. While the government exceeded the ceiling after three months of the first one, it observed the wage restraint. Following a sharp fall in coffee prices in 1979, the government asked the IMF for another standby loan to offset the balance-of-payment deficit. This was, however, delayed for a year, putting the government into a serious balance-of-payment problem. Rather than scale down on government spending in response to the end of the coffee boom, the government approached the WB for support, which they received in the form of structural adjustment lending (SAL) in March 1980. This started a process by which the government played one donor against the other.

This first WB SAL to Kenya, amounting to US$ 55 million, focused on Kenya's industrialisation strategy outlined in the Fourth Development Plan of 1979–83. The plan sought to reorient Kenya's industrialisation policy to be more outward looking. Initiated by the Kenyan government, the WB simply added two conditions regarding budgetary controls and the monitoring of external borrowing. Since the government had approached the WB about a balance-of-payment deficit, the WB calculated that the deficit was transient and that input in the industrialisation strategy would contribute to the resolution of the deficit. The WB was wrong. The economic crisis was severe and prolonged, causing a rise in real interest rates and consequently rendering the debt service position unmanageable (Grosh 1991: 3). Exports declined, private sector investment dwindled further and inflation rose to 20 per cent in 1982. The WB admitted that there was 'little progress' in reorienting the industrial sector and the criteria for evaluating success of projects were vague. Having failed, Kenya returned to the IMF in 1982 for another standby loan. The loan was awarded, again with a ceiling on budget deficit and on the net credit to the government and with a commitment to a programme of 'progressive import liberalisation in the medium term' (Mosley 1991: 275). The government made some strategic moves during the term of this agreement. It devalued the exchange rate by 15 per cent in September and by 14 per cent in December 1982.

Two interesting dimensions of lasting consequence to Kenya's relations with the WB/IMF should be noted at this point. First was the high level of overlap in Kenya's negotiation with each of these organisations. The overlap was an important avenue through which the Moi government played one donor against the other so as to maintain an intermittent adjustment record. This was the case between 1980 and 1982 when Kenya's relations with the WB declined but those with the IMF warmed. After being disappointed in 1980, the WB seemed eager to negotiate a second SAL with Kenya in 1982 in spite of the failure of the first SAL. This second SAL focused on unfinished trade policy of the first SAL. It also included an agricultural component asking for liberalisation of maize marketing and land reform. It asked for action in the areas of interest rates, in the energy and parastatal sectors and in family planning (Mosley 1991: 283–4). This second SAL was comprehensive to the extent of guaranteeing its own failure given the bad macroeconomic context within which it was to be implemented. By the end of this loan agreement period, only one-third of the conditions on trade policy were implemented. The relations between the WB and Kenya worsened following Kenya's failure to meet the conditions on liberalising cereal marketing. At this time, relations with the IMF improved making it possible for Kenya to get an alternative source of funding to substitute that denied by the WB. This poor co-ordination in policy advice and timing in policy action explains why, shortly after suspending support, the WB shifted into sectoral lending in the 1984–89 period. The same problem of poor co-ordination among multilateral and bilateral donors emerged in the 1990s.

The second dimension was that of political legitimacy of reform. Kenya's relations with the WB/IMF was characterised by the ascendance of a triumvirate of technocrats under whose leadership negotiations with the donors were conducted. Three influential bureaucrats, Philip Ndegwa, the governor of the central bank, Harry Mule, the permanent secretary to the treasury and Simeon Nyachae, permanent secretary and, from 1984, head of the civil service influenced government issued policy papers between 1980 and 1986. This impacted negatively on the ability to implement institutional reforms that required political clout, inter-ministerial networking and support. The lack of political clout among technocrats partly explains why agricultural based changes calling for land reform and privatisation of maize marketing were difficult to attain. The political stake involved in these reforms combined with the colonial legacy of state control of cereal marketing to make it a particularly difficult sector to reform. For example, the condition on liberalisation of maize marketing was included in the second SAL package at Mule's request. Hoping to use the WB to institute reform in the cereal-marketing sector, Mule was targeting an area of reform with a history of intense government control, control that favoured people with good political connections. But such reform was difficult to attain because it targeted the oligopolistic rents accruing to those who benefited from maize control. In other words, there was profit in maize control and every reason why leading politicians and business-people close to the centre of power would want to maintain control. While the WB's decision to require privatisation of maize marketing could have been a good one for the small-scale farmers, it was obviously foolhardy to expect a regime that benefited from maize control to implement and oversee the reduction of its largesse, even if it was ill-gotten (see Mosley 1986; Ikiara et al. 1995; O'Brien and Ryan 2001: 503–5).

The question of technocrats raises issues regarding ownership of the reforms. Their dominance in negotiations had serious political implications that donors failed to face. By limiting negotiations to a few technocrats, the donors were in effect depoliticising the reform process and ignoring the wider public, the very constituency that needed to legitimate the reforms. There was very little consideration that the public had a stake in the reform process and outcome since they were affected by the adjustment conditions. The donors preferred an undemocratic process in which negotiations with technocrats foreclosed public debate regarding the appropriate policy priorities needed to revitalise the economy. As such, they made 'secret' policy decisions they wished to implement unimpeded. The WB/IMF policy positions came across as sacrosanct and right, only requiring the approval of the technocrats and the president to be implemented. In the 1980s and early 1990s, the WB/IMF succeeded in having most of their policy decisions passed in parliament with little, if any, debate. After all, Moi was at his most authoritarian then.

The emphasis on technocrats depoliticised the reform process by shielding negotiation from potential dissenters. This approach contradicted donor rhetoric about participatory development, democracy and good governance. It prevented popular discussion of policies before they were enacted; yet the same people who were denied access to the decision-making process were expected to implement them or bear the cost and consequences of implementation. Reform began to appear more as a transaction between the technocrats and the donors with the donors putting up several conditions and using the next loan tranche to induce implementation. Implementing ministries were sidelined even though their compliant implementation was required for the success of the reforms. Depoliticising the process simply compounded the problem of ownership of the reform process, prompting one politician to complain that technocrats alienated the cabinet from the reform process. No wonder the reform process came to be seen in political circles as the work of the technocrats and was consequently frustrated by the key members of the Moi regime who stood to lose.

The technocrat phenomenon snowballed into another problem affecting reform: the up-down, on-off experience. In order to push reforms through, technocrats needed presidential assent and support. This meant that they had to get willing ministers or civil servants with a favourable hearing at State House in order to have their way. By relying on the technocrats rather than working for broad consensus, the donors allowed an intolerable level of uncertainty that depended on the political fortunes of each technocrat. Both Ndegwa and Nyachae received a favourable hearing from Moi in the 1980s. But in the 1990s, Nyachae's political clout waned. It is not surprising that the level of commitment to reform was higher during the Ndegwa era. Similar bold moves in reform were made between 1993 and 1995 when Musalia Mudavadi (Moi's nephew) was Finance Minister. With Benjamin Kipkulei as Permanent Secretary and Micah Cheserem as Central Bank Governor, Mudavadi was able to effect some level of fiscal discipline and implement some reforms. However, this guaranteed only temporary reform gains that would be reversed once the key players in the ministry lost their political clout.

Overall, it is clear that Kenya did not meet most of the conditions on structural adjustment lending in the 1980s. Of the nine conditions in the agricultural reforms, only four were fully implemented by 1984. The rate of slippage was approximately 50 per cent if double emphasis is given to industrial and agricultural reforms. In fact, the bank officials anticipated areas of conflict when drafting lending agreement and imaginatively 'used ambiguity as an instrument of resolving potential conflict' (Mosley 1991: 289, 293). The WB's privatisation and liberalisation regime was also impractical since it came at a time when Kenya was facing serious balance-of-payment deficits.

Donor Aid and Political Authoritarianism

It seems therefore that getting the politics right should have been the donor priority. But most lenders at the time treated development and democracy as trade-offs. This is the logic that explains donor attempts to depoliticise the reform process. Consequently, the depoliticisation of financial aid assisted the Moi regime to entrench its authoritarianism by concentrating the power over reform in the hands of the president. Instead, lenders worried more about the existence of anti-reform elements within the corridors of power – something they treated as a typically African aberration. Africanist literature on the SAP has demonised anti-reformists within African governments as rent-seekers or patrimonialists who inhibit the potential for growth by inducing additional rent-seeking costs (see variations of this argument in Sandbrook 1986; Hyden 1987; Chabal and Daloz 1999). But as Khan and Sundaram (2000) argue, there is no clear and incontestable link between rent-seeking, inefficiency and lack of growth. Success in reform does not therefore depend on the absence of rent-seekers but on the environment that lays out the rules of political negotiation.

In depoliticising the reform process in Kenya, the donors in turn faced a hide-and-seek game between the country's leadership and the donors leading to the bastardisation of the reform process. Done through what George Ayittey describes as Moi's 'Massamba ritual dance', the key elements of this game consisted of:

> … one, Kenya wins its yearly pledges of foreign aid. Two, the government begins to misbehave, back-tracking on economic reforms, and behaving in an authoritarian manner. Three, a new meeting of donor countries looms with exasperated foreign governments preparing their sharp rebukes. Four, Kenya pulls a placatory rabbit out of the hat. Five, the donors are mollified and aid is pledged. The whole dance then starts again.[1]

The dance steps were related to, and determined by, trends in local politics. Moi would conduct a regular reassessment of his political fortunes and apply his mastery of the Kenyan political environment to reshuffle the cabinet and transfer the technocrats thereby denying donors their favourite technocrats. This normally upset the negotiation process since preferred ministers or technocrats were shunted to new and, at times, less glamorous government ministries. This shuffling produced an on-and-off, stop-and-go pattern. Thus, the political will to implement these policies was limited by three factors: the selfish survivalist instincts of the political elite, their genuine concerns about the social consequences of reform and, finally, the effect of reform on state legitimacy.

Most analysts of the reform process are content to blame its failure on bad governance. But the sweeping condemnation of African governments fails to acknowledge that the private gains that presumably accrue to the political class and that motivate their resistance to reform is one aspect among many other explanations for resisting reforms. As many studies have shown, resistance to reform stemmed from numerous other sources, many of which recognised the social consequences of reform and its deleterious impact on the disadvantaged in society and on state legitimacy (Bangura and Beckman 1991; Beckman 1991; Olukoshi 1998). Analysts who associate reform failures with bad government assume that inefficient regimes are necessarily also illegitimate. In fact, what really needs to be explained is how a regime, like the Moi one, survived when it was most inefficient.

Worsening the policy and political environment

The economic reforms of the 1980s in Kenya did, in fact, worsen the policy environment. Rather than promote growth and democracy, they became the basis on which Moi solidified his authoritarian rule. Their piecemeal implementation guaranteed further foreign aid that ameliorated the balance-of-payment and budget deficits and checked inflation while enabling Moi to tighten his hold on state power. As Nasong'o and Oloo show in Chapters 2 and 4, respectively, in this volume, Moi forestalled the formation of an opposition party in 1982 by declaring Kenya a de jure one-party state. During the 1983 elections, Moi edged out of power the remaining pro-Kenyatta leaders and began to set up a new coalition of largely Kalenjin acolytes to occupy the political space vacated by Kenyatta's allies. After the purge of Kenyatta loyalists, Moi acquired new confidence to intensify political repression, state harassment and political corruption. He condoned a series of political harassments and detentions. Oloo, Amutabi and Gimode recount in greater detail, in Chapters 4, 7 and 8 in this volume, the crackdown he launched against advocates of political pluralism first in the university and later among lawyers and politicians. By 1986, detention had become the order of the day. Moi gradually constricted the space for free expression, speech and assembly by spreading a network of special branch spies across the country and creating despondency and fear among people. The masterstroke in this regard was the formation of the KANU Disciplinary Committee (KDC) in January 1986.

Unlike Kenyatta, who left the party in abeyance and relied on the provincial administration as his instrument of control, Moi reconstructed KANU into the most powerful organ of his regime. He declared that 'the party is supreme' over parliament and the High Court (*Weekly Review*, 21 November 1986: 9) and shifted decision-making processes from the executive and the legislature to KANU. To silence party members and especially the MPs, Shariff Nassir, a close ally of the president, recommended that 'if members of parliament talk loosely and at whim, the party should be empowered to discipline them' (*Weekly Review*, 7 November 1986: 4). By emphasising KANU as opposed to the parliament, Moi gained several advantages. First, KANU sponsorship was required to vie for electoral mandate. It vetted and controlled access to parliament and prospective politicians needed it to be elected to parliament. Second, it was an informal non-state grouping effectively controlled by Moi and an inner core of loyalists whose support Moi used to purge radical politicians from the party. Through KANU, Moi vetted and controlled access to parliament for those politicians who failed the party 'loyalty test'. He aimed to ensure the 'party's precedence over parliament in national political matters' (*Weekly Review*, 7 November 1986: 6) and enlisted the help of an inner core of KANU loyalists, including Nassir, Burudi Nabwera and Okiki Amayo among others, who supported moves towards establishing KANU as the supreme organ of Moi's regime (Widner 1992). This core dominated the KDC and perfected a procedure of witch-hunting and punishing politicians considered less loyal to Moi.

The KDC played a significant role in spreading fear. Its indices of measuring loyalty to the president were parochial and selfish. It became a forum for witch-hunting where members were suspended for silly reasons. Some were suspended for merely associating with Charles Njonjo, others like Joseph Munyao for 'showing disrespect and contempt' for the district KANU leaders. Kimani wa Nyoike was suspended for 'disloyalty' to the party president while Peter Okondo, knowing what appearing before the committee meant, simply wept. Political rivals trumped up charges to eliminate competition. Given the overbearing presence of Moi in KANU, the KDC effectively closed the space for autonomous political organisation and action. During the 1988 general election, expulsions from KANU prevented many people from seeking elective mandate. Those who went past the party censor faced a highly rigged election. The 1988 elections went down in Kenya's political history as the most defective. Conducted through the queue voting method in which voters stood behind their candidate or his/her representative, this election eliminated the secrecy of secret balloting and records in case of a re-count.

By shifting supremacy from parliament to the party, Moi concentrated extralegal power in the presidency. On 21 November 1986, the Attorney-General had introduced a Constitutional Amendment Bill that removed the security of tenure for the Attorney-General, the Auditor-General, and put the judiciary at the mercy of the president. As Gimode (Chapter 8 in this volume) recounts in detail, this extensively damaged the independence of the judiciary to preside fairly over politically sensitive cases.[2] Because of this, it was possible for the state to put up weak politically motivated cases against the advocates of pluralism and win. Such cases were often presided over by judges of dubious qualification or the accused were charged on flimsy grounds and at weird hours of the day (*Africa Watch*, 1991: 129–58). At some point, foreign judges were hired, and it is no wonder that the abuse of the judicial system peaked in the era of Chief Justice Allan Hancox in 1989. Hancox was so partisan as to counsel lawyers to be loyal to the president (see *Nairobi Law Monthly*, no. 36, September 1991; Mutua 2001). The absence of an impartial system of arbitration led to wide human rights abuses and intensified political corruption.

The constricted political space allowed the regime to intensify the plunder of the economy. Political patronage became an expedient alternative to merit. Patronage supported inefficiency and economic plunder in the civil service and state enterprises where the reward system did not favour hard work and innovation. Government ministries and state corporations were affected the most by these developments. Corruption came to encompass acts of mismanagement, irregular tenders, theft, phantom payments, malfeasance and impunity. These corrupt practices emanated, in part, from greed among senior civil servants and politicians and also from legitimate concerns about low wage levels and unaffordable prices for basic items. Ministries and state enterprises were affected by lax management and inability to control budgets. The poor performance of state enterprises like the Kenya Post and Telecommunication Corporation (KPTC) in the early 1990s reflects the inept leadership of its managing director, arap Ng'eny. In 1990, the KPTC failed to remit deductions totalling Kshs. 176.4 million from salaries to different income tax and related social security institutions, this at a time when the managing director had loan arrears of Kshs. 1.8 billion (Kibwana et al. 1996: 72).

Other corporations such as the National Oil Corporation, Kenya Airways, National Housing Corporation, Kenya Railways and Kenya Ports Authority were also seriously affected by corruption.

Corporations charged with delivery of important services like the KPTC and the Kenya Power and Lighting Company slackened, followed by a noticeable decline in public confidence (Kibwana et al. 1996: 72–3). State enterprises in agriculture like the National Cereals and Produce Board (NCPB) became guzzlers of public funds. It is estimated that in 1987, the accumulated NCPB debt was the equivalent of 5 per cent of GDP (O'Brien and Ryan 2001: 504). The board had poor storage facilities, expensive middlemen and a virtual monopoly over the movement of Kenya's staple cereal – maize – from the producer to the market. As its debt grew, the Board relied on the government for subvention. Similarly, other state marketing boards such as the Kenya Meat Commission, the Kenya Co-operative Creameries and the Coffee Board of Kenya did not do well during the same era. It is within this context that the BWI requirement for privatisation of state enterprises and elimination of corruption should be understood.

Although continued flow of aid helped entrench authoritarianism, it also motivated opposition to the Moi regime. The broad outline of opposition politics is discussed by Nasong'o, Oloo and Amutabi in Chapters 2, 4 and 7, respectively, in this volume. Suffice it to note that Moi's authoritarianism inadvertently created a cadre of politicians out-side parliament whose role in opposition politics and their impact on the reform process are notable. But these constituted an unstable opposition alliance of *wealthy politicians* and *veteran politicians* with con-siderable mass appeal, especially among unemployed youth and uni-versity students in urban areas. These were joined by a cadre of underemployed and underpaid lumpens in the towns composed of *matutu* touts, hawkers, vendors and idlers like street boys. Not to be left out were people in the middle class. Though these identified more with the bourgeois class, the changing economic situation in the 1990s made it extremely difficult for this group to maintain its class position (Holmquist et al. 1994: 90–99).

Except for the wealthy bourgeois group, most of these groups were equally frustrated by the difficulties resulting from government ineffi-ciency. Basic services such as processing of the national identity card and a birth certificate, and provision of quality education, health ser-vices and employment were inaccessible. The frustration combined to generate wide support for veteran politicians who, joined by firebrand lawyers like James Orengo, advocated political pluralism and took the ground of dissent from parliament to otherwise apolitical arenas like the church, funeral gatherings and weddings where no state licence was required to gather. Together, these politicians in collaboration with an emerging coalition of civil society organisations exerted pressure on the regime to open up the political space. Their message resonated with urban crowds that experienced the effects of economic decline and the SAPs. Streets therefore became major sites where people voiced disapproval of the government and the donor policies. Hawkers and vendors became conduits of spreading anti-government messages through pamphlets, music cassettes and gutter press. Music cassettes praising the advocates of political pluralism emerged from the backstreets. By the early 1990s, special branch spies and police were unable to stem this trend.

The second force the regime influenced was the BWIs and other bilateral donors whose ideas on democracy shifted in 1989. This shift was first articulated in Kenya by the US Ambassador Smith Hempstone. This formally marked the use of political conditionality in aid disbursement. Political conditionality energised local struggles for political pluralism but with divergent economic and political consequences for the unstable alliance of pro-democracy advocates identified above. It forced Moi to repeal Section 2(A) of the constitution and accede to multiparty democracy in 1990. But the interest of the donors in all this did not necessarily dovetail neatly with those of the locals. With the advantage of hindsight following the 2002 elections that swept away the Moi regime and brought to power key pro-democracy opposition leaders of the 1990s, one can roughly identify the following stakes with four groups that made up the opposition at the time, interests that did not always coincide. The first group of wealthy opposition politicians were interested in raw power and economic gains that access to the state promised. Matiba summarised this motivation in the slogan 'Moi Must Go' but it is Kibaki's Democratic Party that exemplified this interest. Most of such politicians were united by their commonality of grievances against Moi. After all, they (Matiba, Kibaki, Charles Rubia, Njenga Karume, etc.) were 'literally almost creatures of the [KANU] state' (Holmquist et al. 1994: 98). For them, removing Moi from power without radically changing the institutional base of that power was enough.

The second group was made of the middle classes and dominated by a cabal of urban-based lawyers and leaders of civil society organisations discussed in this book by Nasong'o.[3] Their claim to national glory was pegged on their belief in human rights. While the first group had clear economic stakes in the political process, the second located their contribution in the legal realm as advocates of a just and fair legal and economic system that guaranteed basic human rights and fairness before the law. For this group, among whom were Kivutha Kibwana of NCEC, Willy Mutunga of the 4Cs, Kiraitu Murungi, Gibson Kamau Kuria and Gitobu Imanyara, their battles against the Moi regime rested on the belief that political pluralism would thwart many of Moi's excesses and limit his ability to manipulate the system to his advantage. Their support for multiparty politics was based on the assumption that this would limit or end Moi's rule and bring in a new and more responsible government. But this group based its struggle on individual rather than communal rights. Because it focused 'mainly on the protection of individual rights within the context of a more accountable unitary state, [it has treated] discussion of decentralization, and therefore communal rights, … as illegitimate' (Barkan and Ng'ethe 1998: 45). Thus, its appeal across constituencies was episodic and limited.

From the first two groups one can hive off a small group of veteran politicians and activists whose identification with the political and economic reform agenda went beyond the 'Moi must go' sloganeering and focused on institutional reform. This group was principally convinced that the key to reform resided in the overhaul of the institutions of governance that predisposed leaders to authoritarianism. They focused on constitutional review processes and related reforms that could ensure equity in resource allocation. This group has survived the test of time more than two years since their comrades took the reins of power under the Kibaki regime. They are still involved in the fight for constitution review and have rejected the temptation to take up positions in the new government.

Finally, there was the generality of Kenyans who actively supported and joined calls to civil disobedience that were meant to force the Moi regime to reform. This group alarmed the Moi administration and the donor community by the sheer weight of the numbers they brought to street demonstrations and work boycotts. Since it constituted the majority in the WB/IMF sponsored retrenchment and divestiture programmes, it experienced the most serious effects of inflation due to liberalisation of exchange control systems and deregulation of price control, and it faced the most serious consequences when the government cut back on employment and other social welfare programmes. Obviously, the interests of each of these groups do not always coincide and have shaped the discussion of reform in diverse ways. Aside from these four groups are the donors and the politicians within KANU whose disagreement with the wealthy opposition politicians was a matter of form rather than substance. When factored in, they further complicate the possibility of any assumed consensus on the aims and procedure of reform.

Failure of the reform programme

The failure of the reform programme in Kenya must be located in the complex and conflicting interests of each of the groups identified above and the false promise by donors that a stable environment would attract foreign investors. A decade after privatisation began, estimates show that 'the annual inflow of net foreign direct investment in Kenya fell by 90 per cent from 1980 to 2000'. Kenya received US$80 million in new foreign investment in 1980 but only US$44 million in 1995 (*Daily Nation*, 2 March 2004). Few foreign private businesses are attracted into a local environment in which the transaction costs of running a private business are high. In the 1980s and 1990s, transaction costs increased not simply because of rent-seeking, as Brown suggests in Chapter 10 in this volume, but mainly because of collapse of infrastructure (as a result of the low premium placed by reform measures on investment in infrastructure) and also government intransigence in fighting corruption. Because of the inability to invest in infrastructure, some foreign companies such as Overseas Motor Transport Company, the owners of Kenya Bus Service, closed up their businesses (Opiyo 2004). Clearly, this was in part a consequence of the anti-state message contained in the reform package (Mkandawire and Soludo 1999).

The anti-state message reduced the role of the state to that of 'night watchman'. As the state vacated, so also was it able to shirk its basic social welfare responsibilities with impunity (Aina 2004: 8–9). At times, it unleashed private but state-backed entrepreneurs to cash in on its absence. This has in turn blurred the distinction between public and private responsibilities, rendering the assumption that the private is efficient and the public inefficient baseless as these two interpenetrate in complex ways. Yet the argument for rolling back the state resonated very well with the wealthy opposition politicians and a section of KANU politicians, though there was some ambivalence within KANU that explains the emergence of pro- and anti-reform camps. As leaders of the various political parties, the wealthy opposition politicians jumped on the bandwagon of donor reform with the aim of exploiting its devastating economic and political effects to defeat Moi. Viewing Moi as an impediment to their interests, this class of parasitic politicians supported the donor call for market-based reforms, but not always for the same reasons as the donors themselves. Their support for reform was a thinly veiled calculation to expedite Moi's defeat and not for a total overhaul of the structural guarantors of authoritarianism and poverty. FORD-K was particularly adept at this calculation. In 1993, when the effects of partial liberalisation of the foreign exchange control system caused shocks in the currency markets, which precipitated a phenomenal devaluation of the shilling against the hard currencies, FORD-K threatened 'to lead countrywide demonstrations if the government did not move to control the spiralling increases in the prices of consumer goods' (*Weekly Review*, 26 March 1993: 17). This statement contradicted its party manifesto that supported accelerated economic liberalisation. Obviously, the party was 'determined to take advantage of the difficult economic times to achieve its political objectives' (*Weekly Review*, 26 March 1993: 18).

The ambivalence among KANU politicians with respect to privatisation was because privatisation held the potential for political corruption for some as opposed to others. This became very explicit in the mid-1990s with a split between KANU-A made of alleged pro-reform leaders like Simeon Nyachae and KANU-B made of so-called anti-reform leaders like Nicholas Biwott. While it was acknowledged that privatisation threatened to withdraw their easy sources of largesse, it nevertheless presented an alternative source of easy wealth if they controlled the process and implemented the process on their terms. Under extreme donor pressure, KANU politicians and their allies eventually saw in partial privatisation opportunities to undervalue government shares in state enterprises and sell them to well-connected private businessmen or to quietly dispose of parastatals without providing any information to the public on the valuation of the enterprise and payments. But the parastatals that ended up being privatised were those considered less strategic to their political interests. Thus, Kenya Cashew Nuts Limited was sold in complete secrecy to a number of businessmen loyal to Moi while the government conspired to undervalue Kenya-Re and sell it to preferred buyers at a ridiculously cheap price. This plunder was facilitated by the fact that there was no law regulating privatisation (see Cohen 1995: 32).

Matters have not been helped by the fact that donors were suspicious of public debate of the reform process. After all, reforms contained harsh economic prescriptions and most of them produced disastrous consequences like sharp rises in consumer prices. In Kenya, such policies affected the prices of basic consumer items such as toothpaste, bread, cooking fat, petroleum products, timber products, cement, corrugated iron sheets, baby foods, chocolate and paper products (*Weekly Review*, 26 March 1993: 19). These policies could never pass the test of democratic debate. Second, harsh prescriptions threatened serious political consequences that made the government reluctant to implement them unless under extreme pressure. When reform consequences threatened to take effect in Kenya in 1993, the government suspended negotiations with the WB/IMF arguing that they set 'unilateral, harsh and dictatorial conditions'. The government correctly argued that the IMF conditionalities remain 'completely oblivious of the hardships their prescriptions were causing the country' (*Weekly Review*, 26 March 1993: 15).

The finance minister, Musalia Mudavadi, explained that IMF prescriptions would cause instant collapse of a large number of companies, bringing mass redundancies and massive recession affecting both private and public sectors. He charged that 'high interest rates will stifle agricultural activity, lead to food shortages and make essential commodities unaffordable to a majority of Kenyans' (*Weekly Review*, 26 March 1993: 15). Thus there were legitimate reasons for state resistance to reform in Kenya. Above all, donors were also to blame in the reform process. Their commitment to political reform was inconsistent (*Africa Confidential*, 34, 4, 8 January 1993). This inconsistency reinforced Moi's intransigence and authoritarianism as donors repeatedly undermined domestic efforts to secure far-reaching political reforms in Kenya by supporting only minimal reforms to the constitution and rewarding the Moi regime 'for modest achievements in economic governance', providing a disincentive to increase political liberalisation. They accepted sub-optimal standards in their evaluation of election results and 'deliberately suppressed evidence that KANU had not legitimately won a majority in parliament' (Brown 2001: 731, 734–5).

The government suspension of negotiations with the WB/IMF in 1993 was in response to stringent IMF conditionality for further disbursement of aid. In the 1990s, the IMF began to shift the goalposts each time the government attained one requirement for further aid disbursement. This strategy began in November 1991 when donors decided to subject the Kenyan government to an 'excessively wide range of conditions requiring simultaneous policy reforms across the many sectors of the economy' (*Weekly Review*, 26 March 1993: 16). They subsequently shifted their priorities to include new ones once the government attained a previous priority condition. The 1992 elections were one such target. The government hoped to use the elections to unlock the door to quick-disbursing adjustment credit of US$ 50 million held since 1991. When the election failed to mollify all the donors, Moi threw a tantrum that paid off. He scrapped the IMF-directed economic reforms in March 1993. This alarmed senior WB officials, who flew into Nairobi, and in April the WB vice president for Africa, Edward Jaycox, announced the release of US$ 85 million for the export development programme (*Africa Confidential*, vol. 34, no. 20, 8 October 1993).

Consequently, Moi emerged from this gamble stronger than his bargaining power allowed. After all, he had started from a weak bargaining position and won concessions from donors (*Africa Confidential*, vol. 37, 8 April 1996). By 1996, Moi was regaining his foot vis-à-vis the donors. Donors meeting in Paris on 22 March 1996 decided to disburse US$ 730 million to Kenya even though the conditions set in November 1992 had not been met. As *Africa Confidential* argued, the IMF's main condition relating to a full prosecution of the Goldenberg case had been ignored. Instead, the government purchased a presidential jet worth US$ 60 million from the Netherlands and proceeded with the construction of Eldoret Airport.

The government reluctance to institute the reform measures was also due to the fear that this would completely eliminate state legitimacy and allow the political opposition to take advantage of the negative political impact of donor prescriptions. Such a possibility resided with urban crowds predisposed to street protests. But when opposition politicians called on donors to withdraw aid and yet organised rallies to protest the rising cost of living, the government responded with new propaganda blaming the opposition for the bad economic situation. In what became a key KANU plank of twisting reality for political expediency, Moi charged that the opposition remained 'callous and unmoved by the groans of Kenyans who are suffering under the current economic hardships' (*Weekly Review*, 26 March 1993: 17). He presented the donors and the opposition as anti-people and himself as more concerned about Kenyans, thereby shifting the blame from the government.

But in reality, the wealthy opposition politicians, elements in KANU and donors all used the lower classes as mere pawns in a political chess game whose stake for the upper class/political elite was control of state power for personal gain. The elite and donors all held the street protestors in great suspicion. For instance, with investments of over US$1 billion, the British were especially suspicious of mass action in the street and 'preferred order to freedom' (Hempstone 1997: 39 and 109). Like the British, other bilateral donors preferred piecemeal and staggered reforms seeking, in the process, to influence changes in Kenya in a manageable way. In contrast, the lower classes were committed to the struggle for reforms that would improve their lives, they wanted to sweep away the oppressive state. Through street demonstrations, riots and worker strikes, cadres mobilised for complete change, seeking in their struggles to mitigate the harsh consequences of kleptocratic rule and donors' shock therapy. University and tertiary college students who mounted eventful demonstrations against the government and SAPs best exemplified the views of this category.

Questioning the notion of 'Silence, Development in Progress'

In Africa, there is a negative correlation between SAPs and democratisation. Africa's star adjustment performers have tended disproportionately to be military leaders like Rawlings of Ghana and Museveni of Uganda (Beckman 1991; Olukoshi 1998: 20). Such regimes relied on a high level of secrecy in designing SAPs. However, in Kenya, the 1997 election marked a turning point in BWIs' relations with the Kenyan public as far as secrecy of reforms were concerned. The public and parliament reasserted their interest in the policy dialogue between the Kenyan government and the BWIs. I conclude with three examples to illustrate how the authoritarian nature of the donor reform process and the choicelessness they promoted were questioned (Mkandawire 1999). These cases summarise with remarkable clarity the preferred donor approach termed, in Joseph Ki-Zerbo's apt words as: Silence, Development in Progress. These include the Kenya Anti-Corruption Authority Bill, the story of the 'dream team' and the case of the Donde Bill.

The *Kenya Anti-Corruption Authority* (KACA) *Bill* was introduced in parliament after a bench of three judges sitting in December 2000 found the original act that gave KACA the power to investigate and prosecute cases to be unconstitutional. When the Attorney-General sought to entrench KACA in the constitution as a response to the IMF conditions through a new bill in parliament in 2001, the general public's reaction to the bill was negative. Unfortunately, this bill came shortly after parliament had secured some autonomy through the establishment of the Parliamentary Service Commission. Also, this bill was introduced shortly after a parliamentary select committee on corruption had issued the Kombo Report that identified several corrupt bigwigs and recommended that they be investigated and prosecuted. The report named close associates of President Moi, including Vice-President George Saitoti, ministers Nicholas Biwott, Julius Sunkuli and Kipng'eno arap Ngeny as well as Moi's son, Philip Moi. The Kombo Report argued that the current Prevention of Corruption Act could not deal with Kenya's plague of 'lootocracy'. Instead, it drew a draft bill that significantly increased the powers and independence of the existing KACA. Though the list of shame was not adopted in parliament when it came up to a vote on 18 July 2000 (*East African*, 15 May 2000, *Daily Nation*, 19 July 2000), it influenced subsequent discussion on corruption and especially the new KACA bill.

The legal tenets that the KACA bill proposed were similar to the Anti-Corruption and Economic Crimes Bill (2000) proposed by the Kombo Report, which parliament had defeated. When the KACA bill came up for adoption in parliament, it did not muster the two-thirds majority required to pass any amendment to the constitution. Most MPs dismissed it as a weak law and sensed in it a political ploy designed to show the donors that there was an anti-corruption law in place, yet the law was too weak to be effective. Furthermore, there were allegations that the bill was drafted by the IMF and handed over to Kenyan authorities to be passed.[4] Even if the bill was not drafted by the donors, they were widely consulted. It is therefore intriguing that the IMF did not object to a flawed bill that would have benefited those who were reluctant to fight corruption. Legislators pointed out three obvious flaws. First, the bill retained a self-serving conflict between the AG and the KACA through a proviso that allowed the AG to take over and override KACA cases. Second, the KACA bill had a generous self-amnesty provision that would have excused those who had committed economic crimes up to 1997. This provision excused the culpability of those in the Kombo report. Finally, the bill was brought to parliament without a broad consensus among parliamentarians and left many wondering why the AG introduced a flawed bill to parliament and ignored all pleas and recommendations to have it revised. Kenyans suspected the government intended that the bill be defeated. Accordingly, Moi would simply respond to accusations that he was unwilling to fight corruption by blaming the judiciary that declared KACA unconstitutional and parliament for refusing to pass the revised KACA Bill, an excuse that cut both ways.

The *Dream Team* was a team of technocrats Moi appointed in 1999 from the private sector to jump-start the economy. Headed by Dr Richard Leakey, Moi's old political foe, as head of the civil service (see *Africa Confidential*, vol. 40, no. 16, 6 August 1999: 4–5; *Daily Nation*, 24 July 1999), it included the former finance director of Barclays Bank, Kenya's largest private bank, Mr Martin Luke Oduor-Otieno, who became the Finance Permanent Secretary (PS); Mr Mwanghazi Mwachofi, the resident representative of the International Finance Corporation in South Africa who became Financial Secretary; Dr Shem Migot Adhola, a Washington-based WB technocrat who became PS in the key Ministry of Agriculture; and Dr Wilfred Mwangi from the International Maize and Wheat Improvement Centre who became Dr Adhola's deputy. Professor Julius Meme, the director of medical services, became the PS in the Ministry of Health while the new PS in the Ministry of Transport and Communication was Mr Titus Naikuni, who had been managing director of Magadi Soda. These appointments were made at the prompting of the WB and were in keeping with a well-known WB practice of encouraging the appointment of WB-connected technocrats into positions of responsibility in government with the assumption that they would have greater commitment to reform (Olukoshi 1998: 34–5).

By appointing this team, Moi hoped that he would redeem his image internationally and use Dr Leakey to bait the donors into disbursing aid. In a radical departure from a previous position,[5] Moi lauded Leakey as 'a man of determination and integrity' who would be charged with leading the 'first phase of a recovery strategy for Kenya'. Moi acknowledged the failures of previous appointees saying that 'the time has come to give public jobs to those who can deliver'. Dr Leakey was to tackle corruption and inefficiency, and he was also a man with the confidence and ability to convince donors to do business with Kenya. Moi declared that 'We have technocrats working for international organisations at the highest level (and) it is to these people that I now turn to lead our recovery and change the culture of corruption and inefficiency in our public service' (*Daily Nation*, 24 July 1999).

But like in many other places where technocrats were appointed with donor support, the Kenyan attempt soon became another fiasco.

First, their appointment was carefully choreographed to produce an immediate response from donors. For instance, on the trip to London where he met Wolfenson, President Moi departed on a British Airways flight, obviously intending this as a sign of his newfound frugality. Normally, he used the presidential jet. Flying in a regular passenger airline, Moi was lauded for his willingness to reform and effect economic recovery. Second, once appointed, the technocrats preferred to keep away from the murky waters of Kenyan politics. This was logical given they owed their position to the donors who also paid their salaries through a loan to the government. But this strategy presented them as being aloof and unsympathetic to the consequences of their reform actions. Third, these technocrats were appointed to clean a civil service made up of equally hardworking officers who had spent long years trying to make a difference with very meagre remuneration and no recognition and under a political and donor regime that undermined and ridiculed them. The technocrats relied on this underpaid workforce to facilitate their work. At times, the technocrats expected these underpaid civil servants to retrench themselves and their colleagues. Worse, the technocrats periodically reported directly to the donors, something that meant they did not have responsibilities to the government and local communities. This arrangement also meant that the civil servants consumed most of their work time writing up periodic reports for the donors.

Fourth, the irony of this arrangement was that Kenyans actually paid the hefty remuneration of the technocrats even though the United Nations Development Programme, the WB and several donors advanced this money to the country through a special fund. When parliament forced the finance minister to reveal how much the technocrats earned, a stunned nation learned that the Dream Team earned a rough total of Kshs. 10.8 million a month (*Daily Nation*, 13 October 2000).[6] This raised the important question of why a country that was economically collapsing should pay the technocrats this much money when it was retrenching people who desperately needed their jobs. It also raised the question why the huge difference in remuneration between civil servants who did most of the work and those few who came in as WB/IMF technocrats.

Fifth, there was no long-term plan to ensure that the reforms that the Dream Team implemented would be sustained. The team was credited with several achievements. Their appointment introduced a new sense of optimism in the reform process that had all but stalled.

This optimism became a new basis of negotiating the much needed support that saw the country through the late 1990s. Dr Leakey managed to retire from the civil service a number of sacred cows whose presence was really a drain on the professionalism of the civil service and promoted corruption (*Sunday Nation*, 26 September 1999). He also put in place a team of people who cleaned up corporations like the Kenya Ports Authority and the Kenya Revenue Authority. He effectively oversaw retrenchment in the civil service even though his actions in this regard had several negative consequences. For instance, it was reported that over 86,000 retirees missed their pension and were living in destitution (*The East African*, 12 February 2001). Nevertheless, Dr Leakey's reforms turned out to be short-lived and, for the most part, ineffective.

When the team's contracts came up for renewal, the Public Service Commission informed them that their contracts would not be renewed under existing terms. The government drastically reduced their salaries and other emoluments. Worsening relations betweenthe WB (which financed the salary of the technocrats under a US$27 million public sector management technical assistance project) and the government prompted this move. The WB also beat a retreat, arguing that it was 'focusing on Kenya's implementation of reforms rather than on the personnel administering the process'. The bank blamed the impasse between it and the government on the 'government's failure to approve the sale of Telkom Kenya and regularise the existence and operations of the Kenya Anti-Corruption Authority (KACA)'. It also blamed the government for the failure to push through parliament bills aimed at laying the ground for good governance, such as the Public Officers' Ethics and Code of Conduct and the Anti-Corruption and Economic Crimes bills. The jobs of the technocrats were 'irrevocably tied up with continued accord between the government and the IMF' (*The East African*, 29 January 2001).

A series of events in early 2001 marked the end of the Dream Team. Leakey resigned in March 2001, three months before the expiry of his two-year contract. In the same month, previously retired civil servants like Mr Joseph Kaguthi rejoined the government, Kaguthi as national co-ordinator for the Campaign against Drug Abuse in Schools. This was an indication that Moi was reverting to his old style. Then it was revealed that Leakey tried to influence the AG to drop criminal charges in the ABN-Amro Bank-John Cato Nottingham case. Such undue influence from the head of the public service compromised the impartiality of the judicial process, prompting Leakey's resignation. On 28 March 2001, Mr Naikuni and Oduor-Otieno were dropped in a major shake-up. In April, the respected Governor of Kenya's Central Bank, Mr Micah Cheserem, was also sacked. By the end of 2001, Kenya was back where it had been before Dr Leakey's eventful appointment.

The *Donde Bill* was introduced in parliament in 2001 to control bank interest rates. It was a private member's bill that challenged the faith in unregulated interest rates. Touted as a pro-people bill, the Donde Bill polarised debate between banks and external donors on the one hand and parliament on the other hand. It therefore set a major confrontation between parliament and the BWI, with the government playing broker in a conflict that boxed it into a tight corner. While the government would have liked to appear pro-people by supporting the bill, it was wary of the consequences such a position would have on donor aid. But even more important was that this bill brought an issue of general interest into the public arena, allowing the general citizenry to debate the merits and demerits of a donor-sponsored reform policy. The act exploded the myth that donor policies were beyond general public comprehension and demystified the secrecy with which government negotiation with the donors took place. As it turned out, many Kenyans actually supported the bill and felt that bank interest rate deregulation allowed local banks to make mega profits through their lending and interest rates. As debate intensified, the democratic verdict favoured regulation of bank interest rates to stem the usurious habit of the banks and scale down the suffering of Kenyans.

Moved by the then MP for Gem, Joe Donde, the bill sought to peg bank interest rates to Treasury Bill rates. The interest rates had been completely deregulated by the Banking Act of 1993. This act was accompanied by the elimination of price control and deregulation of foreign exchange rates. But the deregulation occurred in an environment of fiscal instability that was characterised by weak Central Bank of Kenya supervision of banks. Furthermore, such deregulation did not consider the 'oligopolistic structure of Kenya's banking sector in which a few dominant banks operate in collusion rather than competition'. This prevented lending rates from coming down and allowed the banks to adopt policies that were counterproductive. Rather than lower interest rates to attract borrowers, the banks maintained a high lending rate which, in turn, affected private borrowers, who often ended up paying more than the principal sum advanced.

The Donde Bill sought to introduce ceilings to lending rates in order to ensure better rates for private borrowers. It proposed the establishment of a monetary policy committee appointed through parliament to determine key components of monetary policy. Its baseline aim was to ensure cheap credit for the private sector. The Kenya Bankers Association opposed the bill. They acknowledged that interest rates were too high but argued that the clause that backdated the implementation of the bill would have adverse consequences on their business. Their attempts to stop the implementation of the bill through the court and the parliamentary finance committee failed, prompting the intervention of donors. Led by the WB/IMF, donors feared that by seeking to control interest rates, the bill would undermine the operation of the free market ideals (*East African*, 18 December 2000). The WB/IMF sponsored a conference on economic management in Mombasa in April 2002. The closed-door meeting emphasised the conditions to be met before resumption of lending. Top on the list was the immediate withdrawal of the Donde Bill. Donors lobbied MPs to support an amended version of the bill that the AG had presented to parliament.[7] On the list were also three other bills that had provoked wide rejection from an increasingly assertive parliament. These included the requirement that the 'Code of Ethics for Civil Servants Bill be made law, anti-corruption courts be established and [further required] the immediate sacking of civil servants or ministers facing corruption charges in court' (*Sunday Nation*, 28 April 2002). These were also referred to as the donor bill.

The donor approach at the conference infuriated legislators who, in response, maintained their support for the Donde Bill. They 'accused lenders of imposing policies which hurt ordinary people' and called on them to consider home-grown alternatives. They remained categorical that interest rates needed to be lowered. It was revealed that the donor 'policies came straight from Washington without the involvement of the finance minister, who was in turn expected to implement them and involve the people' (*Sunday Nation*, 28 April 2002). Accusing them of dishonesty, one MP wondered why the donors did not transparently act on a few well-heeled individuals who, with donor knowledge, had stashed billions of shillings in foreign accounts. 'If you know that somebody is a thief and you do not follow up to expose him, that is a collaboration' (*Sunday Nation*, 28 April 2002). But the Alego-Usonga MP Oloo Aringo argued that 'the real problem lay with the government which prefers to have dialogue with the Bretton

Woods Institutions and talk to Kenyans through the WB and IMF' (*Sunday Nation*, 28 April 2002). This meeting did not change the fate of the Donde Bill as it was passed in July 2001. Its argument that the banking sector cannot be trusted to police itself and act in the interests of ordinary Kenyans proved very popular, and the array of obstacles placed before the legislators failed to stem its enactment. In short, the Donde Act starkly demonstrates the dilemma donors face when they emphasise transparency and good governance and contravene it in their own actions.

Conclusion

The relations between donors and the Kenyan government have been characterised by meaningless altercations and expediency. There is a recognisable trend in these altercations in which double standards reign on the part of donors in their conditions to the Kenyan government, and where expediency defines the response of the local power barons both in and out of government. Neither of the two groups have identified clear goals against which it is possible to judge how much their development policies have attained their stated goals. On the contrary, the donors and the Kenyan political elite have worked at cross purposes. In the Moi era, this reinforced authoritarianism and facilitated further economic decay and poverty. Thus the challenge for Kenya has not been to identify the main failures of national programs for economic development and growth, but to work out how to install new styles of management that effectively recognise the importance of sound governance for economic development.

The chapter sought to shift the focus of analysis from a perspective that overly focuses on economic reform to a more governance-centred approach of getting the politics right. The focus has been on the nexus between governance and economic reform using the notions of reform ownership and political legitimacy as critical to the success of SAPs. These two notions were avoided in donor discourse and practice. The reform package was an authoritarian shock therapy that elicited resistance from within and went against the core principle of participation in policy design and implementation that was central to a new era of democratisation. It is because of the lack of participation, the secrecy with which reform initiatives were launched and the siege mentality that characterised the whole process that Moi was able to initiate and sustain a 'politricks of reform' that attenuated donors, facilitated further aid flows and at the same time allowed him to intensify internal abuse. By the time the donors got serious with setting and enforcing conditions for further aid disbursement, the KANU regime in Kenya had perfected its procrastinatory habit and enforced high levels of authoritarianism that undermined the potential for economic revival and political liberalisation. The key factor in the eventual demise of the Moi regime was therefore not donor pressure but the resilience of internal resistance and pressure that ushered in the National Alliance Rainbow Coalition in the December 2002 elections.

The chapter identified four groups that played a significant role in pressuring the Moi regime into some cosmetic reforms. It argued that the interests of these four groups did not always coincide in the principled demand for the radical reform of the state. Rather, some of the groups simply sought to seize the state for personal and class interests. Further research into the trials, travails and tribulations of the reform process should focus on the class interests of the opposition coalition that assumed power, with the aim of understanding how these classes have defeated the noble initiatives towards emancipatory politics. What, for instance, is the implication of the president of Kenya, Mwai Kibaki, being the landlord of the World Bank Country Director, Mr Makhtar Diop![8]

Notes

1. 'Aid for Kenya: Stop, Go', *The Economist*, 19 August 1998, quoted in George Ayittey (1999) 'How the Multilateral Institutions Compounded Africa's Economic Crisis', *Law & Policy in International Business*, vol. 30, no. 4: 585–600.

2. See, for example, newspaper commentaries of Chief Magistrate Aggrey O. Muchelule on how politicians interfered with his work and tried to influence his decisions at http://www.nationaudio.com/News/DailyNation/07102002/Comment/Comment5.html, and A.O. Muchelule, 'Corrupting Judiciary: Magistrate's Personal Experience', *East African Standard*, 12 February 2003.

3. Joel D. Barkan and Njuguna Ng'ethe (1998: 46) refers to this group and its dominance of the constitution review process.

4. See Anyang' Nyong'o, 'Flawed Kaca Bill and the Aid Burden', *Sunday Nation*, 19 August 2001.

5. Moi had, prior to the appointment, publicly chastised Leakey as a foreigner and caused a physical assault on Leakey by a mob of pro-KANU supporters in Nakuru in 1995.

6. Dr Leakey and Mr Mwanghazi each received Kshs. 2.4 million a month, Mr Otieno-Oduor and Mr Naikuni earned Kshs. 1.5 million each, while Prof. Adhola earned Kshs. 2 million and Mr Mwangi Kshs. 1.2 million a month.

7. Njeri Rugene and Onesmus Kilonzo, 'Kenya MPs Rebel Against WB and IMF', *Sunday Nation*, 28 April 2002.

8. See Michela Wrong, 'Worldview: What We Can Learn from the Curious Story of the Noisy Party, the Irate First Lady and the World Bank's Top Man in Kenya', *New Statesman*, 23 May 2005, p. 9.

References

Aina, T.A. (2004) 'Introduction: How Do We Understand Globalisation and Social Policy in Africa', in T.A. Aina, et al. (eds), *Globalization and Social Policy in Africa*, Dakar: CODESRIA.

Ajulu, R. (2000) 'Thinking Through the Crisis of Democratisation in Kenya: A Response to Adar and Murunga', *African Sociological Review*, vol. 4, no. 2.

Ake, C. (1996) *Democracy and Development in Africa*, Washington, DC: The Brookings Institution.

Anyang' Nyong'o, P. (1989) 'State and Society in Kenya: The Disintegration of the Nationalist Coalition and the Rise of Presidential Authoritarianism, 1963–78', *African Affairs*, vol. 88, no. 351.

Atieno-Odhiambo, E.S. (1987) 'Democracy and the Ideology of Order in Kenya', in M.G. Schatzberg (ed.), *The Political Economy of Kenya*, New York, NY: Praeger.

Attwood, W. (1967) *The Reds and the Blacks: A Personal Adventure*, New York, NY: Hutchinson.

Bangura, Y. and B. Beckman (1991) 'African Workers and Structural Adjustment, With a Nigerian Case Study', in D. Ghai (ed.), *The IMF and the South: The Social Impact of Crisis and Adjustment*, London: Zed Books.

Barkan, J. (1994) 'Elements and Institutions of Good Governance and Accountability', in O. Owiti and K. Kibwana (eds), *Good Governance and Accountability in Kenya: The Next Step Forward*, Nairobi: Claripress.

_____ and F. Holmquist (1989) 'Peasant-State Relations and the Social Base of Self-Help in Kenya', *World Politics*, vol. 41, no. 3.

_____ and N. Ng'ethe (1998) 'Kenya Tries Again', *Journal of Democracy*, vol. 9, no. 2.

Bates, R.H. (1981) *Markets and States in Tropical Africa: The Political Basis of Agricultural Policies*, Berkeley, CA: University of California Press.

Beckman, B. (1991) 'Empowerment or Repression? The World Bank and the Politics of Adjustment', *Africa Development*, vol. XVI, no. 1.

Bigsten, A. and N.S. Ndung'u (1992) 'Kenya', in A. Duncan and J. Howell (eds), *Structural Adjustment and the African Farmer*, London: James Currey.

Brown, S. (2001) 'Authoritarian Leaders and Multiparty Elections in Africa: How Foreign Donors Help to Keep Kenya's Daniel arap Moi in power', *Third World Quarterly*, vol. 22, no. 5.

Chabal, P. and J. Daloz (1999) *Africa Works: Disorder as Political Instrument*, Oxford: International African Institute in association with James Currey; Bloomington: Indiana University Press.

Cohen, J.M. (1995) 'Ethnicity, Foreign Aid, and Economic Growth in Sub-Saharan Africa: The Case of Kenya', Harvard Institute for International Development, Development Discussion Paper No. 520.

Gibbon, P. (1992) 'The World Bank and Africa's poverty', *Journal of Modern African Studies*, vol. 30, no. 2.

_____ (1995) 'Markets, Civil Society and Democracy in Kenya', in P. Gibbon (ed.), *Markets, Civil Society and Democracy in Kenya*, Uppsala: Nordiska Afrikainstitutet.

_____ (1996) 'Structural Adjustment and Structural Change in Sub-Saharan Africa: Some Provisional Conclusions', *Development and Change*, vol. 27, no. 4.

Grosh, B. (1991) *Public Enterprise in Kenya: What Works, What Doesn't, and Why*, Boulder, CO: Lynne Rienner.

Hempstone, S. (1997) *Rogue Ambassador: An African Memoir*, Sewanee: University of the South Press.

Herbst, J. (1990) 'The Structural Adjustment of Politics in Africa', *World Development*, vol. 18, no. 7.

Holmquist, F.W. et al. (1994) 'The Structural Development of Kenya's Political Economy', *African Studies Review*, vol. 37, no. 1.

Hyden, G. (1987) 'Capital Accumulation, Resource Distribution, and Governance in Kenya: The Role of the Economy of Affection', in M.G. Schatzberg (ed.), *The Political Economy of Kenya*, New York, NY: Praeger.

_____ (2000). 'The Governance Challenge in Africa', in Goran Hyden et al. (eds.), *African Perspectives on Governance*, Trenton, NJ: Africa World Press.

Ikiara, G.K. et al. (1995) 'The Cereal Chain in Kenya: Actors, Reformers and Politics', in P. Gibbon (ed.), *Markets, Civil Society and Democracy in Kenya*, Uppsala: Nordiska Afrikainstitutet.

Kaplinsky, R. (1978) *Readings on the MNC in Kenya*, Nairobi: Oxford University Press.

_____ (1980) 'Capitalist Accumulation in the Periphery: The Kenyan Case Re-Examined', *Review of African Political Economy*, vol. 7, no. 17.

Khan, M.H. and J.K. Sundaram (2000) *Rents, Rent-Seeking and Economic Development: Theory and Evidence in Asia*, Cambridge, UK: Cambridge University Press.

Kibwana, K. et al. (eds) (1996) *The Anatomy of Corruption in Kenya: Legal, Political and Socio-Economic Perspectives*, Nairobi: Clarion.

Langdon, S. (1975) 'Multinational Corporations, Taste Transfer and Underdevelopment: A Case Study from Kenya', *Review of African Political Economy*, vol. 2, no. 2.

Leys, C. (1975) *Underdevelopment in Kenya: The Political Economy of Neo-colonialism, 1964–1971*, London: Heinemann.

_____ (1980) 'Kenya: What does "Dependency" Explain?', *Review of African Political Economy*, vol. 7, no. 17: 108–13.

Maxon, R.M. and P. Ndege (1995) 'The Economics of Structural Adjustment', in B.A. Ogot and W.R. Ochieng' (eds), *Decolonization and Independence in Kenya, 1940–93*, London: James Currey.

Mkandawire, T. (1999) 'Crisis Management and the Making of "Choiceless Democracies"', in R. Joseph (ed.), *State, Conflict, and Democracy in Africa*, Boulder, CO: Lynne Rienner.

_____ (2001a) 'The Need to Rethink Development Economics', in UNRISD meeting, Cape Town, South Africa, 7–8 September.

_____ (2001b) 'Thinking About Developmental States in Africa', *Cambridge Journal of Economics*, vol. 25, no. 3.

_____ (2004) 'The Spread of Economic Doctrines in Postcolonial Africa', Mimeo.

_____ and C.C. Soludo (1999) *Our Continent, Our Future: African Perspectives on Structural Adjustment*, Trenton, NJ: Africa World Press.

_____ and C.C. Soludo (eds) (2003) *African Voices on Structural Adjustment*, Trenton, NJ: Africa World Press.

Mosley, P. (1982) 'Kenya in the 1970s: A Review Article', *African Affairs*, vol. 81, no. 323.

_____ (1986) 'Agricultural Performance in Kenya since 1970: Has the World Bank Got it Right?', *Development and Change*, vol. 17.

_____ (1991) 'Kenya', in P. Mosley et al. (eds), *Aid and Power: The World Bank and Policy Based Lending, Volume 2*: Case Studies, London: Routledge.

Mueller, S.D. (1984) 'Government and Opposition in Kenya, 1966–9', *Journal of Modern African Studies*, vol. 22, no. 3.

Mutua, M. (2001) 'Justice Under Siege: The Rule of Law and Judicial Subservience in Kenya', *Human Rights Quarterly*, vol. 23, no. 1.

O'Brien, F.S. and T.C.I. Ryan (2001) 'Kenya', in S. Devarajan et al. (eds), *Aid and Reform in Africa: Lessons from Ten Case Studies*, Washington, DC: World Bank.

Ochieng', W.R. (1989) 'Independent Kenya, 1963–1986', in William Ochieng' (ed.), *A Modern Economic History of Kenya, 1895–1980*, Nairobi: Evans Brothers.

_____ (1995) 'Structural and Political Changes', in B.A. Ogot and W.R. Ochieng' (eds), *Decolonization and Independence in Kenya, 1940–93*, London: James Currey.

Okoth, P.G. (1992) *United States of America's Foreign Policy toward Kenya, 1952–1969*, Nairobi: Gideon S. Were Press.

Okoth-Ogendo, H.W.O. (1972) 'The Politics of Constitutional Change in Kenya Since Independence, 1963–69', *African Affairs*, vol. 71, no. 282.

Olukoshi, A. (1998) *The Elusive Prince of Denmark: Structural Adjustment and the Crisis of Governance in Africa*, Uppsala: Nordiska Afrikaninstitutet.

_____ (1999) 'State, Conflict, and Democracy in Africa: The Complex Process of Renewal', in R. Joseph (ed.), *State, Conflict, and Democracy in Africa*, Boulder, CO: Lynne Rienner.

_____ (2001) 'Towards Development Democracy: A Note', in UNRISD meeting, Cape Town, 7–8 September.

Opiyo, T. (2004) 'The Metamorphosis of Kenya Bus Services Limited in the Provision of Urban Transport in Nairobi'. Accessed on 29 February 2004 at www.worldbank.org/afr/ssatp/Countries/Kenya/UM/Kenya%20Bus%20Service.pdf

Sandbrook, R. (1986) 'The State and Economic Stagnation in Tropical Africa', *World Development*, vol. 14, no. 3.

Swamy, G. (1996) 'Kenya: Patchy, Intermittent Commitment', in I. Husain and R. Faruqee (eds), *Adjustment in Africa: Lessons from Country Case Studies*, Aldershot: Ashgate.

Tamarkin, M. (1978) 'The Roots of Political Stability in Kenya', *African Affairs*, vol. 77, no. 308.

_____ (1979) 'From Kenyatta to Moi – The Anatomy of a Peaceful Transition of Power', *Africa Today*, vol. 26, no. 3.

Throup, D. (1993) 'Elections and Political Legitimacy in Kenya', *Africa*, vol. 63, no. 3.

van de Walle, N. (2001) *African Economies and the Politics of Permanent Crisis, 1979–1999*, Cambridge, NY: Cambridge University Press.

_____ (2003) 'Presidentialism and Clientelism in Africa's Emerging Party Systems', *Journal of Modern African Studies*, vol. 41, no. 2.

Widner, J.A. (1992) *The Rise of a Party-State in Kenya: From 'Harambee!' to 'Nyayo!'*, Berkeley, CA: University of California Press.

10

From Demiurge to Midwife: Changing Donor Roles in Kenya's Democratisation Process

Stephen Brown

Introduction

Since 1989, almost all international donors have issued statements on how foreign aid allocations would take into account democracy, good governance and human rights in recipient countries. Virtually overnight, with the disappearance of the cold war, superpower rivalry and the East–West ideological battle, domestic political arrangements took a central place in donor development discourse. Whereas pro-Western authoritarian regimes had long been praised for their allegedly higher rates of capitalist-oriented economic growth and superior potential for eventual democratisation, bilateral aid donors, especially the United States, suddenly exalted the virtues of rapid democratisation. Most multilateral agencies were prohibited from expressing a preference for any particular form of government and therefore hid behind the language of good governance, as did some bilateral donors. Thus donors were propelled on to the international stage as central actors in the democratisation process, particularly in Sub-Saharan Africa.[1]

A growing literature examines donors' democracy promotion and questions the strength of their actual commitment beyond the level of rhetoric (Stokke 1995; Crawford 1997; Pridham et al. 1997; Udogu 1997; Hook 1998; Olsen 1998; Carothers 1999; Adar 2000; Burnell 2000; Cox et al. 2000; Rose 2000/01; Katumanga 2002; Brown 2005). In numerous cases, donors turned a blind eye to continued authoritarianism, usually for trade or strategic reasons, either weakly enforcing aid sanctions or failing to apply them altogether. Countries subjected to political conditionality – the tying of democracy-related strings to foreign aid – are usually less important commercial partners or military allies of donor countries. The practice is, therefore, most commonly found and applied more stringently in Sub-Saharan Africa, the world's most aid-dependent and marginalised region, where donor self-interest holds less sway. In other words, African transitions to democracy are more likely to be influenced by international actors than those in other regions. Under these circumstances, it is not surprising that donor intervention has played an important role in Kenya's democratisation process. In fact, donors' coordinated activities in Kenya in 1991–92 are widely recognised as key influences on political liberalisation and the holding of multiparty elections. Still, donors' individual and collective roles have rarely been considered over the longer term and within a theoretical framework.[2]

This chapter argues that the form and intensity of donor intervention has shifted several times since 1989, obtaining significant results but also creating sometimes contradictory effects. While at times donors helped bring about rapid political change, they also sought to shape the outcome of the democratisation process, sometimes holding back aid to prevent the process from taking a form of which they disapproved. As a result, donors are best described as having one foot on the accelerator and the other on the brakes. With multiple donors pursuing differing agendas or disagreeing on the best road to take, one could argue that far more than one pair of hands was on the steering wheel. This analysis begins by providing an overview of post-cold war democracy promotion and presenting the analytical tools to be used to characterise Kenya's recent experiences. It then examines, in turn, four periods in Kenya's history from the point of view of aid and democratisation: the single-party era under President Moi (1978–90), the return to multipartyism (1990–91), electoral authoritarianism (1992–2002) and the Kibaki presidency (2003–). The conclusion sums up the analysis of the Kenyan case and explores lessons for similar analyses elsewhere.

While the rest of this book focuses on a wide range of domestic actors, this chapter's goal is to analyse the role of international ones. By adopting this particular focus, it inevitably overemphasises the donors' role at the expense of long-standing and crucial local contributions to democratisation. I certainly do not wish to imply that donors did or could have suddenly brought democracy to Kenya on their own (though some of them might like to think so!). Domestic and international efforts were undertaken concurrently and often mutually reinforced each other, collectively painting a complex and balanced portrait of the struggles for democracy in Kenya.

Analysing Democracy Promotion

What do donors do to influence democratisation? Most commonly, they communicate their opinions and preferences, through means such as publications and policy statements. Often they offer specific advice mainly to governments, and also to other actors, euphemistically referring to this as 'policy dialogue'. They provide or suspend financial assistance, not only to governments but also to non-governmental organisations (NGOs). They provide some protection for activists, sometimes by pressuring the government on their behalf and reminding the regime that the world is watching; if the situation deteriorates, they can provide individuals with asylum. Donors also bring various opposition groups together, encourage them to co-operate, and bring government and opposition to the bargaining table. By promoting dialogue, donors influence agendas and therefore outcomes, making more probable certain reforms, but also discouraging or even preventing other changes or results. Finally, donors provide assistance to key components of democratisation, such as the organisation, funding, monitoring and certification of elections.

No consensus exists as to donors' motivation for democracy promotion. From a liberal internationalist perspective, a strong normative preoccupation with democracy and human rights emerged at the end of the cold war. The new international context allows states to accord greater weight to their concerns about domestic governance, which had long existed but was overshadowed by superpower rivalry. That is certainly how donors prefer to present themselves, as having long been preoccupied with the rights of the citizens of the recipient country, but only recently able to act. Public opinion, including editorials in influential donor country newspapers, reinforces the embarrassment at being seen as supporting dictators, especially in Africa. From a more 'realist' or 'neo-realist' perspective, donors respond to their own wider economic or geopolitical interests when formulating foreign policy. Democratisation could be, for instance, a convenient tool for replacing old-school autocrats who resisted economic reform with more market-friendly regimes. In fact, donors sometimes explicitly link political liberalisation with economic liberalisation, and free elections with free markets. At other times, democratisation virtually disappears from the donor agenda, for instance when seeking to reward allies for contributions to donors' international endeavours, such as the 'war on terror'.

How can one categorise donors' democracy promotion strategies? Evans (1995: 13–14, 77–81) describes four types of roles that states play in national economic development: custodian, demiurge, midwifery and husbandry. As custodian, the state acts as a kind of regulator and protective security force, assuring that certain basic rules are set and followed. As demiurge (named after a deity that created material things), it plays a more active role in ensuring basic common goods, recognising that no other actor is able to produce them and acts as a substitute for them. Midwifery implies a less proactive role, limiting intervention to facilitation, be it in the emergence of new actors, working with others or encouraging them to work together. Finally, husbandry is similar to midwifery, but implies a more aggressive approach in bringing actors together – sometimes through cajoling or arm-twisting. Though Evans developed this typology to help understand state intervention in the economies of the newly industrialising countries (NICs) of Brazil, India and South Korea, this analytical framework is helpful in examining Western states' intervention in African countries' political systems. I thus use Evans' conceptual tools to analyse the role of international donors in Kenya's democratisation process. The typology does not justly characterise every role that donors play, yet it does help map out the changing patterns and results of donor intervention, including at times a role inimical to democratisation. Like Evans' NICs, donor states can be positive or negative forces, developmental or predatory.

Single–Party Rule under Moi

Prior to 1990, donors showed very little concern for internal governance in their client states. Throughout the 1970s and '80s, Kenya consistently ranked among the top five recipients of official development assistance (ODA) in the region. Its espousal of capitalism and pro-Western alignment made it a trusted ally. In addition, Kenya seemed immune from the violence and instability that characterised many other African nations. Its large number of European inhabitants increased donor interest, especially Britain's. Kenya's qualities shone even brighter when contrasted with its neighbours: socialist Tanzania, cold war hot spots Ethiopia and Somalia, civil war-torn Sudan, and chaotic and conflict-ridden Uganda. Kenya's stability and economic growth earned the country the rare epithet of an African 'success story'. Moreover, according to the provisions of a 1980 military agreement, Kenya provided the US and its allies with a key naval base in Mombasa on the Indian Ocean, which proved useful for the US and UN operations in Somalia and was close to the volatile but strategically important Persian Gulf. In comparison, human rights abuses and restricted political opportunities in Kenya seemed relatively unimportant to donors, as did the increase in corruption and state repression that occurred under President Daniel arap Moi, who assumed power in 1978 upon the death of independence leader Jomo Kenyatta (for the Kenyatta regime, see Chapter 9 by Murunga in this volume).

During this period, aid flows continually multiplied. ODA to Kenya tripled between 1978 and 1990, increasing from $334 million to almost $1.2 billion (see Figure 10.1).[3] The US sharply increased its aid programme in the late 1980s, making Kenya the largest recipient of US and total aid in Sub-Saharan Africa in 1990.

Multilateral institutions were important contributors as well. The European Community's and the World Bank's disbursements grew in the 1980s, especially the latter's. In need of concessional loans, Kenya began a series of Bretton Woods-led structural adjustment programmes (SAPs) in 1986 (earlier but less pronounced attempts towards adjustment

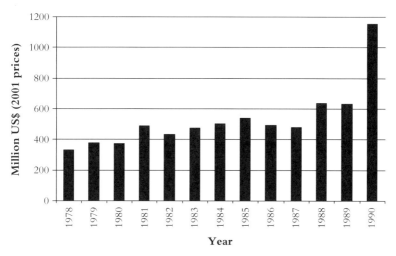

Figure 10.1 Official development assistance to Kenya (all donors, 1978–90).
Source: OECD's International Development Statistics online, http://www.oecd.org/dataoecd/50/17/5037721.htm

in Kenya began in 1981), though their implementation was erratic. The SAPs seriously undermined the base of political support for the government, since, in a fundamentally neo-patrimonial system, patronage is necessary to retain elite and popular support. For example, the international financial institutions (IFIs) convinced the government, in 1990, to reduce real salaries and eliminate some civil service positions, as well as end the practice of guaranteeing jobs for university students upon graduation. Another core element of economic reform, privatisation, diminished the government's ability to use parastatals' financial resources and employment opportunities for private or party benefit. Since these reforms eroded the regime's patronage resources, the government only slowly implemented many of the economic reforms to which it had committed itself, wearing down the patience of donors, including the IFIs. These structural factors, in part, set the stage for the transition to democracy.

Moi's rule was put at a disadvantage by a period of economic stagnation. From 1980 to 1993, per capita GNP grew by an annual average of only 0.3 per cent (though this was still better than the average rate of −0.8 per cent for Sub-Saharan Africa) (World Bank 1995: 162–3; UNDP 1996: 187). For the average Kenyan, living conditions worsened. For example, between 1982 and 1990, real wages fell by 16.3 per cent in the private sector and 22.2 per cent in the public sector (Swamy 1996: 212). Some causes were beyond the government's control, such as the decline in export commodity prices. Other factors, however, resulted from government policies such as shifting economic and political power to the Rift Valley and other regions of the ruling party's power base, whereas the Kikuyu in Central Province were the most dynamic entrepreneurs and agricultural producers, as well as a significant portion of the civil service. Corruption on a massive scale also took a severe toll on the economy. Kickbacks under Jomo Kenyatta's presidency had normally been around 10 per cent of the value of a contract, whereas under Moi they often reached 60 per cent (Holmquist and Ford 1998: 234). In effect, the prebendal Kenyan state was transformed into a predatory one (Thomas 1998: 43).

Prior to 1990, donors virtually ignored the issue of domestic political representation and played little or no active role in promoting democratisation in Kenya. If anything, their continued and growing support for the Moi regime, despite worsening governance and the deterioration in civil liberties, tended to strengthen its hold on power. The only role that donors played in promoting democracy was an indirect and presumably involuntary one: structural adjustment and the continuing economic crisis undermined the regime's ability to finance its clients' loyalty, thus contributing to growing dissatisfaction with the regime (as well as to popular and elite support for political reform). The economic crisis also made the country more dependent on foreign aid and the government more susceptible to policy pressure from donors.

The Return to Multipartyism

Starting in 1990, the US and other donors increasingly spoke out against economic mismanagement, growing human rights abuses and restricted political opportunities. The end of the cold war had decreased the importance of having a solid ally in the East African region, while public opinion and budget deficits in donor countries – among other motivations – prompted bilateral donors to take into account Kenya's domestic politics in their aid allocations. US Ambassador Smith Hempstone's May 1990 mention of tying of aid to political reform marked the beginning of Western donors' active involvement in Kenya's democratisation process. He warned that Kenya was losing the carte blanche it had previously enjoyed. At first, he acted without the support of his counterparts in the Western diplomatic corps or his own government. Most bilateral donors distanced themselves from Hempstone's words, especially the British High Commissioner, Sir John Johnson, who defended Moi's record. Even Washington failed to back up its 'rogue ambassador'; when US Assistant Secretary of State Herman Cohen visited Kenya later that month, he reassured the government that no such decision on political conditionality had yet been made (Hempstone 1997: 94). He also made a point of not meeting with any opposition figures (*New York Times*, 6 August 1990; Africa Watch, 1991: 378). In June, days after British Foreign Secretary Douglas Hurd announced how the British government would attach political and economic conditions to its aid, Johnson announced that his government had no intention of cutting aid to Kenya (Africa Watch 1991: 363).[4]

The following month, Hempstone was the only Western diplomat in Nairobi to release a statement expressing distress at the detention of Kenneth Matiba, Charles Rubia, Raila Odinga and other pro-democracy activists who were planning a rally for 7 July (Hempstone 1997: 104; *New York Times*, 9 July 1990). Several of them were adopted by Amnesty International as prisoners of conscience (see Amnesty

International 1990: 4). Again, Washington's deeds contradicted the ambassador's comments in Nairobi. The day after the arrests, the US government released $5 million in military aid to Kenya.

The US legislative branch, however, took a harder line than the Bush (Sr) Administration. Senator Edward Kennedy called for an immediate cessation of economic and military aid to Kenya. In the first concrete steps taken by a donor, the US Congress rapidly froze the remaining $5 million allocation in military aid for that year, as well as $8 million in development assistance (*New York Times*, 29 July 1990). In October, Congress voted to prohibit the disbursement of economic or military aid unless the judiciary's independence was restored (Kibwana and Maina 1996: 458). In November, three visiting US Senators told the Kenyan government that in order for the US to release $15 million in military aid for the following year, it would have to charge or release all detainees, end the mistreatment of prisoners, and restore freedom of expression and the judiciary's independence (*New York Times*, 16 November 1990). The government complied with only the last demand, restoring judges' security of tenure, but by then it had already replaced the members of the judiciary with those on whose loyalty Moi could not count.

Soon, other countries began to react as well. In mid-1990, Finland, Denmark, Sweden and Norway issued a joint communiqué, threatening to cut aid if democratic rights were not respected. The British government quietly made its displeasure known by calling in the Kenyan High Commissioner in London, but the British High Commissioner in Nairobi remained quiet (Hempstone 1997: 114–15). The British actions were comparatively mild, prompting Moi to thank Prime Minister Margaret Thatcher publicly for her continued support in the face of criticism (Africa Watch 1991: 364). In July, a group of British parliamentarians visited Kenya at the expense of the Kenyan government. After meeting with only ruling party officials – not with a single member of the opposition, nor investigating human rights conditions first-hand – they concluded that Kenya was 'peaceful, stable and democratic' (Africa Watch 1991: 364–5).

After Hempstone, the ambassadors most critical of Moi at the time were the Danish and Norwegian ones, whereas the British, Japanese and German representatives – from three of the largest donor countries – as well as the Austrian ambassador refused to get involved (Hempstone 1997: 95). In October 1990, the Norwegian government protested the kidnapping in Uganda, forced return to Kenya and arraignment for treason of Koigi wa Wamwere, a Kenyan political dissident who had long lived in exile in Norway. In response, Kenya broke off diplomatic relations and lost all Norwegian assistance, worth about $20 million annually. Denmark announced it would cut its aid by one-quarter (about $9 million) because of the human rights situation (*New York Times*, 16 November 1990). Britain's reluctance to criticise Kenya weakened after Thatcher was ousted as prime minister in November 1990 (Throup and Hornsby 1998: 73–4). Nonetheless, the new British High Commissioner in Nairobi, Sir Roger Tomkys, was equally unwilling to issue public criticisms of Moi and advocated applying only behind-the-scenes pressure.

At the November 1990 Paris meeting of the Consultative Group, donors expressed concern for human rights violations and considered the possibility of collectively reducing aid allocations to Kenya (Throup and Hornsby 1998: 74). A number of Western NGOs such as Africa Watch (1991) and the Robert F. Kennedy Memorial Center for Human Rights advocated this. Still, action was slow to come. In February 1991, the US decided to release another $5 million dollars in military aid in order to show 'appreciation' for Kenya's assistance to US policy objectives on Iraq, Sudan and Somalia, including access to Kenyan naval and air force bases (*New York Times*, 3 March 1991; Dagne 1992: 14; Robinson 1993: 63) as well as for assisting with a case of Libyan refugees (Hempstone 1997: 141–2). Days later, the Kenyan government – possibly emboldened by the show of support – arrested Gitobu Imanyara, the editor-in-chief of the *Nairobi Law Monthly*, who had published articles on the opposition and was charged with sedition. Imanyara's arrest embarrassed the Americans and shocked other donors. The US State Department reacted swiftly in issuing a protest and other donors (the Nordic countries, Germany and even Japan) threatened further aid reductions if Imanyara were not freed (*New York Times*, 5 May 1991). In June, *The Times* published an editorial that condemned British equivocation and called for suspension of aid (Africa Watch 1991: 367). The main political opposition group in Kenya, the Forum for the Restoration of Democracy (FORD), also spoke out against Britain's reluctance to criticise the Moi government openly (Mutunga 1999: 216–17, 222).

Later in 1991, bilateral donors and even the World Bank became more proactive. The implausibility of the government's explanation of the murder of Foreign Minister Robert Ouko, with whom they had good relations, prompted them to undertake a few investigations of their own. They found evidence that Ouko had criticised Cabinet Minister Nicholas Biwott and other top-level officials for diverting development assistance for their own profit, including all of Sweden's aid for 1990, and other corrupt practices (Widner 1992: 196). In July, the Nordic countries threatened to cancel $80 million's worth of aid agreements to protest their displeasure with the worsening political situation. Donors began to implement their threats in September 1991, when the Danish government suspended all new aid to Kenya, citing corruption and human rights abuses. The following month, it terminated a rural development programme that it had been financing for 17 years, after an audit showed that most of the $40 million it had contributed had been embezzled. Britain cancelled $7 million in oil subsidies, fearing the money was going to corrupt politicians rather than consumers, and the World Bank decided not to grant a $100 million loan for the energy sector (*New York Times*, 21 October 1991; wa Maina 1992: 124).

During this period, British businessman 'Tiny' Rowland used his newspaper, the *Observer*, to launch several attacks on the corrupt Moi government, specifically targeting Biwott. Rowland was motivated by his company Lonrho's losses to Biwott's business interests in irregular contract tendering (Throup and Hornsby 1998: 84). The *New York Times* also ran an article on 21 October 1991, which highlighted the extent of high-level corruption, singling out Biwott and also naming Moi and a few other members of Moi's inner circle. Adding further evidence to the allegations, the IMF reported that Kenyan accounts overseas were valued at $2.6 billion (*New York Times*, 13 November 1991). Moi responded by promising to set up an anti-corruption unit (which he did only six years later) and by demoting Biwott to a less important cabinet portfolio. In November, a Scotland Yard inspector's testimony implicated Biwott in Ouko's murder, with the alleged motive of preventing Ouko from publicly revealing high-level instances of corruption. This further shocked the donors, and Moi had Biwott arrested; though the latter was remanded at the General Service Unit Commandant's house, he was released after 10 days, never prosecuted and later given senior cabinet positions.

In late 1991, the five most like-minded, pro-reform ambassadors in Nairobi were from the US, Canada, Germany, Sweden and Denmark. When the opposition attempted to hold a rally on 16 November, these and a number of other local embassies protested both the arrest of 12 FORD leaders (including Oginga Odinga, Masinde Muliro, Gitobu Imanyara, Paul Muite and Martin Shikuku), who had called on donors to cease supporting the government, and the government's heavy-handed response, which included the use of riot police. The 'Big Five' bilateral donors named above, plus Finland, Australia and – for the first time – the UK, all issued written or oral protests. The US State Department, Congress and the White House also expressed their concern and the British minister for overseas development, Lynda Chalker, warned that Britain and other donors would be tough on Kenya at the coming Consultative Group meeting – a position opposed by High Commissioner Tomkys (Hempstone 1997: 168, 250–1, 254–6).

FORD lobbied the donors to withhold development assistance. On 26 November 1991, at their World Bank-chaired Consultative Group meeting in Paris, donors decided to suspend new aid to Kenya – amounting to $350 million out of about $1 billion – until corruption had been curbed and the political system liberalised. Donors conditioned resumption of aid to the early implementation of political reform, which included greater pluralism, the importance of the rule of law and respect for human rights, notably basic freedoms of expression and assembly, and firm action to deal with issues of corruption (see Nasong'o 2005: 58–9). Donors did not specify multiparty democracy, but the repeal of the single-party constitutional clause was clearly necessary (Barkan 1993: 91), as was the holding of elections. The US cut $28 million from the $47 million it had been prepared to pledge for 1992 (US Department of State, 1992: 815). Emboldened by the peaceful transfer of power to the opposition in Zambia, the donors promised to review the situation after six months (see Nasong'o 2005, for a comparative study of Kenya and Zambia). Nonetheless, humanitarian assistance continued and evidence later emerged that the regime had exaggerated the number of starving Kenyans in order to receive extra funds from the World Food Programme, which was unaffected by the aid sanctions (Middleton and O'Keefe 1998: 62).

Despite clear warnings, the Kenyan government was caught unawares by the partial suspension of aid. It had apparently expected a rap on the knuckles accompanied by continued financial support. However, the suspension of rapid disbursement aid and balance-of-payments support caused immediate liquidity hardship for the government, including a rapid depreciation of the Kenyan shilling, while its psychological effect was even stronger (Throup and Hornsby 1998: 85). Figure 10.2 illustrates the drastic reduction in development assistance after 1990.

The regime took less than a week to react. Biwott's fall had left the regime hardliners feeling vulnerable, and Moi without his right-hand man. On 3 December 1991, after long asserting that it would never do so, Moi announced that the government would allow opposition parties

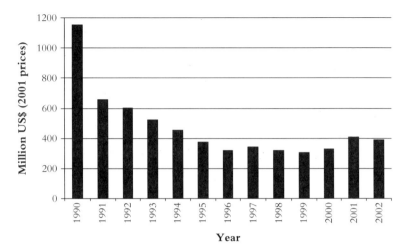

Figure 10.2   Official development assistance to Kenya (all donors, 1990–2002). *Source*: OECD's International Development Statistics online, http://www.oecd.org/dataoecd/50/17/5037721.htm

to register. Within weeks, the government repealed the constitutional article enshrining the Kenya African National Union (KANU) as the sole political party. Arguably, therefore, whereas previous donor support had facilitated Moi's patronage system and bolstered his capacity to resist internal pressure for political change, the aid crunch by the same donors in a changing international context effectively supplemented internal pressures for democratisation resulting in a return to multiparty politics. Still, this was not a complete victory for the opposition. With this move, KANU seized the initiative, since it could control the electoral process and agenda (Throup and Hornsby 1998: 88). It was a 'calculated risk with the regime betting that it was easier to meet the challenge of democracy than run a patronage-based regime without substantial international aid flows' (Holmquist et al. 1994: 99).

During the period from 1990 to 1991, after long ignoring Kenya's domestic political realm, donors gradually spoke out and then applied concrete pressure on the Moi regime to liberalise the political system. Hempstone spearheaded the movement, initially contradicted by messages sent from Washington. Such mixed signals illustrated the conflict between democracy promotion and other foreign policy objectives. Gradually, other branches of the US government and other donors endorsed the ambassador's initiatives and also became vocal in their critique of the Moi regime. Donors overcame their internal divisions to take decisive action by November 1991, when they collectively suspended most new aid. Once this consensus emerged, it took only a few days to convince the Moi regime to end single-party rule.

During this period, donors increasingly played the role of demiurge. They identified the key political change necessary – multipartyism – and, using reduced aid flows as leverage, forced the government to respond to internal popular demands to modify the rules via a constitutional amendment. Donors played a crucial part in helping to create a new political reality in Kenya. The demiurge, having set a new material reality, stepped back to observe its workings. From the donors' perspective, once they had ensured that the basic democratic rules were in place, domestic actors could henceforth compete in the electoral arena as in the donors' own liberal democracies and the electorate would select Kenya's rulers in a free and fair vote. This scenario, however, was far too naive and overly optimistic.

Electoral Authoritarianism

Between 1992 and 2002, President Moi and KANU remained in power, legitimated – at least in part – by deeply flawed multiparty elections held in 1992 and 1997. Though formally a multiparty democracy, Kenya during this period is more accurately described as an electoral authoritarian regime. The precise degree of competitiveness of the elections is highly contested, leaving it open to interpretation whether it would have been possible for the opposition to win had it been united. It is clear that KANU was involved in a wide range of abuses, ranging from ballot box stuffing to ethnic cleansing. Both times, donors took strong measures to make sure that – regardless of such egregious practices – elections would be held as scheduled, that all major parties would participate and that, once endorsed by international observers, election results would be contested only through judicial channels. Between elections, donors virtually withdrew from the political arena, concentrating instead on economic reform. This focus away from politics allowed the regime to act with relative impunity on a number of non-economic issues. As a result, donors wound up helping to keep Moi and his party in power. Donors periodically played important roles, sometimes furthering democratisation and at other times preventing it from entering a phase where change would be more radical and unpredictable.

After Moi legalised opposition parties, donors felt it was important to maintain pressure on the government to ensure that the elections were as free and fair as possible. At the end of December 1991, the

IMF postponed indefinitely the disbursement of a $63 million loan because of economic non-compliance, thus jeopardizing future loans from the World Bank and other sources. Relations between the Kenya government and most bilateral donors – especially the US – were very tense in 1992. The US, Germany and others constantly pressured Moi, in person and in both individual and joint démarches – but not with additional aid cuts – to promote dialogue and make changes that would improve the fairness of the poll. However, not all donors were steadfast in their withholding of aid. In July 1992, France broke ranks and announced that it would release $9 million in aid (Holmquist and Ford 1992: 109). Moreover, the pressure on the government was undermined when, on several occasions in 1992–93, donors, especially the US, strongly encouraged the opposition to proceed under a severely flawed electoral process and accept the results of the poll rather than risk upheaval.

The repeal of the constitutional clause that established KANU as the sole political party permitted the re-legalisation of opposition parties. However, the one-party system was otherwise left intact, including numerous provisions for state repression. KANU benefited from clear and well-documented advantages: the number and size of constituencies overrepresented its strongholds in parliament; the electoral commission was appointed by Moi and was highly partisan; there was a high degree of intimidation, numerous instances of bribery and irregularities in voter registration; the electronic (radio and television) media were strongly biased in KANU's favour; the ruling party used state funds for its campaign; and, not least, the so-called 'ethnic clashes' prevented opposition supporters from voting. To encourage the government to improve the fairness of the elections, the local representatives of nine donor countries delivered a feeble joint démarche to Moi in May 1992, expressing their 'deep concern' – a statement consciously watered down in order to secure as many ambassadorial signatures as possible (Hempstone 1997: 273).[5]

Divisions within the opposition were a clear impediment to the opposition's efforts to replace KANU through the ballot box. FORD, for instance, split into two separate parties – FORD-Kenya and FORD-Asili – and later splintered further. After the legalisation of multipartyism, Mwai Kibaki (a long-term KANU cabinet minister and former vice-president) left the ruling party and formed the Democratic Party (DP). Thus, three major contenders (as well as four minor candidates) vied with Moi for the presidency in 1992, dividing the vote. On one hand, donors made some efforts to get opposition leaders to work more closely together and co-ordinate strategies, for instance at breakfast meetings at the US ambassador's residence. Yet on the other hand they sometimes disapproved and actively sought to dissuade opposition leaders when they did develop joint strategies. For instance, on three separate occasions in 1992–93, donors strongly opposed and helped to end opposition boycott movements, without obtaining any major concessions from KANU. First, in June 1992, DP and many religious leaders called for a boycott of voter registration to protest against the patently unfair playing field. US ambassador Hempstone played a central role in getting them to abandon the boycott. Second, shortly before the December 1992 vote, the three main opposition parties jointly threatened to withdraw from the elections, since they believed a fair poll to be impossible, but Hempstone and others convinced them that to be represented in parliament was better than not being represented at all. Third, after the results were announced, amid accusations of ballot-box stuffing and post-election fraud further distorting the electoral results, donors helped convince the opposition leaders to contest them in court, rather than refuse to sit in parliament. In the end, the KANU-dominated courts ruled against KANU in only one out of 40 cases, leading to a by-election in only one KANU-held constituency.

Once the elections were held, donors were highly reluctant to reject them. Instead, they unenthusiastically endorsed them as having obtained the minimal passing grade, emphasising the 'success' of the voting process on election day rather than the documented unfairness of the campaign as a whole (see Barkan 1993). Though some donors hoped an opposition victory would improve economic management, the main ones were more interested in the process than in the results. They did not necessarily want Moi to be replaced by someone else, but believed that the democratic process would improve political and economic governance through greater accountability, no matter who was in power.[6] In this too, they were mistaken.

Post-election vacillations I: 1993–97

After the 1992 elections, donors greatly reduced their pressure for political change, placing much more importance on economic reform and stability than on democracy. The economic cost of KANU's campaign, combined with other factors, had almost eliminated economic growth for 1992 and 1993 and Kenya defaulted on its debt service for the first time. After repudiating IMF-recommended policies in March 1993, Moi took some macroeconomic measures that pleased donors. The following month, the World Bank disbursed $85 million it had been withholding (Throup and Hornsby 1998: 560–1). The November 1993 Consultative Group meeting in Paris focused on the government's macroeconomic 'achievements' and promises for future compliance, while paying lip service to the issue of improved political liberalisation. Against the opposition's request, most donors resumed balance-of-payment support and new aid, though often at a lower level, and channelled a significant proportion through NGOs rather than the government. They pledged to contribute $850 million, including $170 million in rapid-disbursing aid from the Bretton Woods institutions. In January 1994, Kenya's creditors rescheduled $700 million in outstanding debt. In December 1994, donors pledged another $850 million for 1995, stating their satisfaction with the government's progress in democracy and human rights, ignoring evidence to the contrary.

European donors in particular were divided over the issue of aid resumption. The Scandinavians were especially critical of the Moi regime and resisted any move that could be interpreted as support for the government (Olsen 1998: 355). However, Britain reportedly blocked attempts within the European Union to invoke political conditions (Human Rights Watch/Africa 1995: 2, 13). France, for its part, was uninterested in any form of conditionality that would interfere with debts owed to the French government and French companies (Geisler 1993: 632). Some countries that were particularly concerned with democracy and human rights, notably the US, preferred to resume aid more gradually, dependent on progress on pluralism and ending the continuing 'ethnic' clashes (Throup and Hornsby 1998: 564). However, the US and other donors eased pressure on Moi when the government co-operated with international military and humanitarian operations in the Great Lakes region and the Horn of Africa (Cowen and Ngunyi 1997: 55).

Ngunyi (1997) shows that the donors most committed to political conditionality during this period were the Scandinavians, the Dutch and the Americans. The Japanese, the Germans and the British – Kenya's top three trade partners and aid donors – showed little interest in linking aid to political reforms, whereas the French and the Italians showed none at all. Sometimes there was discord between the donor capital and its local representative in Nairobi. The German government was fairly uninterested in political conditionality, but Ambassador

Bernd Mützelberg assumed the role of a leading donor critic after the departure of Hempstone, whose successor, Aurelia Brazeal, proved to be much softer on the government than Hempstone had been.

By 1995, it was hard to deny that holding by-elections was Moi's only democratic activity (Harbeson 1998: 169). Otherwise, the government was acting in clear violation of democratic principles, including harassing opposition party activists, arresting dozens of opposition MPs and cracking down on critical magazines, newspapers and NGOs. Still, in February, the Bretton Woods institutions approved $310 million in funding for new projects. Soon, however, donors began to turn. Britain reneged on some of its aid pledges when, in July 1995, British Minister Lynda Chalker announced in Nairobi that no new aid projects would be approved until satisfactory improvements had been made with human rights and political and economic reforms (*New York Times*, 29 July 1995). Britain withheld $17 million in aid, the World Bank froze a $160 million infrastructure loan and the IMF delayed a $200 million loan to get the government to free maize prices (*The Economist*, 19 August 1995).

Donors' reticence to provide funding was over both the political and the economic situation in Kenya and it was difficult to disentangle the two. For example, the Bretton Woods Institutions were particularly interested in action on high-profile corruption cases, such as the Goldenberg affair. Corruption notably straddles the political and the economic realms. Both were cited when aid was suspended. However, all the instances of aid resumption to Kenya followed economic reform, either past or promised, or support for Western foreign policy. In fact, there were no true domestic political advances between the 1992 elections and the latter part of 1997.

Post-election vacillations II: 1998–2002

Donor attention returned to domestic political conditions in Kenya in 1997, drawn by the growing number of participants – and violent deaths – at successive demonstrations organised by the National Convention Executive Council (NCEC) under the theme of 'No Reforms, No Election' (see Chapter 2 by Nasong'o in this volume; Mutunga, 1999). On 31 May images of excessive police violence were broadcast around the world. On 7 July, some 20–25 people were killed when security forces repressed the crowds (Barkan and Ng'ethe 1998: 37). The international community was shocked by the images of police brutality against pro-democracy demonstrators. In Nairobi, 22 foreign diplomatic missions signed a joint letter to Moi in July, deploring police violence and urging the government to open talks on legal reforms with the opposition, church and civic groups. A few donors refused to sign the letter, maintaining that both sides had used violence and should be condemned for it (Holmquist and Ford 1998: 239). In Washington, US Secretary of State Madeleine Albright issued a strongly worded statement (*The Economist*, 19 July 1997). Thus physical violence brought many donors together, motivated to an extent by a desire to restore peace but also in fear of mobs taking over.

Sensing growing hostility from donors, Moi postponed the donor Consultative Group meeting scheduled for 21 July. The IMF suspended lending at the end of July, including a $220 million loan, officially attributing its decision to poor economic governance and corruption. The World Bank, the European Union (EU) and several bilateral donors soon followed the IMF's lead and suspended a total of over $400 million in aid, which was $50 million more than in 1991. The donors explicitly urged the government to meet with the opposition (Barkan and Ng'ethe 1998: 37). The aid freeze had an immediate negative economic impact, including hundreds of millions of dollars in capital flight and a 25 per cent depreciation of the Kenyan shilling, causing a rise in the price of imported goods.

Meanwhile, on 8 August, at least 40 people were killed at pro-reform demonstrations (Cowen and Ngunyi 1997: 21). By portraying the demonstrators as 'undisciplined, poor, and out of control', the government fed a distrust of popular mobilisation among donors and opposition parties (Holmquist and Ford 1998: 243). In interviews and press releases, local donor representatives repeatedly expressed their fear that violent demonstrations could spiral into chaos and civil war. Many donors, some of whom had been financing the NCEC (Sweden, Denmark and the Netherlands), and a number of NCEC members distanced themselves from the increasingly 'radical' NCEC reform agenda. With donor support, opposition and government MPs formed the Inter-Parties Parliamentary Group (IPPG) and signed an agreement on minimal reforms that would allow elections to proceed as scheduled. These were amendments to the Public Order Act, Chief's Authority Act and a few other laws, but left in place most of the restrictions on the operations of opposition parties.

Bilateral donors, especially the four largest ones – Germany, the US, the UK and Japan – enthusiastically supported the IPPG reform package, hailing it as an 'old-fashioned compromise',[7] while the NCEC was allegedly warned by some of its funders, including the Netherlands, that it would lose support if it did not cease opposing the IPPG changes, which it considered 'too little, too late', demanding nothing less than an overhaul of the constitution before elections were held.[8] The IPPG accords, only partially implemented in time for the elections, eliminated a few KANU advantages and loosened restrictions on the opposition. Though they allowed elections to be held as scheduled, they did not create a significantly more level playing field. As in 1992, KANU used its gross advantages, strong-arm tactics and a certain amount of fraud, facilitated by the opposition's inability to unite behind a single candidate, to win the presidency and control parliament in 1997. This led one close observer to rethink the international community's actions: 'Donor pressure ... should, in retrospect, have extended to fashioning broader multiparty agreement on reforming the rules of the game, and perhaps to electing a constituent assembly to draft a new constitution' (Harbeson 1999: 51).

As in 1992–93, donors, in spite of very detailed and critical internal reports, only went through the motions of raising the question of electoral irregularities. Moreover, Canada, the US and France reportedly convinced other donors not to reveal that their own joint observation team had concluded that KANU should only have had a minority of seats in parliament (unattributable interview). The main US elections consultant was likewise instructed to underplay the seriousness of her findings in her report.[9] Though some donors, including the EU and Japan, issued more critical statements, foreign diplomats in Nairobi generally expressed their satisfaction that the 1997 elections were better than the previous ones and thus good enough. Donors thus expressed no support when opposition leaders initially refused to accept the electoral results. As in the period following the 1992 elections, donors turned their attention back to the economic realm, showing little interest in further political reform and retaining lower-level aid, mainly because of economic issues.

In the period 1998–2002 Moi continued to pursue a number of donor-prescribed economic reforms, though erratically and as little as possible without overly displeasing donors, who were reluctant to cut aid further and thus lose leverage. Changes in local diplomatic staff affected donor approaches, making them less confrontational than in 1991–92 and 1997. For instance, German Ambassador Michael Gerdts was a lot less vocal than his predecessor, even after the 1998 murder of a German aid worker, which was possibly linked to government corruption. Overall, bilateral donors looked to Moi to steer the state peacefully, maintain stability and, at the end of his mandate, hand over to a successor. They were not overly concerned with human rights issues and were equivocal in their support for civil society (Southall 1999: 108). Multilateral donors especially wanted policy reform that would favour economic growth. After suspending lending in mid-1997 over corruption and the slow pace of privatisation and civil service reform, the resumption of lending by the IMF was crucial to the Kenyan government because other donors were waiting for IMF approval before restarting their own aid programmes. Though large-scale lending had not yet resumed, multilateral institutions sent mixed signals. In April 1998, for example, the World Bank country director, Harold Wackman, commented publicly that he would prefer to work with 'an efficient crook than a bumbling saint', which was widely interpreted as demonstrating support for Moi and a lack of commitment to improving governance.

In 1999, however, bilateral donors became increasingly outspoken. In February, American Ambassador Prudence Bushnell announced that the US would fund the Kenyan private sector, since aid to government had proved ineffective in improving people's lives (*Daily Nation*, 8 February 1999). Her German counterpart alluded to 'powerful politicians' seeking kickbacks and 'frustrating' three projects his government was funding (*Daily Nation*, 13 February 1999). In June, the Netherlands announced that it was cancelling its aid programme to Kenya, worth about $25 million a year, citing the stalled constitutional reform process, corruption scandals, land grabbing, the slow pace of economic reforms and public sector reform, as well as the non-implementation of some provisions of the pre-election accords (*Panafrican News Agency*, 9 July 1999). Other donors publicly chastised the government, albeit without cutting aid any further. The United Nations Development Programme (UNDP) revealed in September 1999 that the government had failed to account for $43.7 million in aid since 1994. Still, this did not prevent the organization from signing a new $14 million grant agreement with Kenya (*Daily Nation*, 18 September 1999).

Other than the Dutch, donors decided by late 1999 that more time was needed to determine if the recent changes would become more substantial or if they were merely cosmetic. Worried that progress under way might be reversed if they applied too much pressure, donors stopped demanding a resolution of the Goldenberg scandal and tolerated the late debt service payments. By the end of the year, the government appeared to have convinced donors that it would improve economic governance. In response, some opposition MPs and members of civic and religious organisations formed the Stakeholders Support Group, whose primary purpose was to lobby against the resumption of aid.

The World Bank, the UK, the EU and the African Development Bank were all reported to have pressured the IMF to release new funds (*Daily Nation*, 26 May 2000), whereas most bilateral donors remained concerned by Kenya's political situation. Still, worries that the worsening economic crisis 'could culminate in political and economic instability' reportedly swayed donors, including the 'reluctant' US (*East African*, 26 June, 24 July and 31 July 2000). Though the government had not complied with the conditions for resuming aid, the IMF announced in July 2000 that it would renew assistance immediately. As expected, the IMF agreement paved the way for hundreds of millions of dollars in additional assistance from other sources, including from the World Bank, the UK, Japan, Sweden, the African Development Bank and the EU – though the Dutch and the Scandinavians continued progressively to phase out their assistance programmes. In exchange, the IMF and other donors demanded a long list of measures, none of which was directly related to further democratisation.

By 2001, it seemed that donors expected little more from Moi than to hand over power peacefully to a democratically elected successor at the end of his mandate. This issue more than any other dominated the political scene until mid-2002. Though Moi was constitutionally barred from running again for the presidency, he avoided stating explicitly that he would step down. A constitutional amendment or a number of cunning interpretations of the constitution could have allowed him to secure at least one more five-year term. After sustained pressure from donors, civil society and the independent media ensured that no underhanded measures would be taken, he finally announced in June 2002 that he would definitely not be a presidential candidate. It is widely believed that US President Bush and Secretary of State Colin Powell discussed this with Moi when he visited Washington a few weeks before the elections (Brown 2004).

The Kibaki presidency

When Kibaki assumed office in January 2003, donors were highly supportive of the new government. During its honeymoon period, the

Kibaki administration won praise for a number of policy initiatives, especially a crackdown on graft, which had been a key plank in the NARC electoral platform. In 2003–04, donors – including the US, the UK, Germany and the World Bank – contributed hundreds of millions of dollars to the fight against corruption, including support for the office of a newly appointed anti-corruption 'czar'. The IMF resumed lending in November 2003, approving a loan worth $250 million.

Despite initially positive signs, notably in measures against corrupt members of the police and the judiciary, it became clear in mid-2004 that large-scale corruption was still a considerable problem in Kenya. Scandals emerged over the procurement of passport-making and police forensic laboratory equipment. In July, donors became more vocal in their dismay with continued high-level graft. British High Commissioner Sir Edward Clay's public pronouncements earned him severe criticism in Kenya. The EU suspended some assistance over the matter. As evidence grew, the media added its voice, more donors joined in and the problem became increasingly difficult to ignore or deny. Western diplomats alleged that corruption had cost the treasury $1 billion since Kibaki took office. In February 2005, the British High Commissioner denounced the 'massive looting' of state resources by senior government politicians, including sitting cabinet ministers. Within days, Kibaki's anti-corruption 'czar' John Githongo resigned and went into exile amid rumours about death threats related to his investigation of high-level politicians. The UK, the US and Germany rapidly suspended their anti-corruption assistance and Kibaki reacted with a minor cabinet shuffle. However, with Githongo's release of a damning detailed dossier on corruption in the Kibaki regime in February 2006, Kibaki was forced to relieve three ministers of their cabinet positions. These included David Mwiraria (Finance), Kiraitu Murungi (Energy) and George Saitoti (Education).

At the root of the difficulties of fighting corruption in Kenya were the conditions that brought Kibaki to power and his dependence on a very loose and disparate coalition to be able to rule. To maximise his electoral chances, he accepted into his alliance, shortly before the 2002 elections, a number of senior KANU officials who defected at the last minute, several of whom were deeply implicated in the worst abuses of the Moi regimes, including the 'ethnic clashes' and massive corruption. This was a pointer to the fact that the new Kibaki regime would not radically break from the KANU mode of politics and governance. This explains why, faced with an uproar both internal and external over 'new corruption', all Kibaki could do was effect a half-hearted shuffle of his cabinet (see Murunga and Nasong'o 2006). Indeed, in a system that though formally democratic is still neo-patrimonial, Kibaki allows his ministers a wide margin of manoeuvre to ensure their continued support. The government turns a blind eye to much corruption, both past and present, to ensure its own survival. In fact, faced with failing support from one faction of his NARC alliance, Kibaki brought KANU sitting MPs into cabinet in October 2004. It is unlikely, given his reliance on corrupt senior politicians, that Kibaki will willingly prosecute his own cabinet ministers, unless his hand is further forced by Kenyans with appropriate assistance of donors or he no longer has to rely on their support to keep governing.

Donor Role: An Evaluation

In the period 1989–91, donors played a demiurge role in Kenya's democratisation in the sense of contributing to the re-establishment of a multiparty system. Thereafter, donors basically abandoned the demiurge role. This in itself is not surprising, since, once the new rules were in place, it would be expected that donors play a custodial role in ensuring that these rules are respected. However, donors failed in this role with respect to the 1992 and 1997 elections by discounting the myriad campaign and election irregularities, as well as by endorsing the unfair elections, even suppressing evidence on the extent of government electoral fraud and the illegitimacy of KANU's majority in parliament. Moreover, donors underemphasised the shortcomings of the new rules in establishing a system in which various parties could compete democratically.

Between elections, donors generally avoided action as custodians of democracy by not protesting post-electoral political backsliding and by eschewing further use of political conditionality, with a few notable exceptions related to corruption. Some progress in or promises of economic reform were generally sufficient to forestall any further punitive actions. Donors appeared determined to give the Kenyan government a series of fresh chances, hoping each time that it would honour its pledges, despite its repeated failure to do so in the past. Donors' primary concern appeared to be the avoidance of any path that could lead to a breakdown of the political and economic order. On occasion, their effectiveness was reduced by a lack of agreement and co-ordination amongst themselves. In addition, Moi's regime was also exceptionally adroit in resisting pressure. In 2002, however, donors' custodian actions did help ensure that Moi did not run again, paving the way for a series of events that made an opposition victory possible (see details in Brown 2004).

Donors also sporadically played a role in husbandry. In both 1991–93 and in 1997, donors co-ordinated their actions and international involvement helped bring about incremental change and modest last-minute compromises that did not significantly modify the political landscape. The momentum created by aid suspensions in 1991 and 1997 was not allowed to reach its full force. Donors deterred opposition parties from confronting the government other than through elections and court cases, even though the government dominated both the electoral and judicial systems. In 1992-93, donors deliberately undermined concerted opposition efforts to pressure for a more thorough rewriting of the rules through boycotts and demonstrations. In 1997, the multilateral institutions' suspension of hundreds of millions of dollars in aid prompted KANU to seek an accommodation with the opposition parties, while bilateral donors twisted the arms of opposition parties and civil society organisations to garner support for the ineffectual IPPG accords.

The least visible role that donors played was as midwife, mainly their actions to encourage opposition parties to co-operate and avoid splitting the opposition vote. The US-led efforts were in vain in 1992, and calls for a united opposition front also went unheeded in 1997 until the emergence of NARC that finally ousted KANU in 2002. Under Evans' typology, donors began Kibaki's term as midwives of change in one specific area, seeking to facilitate additional state transparency and accountability. They did this, among other things, by providing material and moral assistance for institutionalising the fight against corruption. Halfway through Kibaki's mandate, faced with growing evidence of the size of the problem and the lack of political will to address it, donors turned to a more proactive and antagonistic role. Whether it is best characterised as husbandry or custodial remains to be seen, as does the form of donor intervention – if any – in other pressing issues of democratic reform, such as the long-overdue constitutional reforms.

Conclusion

During various periods, donors assumed different types of democracy promotion roles. Of interest is not just the degree of their involvement but also the form that it takes. Prior to 1990, they played no real direct role, while their general support for the Moi regime helped reinforce continued authoritarianism. Between 1990 and 1992, most bilateral donors followed the US ambassador's lead and increasingly acted as demiurges, adding their voices to domestic calls for political pluralism and backing this up with aid suspension. This caused the Moi regime to immediately modify the constitution, though not effect any further changes to permit free and fair electoral competition. Donors then abandoned the demiurge role and failed to recognise the significance of incomplete democratisation. They subsequently failed to live up to a custodial role, endorsing two sets of patently unfair general elections in 1992 and 1997, thus providing legitimacy to Moi's continued rule.

In the period immediately before and after those elections, donors assumed a role in husbandry, actively promoting, sometimes rather forcefully, a few 'compromises' (better described as minor concessions by the regime or major ones from the opposition) that would allow the holding of elections and the acceptance of officially announced results. Also preceding elections, donors occasionally played the role of midwives, encouraging the opposition to form a more united front. Following elections, donors showed very little interest in further democratisation, preferring to concentrate on economic issues. A partial exception is the question of corruption, which is also a political problem and became a central consideration in aid suspension by the Dutch in 1999 and a number of key donors in 2005. Though initially central to political liberalisation in 1991 and 1997, donor intervention has since 1992 actually impeded further democratisation on several occasions, most notably in instances of opposition boycotts and large-scale protest movements. Each time, donors appear to be motivated by concerns for stability and risk-avoidance, even though the uncertainty and violence that could accompany more rapid and radical change can produce a more robust democracy (Casper 2000).

How could donor democracy-promotion efforts have proved to be more successful in Kenya and by extension be more effective elsewhere? It is clear that the demiurge role involves the most active intervention and co-ordination, and requires a deeper understanding of the minimum requirements for a democracy to flourish. It is therefore most difficult to sustain. The custodian role requires a stronger commitment to seeing through all the changes that have been mandated and respect for the rules that have been agreed to. This enters into conflict with other donor interests, including economic reform and security issues. The donors' efforts in husbandry proved more predatory than developmental, which Evans would explain by too much autonomy in policy making. His recommendation for the achievement of the best results in industrial development is 'embedded autonomy', whereby state actors have organic links, sometimes informal, to other actors who neither dominate nor are dominated by the state. Evans ultimately expresses a preference for the midwife role, whose less aggressive interactions ensure the most productive results.

This chapter gives credence to a call for greater embeddedness of donor strategies in Kenyan civil society. Democratisation advances have occurred as a result of close interactions between donors and Kenyan civil society organisations, while each set retained its autonomy. Donors should neither expect Kenyan actors to follow blindly their preferred strategies, nor be expected to support blindly any or all civil society initiatives. Though achieving a consensus is complex and difficult, greater donor attention to domestic priorities and strategies is more likely to produce a road map to a sustainable democracy in Kenya.

Notes

1. By donors, I refer to bilateral governments and multilateral agencies that provide development assistance. Since much of the assistance is in the form of loans, 'lenders and donors' would be a more accurate term. However, in line with common usage and to avoid the clumsy formulation, I refer to them here simply as donors.

2. For a conceptualisation of transition and democracy, see Chapter 1 by Nasong'o and Murunga in this volume. *Political liberalisation* refers to the opening up of the political system to greater competition, whether or not it actually leads to democracy.

3. Unless otherwise stated, all aid disbursement data are gross figures expressed in US dollars, adjusted to 2001 prices, and are drawn from the OECD's International Development Statistics online, http://www.oecd.org/dataoecd/50/17/5037721.htm. Gross figures are used, rather than net, to exclude loan repayments, since the latter reflect conditions at the time of the loan and not at the time of repayment.

4. The UK, historically Kenya's main aid donor, had strong economic ties with Kenya and a close relationship with its government. The British had trained Kenya's police, army and secret service, while their ruling Conservative Party had a number of links with KANU. In addition, the British government was concerned with the future of Kenya's 70,000-strong Asian community, many of whom had a right of abode in the UK, according to a British High Commission document cited by Hempstone (1997: 109).

5. For the most in-depth account of the 1992 elections, see Throup and Hornsby (1998). For an analysis of the 'ethnic clashes' and donor responses to them, see Brown (2003).

6. The opposition leaders presented no threat to Western interests, since all were committed to debt repayment, continued macroeconomic reform and private investment as the motor of growth (Holmquist and Ford 1994: 7). Had the democratisation movement been led by a mobilised peasantry, industrial working class or proponents of the populist economic policies that were common in the 1950s and '60s, donors and the middle classes might have opposed multipartyism (Holmquist et al. 1994: 101).

7 Author interview with Sally Healy, First Secretary (Political), British High Commission, Nairobi, 6 March 1998.

8. Author interview with Gibson Kamau Kuria, NCEC Co-Convenor, Nairobi, 14 May 1998.

9. Author interview with Judith Geist, consultant, Nairobi, 15 April 1998.

References

Adar, K.G. (2000) 'The Interface Between Political Conditionality and Democratization: The Case of Kenya', *Scandinavian Journal of Development Alternatives and Area Studies*, vol. 19, nos 2–3.

Africa Watch (1991) *Kenya: Taking Liberties*, New York, NY: Africa Watch.

Amnesty International (1990) *Kenya: Silencing Opposition to One-Party Rule*, London: Amnesty International.

Barkan, J.D. (1993) 'Kenya: Lessons From a Flawed Election', *Journal of Democracy*, vol. 4, no. 3.

_____ and N. Ng'ethe (1998) 'Kenya Tries Again', *Journal of Democracy*, vol. 9, no. 2.

Brown, S. (2003) 'Quiet Diplomacy and Recurring "Ethnic Clashes" in Kenya', in C.L. Sriram and K. Wermester (eds), *From Promise to Practice: Strengthening UN Capacities for the Prevention of Violent Conflict*, Boulder, CO: Lynne Rienner.

_____ (2004) 'Theorising Kenya's Protracted Transition to Democracy', *Journal of Contemporary African Studies*, vol. 22, no. 3.

_____ (2005) 'Foreign Aid and Democracy Promotion: Lessons From Africa', *European Journal of Development Research*, vol. 17, no. 2.

Burnell, P. (ed.) (2000) *Democracy Assistance: International Co-operation for Democratization*, London: Frank Cass.

Carothers, T. (1999) *Aiding Democracy Abroad: The Learning Curve*, Washington, DC: Carnegie Endowment for International Peace.

Casper, G. (2000) 'The Benefits of Difficult Transitions', *Democratization*, vol. 7, no. 3.

Cowen, M. and M. Ngunyi (1997) 'Reconciling Reforms Within a Chain of Events: Prelude to the 1992 and 1997 Elections in Kenya', Nairobi: SAREAT.

Cox, M.G. et al. (eds) (2000) *American Democracy Promotion: Impulses, Strategies, and Impacts*, Oxford: Oxford University Press.

Crawford, G. (1997) 'Foreign Aid and Political Conditionality: Issues of Effectiveness and Consistency', *Democratization*, vol. 4, no. 3.

Dagne, T.S. (1992) 'Kenya: Political Unrest and U.S. Policy', Library of Congress, Congressional Research Service, 19 February.

Evans, P. (1995) *Embedded Autonomy: States and Industrial Transformation*, Princeton, NJ: Princeton University Press.

Geisler, G. (1993) 'Fair? What Has Fairness Got to Do With It? Vagaries of Election Observations and Democratic Standards', *Journal of Modern African Studies*, vol. 31, no. 4.

Harbeson, J.W. (1998) 'Guest Editor's Introduction: Political Crisis and Renewal in Kenya—Prospects for Democratic Consolidation', *Africa Today*, vol. 45, no. 2.

Harbeson, J.W. (1999) 'Rethinking Democratic Transitions: Lessons from Eastern and Southern Africa', in R. Joseph (ed.), *State, Conflict, and Democracy in Africa*, Boulder, CO: Lynne Rienner.

Hempstone, S. (1997) *Rogue Ambassador: An African Memoir*, Sewanee: University of the South Press.

Holmquist, F. and M. Ford (1992) 'Kenya: Slouching Toward Democracy', *Africa Today*, vol. 39, no. 3.

_____ and M. Ford (1994) 'Kenya: State and Civil Society the First Year after the Election', *Africa Today*, vol. 41, no. 4.

_____ (1998) 'Kenyan Politics: Toward a Second Transition?' *Africa Today*, vol. 45, no. 2.

Holmquist, F.W. et al. (1994) 'The Structural Development of Kenya's Political Economy', *African Studies Review*, vol. 37, no. 1.

Hook, S.W. (1998) '"Building Democracy" Through Foreign Aid: The Limitations of United States Political Conditionalities, 1992–96', *Democratization*, vol. 5, no. 3.

Human Rights Watch/Africa (1995) 'Kenya: Old Habits Die Hard. Human Rights Abuses Follow Renewed Foreign Aid Commitments', New York, NY: Human Rights Watch.

Katumanga, M. (2002) 'Internationalisation of Democracy: External Actors in Kenya Elections', in L. Chweya (ed.), *Electoral Politics in Kenya*, Nairobi: Claripress.

Kibwana, K. and W. Maina (1996) 'State and Citizen: Visions of Constitutional and Legal Reform in Kenya's Emergent Multi-party Democracy', in J. Oloka-Onyango et al. (eds), *Law and the Struggle for Democracy in East Africa*, Nairobi: Claripress.

Maina, K. wa (1992) 'The Future of Democracy in Kenya', *Africa Today*, vol. 39, nos 1–2.

Middleton, N. and P. O'Keefe (1998) *Disaster and Development: The Politics of Humanitarian Aid*, London: Pluto Press.

Murunga, G.M. and S.W. Nasong'o (2006) 'Bent on Self-Destruction: The Kibaki Regime in Kenya', *Journal of Contemporary African Studies*, vol. 24, no. 1.

Mutunga, W. (1999) *Constitution-Making from the Middle: Civil Society and Transition Politics in Kenya, 1992–1997*, Nairobi: SAREAT.

Nasong'o, S.W. (2005) *Contending Political Paradigms in Africa: Rationality and the Politics of Democratization in Kenya and Zambia*, New York and London: Routledge.

Ngunyi, M. (1997) 'Why Donors Do Not Care About Political Reform', *Daily Nation*, 20 July.

Olsen, G.R. (1998) 'Europe and the Promotion of Democracy in Post Cold War Africa: How Serious is Europe and For What Reason?', *African Affairs*, vol. 97, no. 388.

Pridham, G. et al. (eds) (1997) *Building Democracy? The International Dimension of Democratisation in Eastern Europe*, London: Leicester University Press.

Robinson, M. (1993) 'Will Political Conditionality Work?', *IDS Bulletin*, vol. 24, no. 1.

Rose, G. (2000/01) 'Democracy Promotion and American Foreign Policy', *International Security*, vol. 25, no. 3.

Southall, R. (1999) 'Re-forming the State? Kleptocracy and the Political Transition in Kenya', *Review of African Political Economy*, vol. 26, no. 79.

Stokke, O. (ed.) (1995) *Aid and Political Conditionality*, London: Frank Cass.

Swamy, G. (1996) 'Kenya: Patchy, Intermittent Commitment', in I. Husain and R. Faruqee (eds), *Adjustment in Africa: Lessons from Country Case Studies*, Brookfield: Avebury.

Thomas, C. (1998) 'L'économie politique d'une succession annoncée', *Politique Africaine*, no. 70.

Throup, D.W. and C. Hornsby (1998) *Multi-Party Politics in Kenya: The Kenyatta and Moi States and the Triumph of the System in the 1992 Elections*, Oxford: James Currey.

Udogu, E.I. (ed.) (1997) *Democracy and Democratization in Africa*, Leiden: Brill.

United Nations Development Programme (1996) *Human Development Report 1996*, New York, NY: Oxford University Press.

US Department of State (1992), 'Fact Sheet: Kenya', *US Department of State Dispatch*, vol. 3, no. 45.

Widner, J.A. (1992) *The Rise of a Party-State in Kenya: From 'Harambee!' to 'Nyayo!'*, Berkeley, CA: University of California Press.

World Bank (1995) *Word Development Report 1995*, New York, NY: Oxford University Press.

About the Contributors

Maurice N. Amutabi earned his PhD in History from the University of Illinois at Urbana-Champaign, USA. He is currently Assistant Professor of History at Central Washington University, Ellensburg. He has published chapters in several books, and his articles have appeared in *African Studies Review, Canadian Journal of African Studies, International Journal of Educational Development* and *Jenda: A Journal of Culture* and *African Women Studies*. He is co-author of *Nationalism and Democracy for People-Centred Development in Africa* (Moi University Press, 2000).

Theodora O. Ayot is currently Associate Professor of History at Northpark University in Chicago, Illinois. She has previously taught at Kenyatta University, Nairobi, Kenya, State University of New York at Fredonia, and served as Visiting Professor at the University of Jonkoping, College of Health Sciences, Jonkoping, Sweden. Her major academic publications include *A History of the Luo of Western Kenya 1590–1930* (1987), *The Luo Settlement in South Nyanza* (1987) and *Women and Political Leadership in Precolonial Period: Case Study of Chief Mang'ana of Kadem in Western Kenya* (1994).

Stephen Brown is Assistant Professor in the School of Political Studies, University of Ottawa, Canada. He received his PhD in Political Science from New York University. His research interests lie in the area of democratisation and the role of external actors, African politics, international development, and North–South relations. He has published articles on Kenya and Malawi in the *Journal of Contemporary African Studies, Third World Quarterly, Canadian Journal of African Studies* and *European Journal of Development Research* among others.

Margaret Gathoni Gecaga obtained her PhD degree from Kenyatta University, Kenya. She is a lecturer in the Department of Philosophy and Religious Studies at Kenyatta University, Secretary of the Ecumenical Association of Third World Theologians, and a member of the Circle for Concerned African Women Theologians (Kenyan Chapter). She has published several book chapters on religion and reproductive health, and religion and social conflict among other topics.

Edwin A. Gimode is a lecturer in history at Kenyatta University where he obtained his PhD degree. He teaches history of religions, history of science and technology, and philosophy of history. He specializes in cultural history and has published a number of works including a book, *Tom Mboya: A Biography* (1996). His articles have appeared in *Africa Development* and *All Africa Journal of Theology*. He also doubles as Deputy Dean of Students at Kenyatta University.

Godwin R. Murunga is a lecturer in history at Kenyatta University, Nairobi. He is currently completing graduate studies in history at Northwestern University, Evanston, USA. His articles have appeared in the *Journal of Third World Studies, Ufahamu, African Sociological Review, Journal of Contemporary African Studies* and *Africa Development*.

Mshaï S. Mwangola is a doctoral student in the Department of Performance Studies at Northwestern University, Evanston, USA. Her research interests focus on endogenous discourses embodied in performance and identity discourses. She has held numerous performances on different themes including some on African women achievers. Her publication appears in *Africa Development*.

Shadrack Wanjala Nasong'o earned his PhD from Northeastern University, Boston, USA. He is currently Assistant Professor of International Studies, Rhodes College, Memphis. He has published chapters in numerous books in Kenya, the US and India, and is author of *Contending Political Paradigms in Africa: Rationality and the Politics of Democratization in Kenya and Zambia* (2005). His articles have appeared in *Canadian Review of Studies in Nationalism, Nigerian Journal of International Affairs, International Review of Politics and Development, Journal of Third World Studies, Studies in Democratization, African and Asian Studies* and *Estudios de Asia y Africa*.

Adams G.R. Oloo is a political scientist and lecturer at the Department of Political Science and Public Administration, University of Nairobi, Kenya. He holds a PhD degree from the University of Delaware, USA. He has authored and co-authored articles on legislative, electoral and constitutional politics in Kenya. His current research is on coalitions and party politics in Kenya.

Index

Abacha, Sani, 48
Abagusii people, 64
Abaluhiya Football Club, 32
Abaluhiya Political Union, 28, 69
Abn-Amro-John Cato Nottingham
    case, 292
Abong'o, Philemon, 79
accountability, 5, 148; collective, 134;
    CSOs lack, 51; political parties, 115
accumulation, state-led model, 268–9
Achebe, Chinua, 206
Adar, Korwa, 219
Adhola, Shem Migot, 290
Adungosi, Titus, 243, 245; death in
    custody, 257
Africa Confidential, 287
Africa: afro-pessimism, 10; Development
    Bank, 321; economic development,
    263–6; intellectuals' role, 200; post-
    colonial states, 228; traditionalism, 29;
    Watch, 309
African Renaissance, 75
Agikuyu, society, 11, 65–6, 68, 72, 73;
    Agikuyu movement, 61; Mungiki
    movement, see Mungiki movement
Agina, Israel, 251
Ajulu, R., 32, 131, 222
Akara, Jimmy, 243
Ake, Claude, 4–6, 8, 53
Akorino religious organisation, 154
Akumu, Dennis, 237
Albright, Madeleine, 318
Ali, Mohammed, 257
All Africans People's Conference,
    Ghana, 145
Amadiume, I., 171
Amayo, Okiki, 279
Amnesty International, 243, 245, 307
Amutabi, Maurice N., 13, 191, 241, 243,
    269, 278, 281
Anderson, D., 72, 76, 83, 148

Anglo Leasing and Finance, 10
Anyona, George, 31, 97, 220, 238, 240–1,
    248; '4 trial', 248
Aringo, Oloo, 294
Arunga, Rachel, 186
Aseka, Eric Masinde, 206, 208
Asian communities Kenya, 142–3
assassinations, 31, 97, 152, 211, 235–7,
    246–7, 249, 253, 258, 309–10
Atieno-Odhiambo E.S., 211
attempted coup 1982, 242
Aubrey, Lisa, 179
Australia, protests, 311
authoritarianism: culture of, 94; electoral,
    302, 313; patrimonial, 13; post-colonial,
    165; pro-Western, 301; secular theories,
    58
Awori, Moody, 112, 156
Ayittey, George, 277
Ayot, Theodora, 12

Babangida, Ibrahim, 48
Babukusu people, 61, 64
Balala, Najib, 150
Balala, Sheikh, 154
Barclays Bank, 290
Baring, Evelyn, 232
Barkan, J.
Basinde Isukha rite of passage, 138
Bayley, D., 228
Benin, 38, 47
Betrayal in the City, 216
Biwott, Nicholas, 285, 289, 309–11
Biya, Paul, 8
Bogonko clan, 64
Bratton, M., 26, 28
Brazeal, Aurelia, 317
Brazil, 304
'briefcase' political parties, 102–3
Britain, see UK
British East African Protectorate, 230

British-American Tobacco Kenya, 102
Brown, Stephen, 14–15
Brownhill, L.S., 76
Bukusu community, 101; Union, 65
Bundu Dia Kingo, Congolese
    fundamentalist movement, 73
Burundi, 166
Bush, George H., 308
Bush, George W., 321
Bushnell, Prudence, 320
Busolo, Saul, 241

Canada, 319
capitalism, gender impact, 173–4;
    pro-policies, 234, 267, 271
Carothers, T., 6–7
Catholic Church, 40; Justice and Peace
    Commission, 107
Ceacescu, Nicolai, 204
Central Organisation of Trade Unions
    (COTU), 31, 98
Chalker, Lynda, 317
Chandhoke, N., 25, 37
Chazan, N., 24–5, 29, 34
Cheserem, Micah, 276, 293
Chiluba, Fredrick, 49
Christian Missionary Society, 142
Christianity, 74; Church of the Province
    of Kenya, 40; conversion to, 81;
    eschatology, 64; groupings, 59;
    polarised, 27; renouncement, 66
Chunga, Bernard, 252–3
civil society, 11, 20, 93; colonial period, 28;
    concept of, 23–4; organisations
    (CSOIs), 25, 34–7, 41, 45, 47–8, 51–2;
    role of, 19
class, 170; analysis, 74; differentiation;
    process, 268
Clay Edward, 322
Coalition for a National Convention, 39
Coast People's Party, 28
CODESRIA 10th General Assembly,
    Kampala, 211
Cohen, Herman, 307
Cold War: end of, 90; Kenyan role, 267
Collaborative Centre for Gender and
    Development, 183
Colomer, J.M., 8
colonialism, British in Kenya, 25, 141, 143,
    146, 175, 178; cash crop farming, 174;

emergency powers, 232–3; ethnicity
    impact, 208; gender impact, 175;
    oppressive legal system, 230; patronage
    systems, 27–8; police legacy, 229;
    repression, 164
commodity prices, 273, 306
Communist Party, Leninist vanguard, 24
conditionality, donor, 282; selective, 302
Conference of East African Women
    Parliamentarians, 182
Constitution of Kenya Review
    Commission (CKRC), 45–6,
    136–7, 283
constitutional reform, 42
corruption, 10, 49, 59, 116, 270, 280–1,
    288–90, 292, 305, 310, 317, 320, 322,
    324
Cote d'Ivoire, as model economy, 266
Cunningham, L.S., 63
currency devaluation, 273

Dahl, R., 92
Danziger, J.N., 169
Davidian sect, Waco, 22
debt servicing, 273; default, 315
December Twelve Movement (DTM),
    244–5; *Pambana* newsletter, 34
decision-making power, 5–6; gender
    discrimination, 166; women
    marginalisation, 179; youth
    marginalisation, 137
democracy: concepts of, 130, 132;
    pre-colonial, 133; varieties of, 4–5
Democratic Party (DP), 82, 99–101, 105,
    112, 282, 314
Denmark aid cut, 309–10
Department of Literature University of
    Nairobi, 238
detention without trial, 234–5, 237, 241–2,
    252, 255–6
development: 'conditionality', 100;
    imperative, 31
Devonshire White Paper, 142
Dini ya Msambwa, 22, 26, 59, 61, 64–5, 85;
    cross-ethnic followers, 27
Diop, Makhtar, 296
Diouf, M., 140, 158
division of labour, 188; sexual, 172–3;
    social, 191
dominant party system, South Africa, 121

Donde, Joe, Parliamentary Bill, 118, 293–5
donors/lenders, 14–15, 285; anti-opposition pressure, 315; authoritarian connivance, 264; Consultative group, 309, 311; CSO support, 51; democratisation strategies, 303–4; disarming of, 272; governance contradictions, 286, 295, 301–2, 312, 318; IPPG report response, 44, 318–19; Moi support, 288, 306, 313, 320, 323–5; opposition funding, 122; poor coordination, 274; pressure, 43, 46, 98, 314; profitability logic, 265; reform depoliticisation, 275–7; US policy, 294
Douglas, M., 61
Dream Team, The, 290–2
Drewal, M.T., 133
Driberg, J.H., 173
drought, 271
Durkheim, Emile, 62

Earth Summit Rio de Janeiro, 218
East African Association (EAA), 142, 231
East African Legislative Assembly, 186
East African Regional Conference on Women Kampala, 185
Education Centre for Women in Democracy (ECWD), 183
Education, gender inequality, 179
Ekeh, P., 28
El-Basaidy, Abdulghfur, 80
elections, 7–8, 131; 1966 'little', 97; 1983, 278; 1988, 38, 279; 1990s, 45, 99, 108–9, 113–14, 121, 313, 319; 2002, 46, 82, 103, 111, 116, 150, 165, 188, 191, 221, 282; Commission (ECK), 115, 314; donor acceptance, 315; focus on, 92; funding, 115; laws, 181; rigging, 270; women's representation, 185–6
Eliade, M., 60
Eliot, Charles, 142
elite(s), 5, 12–13, 67, 91, 145, 176, 270, 288; development ideology, 31; exclusion politics, 171; factions, 42; foreign capital link, 268; GEMA, 32, 180; intellectuals co-option, 222; Kenyatta era, 31; Kikuyu, 69; Luo, 104; -mass relations, 95; post-colonial, 29, 37, 164–5; recruitment by, 202; social aspirations, 201; survival instinct, 277

Engels, Friedrich, 200
Engendering the Political Process Programme (EPPP), 186
Ethiopia, 304
ethnic clashes, politically motivated, 45, 69, 77, 93, 109; 1992, 67; Mombasa, 108
ethnicity: chauvinists, 205; ethnocentrism, 12, 91; economic policy, 306; politicised, 9, 39, 99, 101, 103–4, 111, 123, 142, 185, 208
European Union (EU), 305, 316, 321; aid suspension, 318
Evangelical Fellowship of Kenya (EFK), 68
Evans, P., 304, 324, 326
Ewait, R.H., 230
exile, 200, 204, 244, 248–9

factionalism, 12, 91, 122
Falana, Jilo, 220–1
'fanatics'/cadres, 21
Fanon, Frantz, 134
Farmers' unions, 33
Fatton, R., 171
female circumcision, 66, 81
feminism, Western, 167–8
fiction, works of, 208, 214
Finland protests, 311
folk tales, 140
forced labour systems, colonial, 26
Ford Foundation, 51
foreign capital, Kenya entrenchment, 267–8, 270; investment fall, 284
Forum for Restoration of Democracy (FORD), 38–9, 49, 52, 98, 104, 309; divisions in, 99–100, 111; intellectuals' role, 217; leaders' arrest, 310
Forum for Restoration of Democracy Asili (FORD-A), 101, 105, 110, 112–13, 148, 314
Forum for Restoration of Democracy in Kenya (FORD-K), 101, 105, 110, 112–13, 116–17, 148, 285, 314
Forum for Restoration of Democracy for the People (FORD-P), 101, 110, 118; NARC co-optation, 120
France, 319; Moi support, 314, 316
free markets donor promotion, 304
Freire, Paulo, 203, 205
Fukuyama, Francis, 4

Gachukia, Eddah, 180
Gakonya, Ngonya wa, 70
Garvey, Marcus, 75
Gecaga, Jemima, 180
Gecaga, Margaret, 11
Gender Equality Bill, 118
gender: discrimination, 177–8; gendering, 166–7
General Service Unit (GSU), 42
general workers' strikes 1947, 144
Gerdts, Michael, 319
Germany, 316, 320, 322; aid pressure, 314
Gethi, Ben, 236
Ghana, 48, 266, 288
Gichuru, James, 234
Gikandi, S., 214, 215
Gikuyu culture, 71; Gikuyu Embu and Meru Association (GEMA), 32, 69, 180
Gimode, Edwin, 13, 67, 269, 278, 280
Githongo, John, 322
Githunguri teachers' training college, 144
Gitonga, Afrifa, 5
Goldenberg scandal, 116, 287, 317, 320
good governance, rhetoric of, 301
Gor Mahia, ethnic organisation, 32
governance: concept of, 14, 265; donor contradictions, 295; 'good' rhetoric, 301; overpersonalised crisis, 48
Gramsci, Antonio, 201
Green Belt Movement, 217
Guevara, Che, 200
Gumbonzvanda, N., 181
Gumo, Fred, 148
Gutto, Shadrack, 211

Habwe, Ruth, 180
Hancox, Allan, 280
Harbeson, J.W., 7, 46
Hardinge, Arthur, 230
Harris, W., 203
Hema ya Ngai wi Mwoyo religious organisation, 154
Hempstone, Smith, 247, 282, 307–8, 312, 315
Hinga, Waiyaki wa, 74
Hodder-Williams, R., 28
Hoffer, E., 21
Holy Spirit Mobile Forces Uganda, 59, 62
Honecker, Erich, 204
Hopkins, N., 62

Hornsby, C., 102
Hurd, Douglas, 307

I Will Marry When I Want, 215
Ibrahim, Mohammed, 248
identity: –citizenship relationship, 140; issues of, 188; shared community, 141
Ihonvbere, J.O., 48
illiteracy, 189
Imanyara, Gitobu, 104, 150, 248, 283, 309–10
Imbuga, Francis, 216
IMF (International Monetary Fund), 14, 50, 263, 265; African development assumptions, 266; anti-corruption failure, 289; conditionalities, 286; institutional pressure on, 321; loan postponements/resumptions, 273, 314, 318, 320; negotiations, 287
Imperial British East African Company, 230
Imunde, Lawford, case of, 253
Independence constitution, 176–7
India, 304
inequality, new forms, 140
Institute for Education, 107
intellectuals, 13, 21; academic/philosophical, 206; activist, 202; authoritarian/bourgeois, 204–5; co-opted, 211–12, 221–2; East Africa 1970s, 210; exile, 200; left-wing 33; public spokespersons, 199; 'traditional', 201
inter-generational struggle, 155–9
Inter-Parliamentary Union (IPU), 165
Inter-Parties Parliamentary Group (IPPG), 44, 220–1, 318–19, 324
interest rates, 294; deregulated, 293
Intergovernmental Authority on Development (IGAD), 43
International Finance Corporation South Africa, 290
International Maize and Wheat Improvement Centre, 290
International Federation of Women Lawyers-Kenya (FIDA-K), 184
Iraq, US objectives, 309
Islam, conversion to, 80; Islamic Party of Kenya, 99, 154
Itwíka, 'spirit' of, 132–3

Japan, 316, 319, 321
Jaycox, Edward, 287
Jeffa, Musa, 243
Jeshi la Embakasi, 148
Jeshi la Mbela, 148
Jeshi la Mzee vigilante group, 42, 148
Jirongo, Cyrus, 149
Johnson, John, 307
journalists, repression of, 243
judiciary, politicised, 251–4, 280

Kabiru, Mugo wa, 72
Kaggia, Bildad, 31, 96, 234
Kaguthi, Jospeh, 292
Kakwanja, P., 72, 76, 78
Kalenjin people, 69; Political Alliance, 28;
    warriors, 70
Kamenju, Grant, 210
Kamiruthu village theatre, 215; Group
    (KTG), 31
Kamiti maximum security prison, 204, 235,
    237–8, 243, 256
Kamotho Joseph, 79
kanzala, 217
Kapten, George, 182
Karam, A.M., 188, 190
Karanja, Peter Njenga, 250
Karing'a movement, Kikuya, 59, 61, 64, 66,
    71; political leaders, 69; squatters'
    support for, 85
Karinga Schools Association, 66, 144
Kariuki, Geoffrey, 248
Kariuki, Josiah Mwangi, 31, 211;
    assassination of, 235–36, 257–8, 270
Kariuki, Mirugi, 221, 248
Kariuki, Ngotho, 248, 253
Kariuki, Terry, 236
Kariuki, Wang'ondu, 243
Karua, Martha, 186
Karume, Njenha, 156
Karura Forest campaign, 218
Kathangu, Njeru, 148, 248
Katiba Watch, 222
Katumanga, M., 21
Kaunda, Kenneth, 48, 49
Kavirondo Taxpayers Welfare Association,
    142
Kaviti, Jason, 246
Kaya Bombo Youth, 148
Keen, John, 237, 248

kekebo Maragoli rite of passage, 138
Kennedy, Edward, 308
Kenneth, Peter, 112
Kenya: aid flows, 305; as model economy,
    266; European inhabitants, 304;
    governance, 264; growth rates, 267;
    police origins, 229; population ratio,
    136; settler class, 143, 270
Kenya African Union (KAU), 145,
    231, 258
Kenya African Democratic Union
    (KADU), 29, 69, 96
Kenya African National Union (KANU),
    9, 29, 41, 43–6, 48, 50, 69–70, 76–7,
    80, 83–4, 98, 108–9, 114, 117, 119, 154,
    165, 200–1, 207; bourgeois intellectuals,
    213; Disciplinary Committee, 278–9;
    internal struggle, 96; NARC
    co-option, 118, 120; sexism, 185–6;
    youth wing, 147, 149
Kenya African Rifles (KAR), 230
Kenya African Socialist Union, attempted
    formation, 97
Kenya African Study Union (KASU), 145
Kenya Anti-Corruption Authority
    (KACA), 288–9, 292
Kenya Bankers Association, 294
Kenya Broadcasting Corporation
    (KBC), 247
Kenya Cashew Nuts Ltd, 285
Kenya Episcopal Conference (KEC),
    67–8, 153
Kenya Grain Growers Cooperative
    Union, 33
Kenya Independent Schools Association,
    144
Kenya National Congress (KNC), 100, 112
Kenya National Democratic Alliance
    (KENDA), 123
Kenya, National Schools and Colleges
    Drama Festival, 153
Kenya People's Union (KPU), 31, 96, 237;
    proscribed, 240; socialist agenda, 97
Kenya Post and Telecommunications
    Corporation (KPTC), 280
Kenya Teachers College Githunguri, 66
Kenya Times Media Trust, 182
Kenya Youth Foundation Movement
    (KYFM), 40
Kenya-Re, 285

Kenyatta, Jomo, 10, 29, 32, 65, 67, 72, 83, 96, 97, 132–4, 146, 152, 154, 176, 178, 180, 252, 266; anti-intellectual, 211; arrest of 1952, 232; authoritarianism, 30, 177, 269; corruption, 306; death of, 238–9; dominant elite, 31; economic policy, 234, 267, 271; ethnic manipulation, 208; family, 102; release of, 233
Kenyatta National Hospital, 256
Kenyatta, Uhuru, 83, 149–50
Kenyatta University College, 223, 241, 250, 257
Khamati, Yvonne, 150–1
Khaminwa, John, 241, 248
Khan, M.H., 277
Khaniri, George, 149
Khaniri, Nicodemus, 112
Ki-Zerbo, Joseph, 288
Kiano, Gikonyo, 183
Kiano, Janet, 183
Kibaki, Mwai: government/regime, 3, 6, 44, 49, 70, 99, 121, 155, 157, 213, 219–20, 240, 271, 282–3, 296, 302, 314, 321, 324; corruption, 322–3; ethno-regional bias, 9
Kibisu, Peter, 237
Kibwana, Kivutha, 49, 171, 177, 202–3, 217, 219, 221, 223–4, 283
Kijana, Michael Wamalwa, 105, 113, 207
Kikuyu communities, 70, 97, 101, 113; Central Association, 26, 144; Independent Schools Association (KISA), 66; Karing'a movement, see *Karing'a*
Kilimo, Lina, 186
Kimani, Kihika, 79, 83
Kimondo, Kiruhi, 113
King, Martin Luther, 75
Kinuthia, Rumba, 248
Kinyatti, Maina wa, 211, 241, 250
Kipipri by-election, 121
Kipkorir, B., 201
Kipkulei, Benjamin, 276
Kirui, Nancy, 187
Kisumu, 246; Tom Mboya Labour College, 213
Kitsao, Jay, 206
Kittony, Zipporah, 183, 185–6
Kituyi, Mukhisa, 104, 150, 217, 221, 241

Kiwanuka, Semakula, 210
Kodhek, Argwings, 31, 211
Koech, Jogn, 9
Koinange, Mbiyu, 234, 236
Kolloa 1950 battle, 65
Kombo Report, 289
Konchellah, Gideon, 112
Kones, Kipkalia, 9
Kony, J., 59
Kubai, Fred, 145
Kuria, Gibson Kamau, 211, 219, 249, 283; exile, 249

Labour Party of Kenya (LPK), 123
Lakwena, Alice, 59, 62
Lamba, Davinder, 219
Lancaster House Conference, 176; Generation (LHG), 12, 134–5, 145–6, 155–9
land distribution, 69
Law Society of Kenya (LSK), 32, 98, 253
League of Kenya Women Voters (LKWV), 182–3
Leakey, Richard, 290, 292–3
Legco, 143, 145
Lemarchand, R., 170
Liberal Democratic Party, 9, 84, 112, 117; NARC faction, 120
Likowa, Owino, 113
Limuru initiative, 219
Lipset, S., 92
Literature Students Association, University of Nairobi, 152
Lo Liyong, Taban, 210
Lokopoyit, Edward, 256
Lorber, J., 167–8
Lords Resistance Army, Uganda, 59
Lost Generation (LG), 12, 134–5, 156–9
Luhiya communities, 69–70
Lumumba, P.L.O., 44
Luo communities, 64, 69–70, 97, 101, 113; elite, 104; *Piny Owacho* movement, 142; *Taliban* militia, 82; Union, 32; widow guardianship, 207; young people, 138

M'Inot, Kathurima, 219
M'Maitsi, Vincent, 149
M'Mukindia, Kirugi, 112
Maasai United Front, 28
Maasai warriors, 70

Maathai, Wangari, 49, 182–3, 186, 189, 203, 217–18, 220–1
MacKinnon, William, 229
Madagascar, 38
Maeneleo ya Wanawake Organisation, women's organisation, 33, 98, 185; KANU co-option, 183
Magwaga, Ben, 112
majimbo regionalist system, 29; *Majimboism*, 205, 207
Mak'Onyango, Otieno, 243, 252
Makere University, 210
Makwere, Ali, 156
Malakisi riots 1948, 65
Malawi, 38, 47
Mali, 38, 47
Mama, A., 170
Mamdani, Mahmood, 20, 23–5, 210
Man of Kafira, 216
Mango, Christine, 202
Manyara, David, 84
Martin, Dominic, 255
Marx, Karl, 200; Marxism, 169, 208
Maseno University, 212, 224
Masinde, Elijah, 64–5, 70, 85
Matano, Maryam, 186
matatu routes: fight for, 80, 85; Vehicle Owners Association (MVOA), 33
Mathu, Eliud, 143
Matiba, Kenneth, 38, 50, 70, 98–9, 101, 104–5, 110, 150, 155, 247–8, 255–6, 282, 307
Mau Mau, struggle, 27, 62, 66, 74, 77, 85, 146, 232–3; women's role, 175
Mazrui, Alamin, 200, 203–4, 211, 214
Mazrui, Ali, 197–8, 200–2, 210
Mbaku, J.M., 52
Mbarire, Cecily, 150
Mbela, David, 148
Mbiti, Daniel, 206
Mbogo, Jael, 181
Mboya, Paul, 138
Mboya, Tom, 31, 96, 129, 145, 234; assassination of, 97, 235–6, 258
Mbugua, Bedan, 254
Meme, Julius, 290
Mghanga, Mwandawiro, 242, 244–5
military the, junior ranks, 154
Millenarian movements, 22; ideology, 64
Miriti Petkay, 112

Misoi Joseph, 44, 221
Mkangi, Katama, 203, 211, 219, 242
Mobutu, 48
Moi, Daniel arap, 3, 6, 8, 10, 14, 33, 43–5, 48–50, 67, 76, 82–3, 100–1, 104, 108, 111, 147, 149–50, 152, 154–5, 180, 183, 185, 236, 238, 240, 246, 252, 285, 302; anti-intellectual, 211; as Interior Minister, 255; attempted coup against, 32, 242; British support for, 307–9; clientilism, 109; culture of fear creation, 239; donor disarming/manipulation, 272, 287, 295, 319, 323; donor disillusionment, 98; donor support, 320; ethnic manipulation, 208; extralegal powers, 280; NCEC manipulation, 220; police use, 227, 247; PR, 291; purges, 278; scale of corruption, 306; sexism, 182
Moi, Philip, 289
Moi University, 213
Momanyi, Protus, 112
Mombasa: ethnic clashes, 108; US naval base, 305
Mosley, P., 272
motherhood, 168
Movement for Dialogue and Non-violence (MODAN), 44
Movement for Multiparty Democracy Zambia, 49, 50
Mozambique, 38, 47, 166; *Naprama* movement, 59; PR electoral system, 191
Mtimama, William, 112
Mützelberg, Bernd, 317
Mudavadi, Musalia, 149, 276, 286
Muge, Alexander, 154, 201, 209
Mugo, Beth, 186
Mugo, Micere, 250
Muite, Paul, 104, 116, 150, 253, 310
Mukhwana, David, 246–7
Mule, Harry, 274–5
Muli, Matthew Guy, 252
Muliro, Masinde, 38, 49, 99, 150, 217, 237, 310
mumbo cult, 59, 64, 85
Munene, M., 177
Mungai, Njoroge, 234
Mungatana, Danson, 150

Mungiki movement, 11, 59, 68, 70–2, 74–5, 81, 148, 154; armed, 77; cleansing rituals, 73; infiltration, 82; Kairobangi incident, 83; political use of, 84–5; urban vigilantism, 76, 78, 80

Munuhe, John, 241

Munya, Peter (Safina), 84, 118

Munyao, Joseph, 279

Murunga, Godwin, 14, 67, 222

Murungi, Kiaitu, 104, 219, 221, 223, 283, 322; exile, 249

Musuveni, Yoweri, 211, 288

Musyimi, Mutava, 201, 209, 219

Musyoka, Kalonzo, 157

Mutahi, Wahome, *Whispers* column, 209

Mutai, Chelegat (Philomena), 154, 180

Muthaura, Francis, 156

Mutua, Kisilu, 235

Mutunga, Willy, 49, 203, 211, 219, 221, 223, 283

Mwachai, Marere wa, 186

Mwachofi, Mwanghazi, 290

Mwakenya (Nationalists' Union), 244–5, 249, 253, 258; *Mpatanishi* newsletter, 34

Mwakwere, Ali, 112

Mwalulu, Jackson, 150

Mwangale, Elijah, 236

Mwangi, Wilfred, 290

Mwangola, Mshaï, 12

Mwanzi, Henry, 204, 223

Mwendwa, Winifred Nyiva, 180, 185

Mwenje, David, 79, 148

Mwewa, Grace, 186

Mwiraria, David, 322

Mwiria, Kilemi, 202, 221, 223–4

Mzrai D.K.L., 245

Nabudere, Dani, 210

Nabutola, Rebecca, 186

Nabwera, Burudi, 279

Naikuni, Titus, 290, 293

Nairobi, 78, 84, 245; City Council workers, 79; Makadara constituency, 151; University of, 152, 154, 217, 223, 241, 243, 250

Nakuru town, 245

Namibia, 166

Nasong'o, Shadrack, 11–12, 131, 243, 278, 281–2

Nassir, Shariff, 79, 279

National Alliance (Party) of Kenya (NAK), 10, 84, 117

National Alliance Rainbow Coalition (NARC), 10, 46, 48, 111, 116, 119, 165, 191, 202, 217, 222, 224, 257, 296; ethnicity use, 208; infighting, 95; KANU parachutists, 322; Memorandum of Understanding (MoU), 9, 84, 158; NAK wing, 120; promises reneged, 47; unofficial elections, 112; women government members, 186–7

National Cereals and Produce Board (NCPB), 281

National Commission on the Status of Women (NCSW), 183

National Convention Executive Council (NCEC), 41–5, 203, 219–21, 283, 317–18; donor pressure on, 319

National Convention Preparatory Committee (NCPC), 40–1

National Council of the Women of Kenya (NCWK), 184

National Council of the Churches of Kenya (NCCK), 39, 67–8, 81, 107, 153

National Development Party (NDP), 83, 101, 105, 110; dissolution, 117

National Party of Kenya (NPK), 117, 191

National Security Intelligence Services (Special Branch), 234, 242, 251

National Union of Kenya Students (NUKS), 40

National Youth Policy Steering Committee, 136–7

National Youth Service, 147

nationalist movement, 29

Ndegwa, Philip, 274

Ndegwa, S.N., 9

Ndenga, Onyango, 243

Nderi, Ignatius, 237

Ndichu, Stephen, 83

Ndwiga, Ireri, 112

neo-patrimonialism, 306, 323

neoliberalism, 23

Netherlands, aid: cancellation, 320; suspension, 325

Ng'ang'a, Mukaru, 211, 224, 241, 249

Ng'anga, James Maina, 81

Ngala, Katana, 149

Ngei, Paul, 154
Ngeny, Kipng'eno arap, 280, 289
Ngilu Charity, 105, 186, 191, 208, 220
NGOs (non-governmental organisations), 35; corrupt, 51; pioneer, 28
Ngunyi, M., 316
NICs (newly industrialised countries), 304
Nietzsche, F., 205
Nigeria, 48
Njama ya ita (council of war), 133
Njenga, Maina, 70, 83
Njonjo, Apollo, 105, 208
Njonjo, Charles, 96, 236, 241, 279
Njoroge, Daniel, 156
Njoroge, Julius, 113
Njoroge, Nahashon Isaac Njenga, 236
Njoya, Timothy, 201, 209, 219
non-party democracies, 4
Norfolk Hotel massacre, 231
Norway, aid cessation, 309
Nsibambi, Apollo, 210–11
Nthenge, George, 49
Ntimama, William Ole, 9
Nyachae, Simeon, 9, 101, 110, 274, 156, 285
Nyagh, Jeremiah, 201
Nyagh, Joseph, 112
Nyamora, Loise, 254
Nyamora, Pius, 254
Nyang'oro, J.E., 24–5
Nyangira, Nicholas, 203, 211, 224
Nyanjiru, Mary Muthoni, 175
Nyati House, 250
Nyayo Bus Service Corporation, 33
Nyayo house: torture chambers, 250–1, 257
Nyayo Tea Zones Development Corporation, 33
Nyayo patronage system, 69
Nyoike, Kimani wa, 110, 279
Nyerere, Julius, 173, 211
Nyong'o, Peter Anyang, 32, 104, 150, 180, 202, 207–8, 211, 217, 223
Nzeki, Ndingi Mwana, 201, 209
Nzomo, Maria, 170, 187

O'Donnell, G., 6
oaths, 66, 72–3, 77, 81
Obondo, Tom, 113

Ochieng, William R., 200, 210; co-option of, 212–14
Odinga, Oginga, 31, 38, 49, 96–7, 99, 105, 110, 116, 135, 150, 154–5, 201, 217, 234–7, 240, 243, 310; death of, 113
Odinga, Raila, 44, 50, 98, 101, 104–5, 110, 113, 149, 157, 219–20, 243, 248, 251–2, 307
Oduor-Otieno, Martin Luke, 290, 293
Ogego, Peter Oginga, 242
Ogot, Allan, 210
Ogot, B., 63
Ogot, Grace, 202
oil price shocks, impact, 267, 271–2
Ojiambo, Julia, 180–1
Okullu, Henry, 201, 209
Okondo, Peter, 279
Oloo, A., 12, 67, 278, 281
Oloo, David Onyango, 242–3
Oloo, Peter, 243
Olurnsola, V.A., 169
Omamo, Raychelle, 187
Omar, Onyango, 219
Ommani, Javan, 112
Oneko, Achieng, 154, 237
Oniang'o, Ruth, 202
Onyango, C.N., 245
Onyango, Grace, 182
Opiata, Oddindo, 241
Opiyo, James, 250
Orengo, James, 44, 150, 176, 203–4, 217, 219, 281
Oruka, Odera, 206–7
Orwa, Katete, 206
Osundwa, Wycliffe, 112
Otiende, Joseph, 201
Otieno, Alfred, 243, 252
Otto, R., 60
Ouko, Robert, murder of 152, 211, 246–7, 249, 253, 309–10
overcentralisation, 9
Overseas Motor Company, 284
Oyewúmí, O., 168
Oyugi, Edward, 211, 248, 257

P'Bitek, Okot, 210–11
Pal Gai, Yash, 46
parliament: empowerment, 118; limited powers, 119; women's representation, 165–6, 185, 188, 192

participatory development, donor rhetoric, 275

Party of Independent Candidates of Kenya (PICK), 123

patrimonialism, 95

patronage, aid crunch, 307, 312

Pattni, Kamlesh, 116

People's Coalition for Change, 118

personality cult, 180

Petals of Blood, 215

Phillips, A., 166

Pinto, Pio Gama, 31, 211, 234; assassination of, 235, 258

police, 78; elite protectors, 229; politicisation, 231, 249

Policy Advisory Foundation (PAF), 40

political parties, 11, 30, 39, 91; alternative, 20, 38; defections, 99, 111; ethnically based, 94; funding, 102–3, 113–17; ideology lack, 112; infighting, 95; institutional weakness, 101; internal democracy lack, 100, 105–7, 110, 122; opposition, 12, 92; personality cults, 111; sale of, 123; state harassment, 109; theories of, 93; wealthy opposition leaders, 282, 284, 287; youth wings, 147–8

political prisoners, campaign for, 218

politics: alternative sites, 153; environmental, 217-18; gender dynamics, 166, 171; generational, 133–4, 140, 146, 156–7; indigenous systems, 132; military power, 58; multiparty, 47, 90; patronage, 280; post-colonial, 134; pre-colonial, 25; pro-capitalist, 234; street, 282–3, 287; student, 152

popular mobilisation, donor hostility, 318

poverty, 189; feminised, 190

Powell, Colin, 321

Presidency, the, 156, 177; accountability lack, 270 centralised power, 3, 233–4, 264, 269; extralegal powers, 280; Office of, 214, 221, 248

price rises, basics, 286

print media, repression of, 45, 154, 254–5

prisons, beatings, 256–7; maximum security, 235; system, 255

privatisation, 306; IMF demands, 281; KANU ambivalence, 285

profitability donor logic, 265

Public Accounts Committee, 118

Public Investments Committee, 118

public–private dichotomy, 172–3, 175, 178, 182, 191

Rastafari movement, 75

Rawlings, Jerry, 48, 288

Referendum 2005, 10

regional inequalities, 69

Reicher, S., 62

religion: cosmology, 58; movements, 11; new movements (NRMs), 63; –political movements, 61; politicised, 103; symbolic resources, 62

representation, principle of, 91

repression, donor inaction, 305–7; agencies, 13–14

Rika Ria Forty, 27

rites of passage, youth, 138–40

Robert F. Kennedy Memorial Center for Human Rights, 309

Roberts, P., 174

Robinson, C., 200

Rodney, Walter, 200, 210

role socialisation theory, 167

Roman Catholic Church, 67

Rothchild, D., 169

Rowland, 'Tiny', 310

Rubia, Charles, 38, 98, 247–8, 255, 257, 307

Rugumayo, Edward, 210

rule of law, 5

Runyenjes Football Club, 148

Ruto, William, 149

Rwanda, 166; genocide complicity, 204; PR electoral system, 191

Saba Saba massacre, 76, 98, 248

Saba-Saba Aisili, 101, 110

'sacred' the, 60; land, 66

Said, Edward, 197–9

Saitoti, George, 112, 202, 289, 322

Sang, Ewdna, 182

SAREAT NGO, corrupt, 51

Scandanavian countries: aid cut threat, 308; Moi critique, 316

Schmitter, P.C., 6

scholarship, Africanist, 23

secondary school students, 153

secularisation process, 58
Senegal, Marbouts, 63
Seroney, Jean Marie, 31, 238
Serut, John, 112
settler class, Kenya, 143, 270
Shamalla, Japheth, 112
Sharp, L.A., 151
Shaw, Patrick, 237
Shikuku, Martin, 31, 38, 99, 110, 150, 217, 238–9, 256, 310
Shivji, Issa, 210
Sijeyo, Wasonga, 237
Simiyu, V., 132
Singh, Makhan, 145
Smith, D.E., 62
Social Democratic Party (SDP), 100, 105, 191, 208
social movements, 20–2, 48–9; stages, 131
social science, mainstream, 5
Somalia, 304–5; US objectives, 309
South Africa, 38, 166; dominant party system, 121; PR electoral system, 191
South Korea, 304
Special Branch, see National Security Intelligence Services
Stakeholders Support Group, 321
state, the: assets undervaluation, 285; authoritarian, 48, 108; cereal marketing control, 274–5; civil society dichotomy, 23; colonial, 37; colonial deconstruction failure, 13, 29; developmentalism, 34; economic role, 268–9, 271; enterprises, 280–1; ethnic patronage, 100; –intellectuals relationship, 198; liberal theory, 170; NGO relations, 30; one-party, 67; patronage, 121; –party fusion, 114; SAPs legitimacy impact, 265; the, structural–functional perspective, 169
Steiner, F., 61
structural adjustment lending/policies (SAL/SAPs), 19, 34, 59, 263, 273, 288, 306; Africanist literature, 277; conditionality failure, 276; externalities unequal distribution, 50; politics of, 14; state legitimacy impact, 265
Student Organisation of Nairobi University (SONU), 40
students, arrests of, 241
Sudan, 304; US objectives, 309

Sundaram, J.K., 277
Sunkuli, Julius, 289
Supreme Council of Kenya Muslims (SUPKEM), 80
Sweden, 321; aid, 310; Swedish International Development Agency, 52

Taita Hills Association, 26; Mombasa protest, 144
Tanzania, 166, 249, 304
technocrats, political weakness, 274, 276
Tent of the Living God Group, 70–1
Tett, Betty, 186
Thatcher, Margaret, 308–9
theatre, power of, 215–16
Thiong'o, Ngugi wa, 31, 72, 200, 203–4, 211, 214–15, 217, 223, 238, 244, 255
Thuku, Harry, 142, 231
Thungu, Wanyoike, 237
Thuo, Chege, 235
Tolle, Esher, 186
Tomkys, Roger, 309, 311
torture, 249–51, 254
trade licensing policy, 270
trade union movement, 145
transaction costs, business, 284
transition politics, 4–6, 37, 122, 131, 141, 151; personalised, 52; 'strategic', 8; stages, 7
transitional ceremonies, traditional politics, 133
Troon, John, 246
Tuju, Raphael, 112
Turner, T.E., 76

'Ufungamano Initiative' (DPK), 46, 155, 219
Uganda, 4, 59, 166, 249, 266, 288, 305
Uhuru Generation (UG), 12, 134–5, 157–9
Uhuru Park: campaign, 182, 217–18; hunger strike, 249
ujamaa (communalism), 173
UK (United Kingdom) 321–2; aid cut, 317; Kenya investments, 288, 304; Moi support, 308–9, 316; oil subsidies cancelled, 310; oral protest, 311
Ukambani Members Association, 26; Nairobi protest, 144
UN (United Nations): Development Programme, 291, 320; UNESCO, 213;

Fourth World Conference on Women,
Beijing, 184; Somalia operation, 305
underground organisations colonial period,
155
universities, 13, 152, 212; Dar es Salaam,
210–11, 241; Port Harcourt, Nigeria,
204; government spies in, 211, 214,
241; repression, 243
Universities Academic Staff Union
(UASU), 31–2, 221; disbandment, 223
USA (United States of America), 316, 319,
322; Agency for International
Development (USAID), 52; aid
pressure, 311, 314; exile in, 204; Kenya
assistance, 266; Kenya military aid,
308–9; Mombasa naval base, 305;
post-Cold War attitude, 307
USSR (Union of Soviet Socialist
Republics), collapse, 38, 229, 246

Van de Walle, N., 264
vanguardism, opportunistic, 203, 205
violence: culture of, 147, 164, 181;
gender-specific, 182; police, 317–18;
political campaigns, 189
voting, ethno-regional patterns, 122

Wach, J., 60
Wachira, Kamoji, 211
Wachira, V., 237
Wackman, Harold, 320
Wadawida people, women, 139
wage restraint conditionality, 273
Wamalwa, Michael, 149, 156, 219–20
Wamba-dia-Wamba, 25
Wamue, G., 68, 73, 75
Wamwere, Koigi wa, 84, 221, 244, 248–9,
265; kidnap protests, 309
Wanjau, Gakara, 244
Wanjohi, Nick, 204
Wanyoike, Simon Karanja, 81
Waruinge, Ndura, 80, 81, 84
Wawire, Apili, 112
Welbourn, F.B., 63

welfare cuts, 283
West, C., 167
Williams, P., 216
Wilson, B., 62
Wipper, A., 61
Wolfenson, John, 291
women: capitalist undervaluation, 174;
economic marginalisation, 190;
movement 1990s, 183–4, 187, 192;
parliamentary presence, 165–6;
political marginalisation, 164, 170, 178,
180, 185; pre-colonial societies, 168,
172–3
World Bank, 14, 50, 263, 265, 275–6, 287,
292, 296, 305, 309, 316, 320–2; African
development assumptions, 266; –IMF
overlap, 274; /IMF Mombasa
conference 2002, 294; 'revolutionaries'
of, 211
World Food Programme, 311
World War II returnees, 231

Young Kavirondo Association (YKA-a),
26, 142
Young Kikuyu Association, 26, 142
Young Nyika Association, 142
Young Women's Christian Association
(YMCA), 184
Youth Agenda NGO, 136
youth: alternative politics, 153; as watu wa
mkono, 146–7; diverse definitions,
136–7; non-violence politics, 151;
political engagement, 140, 150, 159;
political marginalisation, 130, 158;
movements, 41; political position,
150; 'political sons', 149; responsibility
readiness, 139; unemployed urban,
50; vigilante groups, 148

Zaire, 4, 48; Budu Dia Kongo, 59;
Kimbanguism, 59
Zambia, 48–50; as positive example, 311
Zimbabwe liberation war, 63
Zimmerman, D., 167